THE FOURTH GOSPEL

THE

HEART OF CHRIST.

BY

EDMUND H. SEARS.

"It is seldom borne in mind that without constant reformation, that is without a constant return to its fountain-head, every religion, even the most perfect, nay the most perfect on account of its very perfection more even than others, suffers from its contact with the world, as the purest air suffers from the mere fact of its being breathed."

MAX MULLER.

BOSTON:
NOYES, HOLMES, AND COMPANY.
117 WASHINGTON STREET.
1872.

RIVERSIDE, CAMBRIDGE:
STEREOTYPED AND PRINTED BY
H. O. HOUGHTON AND COMPANY.

PREFACE.

"THE fourth Gospel is the Heart of Christ," is the enthusiastic language of Ernesti, from whom we borrow the words of our title-page. Expositors both ancient and modern, who regard the four Gospels as veritable history, have generally manifested the same preference. "Written by the hand of an angel," says Herder; and Schleiermacher, who with his school delighted in "the mystic of the four Evangelists," says that his soul must have been pervaded by eternal childlike Christmas joys.

But sentiments of admiration are not evidence to other minds who do not find through John those depths of living water which those who are more contemplative have ever found. No book has been the subject of a more searching or a more adverse criticism than the fourth Gospel. The history of the controversy, with the motives of it, is exceedingly interesting and instructive, and I had sketched it in two chapters of this work, but was obliged to omit them in order to bring the volume within convenient size. It is the controversy of half a century between some of the ablest theologians and profoundest scholars. The historical evidence was first seriously assailed by Bretschneider in 1820, who then published his "Probabilia," and who contended that the author of the fourth Gospel belonged to the first half of the second century, and wrote it with a dogmatic purpose, namely, to propagate the doctrine of the deity of Christ. He was ably answered, and the only change which the whole discussion then produced was a new value placed upon the Gospel of John. Bretschneider himself retracted his doubts.

But the Critical Philosophy, dating from Kant, and running by a swift and irresistible logic into Pantheism, gave birth to a new school of Biblical criticism ; a criticism vastly more ingenious than the old rationalism, and wrought of finer threads than it had ever spun. It finds its ablest expounder in Ferdinand Christian Baur, an Hegelian of the left wing, that is, the pantheistic, who breaks up the whole New Testament Canon, and runs it anew in pantheistic moulds, fortunately with the calmness and the icy clearness by which his style is distinguished. He furnishes Strauss, we think, with all the ideas and arguments which a Christian believer would care to notice or answer. Whatever we say of his criticism, and the philosophy that determines and inspires it, his three works, the History of the Christian doctrine of the Trinity, of the Atonement, of the Christian Gnosis, place the student of Christian history under immense obligations.

Where learned men have disputed, unlearned men are apt to think there must be hopeless uncertainty. They do not remember that when learned men dispute with theories predetermined, their disputes are only the play of hypotheses, and that the verdict of the common understanding is better than theirs. That the hermeneutics of the Tübingen School are a dance of this sort, is shown by the constant shifting of its positions and its mutually destructive theories. There was a pre-determination to make Christianity serve as a mould of Pantheism with its nomenclature unchanged.

Meanwhile as the dust of the controversy clears off, the calm wisdom of Neander, who put in a plea for entire freedom of debate, and who saw what the result must be, becomes apparent. No one went into it with a spirit more sweet and beautiful than his. To his name must be added a list long and illustrious, to enumerate which would be to suggest works of learning and scholarship, the most profound and reverent of this age or any other, especially in the departments of Christian history and evidence. Never was it more signally shown how great is the service of doubt and denial in rendering faith and affirmation clear, pronounced, and intelligent. Not only the sand was cleared away, disclosing the old foundations more deeply and broadly, but new facts were brought to light, and new fields discovered, running down like sunny glades through opening mist to the Personality which the Christian ages date from. The result is that by the verdict of the best scholarship of modern times not predetermined to Pantheism, no facts of equal antiquity, judged by the reasonable rules of historical evidence, stand out in surer prominence than the fundamental facts of the New Testament narratives; no heights of history thus remote lie on the horizon in mellower sunlight or clearer outline. Among the names in this great debate of half a century, whether disclosing the external grounds of Christianity or its divine contents, are, along with that of Neander, Ullman, Dorner, Tholück, Schaff, Julius Müller, Giesler, Olshausen, Jacobi, Hengstenberg, Bunsen, and Tischendorf.

It is not in my plan to write a book of Christian evidences merely, but to evolve the contents of the Johannean writings, which clearly apprehended are their own evidence, and prove Christianity itself a gift direct from above and not a human discovery. But the exposition would not be at all satisfactory, especially after past discussions and denials, if we left out the historical ground of the fourth Gospel, or left it to be suspected that this ground had been shaken or disturbed. We shall see that this has not been the case. Indeed, it is very difficult to make a sharp line of division between external and internal evidence, and show where one shades off into the other, as much as it is to tell where the soul and body are joined together. Brought home to us in their all-reconciling power, the essential truths of the fourth Gospel imply and necessitate the form and covering in which they appear ; or conversely beginning with their historic basis, the evidence grows and brightens all the way inward to the central light which shines out, encircles, and irradiates the whole.

CONTENTS.

PRELIMINARY.

PART I.

THE HISTORICAL ARGUMENT.

PART II.

HISTORIC MEMORIALS.

PART III.

THE PRIVATE MINISTRY OF JESUS.

PART IV.

THE JOHANNEAN THEOLOGY.

APPENDIX.

PRELIMINARY.

"It has always happened that in the ranks of the scientific army some have been found who refuse to credit the marvels which observation is continually revealing on every hand. Despite all the known wonders of the universe the circumstance that the sole available interpretation of observed facts involves some surprising conclusion, is held by such men to be a sufficient reason for rejecting the observations of the most trustworthy. The value of scientific observation seems enhanced in their eyes precisely as its fruits are insignificant." — R. A. Proctor.

THE FOURTH GOSPEL.

I.

THE SUPERNATURAL.

ALL the great religions acknowledge at least two ranges of existence. This material plane of being which we apprehend by the organs of sense, we must believe in, as it nourishes and enfolds us from our cradles. No one ever denied it. Philosophers dispute about the essence of matter; about what is behind these natural phenomena, and whether anything at all; but no one denies that the phenomena themselves exist. Those who deny the existence of matter only deny that it exists in itself, or in other words that it has any substratum of its own. The world of sight, sound, and fragrance that lies over against the senses and through them becomes an object of perception, is believed in alike by peasant and philosopher, and this by common consent we call NATURE or THE NATURAL WORLD.

In this natural world there is nothing stable. All is mobility and change. Not only the animal and vegetable life on its surface constantly disappear and reappear, but the rocks become disintegrated and enter into other forms of existence. Going back through longer reaches of history we find that the oceans and the mountains have been subject to vast changes by subsidence and upheaval, and that the aspect of the earth is transformed from one epoch to another. The very same elements by changes of combination produce the most diversified forms; and the minerals, the waters, the forests, the flowers of the field and the winds that blow over them, are those same elements commingling by new affinities and proportions, giving the endless ebb and flow which we delight to witness around us in the sea of matter. Man himself is involved in these perpetual revolutions. He appears on the surface of nature, is dominated by it through the stages of his threescore and ten, and then melts into its bosom and disappears. The order of sequence, according to which all these changes take place, we call by universal consent THE LAWS OF NATURE. To discover these changes and recombinations by patient observation or by subtile analysis is the business of science; to group them in their class and order and so determine their law of sequence is the business of natural philosophy.

The Christian believer acknowledges another and higher range of existence. Nature, we said, discharges man from her keeping and domination, and all that the senses knew of him dissolves and recombines in her earths and ethers and flowers. So one hundred generations have passed away since Christ appeared upon the earth. More than three hundred generations have come and gone since the creation of man, all of whom nature nursed on her bosom and then received back their crumbling forms and sent them anew into her unending circulations. The number of human beings then who exist at this moment on the surface of the earth, compared with those who have existed, is only an insignificant fraction of that whole which we call humanity ; only as a single page of one great volume ; only as the last cluster of leaves that flutter in the great forest that has shed its foliage.

If man lives only within the conditions of nature and is only returned into her endless circulations, then the natural world is the only one that exists to him, and he may expect to know of nothing beyond its phenomena. But Christianity affirms that when nature quits her grasp upon him, he still lives on, that only his visible coverings dissolve and recombine with the natural elements, while the man himself emerges beyond her sphere, subject no longer to her conditions and laws. It follows, of course, on the Christian theory, that the three hundred generations of human beings whom this natural world has discharged from its domination are still alive and active. Hence Christianity affirms a sphere of life above nature, more vast and more thronged with people, and whose empire is ever enlarging, since the stream of existence has discharged its immortal contents for more than six thousand years into those endless abodes.

This higher range of existence is called by common consent THE SUPERNATURAL, because it is above the dominion of natural law. This is what men generally mean when they speak of a supersensible or supernatural world. This preëminently is the sense apprehended by Christian faith when it transcends the sphere of natural change and sees the things that are invisible. Every one has a right to make his own definitions, but he is bound consistently to abide by them when made, and not confound things eternally distinct in themselves.

The word nature doubtless is made to have other significations, and indeed passes through an extended range of secondary meanings. We sometimes speak of the nature of man as meaning the whole aggregate of human qualities which make him what he is. Then again we discriminate and speak of his physical, intellectual, and spiritual natures. One who is disposed to play with words may call all beings and things from the mineral up to the highest angel created *natures*, and then by this definition he may deny that there is anything above nature except God Himself. Or he may follow up this game of words yet farther. Cicero writes a treatise, "De Natura Deorum," and we speak familiarly of the Divine nature, meaning the sum of Divine qualities and attributes ; and one who should be so disposed, and could afford the time for such logomachy, might place all beings and things, including God Himself, under the category of nature; and then of course it would be very easy for him to prove that the supernatural has no existence.

Plainly nothing is gained by these tricks of language. The words *nature* and *supernatural*, or the nature-world and the spirit-world, whether put in contrast or correlation, have a meaning fixed and well apprehended in the popular judgment, and we gain nothing but confusion when we try to disturb it. Herein moreover the popular judgment and the most philosophical are in perfect agreement. With both alike, the nature-world is this range of existence conditioned by time and space, and subject to the laws of space and temporal change; whereas the range of existence conceived as out of time and space, and therefore beyond the dominion of natural law, is the supersensible or supernatural world. Thus Kant uniformly discriminates these two spheres of being, — nature, the realm of sensible phenomena conditioned by space; and a cogitable world above space defecated of sense and free of natural law, and therefore supersensible and supernatural.[1]

Of these two ranges of being thus discriminated, how they are related and how contrasted, which is the substance and which the shadow, there is an immense divergence of opinions and beliefs. By the

[1] See chapter iii. of Semple's *Metaphysic of Ethics*; or see Kant's *Kritik of Practical Reason*, passim.

Christian theory man is the connecting link between them. He lives in both. He is the child of nature, and at the same time the heir of immortality. But that is first which is natural, and afterward that which is spiritual. He is born with only a natural consciousness, and the heavy wrappages of sense become the first basis of his existence. He is involved in nature, and he may even pass through all her transformations from the infant to the man, with hardly a dream of aught else than the natural life. Then the supernatural will be to him a phantasy and a chimera. He may honestly deny its existence altogether. Dominated by sensible appearances what more strange than to suppose a man can be alive after he is dead? Beyond sense the imagination "stretches out the stones of emptiness," and to think of that infinite vacancy as our final abode, or as capable of yielding a revelation to us out of its eternal silence, is to such a man the most hideous of all absurdities. Men have lived and passed away from this plane of being with no belief in any other, simply because none other than the natural consciousness was awakened within them; or, in other phrase, because they only lived and died as natural men.

Just removed from this state, and rising out of it, are the first faint dawnings of the supernatural, the first guessings and gropings towards it. But as yet it is apprehended only as dim and spectral. Thus the ghosts of Homer live in the underworld depleted of all that fresh and throbbing life which they lived on the earth, and are described as the fleeting shades of what they were. What a contrast between the Greece that flourished on the sun-bright hills and plains and breathed her transparent ethers and developed into graceful and glorious manhood, and the Greece of her spirit-world reduced to its pale and ghostly existence, and pining for terrestrial air! Not yet did the common mind or even the minds of the poets themselves come to any practical faith in the Supernatural. For with individuals and peoples not yet evolved from the despotic grasp of nature, this world is the substance and the other is the shadow.

Removed somewhat farther from sensuous unbelief, and indicative of a higher intellectual culture than blind instinctive gropings, is that faith which comes from the deductions of the reason but which refuses to affirm aught else than the simple fact of the supernatural. This is the position of Kant, who declines to accept the doctrine as the gift of revelation, but only as his own conclusion from a well-constructed syllogism. He does not pretend to prove it with "apodictic certainty," and he protests that we have no right to envisage it to the eye of faith, for then we fly off among the chimeras of the fabulists and poets. We must cogitate the supernatural and describe it only by negatives. It is the absence of nature; it is spaceless and timeless; it is the perfect defecation of all sensuous life, and beyond this, says Kant, the reason has no right to go.

A more full and affirmative faith than this is quite conceivable. It is conceivable, that is, that the supernatural may not only be believed in as the result of a syllogism and a balance of probabilities, but may be envisaged to the eye of faith; that man no longer involved completely in nature but evolved in part from her despotic grasp, and having a higher consciousness clearly and divinely opened, may be so brought front to front with super-sensible realities that their gleaming ranks and far-dissolving perspectives shall lie on the soul as brightly and surely as Nature does on the organs of sense, and that the consummation of our religious faith and Christian culture shall give us, the supersensible world the eternal reality and Nature its feebler adumbration, — that the sun-bright substance itself, and this the moving shadow projected on the dial-plate.

But is there any probability that such a disclosure as this will be given to mortals? Let us see.

Once admit the simple truth of man's immortality, and how vast and far-reaching are the conclusions that flow from it! How dull and laggard are our minds in coming up to the reality! There are to-day about a thousand million human beings upon the earth. At the end of a year, twenty millions will have passed away from it and twenty millions newborn will have come in their places. Hundreds are going and hundreds coming while I write these sentences. In less than fifty years, a number equal to the whole thousand millions will have put on immortality, and an equal number will have filled up the earthly ranks thus broken. The successive generations that have passed on within eight thousand years, the time during which man has probably been an inhabitant of the earth, would number by a moderate computation, one hundred times a thousand millions of people. This great multitude, moreover, are our own kith and kin ; our brethren elder born, whose hearts have throbbed with the same passions and yearnings and aspirations. And unless the mighty prophecies that go up from our collective humanity are a mockery and a lie, unless the groanings of the creation and its travailings in pain fail eternally of deliverance, then that great company of these uncounted millions who aspired to a better state, have had their hopes fulfilled ; have risen to an existence which has been brought into nearer communion with the Divine, and been enriched and ennobled by being freed from our earthly incumbrance. How immeasurably then in height, in breadth, in dignity, and power, does the supernatural transcend the natural ! And when we speak of humanity only as pertaining to the race on earth, how do we narrow down the conception and degrade it ! If those uncounted generations of men and women have not been disrobed of their humanity by death, but if on the other hand it throbs with a diviner love, then the pulses of their being still beat in harmony with ours as one family of the living God, and like God Himself, are nearer to us on the spiritual side, because there are no walls of flesh between us.

"But then our concern is only with the practical; with our duties here upon the earth, and our fellow-beings who share with us its trials and sorrows. We must relieve the burdens which we can touch now and here, and not follow our imaginations into realms which are uncertain and remote."

Only with the practical! Do we become practical only by bending prone and working mechanically with our hands, without any faith to inspire our industries and turn them to works of love or alleluiahs of praise? Does the practical consist only in finding the swiftest methods of locomotion in the barter of commodities, in changing money, and in handling dirt? And when you speak of our fellow-beings as part of the great orb of humanity in which we are all insphered and involved, must we think of it only as it rounds outward and downward among Africans, Patagonians, the Chinese, and the Esquimaux; or must we think of it also as it rounds upward into light, and expands in those continents vaster and more densely peopled which lie in a broader and warmer sunshine from the eternal throne?

"The burdens which we can touch now and here!" What were the burdens which lay on the minds of the two thousand of our fellow-beings who have died since I began this chapter an hour ago? What are the burdens on the minds of the three hundred and fifty thousand whose feet are now stumbling on the last verge of mortal existence which they will quit forever before eight days have elapsed; whose failing eyes look for the twinkle of some star in the darkness of the infinite Beyond? What are the burdens on the minds of the twenty millions who are crowding after them and will follow them before the year has closed? What are the burdens now and everywhere on our toiling, hoping, and aspiring humanity, conscious of the rapid changes of time, and groping for a foothold on the solid floors of eternity? They are not burdens which any "practical" man can touch unless he has stood himself where the clouds have been rifted above him and disclosed those higher and broader continents reposing in the peace of God.

"Our concern only with duties here on the earth." Yes, — but very possibly a view from the earth's illumined summits rather than its hollows and flats will show us what those duties are. Some centuries ago the philosophers thought that this earth was the centre of the universe and the most important part of it; the sun, moon, and stars being lamps for philosophers to see by. Even Plato thought the earth was the first and oldest of the sidereal gods, and at the centre of the axis of the Cosmos regulating the movement of the whole. They did not imagine that the earth, and the whole solar and planetary system to which it belongs, were but the lackeys of vaster systems which wheel them at will through the fields of space, and that the radiance of our brightest summer's day would be but a dimly lighted candle in the near presence of those monarchs of the skies whose thousand-fold blaze would turn us to ashes if it were not cooled and softened by distance. Very possibly it may be found in like manner when the sphere of our knowledge rounds upward as well as outward and downward, that it will show us relations and harmonies of which before we had never dreamed ; and that we should find the supernatural realms of being running into the natural, and controlling the latter with attractions and repulsions which we should be much wiser and better for knowing. Who shall decide beforehand and deny the probabilities as to whether the Divine Providence will openly disclose to us those supernatural realms where our humanity is glorified, compared with which all our little day on the earth is but the prologue of a mighty drama!

Once admit that man is immortal, and that death is only a physical change, and we shall find that many of the fallacies of naturalism are speedily dispelled. Naturalism, for example, scouts the idea of a "personal devil" as one of the chimeras of superstition. But personal devils have trod the earth for ages. What is the essence of deviltry but the inversion of the powers of man, turning them against God, against society, and against humanity. What but this has gendered the wrongs, the murders, the cruel oppressions which have afflicted the world? Men who incarnate deviltry here leave this world by the hundred every week simply by dropping their mortal coverings. If death has not extinguished their being, it follows by the plainest and shortest logic that the personality of the devil, whether individually or in the complex, is one of the stern facts of the universe both on its mortal and immortal side, and that those who deny it slide into the very superstition which they charge upon orthodoxy, viz., that there is some moral magic in death-beds to change sinners into saints. Possibly when the supernatural shall disclose itself as that other hemisphere of our humanity, where it culminates continually, we shall find that our ascetic and our blindfold theologies alike will have their superstitions sifted out of them; and that to split the universe by a horizontal line and leave the natural below to itself, is to leave it to bewildering fantasies, or, what is quite as bad, leave it to gravitate heavily into dust and mire.

II.

MIRACLES.

A LIVING writer defines a miracle thus: "An event inexplicable from the effect and concurrence of finite causes; which appears as the in-working of the supreme infinite cause, or God, for the purpose of proving to the world God's nature and will; especially of introducing a Divine Messenger, of holding him to life, guiding him in his work and authenticating his credentials with men; this divine wonder-working so shaping itself as to operate through the messenger as a power conferred upon him once for all to bear witness concerning Him; its efficacy connecting itself with an appeal to God on the part of the wonder-worker, so that God Himself on his account breaks through the chain of natural events and lets the supernatural come in." The writer cites alleged examples of such Divine interference: the miraculous birth of Christ, his exceptional childhood, the scene at his baptism, and his ascension.[1]

A most lame and lumbering definition, implying all through that miraculous power is one superimposed from without, standing apart by itself, as in

[1] Strauss, *Leben Jesu fur dar deutsch Volk bearbeitet*, p. 146.

some sense hitched on, not rather the exaltation of the faculties themselves under the action of universal laws, natural, spiritual, and divine.

We hold this definition utterly unwarrantable from any claims which Jesus ever made in his own behalf, no way applying to the events cited or to any facts of the New Testament, practically false and philosophically absurd. If God is immanent in nature and in man, and the supernatural is involved in the natural, there can be no such thing as "interference" or "breaking through." Nature is the perpetual efflorescence of the Divine Power; the natural is the unbroken evolution of the supernatural; history from the first man to the last is the progressive unrolling of the plan of the infinite Providence in which great events and small are taken up and glorified. Who but an atheist doubts "the inworking of the supreme infinite cause." And who but those who ascribe the authorship of nature to a mechanic and not a Creator, believes that this inworking is exceptional and not universal, intermittent like the winding of a clock and not freshly creative every hour? Who among the myriads of messengers which God has sent into the world, ever came without being "introduced" and "authenticated" by the Divine power operating through Him and passing into works that bore witness to his message?

A miracle, as we apprehend it, is exactly what is implied in its etymology, — a surprise. It is an event so unlike anything in our previous humdrum and shallow experience that we cannot group it under any law of sequence, and so it stands forth as a wonder. If a child who had never heard the thunder, were caught in the field by a tempest and involved in a blaze of lightning, he would think "the chain of natural events" broken through, and very likely believe as they did in the childhood of the race that God had spoken from the clouds. The white men told the Indians that on a certain day and hour the sun would hide his face, and the earth at mid-day be covered with darkness. The hour came and the darkness came; the Indians fell on their faces in terror and worshipped the white men as endowed with supernatural knowledge. A man who had been dead four days opens his eyes and rises from his coffin, and strikes dread into the standers-by. A young woman dying at Naples, describes a wedding scene exactly to the life and at the moment of its occurrence in the dear old home across the Atlantic, hears delightful music perceived by no one else, looks up and exclaims, "How beautiful!" and passes away from earth. What is the work of science but to group all the miracles in the natural world under the laws of matter, and what is the work of philosophy but to group all other miracles under laws intellectual and spiritual?

Law is simply the order of sequence which governs all phenomenal changes, whether in the realm of matter or the realm of mind. When we say that the laws of nature or of spirit are "uniform," we mean not that they give a monotonous sameness through all the centuries, but that the same antecedents being given the same consequents will be given also. Like causes under like conditions will be followed by like results. If I planted corn last year and reaped the harvest, I have a right to expect that the same seed this year, in the same soil with the same culture and the same climatic conditions, will produce the same harvest again. But if the harvest should totally fail this year while all the antecedents appeared the same as the year before, it would be sheer stupidity in me to imagine that the chain of natural events had been broken through and not rather that some of the antecedents had eluded my intelligence. The consequents I can cognize, for they stand out palpable before me, but what conceit must that be which claims to cognize all the antecedents which lie hid in the secret laboratories of nature, which run back to the birth of time and into the unknown eternities themselves?

If by "the uniformity of the laws of nature" we were to understand only an unchanging series of phenomena repeating itself age after age, coming round and round in the same cycles, we should have a theory of the creation utterly belied by the facts of the case. Looking out from our little moment in time, and our little mole-hill in space, we might perhaps affirm this kind of uniformity, for the seasons revolve, and even and morn alternate now just as our fathers and grandfathers had described them. But how was it in that period before the seasons began their flowery circuit; before Day lit up its solar splendors, or Night quenched them with cooling shade? How was it when our earth hung in space as a mass of molten lava, or when the seas covered its whole surface boiling hot and void of organic life, or when the Laurentian hills peered above the surface and lifted slowly their drenched and solitary heads above the boundless waste of waters, the first born children of this habitable world?[1] Looking back, not through our own little day, but through nature's periods and cycles, we see her moving not in a "uniform series," but RISING WITH SPIRAL MOTION from lower to higher, never repeating herself, never completing one circle except on a loftier plane than the previous one, and toward which all previous ones were the prophecy and aspiration. The Positivists will have it that temporal change succeeding to temporal change, phe-

[1] What we call "the New World is in fact the Old World," says Agassiz. "The Western Continent was the earliest upheaval; and the first land that peered above the waters was not the highest mountains, which are of later date. Along the northern limit of the United States, bordering upon Lower Canada, there runs a low line of hills known as the Laurentian Hills. They are insignificant in height, but the earliest land that lifted itself above the waters. The earliest forms of organic life may now be studied along what was then the beach of an almost boundless sea." — *Geological Sketches*, chapters i. and ii.

nomenon antedating phenomenon, exhausts the idea of causality, thus affronting our intelligence with the doctrine that the effect can rise above the cause into a new and loftier series. For if nature herself gives us instead of a monotonous circuit in the same grooves, a constant movement out of them into higher ones from indistinguishable chaos through the ascending scale of life and order up to man, the majestic coronal of all, then when we speak of the "uniformity of nature" we only talk foolishness for the purpose of blinking the glories of the Godhead, immanent in phenomena and authenticating all their vanishings and reappearings.

A miracle is a surprise, — but to whom? Not to higher intelligences who see the interiors of nature and know what is about to be from the unbroken links of the ascending series; not to Him who fills those interiors with reality and floods them with his life; but to us who see but one link of the chain; who are ignorant of the long line of antecedents and who stand where the result first breaks upon human sight. An eclipse was a surprise till the laws of planetary motion were discovered and revealed it in accord with the harmonies of the spheres; the first advent of man on the green earth was a surprise to the brutes below him; the first angelophanies to men were a surprise to the infant race, and every Divine epiphany on a higher plane than a previous one, which should date a new dispensation or a new cycle of the endless years, would be at its commencement a surprise to the subjects of it, whether angels or men. But what dullards must we be to stare into the heavens and declare the laws of the universe broken through simply because we could not see those infinite antecedents and their unimaginable consequents, which make up the supreme order of the creation whereby it ascends and reflects the Adorable Perfections with nearer and brighter refulgence!

The changes of a single day are miracles to the ephemera that swarm into existence and die between sunrise and sunset. Supposing them endowed with some sort of puny intelligence, what a surprise it must be to them when they emerge from the surface of the water and bathe their wings in light; when the wind sweeps them from the air; when they expire in the sun's last rays and the three hours that span their insect life are closing! The changes of the four seasons are miracles to the tribes that live and perish in their annual revolutions. The transit of the earth from one epoch to another is miraculous, seen from our finite or merely natural side of things. Every new epoch transcended all the experience of a former one, and came upon it as a surprise. The shell-fish of the silurian beach, if they could have thought and spoken as expounders of naturalism. would have treated as incredible the first rumors of four-footed beasts and creeping things, for would not mollusks and bivalves have been to them the finale of this lower creation, not buffaloes and stags with antlers? And then the mammals of the tertiary period, who inhabited the green earth and cropped its herbage alone for unknown ages, would have been equally surprised when man came as the lord of all. As if quadruped existence and not biped were not conformable to all experience, and the highest to be conceived or desired! As if any other were not anomalous and monstrous and a "breaking through" of the laws of nature! And the new race of men, looking from the natural side only, ignorant of aught else than their own short epoch of a few hundred years, might perhaps claim themselves as the last and highest evolution of Divine energy; and if by some new epiphany a style of life not animal, nor human merely, but ESSENTIALLY DIVINE, should appear upon the earth with attendants and environments transcending all past experience, and inaugurating a new series of years and centuries, they might very likely think the order of the universe disturbed and its laws broken through, and try to sink the fact from its appropriate rank, and shut out the solar splendors of the Godhead.

What can be more childish than to make the experience of what has been the measure of all that shall be? And yet this is the whole pith of Mr. Hume's argument against miracles which Strauss has served up anew as unanswerable. The alleged facts of the Gospel narratives — the birth of Christ from no human paternal line, his exceptional childhood, the angelophanies that attended him, his healing diseases by his touch, his raising the dead, his own resurrection and ascension — are unlike any former experience, and therefore incredible. They are violations of nature's laws, and cannot be proved by testimony. The answer plainly is, How do you know the laws of nature except from phenomena? And whether such phenomena have taken place is the very question in hand. If they did take place, they are consequents palpable to the eye, but whose antecedents belong to the infinite laws of order which you cannot measure, since they are out of sight. The same consequents were never given before because the same antecedents were never given. If we are told that Jesus raised the dead, and restored the blind, and walked the waves, the credibility of the alleged facts will depend altogether upon the question, Who was Jesus? and that again must be decided by the amount and quality of moral and spiritual power with which He moves upon the world, and possesses and changes the heart of humanity. Behold the man, and look before and after, and then say, Does he inaugurate a new epoch; is here a transition period in the ascending Divine series? Is here a new Divine epiphany through the interiors of nature whereby it ever rises and becomes the more transparent type and robe of the Divine Wisdom, Love, and Power?

If so, we may well expect it will have some attendants and environments which belong not to any foregone history, — just as the sun new risen gives shapes and colors to the breaking and purpling clouds which they never had under the colder and feebler lustre of the morning star.

If a miracle is that which "lets the supernatural come in," what are all the on-goings of nature but miracles, unless we take the position of blank atheism? They are the continuous enunciation of some vast intelligence, which is a perpetual wonder, because it transcends our highest thought and comprehension. The highest significance of the miracles of the New Testament consists mainly in the fact that they show more entirely the control of mind over matter, or the sovereignty of spiritual volition in natural things. The same is verified in our experience every time a muscle moves at the touch of a human will, and more divinely and grandly whenever a new phasis of nature evolves freshly the volition of God. The works of Jesus which "let the supernatural come in," are after the analogy of all human works in which mind is plastic over matter, or in which the higher subordinates the lower. The difference is that in Jesus Christ, as the New Testament describes Him, there was a degree and quality of spiritual power, such as we do not find in ourselves nor in people around us, and therefore the subordination of external nature was more signal and complete, and breaks upon us as a surprise.

Law, seen from the Divine side of things, is not the order of sequence which governs the phenomena of days and years only, but of the ages and cycles of endless existence. Even if it be true, as some theorizing astronomers tell us, that the planetary orbits are growing less, and that the travellers of the heavenly spaces must one day mingle in the solar fires out of which they came, who would doubt that the grand winding up must be as much under the laws of the supreme order as the folding up of a flower at evening; preparatory for a new unwinding of the system of nature; of its higher and sweeter efflorescence out of the immanent life of God and a more sublime procession of the heavenly travellers on their endless way?

A miracle is a surprise, — but to whom? To those, of course, all whose habits of thinking have been formed within narrower boundaries, or on a lower plane of existence than the one which the miracle breaks open to their gaze. Plough into the earth deep enough and turn over the furrows, and the earth-worms writhe in their distress, brought too suddenly into the light and air. So with us when a higher realm of truth breaks upon us too suddenly. There are habits of culture which only develop the natural mind; that is to say that order of the faculties which hold us in close relationship with the natural world. Those faculties may be sharpened to an indescribable keenness, till the intellect penetrates outward into space and downward towards the monads, and imagines that the mysteries of the universe are well-nigh solved. A man, perfected exclusively in this sort of culture, never thinks of the universe as more than one story high. A whole people or a whole period of time may be educated mainly to habits of natural thinking. The progress of the collective human mind is not on a narrow and straight line; its progress is like that of a noble ship freighted with the wealth of all the zones, but which tacks to every gale and makes a broad belt that ripples the whole surface of the sea. The ancient supernaturalism was without science, one-sided and baseless, and so running into driveling superstitions. It must always be so when the supernatural is not complemented by the natural, or does not rest upon its solid floors. For the last two hundred years, the van of discovery has led the way down deeper and deeper into sense, till the great verities of immortality seem like a floating and vanishing tradition, and miracle is synonymous with monster. The supernatural, no longer evolved in the disclosures of an irresistible Providence, is left very much to those who knock at the closed doors or rap out responses upon tables. Meanwhile, it requires small gift of prophecy to foretell the result. As surely as the supernatural rests on the natural as its solid flooring, so sure is it never to fall through, but gain security by all the explorations of natural law. As surely as body involves spirit, and the natural world involves and exfigures the spiritual, so surely is the most perfect knowledge of natural law to become the ground of a supernaturalism reformed, illustrated, and purified of old superstitions and errors. The age has veered so far senseward that we may conclude it has touched its boundary line. There are indications that the tacking and veering towards the opposite quarter have begun already, and the only apprehension is that the refluent wave may be too sudden and violent. That we are on the verge of a new epoch when the Spirit of God will utilize the accumulated knowledge of the modern age, taking up science, art, philosophy into a higher unity, there to make them resplendent with a light which is not their own, and the servitors of a more comprehending and adoring faith, there are tokens already both in the earth and the sky. And in that day, when the supernatural and the natural, no longer halved and sundered, are harmonized in one, we shall find the latter the medium through which the other appears more perfectly; and then special miracles will cease only because the whole cosmos is miracle, and more intelligently and completely than to the eye and ear of Plato reports the mind of the Supreme and the music of the upper spheres.

The tendency of our modern thought has been to narrow in the domain of miracle, and finally enclose it by the boundaries of Palestine and the first and last decades of the first century. Within that little province of earth and in that Long Ago you may believe miraculous power was adjoined to a few men so as to enable them to prove certain doctrines of religion, and especially the resurrection and the future life. Ever since all demonstrations from a higher world are to be ruled out as pretense and imposture touching on the special domain of the New Testament. Meanwhile the small space of earth and the small fragment of time made sacred by miracle, recede in the dim and vanishing past, and become altogether spectral to the natural common mind ; and so the idea of the resurrection and immortality belong to the speculations of ancient days. And in what way has this growing skepticism been prevented from eclipsing the faith of mankind altogether ?

The personal history of those who have been caught up nearest to the heart of God would perhaps show that the disclosures which Strauss calls "interference," have never ceased in any age of the world. Miracle, — regarded as that inner and open door where "the supernatural comes in," — always has been and always will be. Its form and its methods may change as the world changes, but the substance and reality are preserved. Just in the degree that an age becomes shut in by sense, the sphere of miracle is withdrawn from the gaze of the street and the market-place, and from all physical demonstration, to that realm of spirit, where only the heart of God beats audibly to the heart and ear of our redeemed and regenerate humanity. He will not strive nor cry amid the coarse dissonance of earthly sounds, only to be rejected and scorned. But the work of the Holy Spirit in the spiritual nature of man, melting through its depravities and evolving a new creation out of its primal chaos, giving to it ever clearer openings,—this has been the miracle wrought ever anew through all the Christian ages. Said Jesus to the people who were amazed at his power of healing the sick, Greater works than these will the Father do that ye may marvel ; referring to that life whose throes were already commencing in the spiritual graves. Those who have been caught inward by the Spirit of God and sealed by its power, will often tell us, not aloud, but in tears and in tremblings, lest the world outside should hear and laugh, of the guidance of a Divine hand never out of sight, and the mouldings of a Divine power more wonderful than that which projected the forces of nature. The moral creation, though rising unseen to carnal eyes, is quite as miraculous as the natural. It is very interesting, sometimes, to hear not only individuals, but families, recount their history ; how events have been shaped and unified by tractations which none but they could see ; how mountains have been removed, and brazen bars cut in two, and victories achieved in answer to the prayer of faith ; how amid conflicts and temptations and the clouds of dust which have risen over them in the race of life they have had tokens of the power that insphered them, tenderly moving behind a veil lest its too great glory should drown their human personality, yet making rents here and there where watching faces looked through ; above all, in those hours of supreme trial when families break up and the last adieus are spoken, seeing the gates flung wide, where the steps lead away from earth and mortality into climes where death shall be no more. When science looks upward instead of downward, and becomes transfigured in a light higher than its own, and sees all its facts taken up and rearranged under laws of a wider and more comprehending unity, the earth will reflect the peace of heaven and mirror its verities anew, repeating, though on planes of existence vastly broader and more secure, the times of which Wordsworth sings, when the Divine Messengers crowning the sovereign heights of the world —

> " Warbled for heaven above and earth below,
> Strains suitable for both."

III.

THE IMMANENCE OF GOD.

IF, as Christianity assumes, man while involved in nature and clothed in its forms, is at the same time intrinsically immortal, and as such is to be evolved out of nature and rise above it, it follows that he is the subject now and here of both ranges of existence. He is natural and supernatural. By his natural organs he is placed in open and necessary relations with time and space; by his immortal faculties he is placed in necessary relations with a supersensible world. He is not always conscious of these higher relations. The babe is locked fast in sense and knows only of sensuous things. There are those, we have said, who scarcely in this life get released from this despotic grasp. But a spiritual nature with its unmeasured possibilities, is in abeyance, securely enfolded, and ready under the appliance and culture adapted to it to open down into the consciousness and arouse the soul to aspirations and reachings towards what lies beyond nature and is independent of her growths and decays. Hence the *involution of the supernatural in the natural and the immanence of God in humanity.* On the first awakening of a consciousness, higher than that of mere natural life, all men have intuitive notions of spiritual and divine things. Then into every soul comes an influx of the supernatural, and breathings from the Lord, which are deeper than all human teachings, and without which all human teachings were in vain. Our minds open inward as well as outward, and thence run along into our souls as on electric wires the tidings that are not of earth; inspirations of God of a moral law and of a life to come. Were it not for these inspirations, the eternal life might as well be preached to trees and animals as to human beings. Granted Mr. John Stewart Mills' theory of "association" and cumulative traditions; they must have had a clear solid ground to start from, a native stock to be grafted upon, or they might just as well have started from the coral or the oyster as from a human soul. There was at the beginning the involution of the supernatural in the natural, else we might teach and preach to all eternity and get no evolution; there must be the immanence of God in man, and he must be capable of becoming conscious of it, else we might just as well offer symbols of worship to the bats and owls as to men and women. With all alike this is the prime ground of culture, from the first bishop of Christendom to the half idiot savages of Sidney Cove. These divine instincts, therefore, possible or actual, are in every man; for every man as to his interior mind belongs to a spiritual world and is capable of being placed in communion with eternal things. But let us discriminate. When we say that God is immanent in humanity, we do not mean that the DIVINE SUBSTANCE is included in man. The Christian conception of God, as we apprehend it, is, that from the Divine Substance and personality are the forthgoing energies that fill the circuit of his universe, so that all things in their inmost nature are receptive of them and exist by them. This influx from the Divine Personality is not to be confounded with that personality itself. If God were present personally in nature and not by influx, then nature itself were one great Fetish, and the idolaters were right who worshipped the sun and the stars. If God were in man personally or by his own essence, man himself would be God, and not his dependent creature, receptive of Divine inspirations. In man and in nature alike, in the child at play and in the flower which he plucks from its stem, there is the unceasing influx of the Divine, and out of this they draw their breath, and suck the life that warms and feeds them. But nature is not conscious of this Divine life out of which it grows and blossoms ; man, when his higher consciousness is opened, has convictions, desires, and aspirations, which he knows must come from Divine imbreathings and urgencies ; and so he bows and worships and returns to God the love which he receives. This distinction between influx and personality, between the Divine immanence and the Divine essence, though sometimes lost sight of, we think is plain and obvious. It should be kept steadily in view, as we shall see by and by, if we do not see already in the naked statement itself that the distinction saves us from fetishism when we make God immanent in nature, and from pantheism when we make Him immanent in both nature and man.

It hence becomes very plain, too, what we mean when we speak of intuitions of God, or inward beholdings of the Deity. Construed literally it has no meaning whatever, except to the pantheist himself. Intuition is simply the survey which one takes of the contents of his own consciousness. It is to the internal phenomena of mind, what perception is to the external phenomena of nature. Perception, if it be clear and accurate, gives you what lies without you in sharp outline and just perspective ; intuition, if it be clear and accurate, catalogues aright the facts of consciousness in your experience, intellectual and spiritual, and gives the soul's perspectives to itself. Of course there can be no intuition of God, since He is not included in the contents of consciousness, and could not be, without the destruction of the human identity and personality. Our mental perspectives, present or possible, opened already, or which may be opened, give us our own, and the limit where they fade off and dissolve in darkness, is precisely where our identity and personality terminate.

But though God Himself can never be the content of the human consciousness, his highest and best work can be. My consciousness at one time may give me an inward scene of moral ruin and disorder. I may see a creation rise out of this chaos more goodly and fair than the order of external nature; changes may be going on within, more auspicious than all the ongoings without; experiences more rich than the regalements of sense; a sunshine from the divine face more bright than summer glories; a peace more sweet than the tranquillity of the morning; affections purged of self and enlarged to universal love; calls to duty more loud and clear than matin bells; strength to suffer and to do that comes by prayer; a power back of my personal volitions, transfusing my whole being and creating it anew; convictions of truth growing bright to the perfect day; all these may come within the range of my intuitions, and beget a faith in God which nothing can shake, and a knowledge of his goodness and power worth more than all the deductions of the understanding. It comes not from inward beholdings of the Deity, but of what He does; beholdings of such work of grace and power as I can ascribe to neither man nor angel, and which bring repose under the shadow of his wings.

PART I.

THE HISTORICAL ARGUMENT.

"One do I see and twelve; but second there
Methinks I know thee, thou beloved one;
Not for thy nobler port, for there are none
More quiet-featured. Some there are who bear
Their message on their brows; while others wear
A look of large commission, nor will shun
The fiery trial so their work is done.
But thou hast parted with thine eyes in prayer,
Unearthly are they both; and so thy lips
Seem like the porches of the Spirit-land;
For thou hast laid a mighty treasure by
Unlocked by Him in Nature, and thine eye
Burns with a vision and apocalypse
Thy own sweet soul can hardly understand."

CHAPTER I.

GNOSTICISM.

THE problem of evil has always been the most stubborn and difficult, whether without Christianity, or within it, and under its resolving light. No Pelagian theories can relieve the burdened consciousness from the fact of inhering corruption. It has existed under every form of religion, from that of the Hindus down to the last modification of New England Calvinism; and the wit of man has been taxed to the utmost so to dispose of the fact as to clear the divine character of all responsibility about it.

It was this laudable motive which gave rise to the most daring system of speculation known in the history of opinions. That system began to appear soon after the ascension of Christ, and grew into gigantic proportions by the middle of the second century. It was the most formidable heresy that threatened Christianity, and overlaid its first purity; and though finally thrown off, and left behind, it imparted to Christianity a direction and coloring which it had for centuries, and of which it is not wholly relieved to this day. There are unmistakable allusions to it in Paul's epistles; it is a clearly established fact that the Apostle John came in contact with it; it is openly assailed in the epistle which bears his name; and portions of the fourth Gospel, quite unintelligible otherwise, are tolerably well understood when we know that they were written with the haunting presence of this growing heresy. The argument for the genuineness of the fourth Gospel cannot be seen in its entire force without some knowledge of the contemporaneous Gnostic opinions.

Gnosticism was a composite of at least four other religions, — Parseeism, once the dominant religion of Persia; Hellenism, as modified by Plato; Judaism; and Christianity. These four were variously combined; and, according to the proportions of the mixture, the new compound very much resembled Christianity, and did not greatly obscure its essential truths; or it so distorted and annulled them that their native simplicity, power, and beauty, were entirely gone.

Gnosticism was an attempt to combine Dualism with Christianity. Dualism asserts the doctrine of two original eternal principles of good and evil; hence two primal uncreated realms of Light and Darkness, of immaculate purity and essential depravity. One was the realm of pure spirit, at the head of which was God Himself; the other was the realm of matter, — dark, chaotic, and evil. These two eternal, original principles lie at the foundation of the Parsee religion; and with equal distinctness, though with less active antagonism, they are the basis of Plato's philosophy as developed in the Timæus. This Dualism invaded Christianity, — from Persia through Syria and the Syrian Theosophists; from Plato's philosophy through Alexandria and its Platonizing Jews and Christians. They formed a composite which we will briefly describe, inasmuch as it has an important bearing on the exposition and evidence of the fourth Gospel.

For a long period the boundary line between these two kingdoms of Good and Evil had not been passed over. Each existed apart in its own isolation, — one in its transcendent excellence and glory; the other as the outlying chaos, conceived sometimes as inert and dead, sometimes as seething with corruption, always as disorderly and wild. But it was inevitable that the kingdom of light should approach nearer and ever nearer the kingdom of darkness. For God — the primal infinite good — was ever sending out emanations from Himself. These at length hypostasized in the angelic powers that circled Him about and stood nearest to his throne. But out of these highest and nearest of the heavenly powers came forth emanations in turn, and these hypostasized farther out and lower down. From these latter came forth other emanations; and, with every remove from the infinite original source, the eternal perfections were reflected more dimly. Of course these waves of emanation can be extended indefinitely; and you can cogitate any number of heavens to suit your fancy, — from the inner circle, most resplendent about the throne, to the outermost limit, the Chinese wall of the upper celestials that bounds them from chaotic darkness and death. These powers thus created successively were called Æons, and the whole realm, from the centre to the circumference, was the *Divine Pleroma*, because within these limits God reigned in the fullness and completeness of his perfections.

Thus far there was no mixture of the two realms. But at length the emanations streamed over the Chinese wall into the realm of dark, dead, chaotic matter. The angel on the outermost limit rayed into it, and fructified it. Hence a new world arose, — this world we live in of mingled good and evil. It was not created by God, the supremely good, who never appears directly and openly in it; it was formed by the angel who was lowest down and next to it; whose emanations streamed into it, and took on a covering of matter. Hence this angel was called the World-former. Or, again, he was called the Logos, or Word, because a ray from his reason pierced the realm of matter, and took its clothing thence. Hence the complex nature of man. His most external nature is material. It is the hylic coat which he wears, always corrupt and poisonous, the seat of all his temptations and woes. Within this is his soul, which is an emanation from the angel World-former, and therefore his psychical or soul-nature is a ground of communion, not with the Supreme Good, but only with the World-former who made him and ranks just above him.

There is in man, however, as in the Æons or angels above him, an inmost principle of the supremely good and perfect. Because every tier of being which creates a next lower one is a medium, though unconsciously, of the infinite and primal life, and that life therefore is immanent in all created things. But, before it has reached man, it becomes imbedded under so many strata that it comes not generally into the consciousness. Hence the Logos, or World-former, who made us and all terrestrial things, and who is the immediate ruler of this lower sphere, while he thinks he made it and rules it from himself, is really and unconsciously the organ and instrumentality of the Supreme Divinity. Hence man has a threefold nature, — the hylic or fleshly one, which is outermost; the soul-nature, which is next inward, and which is an emanation of the World-former; and the deepest and inmost of all, buried far beneath the consciousness of common men, the spiritual or pneumatic nature, which is the pure emanation of God himself.

The sum is, this is too bad a world to be regarded as the handiwork of a perfect Being. The essential evil of matter, and hence the utter depravity of the fleshly nature, lie at the foundation of all the Gnostic systems.

It will be seen at once how Christianity, on the

side of Judaism, holds out an irresistible lure to the first theosophist who might choose to dovetail Gnosticism into it. The wonder is that they did not interpenetrate so tenaciously as to defy the wit of the Church fathers to break them off from each other and keep them asunder. The problem of evil, if not solved, was at least artfully *dodged*, at a time when it was the hardest and the sorest; when the whole creation was groaning and travailing in pain. The Divine character stands clear of all responsibility touching its origin. Not only so, but the Old Testament history, and the whole dispensation of Judaism, the stumbling-block of the Christian believer, can now be fitted in with Christianity with marvelous symmetry. Nothing is easier. The God of the Old Testament, sternly just, sometimes with changeful passion and consuming anger, was not the God of Christianity, but the World-former himself, ruling his own kingdom and trying to hold it in its wild disorder. Confessedly, the Being who fashioned this world, and governs it, is the Jehovah-angel of the Old Testament. See thus how the threefold nature of man is marvelously displayed! The heathen — lost in thick darkness, and worshipping devils — are those on whom the hylic coat of sense and matter hangs thick and heavy; and the soul-nature, even, is lost under it, and comes not into consciousness. Only a few chosen people have had this consciousness awakened and so brought into acknowledged relations with the

World-former who governs them. These are the Jews, — not the chosen people of the Supreme God but of the World-former, who has parted them off, and, with constant watching and sore trials of his patience, keeps them in external order by rigorous commandments and temporal judgments. The World-former, with his Jews, expected a Messiah; but it was only a temporal one, who was to extend, not his own reign, but that of the World-former himself. The Messiah was to be *his* subject and conquering vicegerent. A few, however, there were whose pneumatic or deepest natures had been touched and vitalized. Beneath the covering of flesh and sense, beneath even the soul-nature itself, a chord was touched in their profounder contemplations whose vibrations thrilled beyond the World-former, even up to the First Good, First Perfect, and First Fair, and gave them communings with the Highest. Such minds were choice and few; but they waited and watched for the true Christ, and they indicated his possible achievement in human nature. By this clever dovetailing, Christianity is relieved of all difficulty arising from its connection with Judaism, and Judaism adjusts itself easily in a grand system of the Universe.

The World-former does not know that there is a sovereign hand that uses him and turns him whither it will. He thinks he is acting only from himself and for himself, and never dreams that he is preparing the way for a higher Æon to come and supersede him. But such is the fact, and in the fullness of time the pneumatic Christ appears. But He must not take upon him our flesh and blood. Nothing could be more abhorrent to Gnosticism than to bring the Highest in contact with corrupt and poisonous matter. His immaculate purity must be kept clear of its stains. How, then, can the Christ, either as the Highest himself, or as his first Æon, get introduced into this bad world to save it? In either of two ways.

Jesus Christ was, in fact, two persons in one. Jesus was a mere man of Jewish descent, born like any other man. But he was of pious disposition, and went to the Jordan to be baptized. Then the Æon Christ descended, and entered him, and acted and spake through him ; and so from that period his marvelous history unfolds, and the wisdom of God drops from his lips. The Jews arraigned and crucified the man Jesus. They thought to have killed the Christ, but him they could not touch. Before the crucifixion the Æon Christ re-ascended to his skies, and only a man like us died upon the cross. Hence his exclamation in that awful hour after the God had gone up and left him, "Why hast thou forsaken me?"

Or there is another way by which Gnosticism, always abhorring the touch of matter, eludes the difficulty. Some Gnostics held that Jesus Christ was one person, but that there was no incarnation at all; that He did not come in the flesh, but only in divine shapes that took its image and likeness. The angelophanies of the Old Testament, they said, were not material forms, but celestial substances taking on the appearances of the human figure. Even so the Christ that appeared in Palestine was not clothed in veritable flesh and blood, but only in its semblance and effigy; for it is in the power of God at any time to evolve this appearance out of Himself, and project it into this lower world. The Jews thought they crucified a man: but therein were they deceived, and their impotent rage defeated; for the agony and the death were only phantasmic, while the real Christ within the outward semblance was untouched by the spear and the nails.

Not all men can rise out of hylic darkness, or out of the hard service of the World-former, to the knowledge of the pneumatic Christ and communion with the Highest. It is only those whose inmost natures have been quickened and unfolded. These can appeal to their highest consciousness. They have done with the poor outward letter of the Jewish World-former, and have intuitions of the supreme Deity. They look down with pity upon those still held in bondage, whether to the Jewish letter or to the poisonous coverings of flesh and sense.

Gnosticism prevailed extensively during the second century, and did not become extinct before the middle of the fourth. Men of wealth, nobility, and intelligence, embraced Christianity under some Gnostic form ; for it fostered mightily that serene self-complacency which makes men well-pleasing to themselves, and lifts them above their fellows. It exerted, however, other and more lasting influences. Its prime article, the essential evil of matter as the deadliest foe of the internal man, led on to asceticism and the maceration of the flesh. It made marriage odious, and all sensual pleasure corrupting and vile ; it made all nature but a blight, an incumbent curse upon the spirit ; and either its direct influence, or the ground principle out of which it grew and flourished, sent the monks into the monasteries or the deserts, doomed the priests to celibacy, and wrenched human nature itself into frightful distortions. The Church excluded Gnosticism, but not till its virus had entered her veins and exerted a potent influence in shaping both her theology and institutions. Augustine, her greatest theologian, came into the Church out of one of the forms of Gnosticism, and through him it flings its long shadow down the centuries, even over the theology of the modern age.

Not only the orthodox, but the heretic theologies were sometimes determined either directly by Gnostic influence or by the fundamental principle from which it comes. Arianism is not a system of dualism : it does not assert an eternal primitive matter ; but it abhors to bring God in contact with matter, and so makes Christ a sub-deity or Æon under him, created out of nothing, that he in turn might create the world and become incarnate in time. Therefore nature would not lead us directly up to the supreme God, but to the sub-deity who created nature, who became incarnate within it, who intercedes for us, while the Supreme himself dwells apart, never passing over into the finite except through the mediating Christ and his angels.

The Gnostics began to appear soon after the ascension of Christ, and during the second century their spread was rapid and wide. Gibbon says they "covered both Egypt and Asia." They were polite, learned, and wealthy, and highly self-exalted. They had their congregations, their bishops and doctors, and sometimes mingled imperceptibly and extensively among the congregations of the faithful. They condescendingly accepted Christianity in full ; but, as they drew it up and absorbed it in their own pneumatic consciousness, they held it sublimed in a higher Gnosis, — a very different religion from that of the vulgar Christian multitude around them. They were shy of martyrdom, and could evade the authorities. They could not always be distinguished from the Catholic Christians, with whom they had no hesitation to commune and worship ; but there was one subject by which they could generally be discovered and sifted out. If questioned touching the resurrection of the dead, they would "look foolish," says Tertullian, and finally disclose themselves. The resurrection of the material body was abhorrent to their whole system of faith.

Of course such a system, ramifying into the most vital part of Christianity, adhering as a parasite, and threatening to suck its life-blood, was not extruded and left behind without sharp and persistent controversy. The controversy begins with Paul, who gives a side-blow here and there at the incipient heresy; John stops in his exhortations of brotherly love to launch his anathemas against it; Polycarp, the disciple of John, and the saintly martyr, ascribes it to Satan; Irenæus, the disciple of Polycarp, wrote to refute it; and Tertullian, at the close of the second century, employed his rough and fiery eloquence to denounce it.

CHAPTER II.

SAINT JOHN AT EPHESUS.

PERHAPS no country on the face of the earth has been the centre of influences more subtile and pervading than Ionia, so far as those influences have been extended by means of literature. It shaped the intellect of the world in its finest moulds, for it was plastic over the mind of Greece; it has determined most profoundly its religious culture, for those writings of the Christian canon which appealed to the deeper consciousness were produced within its transparent and inspiring ethers. In our gross and sleepy occidentalism we constantly lose sight of the educative power of nature under conditions such as we have never experienced and hardly imagined, over those minds which have produced the master-pieces in art, in literature, and in religion. This little Greek province of Ionia has given us Homer and the Iliad, and made all other poetry but a broken strain; it has given us the fourth Gospel and the Apocalypse, which find us at the close of eighteen centuries veiling our sight before the too burning disclosures of the Godhead. It has given us a language whose sound is music and whose touch can bring the subtlest thought within its soft and delicate shadings. If it is bad philosophy to say with Mr. Buckle that man with his culture and his religions is the mere product of his environments, so it is equally bad to say that God is only a great Magician, who works without means and without law, and not the Infinite Providence who works both within man and around him by his immanence in both nature and humanity.

Ionia lay upon the western coast of Asia Minor, mainly between two rivers, though extending a little beyond them; the Hermus on the north and the Meander on the south. It was about one hundred miles in length, and less than half that average distance in breadth, therefore comprising less territory than the little State of Massachusetts. Two beautiful islands belonged to it, separated from it by narrow straits; Chios towards the north, and Samos towards the south. Besides the two rivers already named, there is a third, the Cayster, which flows between them, at whose mouth stood the city of Ephesus. These three rivers find their way to the sea through valleys of surpassing fertility, and the coast from river to river is skirted by a belt of land, winding with the winding coast, fronting the islands which lie off as gems upon the sea, teeming with luxuriance and gleaming in the gorgeous beauty of an oriental clime. Its climate, though the most charming in the world, is not one which melts and debilitates. Its brilliant atmosphere taken into human lungs, is a perpetual stimulus, sparkling through the blood and through the brain, and thence through the soul itself, to sharpen its faculties and inspire its imaginative powers.

This was Ionia; colonized from the selectest portion of the Greek race, a thousand years before Christ. Twelve Greek cities rose along the coast, and upon the two islands, confederate for the purposes of government and religion, and the common life and culture which give birth to art and literature. Architecture attained here its finishing grace in the Ionic column. Genius not only sung its sublimest epic in the Iliad, but language itself, newly modulated, had a breezy lightness and softness in the Ionian lyrics which became the models of Greece.

Mark the indentation of the coast and the islands by which Ionia opens towards the Ægean, and invites the commerce of the world! Mark the three rivers winding through fertile meadows by which it opens into the interior of Asia. By a magnificent Roman road which crossed the table-lands of Phrygia, and passed over the ridge of Taurus even to the river Euphrates, the cities of Ionia became the marts of an immense trade which set from the interior towards the Mediterranean sea. Consequently this little Greek confederacy, though small in territory, became the centre of a widely-extended influence upon oriental life, religion, and manners.

Ephesus was the metropolis of Ionia, and under

the Empire was the chief city of proconsular Asia. It stood at the mouth of the Cayster, on the southern bank of the river, extending over a wide plain and up the slopes of a mountain ridge called Coressus, which shut it in from the south, and up the slopes of another ridge on the right, called Mount Prion, which shut it in from the east. Within this brief space the oriental Greek wantoned and reveled, as if life were given for a perpetual holiday, and its main business were to enjoy the charms of earth and sky, and breathe the exhilarating airs. Near the banks of the river northeast of the city, rose the temple of Diana, one of the seven wonders of the world, with its one hundred and twenty-seven columns sixty feet high, each the gift of a king, and in which the Ionic style of architecture culminated in its highest perfection. On the side of Mount Prion was the theatre, with its immense circular rows of seats rising one above another, open to the brilliant sky, crowded often with the vast multitudes, not always like the mob who shouted "Great is Diana of the Ephesians," but answering with acclamations to music and song, sometimes perhaps to works of genius in a language whose vowel sounds made it the softest and sweetest that ever fell upon human ears. Southeast of the city and between Coressus and Prion was the gymnasium, where the exuberant life overflowed in athletic games. The annual festival held in honor of Diana, exhibited the rites of the Greek oriental religion.

What a contrast to our Puritan solemnity and sobriety! It was called "the common meeting of Asia." It was held through the month of May, and it drew throngs of devotees with their wives and children, not only from along the coast but from far away in the interior, who came for dance and song, for the amusements of the theatre and the gymnasium, for the rites of Diana, whose image was enshrined within the long, brilliant rows of colonnades, where came the vast and winding processions of joyous worshippers. The Asian Diana personified the all-fructifying and nourishing powers of nature, and hence her festival was held in the vernal season, when all nature was storming into life, and it made the days and nights of the month of May "one long scene of revelry."[1]

Partly within the limits of Ionia, partly just beyond in the neighboring provinces, were the cities which were to contain the seven churches, holding "the seven golden candlesticks," to bear aloft the light of Christianity to this portion of the eastern world. Not very far off is the little island of Patmos, unlike the others which gem the waters with green, but rising as a bald and barren rock out of the Ægean sea.

We have said enough fully to possess our readers with the idea of the vast importance of Ephesus as one of the strongholds of the pagan religion, one of the keys of its position which Christianity would be

[1] Conybeare and Howson's *Life of St. Paul*, vol ii. p. 79.

likely to take and hold. Notwithstanding the stimulating powers of nature amid which they lived, and the glorious traditions that urged them from behind, and the models of intellectual beauty which charmed their imaginations, the Asiatic Greeks sank into degeneracy and decay. An effeminate and voluptuous race read of the heroes that thundered through the Iliad without a spark of heroism in themselves. Religion itself became to them, not a light which leads upward into life, but which lured them downward into death. It was made to throw its consecrating veil over the most brutalizing sensuality, and the sacred groves concealed abominations which would bring a blush upon the face of the open day. We do not know that the groves of Mount Prion, like the groves of Daphne near Antioch, were consecrated to lust, but it is very certain that manhood and womanhood in the oriental Greek cities were infected with the common leprosy and sank down in Asiatic effeminacy and corruption. The cities of Ionia were not an exception. Their history illustrates the great truth that without a religion which brings life and health to the soul, the most illumined page of nature will grow dark to it and the most brilliant atmosphere, though drank as a constant elixir out of heaven, will not save it from consumption and death.

It is certain that the Gospel was preached at Ephesus by Paul soon after the middle of the first century, and that a church was gathered there whose influence extended rapidly through the neighboring country. Its converts were drawn first from the Jewish synagogue, but afterwards and mainly from the Greeks and orientals, more curious to know and more quick to receive and understand the truths of the new religion, and doubtless yearning towards the light out of the depths of their own degrading superstition. At the end of three years even the magnificent temple of Diana began to be deserted of its worshippers, its long processions to be thinned out, which shows how deep was the hunger of the multitudes and how directly Christianity went to their sorest needs.

We find the Apostle John, as early as A. D. 60, according to the New Testament narratives and epistles, a colaborer with the Apostles in or near Jerusalem. He then vanishes from history; but he reappears at Ephesus towards the close of the century, where memorials of unquestionable authenticity fix the last scenes of his life. We cannot mistake the exigency which brought him hither. Christianity had broken away from the synagogue, had shivered in pieces the Jewish shell which sought at first to confine it, and thrown itself on the vast floating waves of gentile peoples as a religion for humanity itself, which it was to renovate and redeem. It had already penetrated far beyond the limits of Ionia, and its leaven was fermenting and heaving the masses with life. "The seven churches that are in Asia" had arisen and were flinging their constellated light through the darkness. We knew from the letter of Pliny to Trajan, written soon after the close of the century, how wide and deep throughout this region the influence of Christianity had become. "The contagion of this superstition," says he, "has not only seized the cities but the villages and open country. The temples are well nigh deserted, the sacred rites for a long time have been intermitted, and victims for sacrifice are rarely purchased." But just in the degree that Christianity extended its influence would its native purity be liable to be over-clouded and its sharply cut lines of demarcation to become wavy and dim. This was the case among the Asiatic Greeks, and especially at Ephesus, the heart of the country whence the tides of life were constantly flowing, and into which they constantly returned. Metaphysical, subtle, curious, both analytical and constructive, and imaginative in the highest degree, with a language flexible to all the ranges and reaches of thought, the Greek mind was now to receive and act upon Christianity, and give it all its possible changes and combinations. Gnosticism was already at Ephesus. Cerinthus, a Hellenistic Jew, had come from Alexandria and adopted Christianity into his all-absorbing system of belief. Judaism had before been received into it. He made Jesus and Christ two persons. Jesus was a man like other men, with a human father and mother, but at his baptism the higher Æon, Christ, descended and entered him as the Holy Spirit, but ascended again and left him before his crucifixion. Cerinthus would hear and know nothing of a suffering and dying Messiah, but only of a heavenly one whose splendor was undimmed and untarnished by flesh and sense, and of whom the man Jesus was not an incarnation but only the passive organ and vehicle. This man was at Ephesus in the last decade of the first century.

Almost everything else was there at this conflux of the Eastern religions and superstitions. The arts of magic which are always in vogue where there is no enlightened faith in the supernatural, were prac ticed by strolling astrologers who infested every principal city from the Euphrates to the Tiber. They, too, were at Ephesus, exorcising demons by charms and incantations. The worship of Diana of the Ephesians had become a species of sorcery. The silver shrines bearing the image of the goddess with magical letters — the famous "*Ephesia grammata*" — were worn as charms and amulets by votaries from all the provinces of lesser Asia. Moreover, a more fantastic Gnosticism than that even of Cerinthus had been imported and diffused from Syria. Abhorring the idea that God could appear in this bad world directly and thus stain with matter his immaculate purity, it made God himself a great magician who could bejuggle the senses of men by projecting appearances upon them, which appearances.

though not matter, were the semblance of it without its substance.

It is certain that John was in Ephesus in the last decade of the century presiding over the constellated churches of that region, purging them from corruption and guarding their purity. It is certain that he here met Cerinthus and opposed him. The immediate disciples of John so reported, and there is not the least reason to question their truth. Many anecdotes are told of him; of his meeting Cerinthus at a bath and fleeing instantly away from it; of his apostolic watch and tender care over the churches of Asia; of his going into the fastnesses of the mountains to reclaim a young man who had apostatized and joined a gang of robbers — such as is well-known infested the provinces when fleeced by the Roman proconsuls; of his serene and beautiful old age, when too weak to walk alone he was borne into the assembly and out of it with exhortations to brotherly love ever upon his lips till the monotony tired them; of his banishment to the island of Patmos in the persecution under Domitian, and his return thence in A. D. 97; of his death about the close of the century when past the age of ninety; of his burial-place which Polycrates, bishop of Ephesus, towards the close of the second century, speaks of as a sacred spot well known in his day to the Christians of that region who cherished tenderly the local traditions of the beloved disciple. The anecdotes are strikingly characteristic, allowing in the details for some additions and colorings, just such as a fond and gossipy tradition would be likely to give.[1]

That the Apostle was called to a post where Christianity was centralizing its forces at the most fearful crisis of its history, — a post which needed the personal presence and commanding authority of one who had not only seen and heard the Lord Jesus in the days of his earthly life but who held open converse with Him still; that not only the exigencies of the times called him there, but the Divine Providence openly manifested to protect the nascent church and the rising faith, — is perfectly plain, we think, from all the memorials of this period both sacred and profane. It is convincingly evident when you study the Johannean writings and character and regard them as a collective force, thrown in at one of the most perilous conjunctures in human development to control it and guide it and hold it under benign spiritual laws. Christianity had escaped one danger and had fallen upon another vastly more threatening, and was in the breakers already. It had broken the bondage of Judaism, thanks to the intrepid power and inspired logic of Paul; and the poor and vanishing sect of the Ebionites which the Church had fairly thrown off was the last fragment of the broken chain. It had cleared the synagogue completely, and on the side of the Jew the peril was

[1] Eusebius H. E. iii. 23, 31; iv. 14.

past. Not so on the part of the Greek whose nimble intellect and soaring imagination could put all the philosophies and religions of the world together and fuse them through every changeable and gorgeous shape which could captivate the fancy of man, inflame his passions, or flatter his pride. Christianity, left to its natural course as a mere human system evolved out of the common and seething mass of opinions, would not have brought down the proud imaginations and humbled the philosophies of this world at its feet. It was in imminent danger now of being drawn up and absorbed by them; of serving as the fringe of a new Pantheism, or having a place in a heathen Pantheon enlarged and decorated for its reception. Such plainly was the crisis when John went to Ephesus.

John lived "to the times of Trajan," says Eusebius; and others say more definitely that he died in the third year of that emperor's reign, that is, in the year 100, at or near to its close. His death at least could not have been earlier. This does not rest on any uncertain tradition. We know it from other data. Polycarp, a disciple of John, who had drank deeply of the same spirit, was placed by him over the neighboring church at Smyrna, one of "the seven churches in Asia," the light of whose golden candlesticks the Apostle watched from Ephesus and labored to keep undimmed. There Polycarp lived and preached ever after, and there he suffered martyrdom in the year 167. He was then eighty-six years old, as he says to his persecutors when they urged him to abjure his Saviour: "Eighty-six years have I served Him." This is contained in the letter of the church at Smyrna, written by eye-witnesses describing the beautiful and triumphant death of that aged bishop and reporting his words.[1] This would give barely twenty years of his life as falling within the first century. He could hardly have been younger than that when John placed him over the church at Smyrna, and it becomes more probable that the Apostle lived past the century than that he died before its close. We know from Pliny's letter to Trajan already referred to, written close upon this time, that Christianity had then become widely diffused in Asia Minor, and that the heathen temples were becoming deserted of their worshippers.

[1] This letter has some marks of embellishment from a later hand, but we regard its facts and dates as authentic. It is given by Eusebius.

CHAPTER III.

THE JOHANNEAN WRITINGS: THEIR CONGRUITY, INTERIOR RELATIONS AND IDENTITY OF AUTHORSHIP.

TAKING for our present purpose the fourth Gospel, the Catholic Epistle, and the Apocalypse, and the memorials of John found in the synoptics, a character rises before us sketched and shaded with marvelous symmetry, consistency, and grace, and a class of writings present themselves, whose interior relations are of a most extraordinary kind. The character is such that no writer of that age would have created it as fiction, and the relations of these writings are not only impossible, but unimaginable on any theory which does not make them the production of one mind and genius.

To suppose a set of myth-makers of opposite opinions and tendencies, scattered through half a century and half of the then civilized world, to have left a mass of documents, partly forged, partly compiled from uncertain tradition, partly made up of imaginations taken unconsciously for facts; that these were thrown hap-hazard together, and that out of them emerges a character of such freshness and originality as that of John, of tints so rich, and varied, and delicate, and yet so harmoniously blended, — to suppose this would be supposing no less than a moral miracle. We are not saying that this character is unimaginable or beyond the reach of creative art under a single and very skillful hand ; we are saying that such compilers could no more have produced it, and that by accident, than a hundred Greek slaves could build the temple of Diana by throwing down at random their cart-loads of stone and mortar.

The character of John is composed of two vastly differing elements, rarely found in such combination except under the transfusing power of the Christian spirit, but found there in its perfection and consummation. These two elements are very great masculine strength, joined with affections so overflowing and tender, that the strength is concealed under their profusion, except when occasions and emergencies bring it to the test. The granite is hidden under the tendrils that overhang it with flowers. It is only by assuming that these two elements are inconsistent with each other that the critics have raised their objections against the congruity of the canonical Johannean writings, whereas to blend them together is the great achievement of Christianity in human nature, and the blending is most perfect when the disciple leans most intimately on the bosom of his Lord. The combination does not impair the masculine intrepidity, but preserves it and tones it, though concealing it sometimes under the mildest of womanly gentleness. That there was this native hardihood in the favorite disciple, intensified even to savageness, there are indications which cannot be mistaken. The two sons of Zebedee were called "thunderers," and that the surname was descriptive of natural traits, is shown by the fiery zeal which prompted them to invoke the lightnings to blast the Samaritan city which refused them hospitality. This, it must be remembered, was in the first stages of discipleship, while as yet they understood the Messiah's kingdom to be one of temporal power and magnificence, and aspired to its chief honors and rewards. Not yet had the deep and abundant fountains of love been called forth to their overflowing. But even when this is the case, and when they trickle forth in all their tenderness, spreading everywhere the most delicate verdure and bloom, we are never allowed to forget the rock-ribbed back-ground which supports the whole. Something reminds us even in the softest refinement and spirituality of the favorite disciple that these come not out of weakness and shallowness. When Jesus was arrested in Gethsemane, the disciples dispersed and fled for their lives. But there was one exception. We follow on, and in the open court of the High Priest's palace where Jesus is brought for insult and mockery, appears the youthful John who had kept close to his Master. Peter follows cautiously at a distance, and is let in through John's intercession; but Peter's courage soon gives way amid the appalling scene. At the cross again, under the storm of rage, and amid the scoffs and wagging of heads, Jesus looks down and sees a single disciple standing close by. It is John again, — the same who drank in the divine love on his breast with a tenderness which was more than woman's, and who when the storm came which sifted his followers like wheat, evinced a greatness and strength of character beyond that of common men. It shows us, what history and experience teach alike, that in the most trying emergencies, the gentlest natures are the strongest, provided the divine gentleness has made them great.

There are three principal documents extant which the churches ascribe to the beloved disciple, — the fourth Gospel, the Catholic Epistle, and the Apocalypse. That the first two were written by the same hand, is shown from internal evidence which cannot be resisted. An imitator or forger might have strung together phrases culled out of the fourth Gospel such as occur in the Epistle, but he never could have so made it live as to preserve the spirit that breathes through it spontaneously and gives fragrancy to the whole. The theology of the fourth Gospel, the doctrine of the Logos, is here set forth, not only in the terms but with the unction known only to the beloved disciple. But this is not all. The very atmosphere of Ephesus is felt in every chapter of the Catholic Epistle. Through every one there is an outlook upon the Gnostic heresy confronting us in some shape. In the opening passage we have it full in the eye, as if in the first stroke of his pen the writer was refuting the false teacher who turned the Christ into some intangible unreality or phantasm, "that which we have heard, which we have seen with our eyes, which we have looked upon, and OUR HANDS HAVE HANDLED of the Word of Life." Every sense that can testify is appealed to. Not only so. We have it asserted and reiterated that "Jesus is the Christ," and he who denies this is a "liar." This finds its point and burden of meaning when we have Cerinthus in full view, asserting that Jesus was not the Christ, but that He was one person, and Christ who never came in the flesh was quite another person. By this, says the writer of the Catholic Epistle, ye shall try the spirits and distinguish them. "Every spirit that confesseth that *Jesus Christ is come in the flesh* is of God, and every spirit that says Jesus Christ is not come in the flesh is not of God, and this is that spirit of anti-Christ whereof ye have heard it should come, and even now already is in the world."

That "sin is a transgression of the law," and that "he that doeth righteousness is righteous," sound very much in our modern ears, like saying sin is sin, and virtue is virtue. Not so in presence of a heresy which allowed men to grovel in the stye of sensuality, and yet promised to keep their inmost souls separate and immaculate before the Highest. In the whole cast and style of this Epistle we not only know that the spirit that gave form and coloring to the fourth Gospel is with us, but that the very same moral atmosphere which lay upon lesser Asia at the close of the first century, is all around us.

But the commingling of the two elements in the Catholic Epistle is such as nature and not art must have given them. Through the abounding tenderness, whose language is ever reiterated, breaks the most severe and wrathful denunciation. Almost in the same sentence come the blessings and the curses. The words "little children," which should rather be rendered "my dear children," with fond allusions to the divine love and fatherhood, alternate with "murderer," "liar," and "anti-christ," and "children of the devil," applied to the heretics of his day. In the disciple leaning on the divine breast and drinking its love, we never quite lose sight of the darker background of character in the man who invoked lightnings on the Samaritans.

But more remarkably and unmistakably do we find all this in the Apocalypse brought out in such wise as no human imagination could have invented. It is no part of our work to expound the Apocalypse, but we affirm that its congruity with the other Johannean writings is most remarkable, and they run into each other by relations exceedingly subtile and pervasive. This fact we know is not generally acknowledged, but it will be obvious to the reader the longer he studies the contents and interior relationships of these writings.

The Apocalypse as is now generally conceded is the writing of John the Evangelist. Doubts, it is true, were entertained on this point in the third century, and there were some Greek churches which did not receive it. But there were obvious reasons. From the nature of its contents it was not read in the churches, and therefore was not so publicly known as the four Gospels. But it was early attested and commented upon ; and modern investigation and criticism render a verdict in favor of its genuineness which is emphatic and substantially unanimous. Perhaps, however, the Tübingen critics would not have been quite so swift in claiming the Apocalypse as the work of John, had not its contents on superficial examination indicated a different hand from the one which wrote the fourth Gospel, and afforded therefore new ground from which to assail the genuineness of the latter. Both, so we are told, could not be the productions of the same mind, so totally diverse are they in matter and style. One has an artless or else exceedingly artful simplicity ; the other an unwonted gorgeousness and grandeur ; one is in comparatively pure Greek ; the other is in bad Greek, and constantly violates the structural rules of the language.

A comparison of these two works reveals some of the most profound and subtile of psychological phenomena, and those which are the most infallible of all circumstantial evidence. When we open the Apocalypse, we are called upon to recognize at once a new mental condition and one professedly abnormal. It is the state of seership, out of which some of the old prophets, Isaiah and Ezekiel for example, and David sometimes, prophesied and wrote. It was produced from a state described by the author himself as ἐν πνεύματι. No critic who refuses to take this into the account can say anything of the Apocalypse, whether of its form or essence, which is of the least value whatever. No critic, we think, who does take this into the account and understand its bearings, will rise from his investigation with any doubt that the same hand wrote this book that wrote the fourth Gospel and Catholic Epistle, and that the same personality and lines of character which appear in the latter two, are intensified in the former to their sublimest consummation.

Says Mr. J. J. Tayler in his treatise on the fourth Gospel, "No living writer has exhibited a more remarkable change of style in the course of his literary career, than Mr. Carlyle; yet if we compare his 'Life of Schiller' with his 'French Revolution,' or his 'History of Frederick the Great,' notwithstanding the great disparity of form, every reader of ordinary discernment will recognize the same fundamental characteristics of his peculiar genius in his earlier and his later works." The same, he says, is true of Milton. "Apply this standard to the two books now under consideration, and the conclusion," he says, "will be irresistible, that if the Apostle John be the author of the Apocalypse, he cannot have written the Gospel; if he wrote the Gospel, he cannot be the author of the Apocalypse."[1] He then goes on to prove that the Apostle John *did* write the Apocalypse, the early testimony being nearly unanimous on that point, and therefore he did not write the fourth Gospel. Theodore Parker, and more recently, Professor Davidson, come to the same result, and they echo the Tübingen critics generally.

It never seems to enter the conception of any of these writers that there is any such condition of the human faculties as *seership*, or if they do that it is anything else than a normal exercise of the imagination, as in the case of Milton and Carlyle. The very stand-point from which John says he wrote the Apocalypse, and which determines the very nature and style of his production, they ignore altogether, or have not the remotest idea of, and so their volumes of criticism are not worth the paper they have wasted.

There are three modes and degrees of apprehending truth. It may be reasoned and proved argumentatively by strong intellection like that of Paul; it may be perceived intuitively under the inspiration of the heart, or it may be visioned objectively by representatives and symbols, when the prophet becomes a seer. The deepest and clearest intuition is nearest to the state of the highest seership, and if John drank

[1] Pages 13, 14.

the deepest and clearest draughts of the divine love he would be the one of all the twelve on whom the Apocalypse would open its magnificent scenery.

We do not say this, believing that the seership of the Apostle was a natural development of his faculties, but simply supposing that the Divine Providence never acts by magic; that the Spirit does not select its instrumentalities arbitrarily, but those best prepared naturally and psychologically for its highest inspirations and disclosures. The evidence we are about to unfold, however, is all the same, whatever view we take of the inspiration of these writings.

When the mind of a speaker or writer passes from its normal state to that of seership, two things are to be observed. He speaks thereafter not from himself, not according to his own tastes and models. His will no longer determines either his style or matter, but both are determined by the uncontrolled spontaneities within him. Hence the higher prophetic style is never that of simple narrative or voluntary utterance.

But neither again is it a style arbitrarily induced upon the writer, and altogether foreign to him. Because in the seer his subjective state becomes objective. The truth that lay in his mind, or was bodied in his speech in the form of metaphor, now passes out of his mind, and the metaphors become the living beings and the moving panorama of an objective world. Therefore, while the seer does not speak from his own personality but from a consciousness deeper than his natural one, his personality, nevertheless, does not disappear. Rather it reappears, though changed and sublimed, in a higher order of mental and spiritual phenomena. The Spirit that breathes through him and makes him its organ, takes the things of his memory and the whole treasury of his imagination and experience, and recombines them with the figures of its own more vast and illuminated perspectives. Consequently, the idiosyncrasies, mental, moral, and spiritual, the characteristics of the individual in his normal condition, are to be traced always in the seer, though heightened and intensified. Ezekiel is not Isaiah, and neither of these prophets retain their simple narrative style when they rise into the heights of seership, though their characteristics are sublimed without being lost. David passed the years of his youth tending his father's flocks on the plains of Bethlehem, and so afterwards in his highest moments of inspiration his figures of speech are drawn from a shepherd's life and from pastoral fields. If his inspiration had become vision, unquestionably his figures of speech would have taken form and coloring, and unrolled to his eye an objective world showing in mystic light "the green pastures" and "the still waters."

Now let any one compare the fourth Gospel with the Apocalypse, and he will be surprised to find how constantly the metaphors of the former pass into the latter and become the living figures of its ever shifting panorama. This is the more remarkable as these figures of speech are altogether peculiar and strictly Johannean. The fact is illustrative of a profound psychological principle, but it is a principle which no fabricator of that age would ever have dreamed of availing himself of. We will give some very striking examples.

The first chapter of the fourth Gospel, in that portion of it which opens the personal biography of Jesus, describes a scene which evidently glowed vividly afterwards in the imagination of the Evangelist. The Baptist, seeing Jesus coming, waves his hand, and says to his disciples, "Behold the Lamb of God that taketh away the sin of the world." The mind of John dwelt fondly upon the image, for the same is repeated soon after and graphically described. The next day the Baptist stood, and two of his disciples, one of whom was evidently the Evangelist himself. On looking on Jesus *as He walked*, he saith, "Behold the Lamb of God." By none other of the Evangelists is Jesus ever called the Lamb, and with a single exception the figure is used by no other writer of the New Testament. It occurs in 1 Peter i. 19. But at the beginning of the fourth Gospel, it evidently describes Jesus as the coming sacrifice, and implies as well a certain grace of person and charm of manner which had won at first sight the heart of John.

A lamb offered in sacrifice is a beautiful figure of

self-oblation, but not likely to be selected by any writer under ordinary conditions, as the symbol of regal power and authority. But we open the Apocalypse, and lo! the image of the Lamb reappears, not now as a figure of speech, but in living objective form, and around it all the figures of the moving panorama are grouped in their rank and order. And when the ritual of heaven is described, and we look up through "the ten thousand times ten thousand and thousands of thousands," and the angels about the throne, and the four-and-twenty elders that cast down before it their crowns of gold, and the eye at last sees the central figure of this ascending homage, it is not an oriental monarch sitting in regal splendor, but A LAMB AS IT HAD BEEN SLAIN. The figure occurs more than twenty times in the Apocalypse, but now always hypostatized. The figure stands conspicuous at the opening of the fourth Gospel, and tones it throughout; the figure hypostatized determines the whole drama of the Apocalypse, and draws around it the heavenly alleluiahs.

The doctrine of the Logos, or Word, is not peculiar to the Johannean writings, but its form of statement is.

Nowhere else in the New Testament except the Johannean writings, nor indeed in any writing of the first century is Jesus Christ called the Logos. In the proem of the fourth Gospel the Logos is distinctly personified, and in such wise that it has baffled the commentators ever since; and in the very first verse of the Catholic Epistle it is personified again in like manner. It ceases to be an abstract term, and is something which men have "seen" and "handled." This is specially and emphatically Johannean, and, as we shall see by and by, was designed to turn the divine truth with its boldest and brightest front against the Gnostic heresies.

We should naturally expect that the Logos would reappear in the Apocalypse. It does; and it is not only hypostatized, but dramatized, and goes forth as a fierce warrior and an almighty King, armed against the enemies of truth, and riding them down with garments crimsoned with their blood.

"I saw heaven opened, and behold a white horse; and he that sat upon him was called Faithful and True, and in righteousness he doth judge and make war. His eyes were as a flame of fire, and on his head were many crowns; and he had a name written that no man knew, but he himself. And he was clothed in a vesture bathed in blood: and his name is called the LOGOS OF GOD. And the armies in heaven followed him upon white horses, clothed in fine linen, white and clean. And out of his mouth goeth a sharp sword, that with it he should smite the nations; and he shall rule them with a rod of iron: and he treadeth the wine-press of the fierceness and wrath of Almighty God. And he had on his vesture and on his thigh a name written, King of kings, and Lord of lords."[1]

[1] Rev. xix. 11–16.

It is alleged by some of the critics that the Logos doctrine was borrowed from the later Platonists, and that it fixes the date of the fourth Gospel towards the middle of the second century. Here in a work acknowledged to be John's by these same critics, the Word is not only hypostatized already, but clothed with Divine attributes like the Word of the Golden Proem.

Our next illustration is of even more remarkable significance. The opening chapters, both of the fourth Gospel and of the Catholic Epistle, describe the Word as the Beginning and the Ultimation; as existing ἐν ἀρχῇ, —in the prime central principles of Divine being; and again as the Word made flesh—σὰρξ ἐγένετο,—as existing in the lowest and outermost things. In the Catholic Epistle it is, "That which was *in the Beginning*," and, "That which *our eyes have seen and our hands have handled.*" This goes to the profoundest metaphysics of the New Testament. Moreover it is in a form exclusively and intensely Johannean. The thought may be gathered and deduced elsewhere, but it never runs into this peculiar mould. But open the Apocalypse, and this profound metaphysic becomes the grandest objective reality, rising on the sight in glorified form and with overwhelming power and effulgence. The Beginning and the Ultimation, the Alpha and the Omega, appears as one like unto the Son of man, his countenance as the sun shining in his strength, his hairs as white as wool, and his feet like brass refined and burning, — that is, He is divine not only ἐν ἀρχῇ — in first things, but in their lowest natural forms and ultimations. The conception was not only above the age, but above all the ages. Its formulation, as found in the Johannean writings, is not only original and peculiar, but it transcends the profoundest deep of Greek metaphysics and the loftiest flights of poetry.

Another figure which has become common currency in the speech of Christendom, but which is altogether Johannean in origin, is that of water not used as the symbol of baptism, but as representing the power of truth to refresh the soul and slake its thirst; and of bread to satisfy its hunger; making Jesus Christ, by a bold metaphor, both water and bread from heaven. There is nothing of this in the synoptics, but it characterizes the fourth Gospel throughout. The imagery clung delightfully to the mind of the beloved disciple, and those discourses and conversations of Jesus in which it abounds are fondly remembered and reproduced in all their tenderness. In the conversation with the Samaritan woman, the Christ is "living water," or, again, a fountain of water in the believer bubbling up unto everlasting life, — that is perpetually, and diffusing verdure and bloom over all the scenery of the soul. He offers Himself as food and drink, and so merges the literal sense in the spiritual, that some of his followers misunderstand Him and go away. "Who can hear such sayings?" And in the last jubilant day of the Feast of the Tabernacles, when the long winding procession brought water from the springs of Siloam, circling the altar and pouring it out as they chanted, "Behold, we draw water from the wells of salvation," a loud voice startles the crowd and commands them. Evidently there was a prophet-tone in the words that broke in upon the ceremony and arrested it. Jesus "stood and cried," "If any man thirst let him come unto *me* and drink. He that believeth on me out of his heart shall flow rivers of living water."

Turn to the Apocalypse, and what before was bold metaphor and graphic description passes into the objective scenery of the seer. It is no longer in the mind, but visioned as out of the mind; unrolled as the land of Paradise through which crystal streams are flowing, between rows of trees, margined with eternal green. The streams flow out of "the throne of God and of the Lamb," along the streets of the New Jerusalem, and on either side are rows of the tree of life. The figure often recurs, but now as actual water visioned and flowing clear as in the last fervent invitation, "Let him that is athirst come, and whosoever will let him take the water of life freely," reiterating the very invitation of Christ in the Gospel, "If any man thirst let him come unto me and drink." The whole is intensely Johannean, and could no more have been fabricated by some writer of the next century than Lear's jester could have fabricated a second Iliad. It is beyond the range of poetic imagination, and beyond Homer himself.

The GOOD SHEPHERD, and the flock as the sheep of his pasture, have been the favorite imagery under which the Church in all ages has delighted to represent the relation of Jesus Christ to his followers. But whence is this imagery derived? Not from the twenty-third Psalm, though it occurs there, David himself having been called from pastoral life. The Church derives it from discourses of Jesus reported in the fourth Gospel, and which are not found in the synoptics, not merely because they were most congenial with the Johannean spirit, but because John only of the evangelists was an ear-witness of their utterance. The parable of the good shepherd was not one of the public proclamations of his ministry in Galilee; it was uttered in the more private colloquial intercourse which he had with the people that gathered around him in and about Jerusalem, whither He had gone up to attend one of the festivals. The Jews were watching Him, and seeking cause for arresting Him. "My sheep," said He, "hear my voice, and I know them, and they follow me. I am the good Shepherd, and know my sheep, and am known of mine." And at the next festival He repeats what He had said before: "Ye believe not because ye are not of my sheep, as I said unto you. My sheep hear my voice, and I know them, and they follow me. And I give unto them eternal life, and they shall never perish, neither shall any pluck them out of my hand." And again, as the door or gate of the field, he says, "If any man enter in he shall be saved, and shall go in and out, and find pasture."

The appendix to the fourth Gospel — for such we regard the closing chapter — was probably added by John's personal disciples from traditions of his discourses preserved at Ephesus. In it the same imagery occurs again with the injunction of the Master, "Feed my sheep, feed my lambs."

It is easy to imagine why this imagery passed thus fully and spontaneously into the discourse of our Saviour. He was brought up at Nazareth; and the vast plain of Esdraelon, with its brooks murmuring towards the sea, dotted over with flocks of sheep, the shepherds going before them, calling the leaders by name, carrying the lambs in his arms, conducting them to green spots by the brook-side, or into the sheep-fold by night, and into the cool shade at sultry noon, must have been the most familiar scenes which Jesus looked upon through his youth and opening manhood. They arrest the notice of the traveller to-day, and bring the peaceful imagery of the fourth Gospel freshly to his mind.

It would be very strange if we did not find it reproduced in the visions of the New Jerusalem. It is there; the vales of Esdraelon idealized and glowing in mystic light become the fields into which the Christ as the Shepherd of the fold shall lead his flock washed in his blood and made white and clean. "They shall hunger no more, neither thirst any more, neither shall the sun light on them nor any heat; for the Lamb which is in the midst of the throne shall feed them, and shall lead them unto living fountains of waters, and God shall wipe away all tears from their eyes."

Light, as the symbol and representative of truth, is a figure of speech found in almost all classes of writing, but it is found in the fourth Gospel as nowhere else. Jesus Christ is there presented, not merely as a teacher to enlighten the minds of men with his doctrine, but He becomes the impersonation of Light itself, and the very sun of the moral universe. This mode of speech characterizes the entire fourth Gospel to such an extent that it has seemed to many to give it a Zoroastrian tinge, and it is difficult to avoid the inference that it has not some tacit reference to the Gnosticism of that day. The Baptist is *a* light local and temporary, but the Logos which was in the beginning with God, and was God, comes into the world as The Light to enlighten every man, and John and all other lights pale before it. The figure used in this way occurs nowhere in the synoptics, and nowhere in the Epistles, except in the first Epistle of John, where God Himself is "Light in whom is no darkness at all."[1] In one of the most

[1] 1 John i. 5.

striking passages of the fourth Gospel the personification is employed early in the morning as Jesus was teaching in the temple. At the hour when the sun was just rising and flinging his beams aslant the gilded dome and roof, and the white marble columns possibly suggesting the figure, Jesus declares, "I AM THE LIGHT OF THE WORLD." [1]

We open the Apocalypse, and in the very first chapter we find that the figure of the Proem is hypostatized as the sun itself of the higher mystic world. The Logos which came before as The Light to enlighten every one, appears now as one like unto the Son of man, his countenance as the sun shining in his strength, standing in the midst of the constellated churches, which like golden candlesticks, borrow their light and trick their beams from Him. The figure recurs again and again, but it is no longer metaphor. It becomes the central luminary itself, diffusing warmth and glory throughout the New Jerusalem, which needs no candle, no sun, and no moon, because "THE LAMB IS THE LIGHT THEREOF.[2]

We cite one more instance of a most remarkable kind. John alone of all the twelve followed Jesus to the cross and stood under it to witness its agonies. Therefore he gives details which all the others omit. None of the synoptics mention the piercing with the spear, but John does it with asseverations which show how deeply the sight affected him.

[1] John viii. 12.

[2] Rev. i. 13–16; xxii. 5.

"One of the soldiers with a spear pierced His side, and forthwith came thereout blood and water; and he that saw it bare record, and his record is true; and he knoweth that he saith true; that ye might believe,"—evidently referring to the doceticism of the Gnostics, who denied the real suffering of the Christ. And then follows the citation of the prophesy, "They shall look on Him whom they pierced."[1]

This quotation is from Zech. xii. 10, and the language, as there applied, has no direct reference to Christ, but to the enemies of Jerusalem in her conflict with the heathen nations. John applies it in a secondary and mystical sense to the men who crucified the Lord.

In the reappearings of Jesus, in two successive scenes, John alone remembers what had so vividly impressed his senses, and through them his imagination at the cross. "Jesus showed them his hands *and his side.*"

Turn now to the Apocalypse, and the same thing reappears in the vision of the seer, sublimed and intensified. The fact, of which John alone of the twelve was the eye-witness, is recalled. Not only so, but the same passage from Zechariah is cited in the same secondary and mystical sense, and the imagery and language of the passage are employed with greater fullness and amplitude. "Behold He com-

[1] John xix. 34-37.

eth with clouds and every eye shall see Him, and *they also which pierced Him*, and all kindreds of the earth shall wail because of Him. Even so, Amen." Both quotations from the same prophecy, made with such peculiarity, point indubitably to one and the same writer.[1] The fact which had impressed the senses of John so deeply and tragically, passes into the imagery of the seer, where that same Christ coming to judgment shall compel those who pierced his side to look upon Him in his open and overwhelming majesty. Dr. Davidson tries to parry the force of this point in a course of remark which we can regard as little better than puerile.

The personal characteristics of the favorite disciple are portrayed not less in the Apocalypse than in the other Johannean writings. Both the prime elements of his character are strongly contrasted, but exalted and toned beyond the power of any human imagination to commingle and harmonize. No chambers of imagery ever opened such treasures of wrath, such storm-clouds, forking lightnings, or showering down fire and hail and bloody rain. The destruction, not of a Samaritan city, but of all the enemies of Christianity, both Jewish and Roman, is seen through the opening ages, and the New Jeru-

[1] The quotation is doubtless from the Septuagint, — *καὶ ἐπιβλεψονται προς με ανθ' ὧν κατωρχήσαντο*, — "they shall look on *me* whom they have pierced." In both cases, in the quotation in the fourth Gospel and in the Apocalypse, the original is changed from the first person to the third.

salem descending beyond adorned and beloved as a bride. The grand and terrific heightened to superhuman intensity, set off in contrast with images of peace more sweet and lovely than the earth alone can furnish, all are there. But the critics mistake, we think, when they suppose the personal feelings and passions of the writer are in the Apocalypse. In the seer they have passed beyond that stage altogether. His personal genius is there superhumanly exalted and idealized, for he speaks not himself but is spoken out of; and the divine pencil takes its colorings from a human treasure-house, where they had been abundantly stored up, and paints the realities which were to be, and whose future the course of Christian history has ever since been filling up.

The style of the Johannean writings, — a subject on which the critics have grievously stumbled, — is exceedingly variant. But it varies as the psychological condition of the historian differs from that of the seer. One writes from his own natural consciousness. The other writes from a profounder consciousness than the natural one, and the style is not his own, though colored by his native genius. One may be perfectly simple and prosaic; the other, when essentially prophetic, is raised to a sphere of thought where the wing of imagination never dares to play, and his style may assume a mystic grandeur beyond that of ordinary poetry.

But we come to another peculiarity of the Apocalypse, and one which seems at first to distinguish it strongly from the other Johannean writings, we mean the "bad Greek," which the critics have made so much account of. This, too, when narrowly scrutinized, remands us to one of the profounder principles of mental action.

When men pass from a normal to a trance condition, or one essentially abnormal, and speak from pure spontaneity, they almost always speak in their vernacular tongue, seldom in a language which has been acquired later. If a German who had acquired English should somnambulize, he would inevitably fall back upon the speech which he learned from his mother's lips, and to which his organs and his interior thought had always been attuned. The reason is plain. In these abnormal moods the voluntary powers are in abeyance, and the involuntary are in full play, and will determine to no speech which is foreign to them and artificial, but only to their own native forms and idioms.[1]

It is a very remarkable fact that the bad Greek of the Apocalypse is Greek *which has been Hebraized.* It is full of Hebrew idioms, which has led the critics strongly to suspect that it was composed originally in Hebrew. Bishop Middleton says that if this could

[1] Dr. Rush, of Philadelphia, who practiced among the German population, said that people who had not spoken their native tongue for thirty years, on their death-beds, with the eternal scene drawing nigh, would talk and pray in the language of their childhood.

be admitted all the difficulties on this score would vanish at once.

It may not only be admitted, but assumed as exceedingly probable, that the Apocalypse, if written by John ἐν πνεύματι, was produced in one of the Hebrew dialects. The Syro-Chaldee was his vernacular, the same which he spoke on the shores of the Galilean lake, and associated with which all the memories of his childhood, youth, and early manhood, and the natural imagery which enshrined them, were stored away in the treasuries of his mind. All his intercourse with Jesus had been in this language, and all the discourses he had ever heard from Him were in the same dialect. It would be strange indeed if after the ascension of Jesus, when intercourse with the beloved disciple was renewed, it had been in a foreign language, and not in the one which they used together when he leaned on the Master's bosom. Inevitably, and by psychological laws, when he wrote ἐν πνεύματι, that is, not by his own will, but out of a profounder spontaneity and under the dictation of the very lips that charmed his younger manhood, the Divine influx would not flow into Greek forms, but into the forms of his native tongue.

The congruity of the Johannean writings with each other and with the character of the favorite disciple, is important not merely as a most decisive argument for the genuineness of these writings, but as helping greatly in their mutual interpretation and in that of the whole New Testament. For it cannot well be denied that the Johannean theology is inmost like the soul in the body, being the central light which penetrates, involves, and transfigures the whole.

CHAPTER IV.

THE SCOPE, PURPOSE, AND SPIRIT OF THE APOCALYPSE.

WE reserve for a separate chapter a difficulty raised by modern criticism pertaining to the congruity and identity of authorship of the Apocalypse and the fourth Gospel. It is this: The temper of the one is wholly unlike that of the other. The temper of the fourth Gospel is sweet and beautifully Christian; the temper of the Apocalypse is fierce, vindictive, and Jewish. Baur sees in the Apocalypse abundant evidence for his theory of two hostile parties in the primitive Church, — the Jewish party, at the head of which was Peter; the Gentile party, at the head of which was Paul; and of course John wrote in the interest of the Jewish party, recognizing throughout the Apocalypse only twelve Apostles, ignoring the thirteenth, telling the churches that Paul claimed to be an Apostle when he was not, and was a "liar" (Rev. ii. 2). We enter not into any examination of Baur's theory, which a late writer we think has put forever at rest,[1] but the purpose and temper of a writing, which comes to us from the man

[1] Fisher's *Essays on the Origin of Christianity*, specially Essay IV.

who shared most fully the confidence of the Lord Jesus Christ, becomes to us a subject of the deepest interest.

At what time was it written? is a question of some importance, and bears incidentally on its interpretation. On this point the traditions of the primitive Church are all in one direction: the Church, that is, of the century succeeding the apostolic age; traditions so early that they almost become the testimony of ear-witnesses. It was written, according to the earliest testimony, during the reign of Domitian, or about A. D. 96. Irenæus, a contemporary of John's disciples, says the Revelation "was seen not long ago, almost in our age, at the end of the reign of Domitian." Melito, bishop of Sardis, one of the churches to whom the Apocalypse was originally addressed, writes as early as A. D. 177, and receives the Apocalypse as that of John; and Justin, writing in 140, and at the city of Ephesus, the scene of John's last labors, and when hundreds were alive who had seen and heard him, refers to the book, and quotes it. Tertullian, about A. D. 200, says, "We have churches which are disciples of John;" and referring to the Apocalypse, "The succession of bishops traced to the original will assure us that John is the author." Clement's testimony is to the same purpose. The churches which had the best means of knowing, not only testify unanimously to the Johannean authorship of the Apocalypse, but also to its date; and the testimony begins so early that it is virtually that of men who had seen the beloved disciple, hung upon his lips, welcomed him home from his banishment in Patmos, and saw him laid in his final rest at Ephesus. It is concurrent to the same result. — John's banishment was in the persecutions under Domitian, at which time he had his visions; that is, about A. D. 96, the last of that tyrant's reign.

Why have subsequent criticisms, some of them ancient but most of them modern, endeavored to set aside this early testimony? Almost solely for the reason that the eleventh chapter of the Apocalypse is supposed to refer to Jerusalem and the temple as if they were yet standing. Jerusalem was destroyed A. D. 72. Therefore — such is the logic, — the book must have been written before that time. The banishment to Patmos must have been during the persecutions of Nero, or about A. D. 66.

We shall see that the supposed reference to Jerusalem and the temple is an argument which has not the least validity. Aside from this, it is to be observed that the persecution under Nero was local, and there is no historical evidence that it extended to Asia Minor. Then there is no probability that John was at Ephesus so early as 66, or that the seven churches, with the exception of the church at Ephesus, had even an existence. Paul preached at Ephesus A. D. 55, and gathered a church there. About three years after (58), on his return to Jerusalem from Corinth, he meets at

Miletus the elders from Ephesus, when occurred that scene of tenderest pathos which Luke has described. In the year 62 Paul writes his letter to the Ephesians from Rome. In the year 67 he is at Ephesus again, and writes thence his letter to Titus. In the year 68 he is in prison again at Rome, where he was beheaded under Nero. These dates may not all be exact. We take them from the careful chronology of Conybeare and Howson, and we have no doubt they are approximately correct. Through the whole there is no allusion to John at Ephesus or to the constellated churches of Asia Minor. We hold the supposition utterly baseless that so early as the year 66 Christianity had thus spread through Asia Minor; that seven churches had been founded there and passed through stages of growth, corruption, and declension, like some of the seven churches to which John first published his revelations. The internal evidence, as well as the historical, point to the close of the century as the true date. When John wrote the Apocalypse, therefore, Paul had been dead twenty-eight years. John, at the time of writing, was placed over a church which Paul had founded and nourished with vast sacrifice and toil. John had entered into his labors and built on his foundation. Even allowing there might have ever been any division between them — of which we have not a shred of evidence — the notion that John would go twenty-eight years out of his way to shout "liar," over the grave of the great martyr, is rather too absurd for refutation. In the passage cited reference is made not to one man but to a class of men. "Thou hast tried them," he writes to the church at Ephesus, "which say they are apostles and are not, and hast found them liars." That the Cerinthian Gnostics, who we know were at Ephesus, and who pretended to have revelations from the Christ which superseded the apostolic Christianity, are the persons here alluded to seems beyond all reasonable question.

To estimate aright the scope and temper of the Apocalypse we must have some adequate conception of the state of seership from which it professes to have been produced. Professor Davidson, who writes learnedly about this book, has no other notion of that state of mind than the natural faculties excited to unwonted fervor and ecstasy. That "the visions and their coloring were *given*, is an assumption," he says, "which deprives the author of consciousness, and is contrary to the analogy of prophecy." It no more deprives the author of his consciousness, than the scenery of nature given every day to our natural vision, deprives us of our consciousness; and it is not only in analogy with prophecy, but it is prophecy itself in the exercise of its highest function. The seer has opened within him a more interior consciousness, to which the scenery of a higher world is unrolled. That scenery he can describe, and its changes he can note and chronicle, while his consciousness may be as vivid and more so than that of the astronomer when looking at the stars. He sees events in their causes; in those spiritual states and conditions that lie behind and within all material phenomena, and out of which material phenomena are evolved. Those states and conditions he sees represented by appropriate symbols. Those symbols may be given entire, or they may be in his own memory, the treasures of his own imagination; as in the case of John, whose mind was aglow with the imagery of the Savior's discourses fondly preserved and dwelt upon. In either case they are no longer his own, after they have passed into scenery which symbolizes the spiritual truths and realities of which all earthly realities are only the outcome and ultimation. To illustrate: the seer beholds in vision the sun in sackcloth and the moon turned into blood. Does this foretell an eclipse of the sun and moon in the natural world? Nothing of the kind. It represents the divine light and love extinguished in human souls, and the woes and calamities that are sure to follow. He sees a conqueror, whose name is Faithful and True, riding upon a white horse with a sharp sword issuing from his mouth. Does this mean that we are to look in the natural world for a man on horseback with the same appearance and name? Nothing of the kind. It represents plainly Divine Truth in its triumphal power. He sees a city lying waste, and the temple in it about to be thrown down.

Does this mean that some city answering to it in appearance is to be destroyed? Nothing of the kind. It means that a system of religion is to be overthrown whose worship has become false, and whose unitizing life has gone. In short, the psychological condition of the seer is such that he sees SPIRITUAL THINGS REPRESENTED BY NATURAL THINGS. We shall turn his vision into delirious nonsense when we interpret him as representing *natural things by natural things.*

And yet this is precisely what a long series of interpreters, ending with Professor Davidson, have been trying to do. Swedenborg is the only interpreter we have ever met with who does not flounder in this interminable slough. He keeps consistently on the spiritual plane, and though we do not pretend to understand his entire exegesis, we believe his method is the only rational one for interpreting a purely symbolical book, and that in the work under consideration, it unfolds some of the profoundest truths that ever searched the nature of man.

The eleventh chapter speaks of "the temple of God," as seen in vision, and which the angel was to measure with a reed, and of the great city which spiritually is called Sodom and Egypt, where the Lord was crucified. This, say the critics, must mean Jerusalem; therefore Jerusalem and its temple must have been standing at the time. Why do not these critics keep on with this style of exegesis instead of playing fast and loose with it? What do they make of the two witnesses in this self-same city, which were also "the two olive-trees and the two candlesticks which stand before the Lord," and which have power to shut heaven that it rain not for a thousand two hundred and sixty days; whose mouths emitted fire that devoured their enemies, and who have power over the waters to turn them into blood? Were these two remarkable persons living in Jerusalem in the days of Nero? And if the Jerusalem of the eleventh chapter with the temple therein, was the veritable stone-mason work which Titus captured and destroyed in A. D. 72, pray what was the masonry of the New Jerusalem of the twenty-second chapter which was to succeed it and stand upon its ruins? Most remarkable mason-work indeed! A city coming down ready built out of the sky, exactly cubical in shape, its length and breadth and height equal each to twelve thousand furlongs! A city, whose walls and buildings were fifteen hundred miles high, must have had a very wonderful and original style of architecture.

There is no end to these bewildering fantasies when we try to follow the method of these critics, and find in the Apocalypse literal cities and temples, or such people of flesh and blood as Nero, Titus, Vespasian, and Napoleon Bonaparte; or Roman, Parthian, Saracen, and French armies in full costume. When we make the natural imagery in it represent natural persons and things, the confusion becomes worse and worse confounded. When we make natural things represent spiritual things, and those only, light and order will begin to appear.

After the prologue or address to the constellated churches, the Apocalypse naturally falls into three divisions. There are three successive revelations and scenic representations of things that were to be. In the first revelation the Jewish religion is the theme. The quality of its interior life, of its entire system of faith and worship, is explored and laid open; its consummation and dissolution are described, and the quality of that remnant which are to be saved out of it and given to the Lamb. The preparation for judgment, and the execution thereof, are symbolized in successive groups of sublime and terrible imagery. This occupies the book as we read it from the fourth to the twelfth chapters inclusive. The Jewish ecclesiasticism, which had become corrupt and apostate by the sensualization of its faith and worship, is typified by Sodom or Egypt, in which the Lord is crucified; that is, in which the Divine Life is extinguished.

In the second revelation the Roman religion is evidently the theme. It is the city of Babylon, in which the Great Harlot sits upon seven hills. The perversion of all faith, the falsification of all truth used for self-exaltation and arbitrary power; its cruel and depraving influence; the divine judgment that explores and lays open its hideous qualities and dooms it to hell, we understand to occupy the book from the thirteenth to the twentieth chapter inclusive.

These false religions, being adjudged and cleared out of the way by the conquering power of the Divine Word, the hindrances are removed for the New Jerusalem to descend. The Old Jerusalem has vanished, and Babylon has fallen, and now Christianity, the reign of peace and brotherhood, the visible presence of God with men, is to succeed them. It appears to the seer objectively, symbolized by the same sweet and beautiful imagery which glows in the discourses of the fourth Gospel, and in the language of the old prophets ; only what the old prophets saw in twilight, John sees in serene and mellow noontide falling down from the throne of God and of the Lamb. The New Jerusalem has its length and breadth and height exactly equal ; its system of truth and doctrine, that is, neither perverted, nor distorted, nor corrupted, is perfectly symmetrical ; and the city depends not on the lights which men kindle, nor on the light of nature, for "the Lamb is the light thereof." The whole scenery bathed in mystic splendor, is beyond the reach of art, beyond anything which human genius ever produced from its richest treasuries.

Such are the three divisions of the Apocalypse, though the first and second interblend imperceptibly with each other, for the reason that systems of false religion which are there explored and adjudged, have much in common that is corrupt and bad. In the first division the baleful consequences of separating religion from life are described as they never were before or since. The religious faith which has no love in it, in which the last throb of humanity has ceased to beat, leaving it hard, cruel, and deformed, has lost the human features and the human shape, and has become a Great Dragon, drawing the stars from heaven, putting out the benign lights in the firmament of the soul. The worship without faith, rehearsing its dreary litanies, parading its gorgeous forms after they have been emptied of all divine meaning, after all true knowledge of God has leaked out of them, and contempt and denial have come in the place of it, to which the sun becomes black as sackcloth of hair and the moon becomes as blood, has ceased to bless and to save ; and the moral and spiritual chaos that follows is imaged in the falling stars, and the mountains moved from their places. All shades and degrees of the faith in which there is no love of man, and the worship in which there is no knowledge or love of God, are laid open and described. And last of all the religion whose doctrines and forms are used for self-aggrandizement and self-exaltation, in which human ambitions and hatreds are enthroned in the place of God, is explored, and its interior quality disclosed. It is the ecclesiastical power which blasphemously usurps the seat of the divine judgment to tyrannize over the minds and bodies of men, always full of abominations and drunk with the blood of the saints and the blood of the martyrs. This is the great harlot of Babylon sitting on her seven hills. It is the love of power subsidizing the religious sentiment to its infernal ends, and using its machinery not to bless but to oppress mankind, — the worst of the seven plagues that have fallen upon them.

That the Jewish and Roman religions are here explored, and their interiors exposed and adjudged under the "seven trumpets" of God, has been the opinion of Protestant expositors generally. The Jews had crucified the Lord spiritually before they nailed the Lord Jesus to the cross. Within their gorgeous ceremonials the Divine Life was extinct, and charity and humanity had ceased to pulsate through them. Pagan Rome was sitting on her seven hills drunk with the blood of martyrs, and a paganized Christianity was to succeed her with like power over the souls and bodies of men. It is important to observe, however, that not persons nor places, not Jerusalem and its pharisees, nor Rome with its emperors, nor the Roman Church with its papal tyrannies, are to be looked for exclusively in the Apocalypse. Not persons, but states of mind and depravities of heart infesting our human nature universally, are described in the symbolization of the seer;

depravities of which all the Neros and Napoleons are the visible incarnation, and all ecclesiasticisms, used to serve the ends of human ambition and pride, are the body and form.

Faith severed from life, dogma hard and frozen with no pulse of charity in it, worship, whose form stands forth as a gorgeous shell emptied alike of the knowledge of God and the love of man, — these are the same in quality, whether we call them by Jewish or Christian names, and the hatreds and strifes which they engender in the name of religion, are the plagues that fall upon men ; out of these comes the pale horse, and the name of him that sits thereon is Death, and hell follows with him, and power is given him over the earth to kill with sword and with hunger and with death and with the beasts of the earth.

Babylon is Rome ; — human pride and ambition usurping the seat of God, and blasphemously sending forth anathemas in his name. But every church which has done the same is also Rome, and is apostate. The fires of Smithfield are not more lurid than the fires of Geneva ; and the plagues that fall on the bodies of men are not worse than those which blight the soul. Not anything in the natural world, whether of men or cities, appears in the vision of the seer. But the infernal depravities, born of our uncleansed human selfhood, latent alike, reader, in your nature and in mine, subsidizing even the religious sentiment to the service of its own lust, aggrandizement and glory, and pouring out the seven plagues on the earth and on the sea, are the Apocalypse of woe irrespective of person and time ; and if we read it, more willing to be searched beneath it than to judge others by it, no book that ever was written would open into more startling sunlight the pages of our book of life. There is no priesthood, Roman or Protestant, which does not need betimes the exploration of its trumpet voices, to show them whether they are using the forms of Christianity for their own power and glory, or only to bless and save mankind. There is no church, Roman or Protestant, which does not need to have its ruling motive and that of all its members revealed to its consciousness ; and if religion is something apart from life, if faith is divorced from works, held and professed only for a man's personal salvation, and not made warm and radiant with all the charities and humanities, they should find themselves revealed in this book quite as much as the dynasties that have passed away. Not material weapons, not flesh and blood, but evils and delusions of the heart and mind, hinder the descent of the New Jerusalem.

And the New Jerusalem is neither a lo ! here nor a lo ! there. It is not an ecclesiasticism, but a form of faith, of doctrine, and of worship, so warm with the love of the Lord that He abides in the soul, the river of its peace, the fountain of its charities, the inspiration of its tender humanities, after all the old Judaism and Romanism have been adjudged and cast away. It is Christianity unitizing God, man, and nature; making our cleansed and renovated humanity the tabernacle of God with men, and thence turning the earth into Eden, and making it the reflex image of the skies. It descends into all minds, and thence into all the ecclesiasticisms, as we renounce our Judaism and our heathenism for the spirit of universal brotherhood, and then "the nations of them that are saved do walk in the light of it, and the kings of the earth do bring their honor and glory into it."

The worship and ritual of heaven, and thence of the New Jerusalem descending out of it, in contrast with the worship whose interior truths have been falsified or lost, is set forth in one of those chapters which open into the serene vistas of the higher world. The heart becomes tender and warm in the light which comes down through it from the central glory. "God and the Lamb" is the twofold designation of the object of the Christian's supreme worship and love. This does not imply any divided homage, but the Lamb is a predicate of the one divine Being, and sets forth his relations to the creatures He has made. Its essential meaning is sacrifice, and coupled with the divine name it signifies that God himself is one great sacrifice for man. Not alone in the sacrifice on Calvary He gives himself away for the expiation and forgiveness of sin. Beyond its solemn heights and away through the door opened into heaven, He appears as the essential sacrifice given hourly for the redemption of the world. Ever going out of himself, and coming down to our lowly condition, underlying all our weaknesses, and helping us bear up our weary burdens, present in all our sufferings and suffering with us, sinking himself out of sight beneath our mortal infirmities, clothing himself with them, as it were, that He may help us the more ; rejected, injured, wounded, grieved away by our hardness of heart and blindness of mind, his very life killed out of us when striving most to enter and save us, — such is the eternal sacrifice of God ; and so when we look up to the throne with eyes made wet with repentance, we see not the thunder-clouds of wrath but *a lamb as it had been slain.*

Truth, as seen by the pure intellect, is white and silvery ; but truth transfused and made chromatic with the divine love is golden ; and when it rules right royally over the conscience and the life, it crowns us, and we wear it as our diadem of praise. But how prone we are to wear it as our personal adornment ; as something which we have wrought out and perfected, and so make it our crown of pride, to draw with it the admiration and applause of the crowd ! Hence all our priestly ambitions and all the selfish motives by which the rites of worship have been made aglow with strange fire. Hence the controversies that have been waged only for personal victory. Hence our pulpit eloquence is so prevailingly an exhibition of self-love or the love of popular applause, and hence our churches are gathered admiringly around the preacher who expands so largely with the breath of praise, that the Lord Jesus Christ is not seen at all, but is kept behind him out of sight. But when we get gleams of the ritual of heaven, the elders who wear crowns of gold cast them down at the feet of Him that sitteth on the throne, saying: "Thou, O Lord, art worthy." The whole scene, both in the description and the symbolic meaning, is impressive and grand beyond all human conception, and we never read it without being ashamed of the strut and vanity of our ecclesiastical pomps so faintly chromatic with the divine love, nor without an aspiration that the crowns we wear of so lurid and fiery a lustre may be exchanged betimes for the crowns of gold, fit to be cast down in that beautiful ceremonial which ascribes "blessing and honor and glory and power unto him that sitteth on the throne and unto the Lamb, for ever and ever."

How stands the question, then, as regards the spirit and temper of the Apocalypse? Is a book which describes the consequences of divorcing religion from life, and worship from humanity, and dogma from charity, foreshowing the states of mind which ultimate in baleful results by a symbolization, compared with which Homer's battle-pictures are feeble and tame, — written in the interest of humanity or not? Is the book Jewish in spirit which depicts what was false and evil in Judaism, and doomed the Jewish Church to its downfall? It is vain to cite its imagery of retributive wrath, such as "the wrath of the Lamb," "the wine-press of the fierceness and wrath of Almighty God," as if this were descriptive of the temper of the Divine mind, and not rather the results of retributive law in complete operation. That is not a clear and healthful, but rather a confused and weak moral sentiment which revolts against the most thorough exploration of the hiding-places of sin, and the most faithful portraiture of its nature and consequences. All that the Apocalypse described in the realm of causes has had its fulfillment in history. All the thunder-clouds which it painted as hanging over the future Church, have broken upon it with their burden of plague and lightning and great hail. And beyond those thunder-clouds, and only as they clear the horizon, has the New Jerusalem been seen to descend. If it is cruel and vindictive to lay open to our gaze the virus that lurks in false religion or in the uncleansed human heart, and thence poisons the relations of life, making the sweetest fountains run gall and turning the rivers into blood, then the spirit of the Apocalypse is bad. But if it is good for men or for a church to see as in a mirror, the evils that lurk within them, and if unresisted shut them off from heaven both here and hereafter, then the Apocalypse is one of the most humane in spirit of any book that ever was addressed to the human conscience.

Long before our civil war, caused by the rebellion of the slave power against the American government, some of our poet-prophets foretold the conflict and the calamities which it would involve. In the evils of slavery, and the states of mind which it engendered, they saw an Apocalypse of woe, and described it in appropriate imagery. Herein they prophesied not from a spirit of cruelty or vindictiveness, but from a spirit of humanity and mercy. No strains more tender and humane can be found in the compass of modern literature, than the strains of Whittier and Lowell; and yet both prophesied against our modern Babylon in types which come as near to those of the Apocalypse as they could well do without passing into the objective scenery of the seer. Take the following examples from Whittier: —

"Take your slavery-blackened vales,
Give us but our own free gales
Blowing on our thousand sails.

"Live like paupers mean and vile
On the fruits of unpaid toil,
Locusts of your glorious soil.

"Live if it be life to dwell
In your tyrant citadel,
Mined beneath by fires from hell.

"Our bleak hills shall bud and blow,
Vines our rocks shall overgrow,
Plenty in our valleys flow.

"And when vengeance lights your skies,
Hither shall ye turn your eyes,
As the damned on Paradise."

"Hold while ye may your struggling slaves, and burden God's free air
With woman's shriek beneath the lash, and manhood's wild despair;
Cling closer to the cleaving curse that writes upon your plains
The blasting of Almighty wrath against a land of chains."

Or this from Lowell: —

"Out from the land of bondage 'tis decreed our slaves shall go,
And signs to us are offered as erst to Pharaoh;
If we are blind, their exodus, like Israel's of yore,
Through a Red Sea is doomed to be whose surges are of gore."

The inspiration of prophecy, and of poetry which becomes prophecy because the voice of the divine justice speaks through it, approximate both in style and spirit. They divine by a more unerring vision the malign nature of moral and spiritual evil, and select by the same vision the things in nature most fit to represent and shadow it forth. Hence the poet, who is not a mere sentimentalist, approaches the state of seership and sees nature, both in her baleful and benignant phases, the exponent of man in his infernal or his heavenly states; humanity, in fact, turned inside out; and, in the symbolism which he employs, representing spiritual things by natural things, he only gives to the human soul, and thence to churches, societies, and communities, which are the collective man, the mysteries that lie within them; warning them of evils which have not yet passed into history and had their ultimations in heaven or hell. "The wrath of the Lamb poured out without mixture from the cup of his indignation," describes not the essence of the Deity but the aspect of his nature towards men in those false religions which quench his mercy and love; even as the poet who sings of the Eternal Goodness as few poets have ever done, sings also of "the blasting of Almighty wrath against a land of chains."

CHAPTER V.

THE WITNESSES OF THE SECOND CENTURY.

IT becomes important to survey one moment the theatre over which Christianity extended its sway during the first two centuries. The Roman empire was bounded by the Euphrates on the east and the Atlantic ocean on the west; by the Danube on the north and by the African deserts on the south, while in the northwest it crossed the channel and included Britain then sunk in barbarism. The peoples were separated by vast varieties of climate, manners, language, local governments and religions. There were the voluptuousness of the East and the hardiness of the West. There were the hot blood of the South and the cold blood of the North. There were the languages of Demosthenes and of Cicero; there was the Hebrew and its cognates heard throughout the East in the worship of the synagogues and in the marts of trade, and there were the horrid gutturals of the savage in the groves of Germany and on the banks of the Rhine.

Before the close of the second century, Christianity had penetrated this vast region so as to streak the darkness everywhere with light. Churches had sprung up east, west, north, and south. It had even passed over the Euphrates into the great Parthian empire. It had become firmly fixed in nearly all the great cities and centres of population, and thence ramified through the surrounding country. The magnificent Roman roads, radiating from the eternal city throughout the empire over which the life of the world poured its turbid streams, wonderfully facilitated this early diffusion of Christianity. By the year 175 it had spread through Syria, through lesser Asia, through Greece and the islands of the Mediterranean, and entering Egypt it had travelled up the Nile. It was established at Rome, and thence it had gone south and skirted the southern shores of the Mediterranean even into the heart of Mauritania. It had entered Gaul, and had flourishing churches at Lyons and Vienna. Churches had sprung up in all these provinces, sundered some of them from each other by the space of two thousand miles, sundered too by diversities of language and manners, but united internally by a spiritual bond, and having common traditions whose lines converged towards one majestic person who had appeared in Palestine.

Starting now with the last quarter of the second century what do we find? We find A CANON OF SCRIPTURE received and established in all these churches without exception. We mean by this that certain books, regarded *sui generis*, elevated far above the level of common literature, were universally appealed to as commanding authority in all matters of life and doctrine, and read as Holy Scripture in the churches when they came together for worship. Prominent in this canon of Scripture were the four Gospels, as we have them, and in the order in which we have them received as authentic and genuine, and as a legacy to these churches from the hands that wrote them. It is the testimony not of an individual here and there. It is the unanimous testimony of an entire generation. Clement of Alexandria in Egypt, Tertullian at Carthage, Irenæus at Lyons in Gaul, Polycrates at Ephesus, and Theophilus at Antioch, either quote the four Gospels, or refer to them, not as describing their individual faith, but the faith of the churches throughout the then civilized world. Their testimony is not their own merely, but that of the churches thus scattered and separated, whose lines of tradition are unbroken, and all converging to a common centre.[1]

How long must these books have been in circulation to be thus unanimously and universally received? It will flash upon almost any man's common sense that they could not then have been recent and modern, that they must date back more than twenty-five or even fifty years, and that the notion that any one of them originated or took its final

[1] Read Norton's work; Fisher's admirable *Essays on the Supernatural Origin of Christianity*, Essay ii.; or see the evidence concisely put in Tischendorf's tract: *Wenn wurden unsere Evangelien verfasst?*

form after the middle of the century, and thus suddenly found its way as Holy Scripture into churches of different languages, and a thousand miles apart, is one of the wildest absurdities.

But look at the matter in something more of detail. Who and what were the generation of Christian believers living in the last quarter of the second century? Many of them were men and women *who received their Christian faith and nurture from the men who had seen the Apostles themselves and sat at their feet.*

The churches at Lyons and Vienna in Gaul in the year 177 were called to endure a persecution so cruel and vindictive, that it seemed not to have been inflicted by men but by wolves in the shape of men. After the storm had spent its rage these churches sent a letter to the churches in Asia Minor describing the calamity that had come upon them. Eusebius preserves copious extracts from this letter. It is in a triumphant strain, and rises sometimes to a fervid eloquence. This letter quotes the fourth Gospel, once a whole passage *verbatim,* and it quotes the Apocalypse not less than three times. But more than this. Not only the language of the Scriptures enters largely and spontaneously into it, but their very life throbs through the sentences and compels the conviction that these people had the New Testament, and read it as we read it, and bathed their inmost souls in its spirit.

Who were the teachers of this church at Lyons in 177? One was the aged bishop Pothinus, passed now his ninetieth year with his streaming gray hairs, led forth to death for the faith he loved. He was a boy twelve years old while John was living at Ephesus; he had lived in Asia Minor through his boyhood and younger manhood; he must have seen and conversed with the companions of the Apostles, and he was old enough to have seen and conversed with the beloved disciple himself. Another teacher of this church was Irenæus, the associate of the aged Pothinus. Irenæus says the Gospel was transmitted to them in writing and he goes on to specify the fourth Gospel as published by John "while he dwelt at Ephesus in Asia." He cites the four Gospels as we have them, and calls them "the pillar and support of the Church and the breath of life."

Who was Irenæus? Look over the map and you will find the city of Smyrna a few hours' journey from Ephesus. There at Smyrna was one of the constellated churches, and over it presided the saintly and venerable Polycarp, the disciple of John. Polycarp sat at the feet of the beloved disciple and others who had seen the Lord Jesus, and he heard them recount over and over the works which Jesus did and the speech which fell from his lips. Irenæus was a disciple of Polycarp, and heard the same things over from him, and he tells us *how they agreed with what John had written in that self-same gospel which the churches had received.* Says Irenæus in a letter to Florinus, his friend and former fellow pupil with Polycarp, "I saw thee in my youth in lower Asia with Polycarp, — for I remember the events of those times much better than those of recent occurrence; what we learn in fact in our youth, grows with our soul, and grows together with it so closely, that I can even yet tell the place where the holy Polycarp sat when he discoursed, his entrance and exit, the peculiarities of his mode of life, his bodily figure, the discourses which he addressed to the people; how he told of his familiar intercourse with John, and with the rest who had seen the Lord; how he narrated their discourses, and what he had heard from them in regard to the Lord about his miracles and doctrine, all of which, as Polycarp had received it from those who were eye-witnesses of the word of life, *he narrated in harmony with the Holy Scriptures;* these things by the mercy of God then granted to me, I attentively heard and noted down, not on paper, but in my heart, and by the grace of God I continually repeat it faithfully." Irenæus, who brings us thus near to the beloved disciple, wrote with considerable ability against the Gnostics, and other heretics of his day, all of whom he says appealed to the four Gospels and acknowledged them as authority. He cites in this treatise not less than four hundred passages from the Gospels and more than eighty from the Gospel of John. Would he not be likely to know the origin of the book which he quotes as undoubted, having been thus brought almost within hearing where the contents of the book fell fresh from the writer's lips?

There was a man whose birth dates about the year 125, when a great many were yet living who had known John and his fellow disciples. He was educated in a Christian family. Moreover his family was directly connected with John's contemporaries, and seven of its members had held the office of bishop or presbyter. This man was Polycrates. At the date we have assumed, 175, he was fifty years old. A few years later, during the last decade of the century, he became Bishop of Ephesus, and there on the scene of the labor and death of the beloved disciple, he dwells complacently upon his memory, and refers to the place of his sepulture as well known to the Church. He describes himself as "having conferred with the brethren throughout the world, *and studied the whole of the sacred Scriptures.*" There with the fourth Gospel in his hand, transmitted in the church at Ephesus, where it was read and had long been read as the writing of John, having known the men who knew the Apostle, — he uses it as the unquestioned work of the man whose name it bears. In the church over which John himself presided, the custodian of the writings he left, and among which they were read as Holy Scripture when assembled for worship; at a time when his memory was fresh and vivid; when there were men yet living who had seen and conversed with John's disciples,—in this church would John's own successor, who was born near to his times, know what he was doing when he studied the fourth Gospel as the record direct from the hand of the beloved disciple? [1]

Follow another line of tradition remote from Ephesus, but leading up directly to the same source. We have named Clement of Alexandria in Egypt. Who and what was Clement? If we place ourselves in that seat of culture, philosophy, and learning we may be able to appreciate his word and testimony. Here at Alexandria was a Christian church which dated from the times of the Apostles, founded, tradition says, by Mark the evangelist, and destined to exert a wide and plastic power over the opinions of Christendom, indeed, to furnish the moulds in which its theology was to be shaped for eighteen centuries. Here, too, was a theological school where teachers of the keenest insight, of the most affluent learning, enlarged both by study and travel, and of the warmest Christian devotion, prepared their scholars for their future work. Three of these men come within the second century, and, viewed in succession, they

[1] That Polycrates includes the Gospel of John when he says he studied "the whole of the sacred Scriptures," is the inevitable inference from the fact that he not only refers to John as authority in the controversy about Easter, but refers to John xiii. 25, and xxi. 20, where he is described as "he who leaned on the Lord's breast."—*Eusebius*, *H. E.*, L. v. c. 24.

extend nearly through the latter half of it in a continuous line of light, brilliant yet mildly beautiful. Fifteen years of the life of Origen falls within this period. They were years of youth and childhood, but such childhood as might well be called the fatherhood of the man, for they controlled and directed the man that was to be. He was born and nurtured in a Christian home. Leonides, his father, made the boy commit daily portions of Scripture to memory. It was no irksome lesson, but the boy's untasked and inexpressible delight. The questions he asked were beyond his years and beyond the father's scope altogether, but the father so rejoiced and thanked God for this early promise, that he would kiss the boy's breast when asleep as the temple where the Holy Spirit was preparing to dwell. The fourth Gospel became Origen's special study, and the theology of the Proem was with him not only the prime moving power of Christianity, but it explained and unitized the whole system of the universe. As yet, however, it had not opened upon him thus grandly, for he says that in his youth he only knew the Logos according to the flesh. We see him as yet only in his boyhood, committing to memory the Christian Scriptures with the keenest relish under the guidance of a pious father. Who was this Leonides who at the year 185 had a son born in his family whose mind opened with such brilliant promise? He was a man of unusual gifts, and of marked intelligence; probably a rhetorician, and withal so imbued with the ideas and the spirit of the four Gospels which he taught to his children that a few years later he suffered martyrdom for the love of Christ. He had a wife and six other children besides Origen. When the father was thrown into prison, the boy wrote to him: "See thou change not thy mind on our account." He did not change, but cheerfully and nobly died. His property was confiscated, his wife left a helpless widow, and his seven children distributed among the Christian families of Alexandria as a martyr's legacy. What a picture of Christian domestic life in the last half of the first century, and of the power of the Christian Scriptures as then used in families! The birth and education of this pious Leonides must have been some twenty-five years earlier, and they carry us up well-nigh towards the middle of the century.[1]

Origen was the pupil of Clement, whom in the last decade of the century we find at the head of the theological school at Alexandria. How much Origen owed to his master we do not know; only it is certain that Clement, too, delighted supremely in the fourth Gospel, and found in it the central glory of Divine revelation. "The Logos" which was in the beginning with God, "by which all things were made," and "which now has taken the name of Christ," is called by him a New Song. This Logos is "the Sun of the Soul," its informing and indwelling light, the inspirer

[1] Eusebius, *H. E.*, vi. 2.

of all the truth to be found in the old philosophies, the guide of the Christian not only because it has become incarnate, but because its inward shinings bring the disciple to behold its glory in the face of Jesus Christ. He quotes largely from the other Scriptures, but the fourth Gospel with him is the heart of Christianity, and his thought, though expressed more crudely and irregularly than that of Origen, is precisely in the same line of development, and shows that the leading idea of the teacher lived and glowed in the mind of his pupil.

Clement not only quotes the same Gospels which we possess, but assures us that they were handed down to the churches of his day in unbroken line; he gives abridged accounts of all the canonical Scriptures, and particularly one pertaining to the composition of the four Gospels "received from the oldest presbyters." [1]

It becomes a very interesting question, who in turn was the teacher of Clement, and who introduced him to this intimate knowledge of Christianity and the Christian Scriptures? Happily, he has told us in the language of enthusiastic admiration, and this carries us back one step further towards the middle of the second century. The predecessor of Clement in the theological school at Alexandria was Pantænus, who left a name behind him not only distinguished for learning, but fragrant with the Christian graces

[1] Eusebius, *H. E.*, vi. 14.

and virtues. Disciplined in the Greek schools of philosophy, but fired with zeal respecting the divine Word, he preserved "the salutary doctrine as given by Peter and James and John and Paul." Clement found Pantænus in great eminence at Alexandria presiding over its theological school. He had wandered over the earth hungry for the true doctrine; he had found teachers from Greece, from Italy, and from Syria, but not till he found Pantænus was his hunger satisfied. "He was in truth," says Clement, "a Sicilian bee, who, cropping the flowers of the prophetic and apostolic meadow, caused a pure knowledge to grow up in the minds of his hearers." The prophetic and apostolic meadow, whose flowers Pantænus gathered and charmed his hearers withal, was evidently none other than the Old and New Testaments which he expounded to his pupils; which Clement expounded in turn after him, and which Origen in turn expounded after him, and edited in his famous "Hexapla," fragments of which have come down to us, and which was one of the greatest achievements of learning in ancient times.

But who preceded Pantænus in this same theological school? We do not know. But we are told by Eusebius that it had been established at Alexandria from ancient times, and had a reputation for teachers "able in eloquence and the study of divine things." [1]

The "ancient times" of the age of Pantænus carry

[1] Eusebius, *H. E.*, v. 10.

us across the middle of the century and up towards its beginning. They bring us near or into the times of the beloved disciple himself.

Skeptical modern criticism has assumed that the fourth Gospel was forged by some unknown writer in the last half of the second century. We ask our readers here to sum up the facts we have given, that at or near the time when we are told it was thus fabricated, it was universally read as Holy Scripture in the churches, dotting the Roman Empire from the Euphrates to the Atlantic Ocean, and from the British Channel to the African desert; and last, not least, that it was expounded in a theological school which could boast of teachers imbued with all the learning and philosophy of the times, with minds enriched by travel and the study of God's Word; whose special and chosen work was historical investigation; who delighted in John's Gospel as the very heart of Christianity and of all divine revelation; whose succession of teachers ran up in continuous line near or into the days of the Apostle himself; who preserved the accounts of old men who told them how and when it was composed; who gloried so much in its doctrines that they declared them in the face of death; and after all this same fourth Gospel was then a new work foisted surreptitiously upon the Christian public, received universally and suddenly like a flash of lightning, and without a breath of controversy, while the churches that received it, the bishops that read it in the assemblies, the families where the children committed it to memory, and the learned theological school that expounded it, were all innocent as babes of any knowledge respecting its origin! Such are the reasonings of skepticism. It might just as well cut the threads of history from behind us every hour, and make the world of yesterday and the world of to-day disjointed fragments that float at random in the river of years!

We have followed the converging lines of tradition from Lyons in Gaul, from Ephesus in Asia Minor, and from Alexandria in Egypt. We might go to Carthage in Northern Africa, and cite Tertullian with a like result. But let us go east to Jerusalem, where a church existed from the beginning, amid the scene of the Saviour's life, death, and resurrection, and whose first bishop was one of the twelve, — the Apostle James. Placing ourselves at the close of the second century, what do we find? The metropolitan churches, especially those founded by Apostles, very carefully preserved the names in succession of their bishops inscribed on tablets and laid up in their archives. These were diligently examined by Eusebius, and he enumerates in his history the names of all the bishops of the Church at Jerusalem, from the close of the second century up to the Apostle James himself. A fact like this goes to show that tradition, with these churches, was not so loose and floating as is sometimes supposed, especially when it pertained to things held dear and sacred like their canonical books and consecrated names. Moreover Jerusalem was the resort of Christian pilgrims as early as the close of the second century; and yet earlier it is more than probable, and while disciples were yet living who sat at the Apostles' feet and heard their story. Thither they went to see with their own eyes the places trodden by the Redeemer's feet, and to gain knowledge of the localities referred to in the New Testament, that they might read it with better understanding.[1] It is easy to conceive with what avidity a teacher who expounded the New Testament would seek the geography of Palestine, and read it as a living book. Thither went Clement of Alexandria; and we find him there just after the close of the second century. Whom did he meet at Jerusalem? He met Alexander, bishop of the church there, between 193 and 211, who has told us of Clement's visit in episcopal letters, fragments of which Eusebius has preserved. In one of these letters Alexander speaks of Clement as "the blessed presbyter, a man endued with all virtue and well approved, who coming hither by the providence and superintendence of the Lord, has confirmed and increased the Church of God." [2]

But there was another man whom Clement met also at Jerusalem. Alexander was not sole bishop,

[1] *Neander's Church History*, Torrey's edition, vol. i. p. 691.
[2] *H. E.*, vi. 11.

but colleague with the venerable patriarch, Narcissus, who had held the Episcopate of Jerusalem for about twenty years. His name breathed the odors of piety down even to the times of Eusebius. He lived to an extreme age. Alexander says in one of his episcopal letters, "Narcissus salutes you, the same who was bishop here before me, and is now colleague with me in prayers, being now advanced to his hundred and tenth year, and who with me exhorts you to be of one mind."[1] This was in 211. Here was a man whose life spanned almost the whole of the second century; whose scene of active labor and care was the very place where Jesus taught, died, and rose again; who must have been familiar with many who had seen and heard the Apostles; who lived when the fourth Gospel was read in his church and in all Christendom, as holy Scripture, and who began to live when the man whose name the fourth Gospel bears went to his earthly rest. His life fills up the whole space between John and Clement, with not more than the gap of a single year, and probably not even that. He must have known familiarly scores of persons who knew John before he left Jerusalem for his charge at Ephesus. This man, Clement communed with at Jerusalem. We can understand how much his language signifies when he gives us traditions about the four Gospels "*received from aged presbyters.*" The assumption that John's

[1] *H. E.*, vi. 11.

Gospel first saw the light after the year 150, or during the second century even, becomes, if possible, still more absurd.

We ascend the stream. We come into the third quarter of the second century. We can hardly say that the historical evidence grows stronger as we ascend, which were scarcely possible, but it thickens and becomes multiform.

And here at the opening of this quarter we meet with a professed canon of Scripture carefully arranged. We find a list of canonical books dating from about 170, discovered by Muratori, and probably written at Rome, and in this list, Matthew, Mark, Luke, and John, stand in the order as we have them now, and as they had then been universally adopted.

The four Gospels were originally composed and published in the Greek language; that of Matthew being possibly, though not certainly, an exception. It was the vernacular speech of many provinces of the Roman Empire. It had been diffused throughout the East by the conquests of Alexander. The Old Testament had long been popularly used in a Greek version. Greek was the language of scholars; it was to a large extent the language of commerce, and it was preëminently adapted to clothe the ideas of the New Testament and depict the doctrines of Christianity in their minutest and most delicate shadings.

But Christianity soon transcended the bounds of Greek culture, and it became necessary that the New

Testament should be rendered into other tongues. Of course it would be translated very early into the language of Rome, which was spoken throughout the West. It would be translated into Syriac, which was spoken in the East. Accordingly we have a Syriac version called the *Peschito*, generally acknowledged on good evidence to have been made before the close of the second century; and we have a Latin version well known under the *Itala*, made still earlier; for Tertullian used it, as is known by his quotations, and the Latin translator of Irenæus' great work against heresies also followed it. These translations both contain the four Gospels substantially as they have come down to us. Here then is the important fact. The four Gospels before the close of the century, were held as preëminent authority, and translated into other tongues to be quoted and used as such in other communities. But suppose we had *the very Greek text* from which these translations were made, we should then be carried back still farther towards the beginning. Well, that very text has lately been found. We have in the lately discovered "Codex Siniaticus," the identical Greek text out of which those translations must have been made, for the "various readings" of the latter are found in the former, and correspond thereto. This carries us back inevitably to the year 150, and shows that a Canon of Scripture was then firmly established. All the theories recently blown up, assuming the later origin of the fourth Gospel, vanish like bubbles that break

9

in air. We shall see by and by that we are carried back by these ancient documents, not only to the middle of the century, but past it, and up to its very beginning.

Not only translations, but *harmonies* of the four Gospels were made during this period, in which the fourth Gospel was included, and this forms an independent and most conclusive ground of evidence. The city of Antioch, the capital of Syria, received Christianity from the hands of the Apostles themselves. Here in the year 168, we find Theophilus, bishop of the church in that city. Only five pastorates had preceded him in that church, since the times of Paul and Barnabas, who started from Antioch on their missionary journey. It was in the vicinity of Jerusalem and in frequent communication with it, and its bishop must have known familiarly many who saw and heard the personal disciples of Jesus. Theophilus wrote several works, which were extant in the times of Eusebius, who describes them. In one of these he names John's Gospel as a part of the Holy Scriptures, and John himself as a writer guided by the Holy Spirit. But more than this, Theophilus wrote a commentary on the Gospels, including John, showing not only the estimation in which he held them himself, but in which they were held by the churches themselves. His testimony is that of the Christian communities separated by only a single generation from those who had consorted with the Apostles, and received the Gospel from their lips.

Contemporary with Theophilus was Tatian, who flourished as early as 150, a disciple of Justin Martyr, one therefore, who learned Christianity of a teacher whose life began in the first century, and was ten years a contemporary with John. Tatian relapsed into Gnosticism, but he wrote an exegetical harmony of the four Gospels, including the book of John, which he quotes, and which also was extant in the times of Eusebius. His testimony also is that of his times, showing incontestably that in the middle of the second century the four Gospels belonged to the *Canon of Scripture*, so universally received in the churches that they were translated and expounded even as now, as the rule of faith and of life. How long must they have existed to have acquired, by the year 150, this universal and undisputed authority in the churches, East and West, in at least three languages, from the Euphrates to the Rhone, and from the English Channel to the deserts of Africa? That commentaries were written upon the four Gospels, and harmonies made of them, and that they were bound together as a separate and exclusive whole, is a fact of weightier significance even than individual citations. "These enterprises," says Tischendorf, "fall soon after the middle of the second century, and consequently we must assume that the use and acknowledgment of all four Evangelists, in a far earlier period, is fully determined."[1]

[1] *Wann wurden unsere Evangelien verfasst?* pp. 11, 12.

CHAPTER VI.

THE WITNESSES OF THE SECOND CENTURY.

STILL we ascend the stream. We come into the first half of the second century and among a generation, many of whom were contemporaries of the Apostles or of their companions, and co-laborers. Here we find the historical evidence coursing through various channels, yet converging to its single source.

I. The first class of men whom we meet here are those Christian fathers in full reception of the faith of the Church, whose vigorous manhood falls within the second century, but who were born before the close of the first, and whose childhood therefore was contemporary with the later Apostles and their companions. Some of them had seen the last of the Apostles and hung upon his speech. All of them belonged to a period when tradition was fresh, frequent, and direct; when the minds of new converts were eager and inquisitive, and when the times of Christ, and the scene through which He moved, must have been produced in their minds with most vivid and uncoloring sunlight.

First, we meet with Justin Martyr, the teacher of

Tatian. Justin was born not far from A. D. 100. He was a native of Shechem, in Samaria, the Sychar of the New Testament. He was not born, however, in a Christian family, and knew nothing of Christianity till his early manhood. Then in his hunger for divine knowledge, he met a serene old man, of aspect grave and meek, who directed him to Jesus Christ and the Hebrew prophets. He had witnessed the tranquillity of the martyrs and their triumph over torture and death. He became a convert to Christianity. How genuine his conversion was is shown by the fact that he publicly defended it in his Apologies, when he clearly foresaw that the defense would cost him his life.

His pupil Tatian called him "a most wonderful man." Judged by the standard of his own times, his acquirements were remarkable, and by the standard of any times his moral greatness and Christian heroism are worthy of warm admiration. He is an important and most unexceptionable witness to the four Gospels, not only as to how they were regarded by himself, but how they were received and held in all the churches of his day. He gives us an interesting and somewhat graphical view of these churches assembled for worship: "On the day which is called Sunday we all, whether dwelling in the cities or in the country, assemble together, when the memoirs by the Apostles, or the writings of the prophets, are read as long as time permits." Again, he characterizes these memoirs as written by "the Apostles and their companions," thus clearly designating the synoptics and the fourth Gospel. He quotes them so much and so familiarly as to show that his mind was imbued with their spirit, and that their language flowed spontaneously from his pen; and the main facts could be reproduced, says Mr. Norton, from Justin's writings alone, and the passages referred to the places from which they were severally drawn. But the evidence in respect to the fourth Gospel is very striking and doubly significant. Justin delighted in the Johannean theology. It colored his whole mind, and thence flowed into his speech. "The making over of the Logos to Christ," says Tischendorf, "is a deduction from John in many passages of Justin, of which no trace in the synoptics nor in the oldest parallel writings ever occurs to us. So, too, the answer of the Baptist to the inquiring messengers of the Jews is given by Justin word for word as only John reports it; as also he gives the very searching passage respecting the second birth," found only in John iii. 3. These citations compel those who deny the genuineness of the fourth Gospel, to take refuge in the theory of a lost writing which contained a passage as it stands in John. This is the desperate shift of the skeptical criticism. To measure its enormous absurdity requires but a moment's reflection. Justin's first Apology was published A. D. 138, in which he says the Gospels are read in the churches in city and country with the prophets; read, that is, as Holy Scripture. These were the Gospels as he quoted them, — memoirs of Christ written by Apostles and their companions, including, therefore, the book of John as he knew it. Twelve years later, as we have seen, the four Gospels, *as we have them*, were read in all the churches east and west, in Syria, in Rome, and in Africa, and *one of Justin's own pupils* had made a harmony of them which was extant in the times of Eusebius. These critics then would have us believe that within this interval of twelve years, one book of John dropped out of use all over Christendom, covering now its thousands of square miles, and including its peoples of various tongues; and a new and spurious book of John in at least three languages, went into its place, simultaneously and universally, and with the silence of night, as not a lisp of controversy was ever heard about it. This, too, during the lifetime of Justin, — for he lived and wrote past the middle of the century, and when men were giving up their lives for the ideas which these books embodied as the Rule of Faith. It has been said that the science of historical criticism was not understood by these people. We shall see. But granting they had not the keenness of critics they certainly were not fools.

We come next to a very important witness, who is always named as "the blessed Polycarp." We have already referred to him in connection with Irenæus his pupil, but he is too important a witness, not to be evoked in his own name. He not only lived through his youth and younger manhood in intimate and loving intercourse with John, and other Apostles and disciples who had seen and heard the Lord Jesus, but he was installed as bishop over one of the constellated churches — the church at Smyrna, near Ephesus — by apostolic hands. The mantle of the beloved disciple fell gracefully upon him. The sweetness and benignity of spirit largely imbreathed on the bosom of Jesus, exhaled in its benignity and gentleness around "the blessed Polycarp." The same influence inspired him with the intrepidity of Christian heroism. It will be readily understood how by his intercourse with John, not merely the contents of the fourth Gospel, but also some of "the many other things" which Jesus did and said, and which "are not written in this book," entered largely into the memory and the very being of Polycarp, and that he would preach Christ to his flock, not so much from written documents as from this living gospel in his soul. This indeed was the case. It is plain, from the account of Irenæus who heard him, that this was the burden of his discourse and conversation with the people whom he drew around him; and so vividly did he reproduce to them the life and teachings of Jesus, "his miracles and doctrine," as he had "received them from the eyewitnesses," that the picture of the man, and the room where they met, lived afterward in the memory with unwonted brightness, — "the place where he sat, his bodily form, his entrances and walks, and the complexion of his life." Long afterwards Polycarp was quoted as a kind of living Bible, to show what Jesus would have said and taught. Irenæus cites him in his controversy with the Gnostics as "a man who had been instructed by the Apostles, and had familiar intercourse with many who had seen Christ, and had also been appointed bishop by the Apostles in Asia, in the church at Smyrna; whom we also have seen in our youth, for he lived a long time and to a very advanced age, when after a glorious and most distinguished martyrdom he departed this life. He always taught what he had learned from the Apostles, what the church had handed down, and what is the only true doctrine. All the churches bear witness to these things, and those that have been successors to Polycarp to the present time, a witness of the truth much more worthy of credit, and much more certain than either Valentine or Marcion, or the rest of those perverse teachers." [1]

Polycarp suffered martyrdom at Smyrna A. D. 167, being then eighty six years old, as already stated. We have a full and detailed description of his sufferings in a letter from his church at Smyrna to the churches in Pontus, and which Eusebius mostly preserves. It is written by eye-witnesses, and describes

[1] Eusebius, *H. E.*, iv. 14.

the heavenly bearing of the venerable martyr, "filled with confidence and joy, and his countenance brightened with grace." [1]

A single writing of Polycarp has come down to us, — his letter to the church at Philippi. It is written with unction and dignity, and is worthy of its author's fame. It affords evidence moreover the most full and pointed, that when it was written there was a canon of Scripture corresponding to our own, well known and established in the churches. He quotes the New Testament again and again. He quotes Paul's Epistles by name, and quotes them as canonical. "Do we not know, he says, that 'the saints shall judge the world' as Paul teaches?" Again, "I trust ye are well versed in THE SACRED SCRIPTURES, and that nothing is hid from you. It is declared in *these Scriptures*, 'Be ye angry and sin not,' and 'Let not the sun go down upon your wrath.'" But what is directly and forcibly to our purpose, he quotes the first epistle of John *expressly to refute the Gnostics*, showing not only that it was then in the canon, but also how John himself understood and applied it. Referring to those "false brethren," who "in hypocrisy bear the name of the Lord and draw away vain men into error," he says, "Whosoever does not confess that Jesus Christ is come in the flesh is antichrist (1 John iv. 3); and whosoever does

[1] It was evidently interpolated by later hands, but its main facts are regarded as authentic.

not confess the testimony of the cross is of the devil, and whosoever perverts the oracles of the Lord to his own lusts, and says that there is neither a resurrection nor a judgment, is the first-born of Satan." Every sentence here sharply distinguishes the Gnostic heresy. The disciple of John quotes him to rebuke this haunting and hated error. That the same hand wrote the Catholic Epistle, and the fourth Gospel, is to our minds an undoubting conviction, and proof for the genuineness of one is good for both.

But Polycarp nowhere quotes the fourth Gospel, and for obvious reasons. His intercourse with John took place before the fourth Gospel was written, and before that time he was not only possessed with its contents, but the life of Jesus, in ampler scope and more minute detail, filled his memory and glowed in his mind and heart. It is well known that the recital of the events in the life of Christ made up the substance of the preaching of some of the Apostles, and we can well understand with what hunger it would be received, and how fondly it would be treasured up.

But Polycarp is a witness to the fourth Gospel, in a way far more complete and satisfactory than a few quotations could possibly be. Irenæus not only quotes it, but he quotes it as Holy Scripture; and we know both from him and his translator, that the same work which has come down to us, was the one which he had in his hands. But Irenæus sat at Polycarp's feet in Smyrna, heard him recount the narrative and conversation of John and of others who had seen the Lord, the "discourses" of Jesus, "his miracles and doctrine." These, he says, were "in consistency with the Holy Scriptures"; that is, with the fourth Gospel which he held in his hand, and which we have now. The fourth Gospel becomes not merely the testimony of John. It is as if a whole company of eye-witnesses rose up from amidst the constellated churches over which he presided, saying over again the closing adjuration of John's Gospel, "this is the disciple that testifieth of these things and wrote these things, and we know that his testimony is true."

The next witness is Papias, who was Bishop of Hierapolis in Syria, about the year 116. He was a weak, but pious and learned man. He wrote a work in five books called "Interpretations of our Lord's Declarations," which Irenæus had seen, but of which Eusebius evidently had only seen the preface. In the fourth book, as Irenæus read it, Papias says he was an associate of Polycarp and a hearer of John. In the "preface," as Eusebius quotes it, Papias represents himself as an eager and inquisitive hearer of old men who knew the Apostles, and reported largely the discourses of Jesus. The "Interpretations" were evidently expositions of these traditional sayings. He not only knew the Gospels of Matthew and Mark, but tells us how and why they were composed, and he assures us that he had this account of them from John the presbyter, who was a hearer of John the Evangelist and other Apostles. Whenever he met with any of these old men who had sat at the Apostles' feet, he made it a point, he says, to inquire "what was said by Andrew, Peter, or Philip; what by Thomas, James, John, Matthew, or any other of the disciples of the Lord, *for I do not think I derived so much benefit from books as from the living voice of those that are still surviving.*" He does not quote the Gospels, and he does not mention the book of John. Nothing seems more perfectly natural. Let us place ourselves in his position with all the fresh awakened interest in the wonderful events which had taken place, and which were still shaking the fabric of society. The men were yet alive who had conversed with the twelve that gathered about Jesus in Palestine; old men like Polycarp and John the Presbyter, whose memories brooded tenaciously over what they had heard, and whose souls were ripening for immortality under its hallowing sway. How eagerly and fondly should we have turned from the synopsis of books to the conversation of those living men! How inquisitive should we be about all the gossipy details of circumstance; how Jesus looked and how he dressed; what were all his private haunts; what other things he said and did; what were the shinings of his face and what the tones of his voice! This is precisely what Papias evidently did; and he says naively, "I do not think I derived so much benefit from books." He may have referred to the fourth Gospel in the body of his work, for we have only short quotations from its preface. For quite obvious reasons, however, he would not be likely to do so. It was then fresh and recent, and in the hands of those that knew all about it and knew John himself. Not so of Matthew and Mark. Their books were already sixty years old, and had become ancient documents, and the way Papias speaks of them, shows not only that they were well known, but that an interest attached to them as sacred writings, and that how and why they were composed were questions of exceeding interest. "John the presbyter, said this. Mark being the interpreter of Peter, whatsoever he recorded he wrote with great accuracy, not in the order, however, in which it was spoken and done by our Lord." Again, "Matthew composed his history in the Hebrew dialect, and every one translated it as he could." He speaks of these precisely as of writings which had become venerable and canonical. But his testimony for Matthew and Mark is good for that of John also. How preposterous the supposition that the churches which held in their hands the very writings of the Evangelists, and could prove them as such by living men, and the very details of their composition, would throw them away and receive in their place forged or second-hand documents; or that a spurious Gospel of John could have been got up and foisted upon the churches while the persons could be appealed to who sat at his feet! Schenkel fixes the date of the fourth Gospel in the times of Papias, about the year 120: that is, it was got up by some forger, while hundreds were alive who had seen John and drank his discourse; while the writings which came from an apostle's hand were matters of keen interest and inquiry; while John's own church at Ephesus held the legacy of his spoken and written words as sacred treasures, remembered the tones of his voice, and pointed pilgrims to the sepulchre where he slept.

The next witness to the canon of Scripture is the author of the "Letter of Barnabas," probably the same Barnabas who was the companion of Paul, though this is not entirely certain, and is not essential to the present argument. The history of this letter is curious. It was quoted as early as the last decade of the second century by Clement, and quoted as genuine as we would quote one of Paul's Epistles. It was quoted afterwards by Origen, and as the work of Barnabas. It disappeared, and was wholly unknown in modern times till about 1645, when it was discovered, and an edition published at Paris. It was variously regarded. Some thought it genuine, some not. Rosenmüller received it. Mr. Norton rejected it. But thus far in modern times it was only known in a mutilated copy, partly in the Greek original, and partly in an old Latin translation, and a very bad one, the beginning of the former and the end of the latter being lost, and the text of both being corrupt. Its antiquity, however, was indisputable, and it quoted Matthew's Gospel as Holy Scripture, under the formula "*as it is written*," under which only canonical Scripture was ever cited. Here was a hard fact to be disposed of somehow, or we must admit that early in the second century there was a New Testament canon of Scripture. It was evaded in this way. The quotation occurs in the Latin translation, and is a gloss.. It could not have been in the Greek original. "The quotation-form '*as it is written*,'" said Credner, "used for the New Testament books, is for that time unheard of, and without example. On internal grounds we must question the correctness of the text till the contrary is proved to us."

The contrary is now proved. In the "Codex Siniaticus" we have the oldest Greek manuscript which the world possesses. It has just been discovered, and lo! the Epistle of Barnabas reappears entire, not in a mutilated copy, but the whole Greek original. That the work cannot possibly date later than the year 100, the contents, says Tischendorf, unexceptionably show. Others carry the date back as far as the year 80. Turning to the disputed formula, there it is in the old Greek parchment manuscript "AS IT IS WRITTEN," and the smell of gloss all disappears. Tischendorf does not conceal his delight and exultation. "Surely the fact that at the opening of the second century, proof that the existence of an evangelical canon has been found, is a crushing weight against the boundless play of hypothesis in which during the last ten years the history of the New Testament canon has been involved."[1]

Finally, the authors of the Appendix to John's Gospel, furnish, we think, an indisputable proof of its genuineness. The critical reader sees at once that the concluding part was written by another hand. By a still more careful criticism he sees that John's Gospel proper ends with the twentieth chapter, where the writer thus closes and sums up the whole, "And many other miracles truly did Jesus perform in the presence of his disciples which are not written in this book. But these are written that ye might know that Jesus is the Christ, the Son of God, and that believing ye might have life through his name." Then follows the twenty-first chapter, beginning as a separate piece, not at all continuous with what goes before, having throughout the air of tradition, in a different style, and closing with two passages written professedly by another person with idioms and turns of expression which John never uses. It refers to a rumor which had become quite current, that Jesus had told John that he should not die but should sur-

[1] *Wann wurden unsere Evangelien verfasst?* p. 45. It is very doubtful whether Barnabas, "the companion of Paul," wrote this epistle. It contains many silly things, as it needs must, in attempting to allegorize the Old Testament.

vive the rest of the disciples till his second coming. It is perfectly plain, from the writings of Paul and Peter, that the expectation was quite general of Christ's second personal coming; and that the time was so near that some of the Apostles would live to see it, and so would be translated without seeing death. "We shall not all sleep, but we shall all be changed." They seem to have construed the language of Jesus to John as a direct promise that this would be so. It is easy to see that John dying and no Christ appearing, the word of Jesus would seem to be compromised. From this as from other tokens, we think the evidence conclusive that the last chapter is an appendix written after John's death. It undertakes to show that Jesus did not give any such promise, and deeming it important to make known just what he did say, it repeats his exact language, and repeats it twice over: "Then that report went abroad among the brethren, that that disciple was not to die; yet Jesus said not unto him that he would not die, but If it be my will that he remain till I come, what does it concern thee?" Then follow these words: "The person (to whom this rumor referred) is the disciple who wrote these things and testifieth of these things, and *we* know that his testimony is true." No one ever speaks of himself in this way. Then follows the extravagant statement of the closing passage, as remote as possible from the simplicity of John's narrative, and containing Greek idioms which he never uses. "And there are also many other things which Jesus did, which, if they should be written in detail, I suppose that even the world itself could not contain the books that would be written."

We have seen how eagerly and fondly the first hearers of the Apostles hung upon their speech, and how they would ask for the details in the life of Jesus. That this was so at Ephesus, Polycarp and Papias are unexceptionable witnesses as cited by Irenæus. Their reports coming only at second hand, we should receive with much interest, but we should not expect to see things through their eyes in the severe uncoloring daylight as seen through the eye-witnesses themselves. Things would appear very much as in the closing chapter of the fourth Gospel, and their excited wonder and admiration might well dictate the closing passage.

But this appendix becomes a most important and independent testimony to John's record itself. It is wanting in none of the manuscripts, and it becomes extremely probable that it went forth in the first copies from the Church of Ephesus or the constellated churches over which he presided, as their testimony both to the known authorship of the fourth Gospel and to the truth of its contents which they had heard from the writer's lips. We know from other sources that while the hearers of John were yet alive, that is, in the first decades of the second century, the fourth Gospel with its appendix were in the canon of the New Testament, and it becomes almost certain, therefore, that no copies were in circulation without it. The solemn averment, "This is the disciple who testifieth of these things and wrote these things, and *we know* that his testimony is true," becomes that of the Church at Ephesus which had heard year after year the details of the life of Jesus from his lips; which had received the legacy of his written narrative, indorsed it as genuine, and sent it forth to the Christian world.[1]

II. The enemies of Christianity, during the period under review, furnish the same conclusive argument for the fourth Gospel. Conspicuous among these is Celsus, its bitter antagonist, who wrote about the year 150 to refute it. Origen answered him, and has preserved some things which he wrote. Celsus refers to scandalous reports and traditions; says he could bring forward many things which have been truly written about Jesus of a very different character from the writings of his own disciples. These, however, he says he will forego, and proceeds to make use of the four evangelists as the public and sole authority acknowledged by the Church. He refers to all the four Gospels, and quotes them; tries to show their inconsistency with each other, dwells upon the dis-

[1] Norton considers the last chapter of the fourth Gospel as John's writing, except the last two verses. Neander ascribes the whole to another hand. Both consider the whole chapter an appendix.

crepancy between Luke and John, and Matthew and Mark, touching the appearance of the angels at the sepulchre; quotes the synoptics repeatedly, and John several times; seizes upon John's designation of Jesus as "the Logos;" ridicules the idea that blood and water flowed from his side at the crucifixion,— a fact found only in John's narrative. "All these things," he says, "we have taken out of *your own Scriptures,* we need no other witness, for you fall upon your own sword."[1]

There were two classes of Gnostics: there were those who broke with the Church and rejected its Scriptures, and there were those who kept within it and perverted them. Of the former class was Marcion. He flourished between the years 140 and 150. He was the son of the Bishop of Sinope in lesser Asia, was educated in the Christian faith, but fell away from it, and was excommunicated. He rejected the Old Testament as being only the work of the Demiurgus; he rejected John's Gospel, and probably Matthew and Mark, *not because he disputed their authorship,* but because he held the Apostles themselves to be corrupters of the true faith. He retained Luke's Gospel, which he undertook to alter and expurgate, to make it conform to his views. That he was acquainted with John's Gospel is abundantly clear, and has been vainly denied. Tertullian, who writes to refute him, says, "Marcion having got the

[1] See Tischendorf's tract, pp. 27, 28.

Epistle of Paul to the Galatians, who blames the Apostles themselves as not walking uprightly according to the truth of the Gospel, and also charges some false apostles with perverting the Gospel of Christ, sets himself to weaken the credit of those Gospels which are truly such, and are published *under the name of Apostles or apostolic men*."[1] The fourth Gospel is here clearly referred to, and afterwards by name; and Tertullian states the reason why Marcion rejected it. "The Gospel of John would convict him of error." This shows, beyond any reasonable question, that in the year 140 the four Gospels, and John's especially, were universally ascribed by the Church, and its enemies as well, to the men whose names they bear, and that the former held them as sacred and canonical authority.[2]

III. We come next to a very interesting and important mine of evidence which has lately been explored by a highly competent and skillful hand. Every one knows how exceedingly concise are our canonical Gospels; how rigidly they hold the reader to the prominent facts pertaining to the life and public ministry of Jesus; how little they gratify mere curiosity, and how free they are from gossiping details. Their majestic simplicity is strong evidence under the circumstances of a controlling and shaping Providence, for these are very different productions

[1] *Ad Marcion*, lib. iv. c. 3.

[2] *De Carne Christi*, c. 3.

from those which would naturally have been dictated by the private taste and judgment of their authors. But herein was a most tempting opportunity offered to pious fraud to try its hand in filling up the supposed gaps in the narratives. This was attempted very early, and hence arises a *New Testament apocryphal literature ;* forgeries got up by pretended friends of Christianity which they tried to circulate under apostolic or highly honored names. Tischendorf, the prince of scholars in the history and purification of the true text, has made this apocryphal literature the study of years, and they furnish, he says, the completest proof for the earliest reception of our evangelical canon. This holds especially true of two writings : the "Gospel of James" and the "Acts of Pilate."

The spurious "Gospel of James" stands in such relation to our Gospels, which it tries to supplement, that the latter must have been a long time in circulation before the forgery was attempted. There are passages in the writings of Justin Martyr, whose first "Apology" dates as early as 138, which can only be traced to the "Gospel of James," and which show clearly that the work was in his hands. This being so, it must have been written in the first decades of the second century, and therefore Matthew and Luke, which it tries to supplement in matters pertaining to the birth and parentage of Jesus, must fall, beyond question, within the first.

The "Acts of Pilate" refer not only to the synoptics, but to John's Gospel. For this also our oldest witness is Justin. In his first "Apology" he refers to various things foretold concerning the crucifixion, and of Christ's miraculous healing. He gives an account of the trial, death, and resurrection of Christ, and adds, "All this has Pilate, driven by his conscience to become a Christian, reported of Christ to the emperor Tiberius." We have the same in Tertullian given in more detail.

A writing answering entirely to these ancient citations, and bearing the same title, has come down to our time in many old Greek and Latin manuscripts which Tischendorf identifies as the very work quoted by Justin and Tertullian. The work presupposes the records of our first three Gospels, and that of John beyond all question; for while the report of the crucifixion and the resurrection refer to the former, that of the trial of Christ is essentially the report of the latter. An apocryphal book then was in existence in the year 138, based on the synoptics and the book of John. It must have been written some time before to have obtained credit with such a man as Justin. It carries us up towards the beginning of the second century, and therefore the Gospels on which it was based must have originated in the first. "It falls," says Tischendorf, "not as the lightning flashing through impervious darkness, but it is one of the clearest among many rays of light out of the post-apostolic age streaming down to us over the weightiest question of Christendom." [1]

But in quite another way these apocryphal gospels furnish evidence of the true ones. The true ones in their more than Doric simplicity and divine pathos, in moral dignity and ethical tone, and in their direct appeal to the inmost consciousness of human nature, stand forth in contrast with the spurious ones even as God's work in nature stands in contrast with the contrivances of men. This is not a matter of individual taste and judgment. Individuals, as Tertullian and Justin, were deceived. The churches were not, and in no case can it be shown that a forged Gospel was foisted into the canon of Scripture to be generally received. The same spirit that breathed through the letter of the Word breathed also through the heart of the Church, and made its faculty of recognition in the main unerring and its vision clear. The apocryphal Gospels show us indubitably what our New Testament writings would have been if they had been the productions of the second century. All that gave the spurious ones local and temporary currency was the grains of gold filched from the evangelic narratives to incorporate with their tinsel and sand. An epistle, if very brief, might possibly escape detection. But when forgers undertook to write gospels, though they borrowed from the true ones, their own despicable puerilities showed more

[1] *Wenn wurden unsere Evangelien verfasst,* pp. 29–40.

surely in the contrast. They tried the experiment repeatedly. They invented their "Lives of Christ," and these compare with the simple, sublime conceptions of our Gospels, and especially the fourth, as the murky bonfires of midnight compare with the stars that shine in eternal serenity and beauty above them.

IV. The heretics of the Church are a company of important and independent witnesses. There was a class of Gnostics, as already intimated, who did not take their position outside the Christian Church and assail it, but claimed their position within it. They might the more easily have maintained it after the death of the Apostles if there had been no Canon of Scripture by which their notions were to be judged, but only loose and floating traditions. But if there *was* such a canon of Scripture, of course their first object would be to pervert it and bend it to their purpose. We know just what they did since Irenæus wrote to refute them; and Hippolytus who wrote towards the beginning of the third century has given an account of their opinions, and how they defended them, and the works of both these fathers are in our hands. Irenæus says, "So firmly are our Gospels established that the heretics themselves bear witness unto them, and appeal to them to confirm their own doctrine." These heretics belonged to the first half of the second century. Irenæus wrote about twenty years after their time. His words give the pronounced judgment of the second half of the second century on the first half; and more than this, we have detailed accounts of the writings of these heretics which confirm the judgment.

Among these heretics Valentine stands conspicuous. He came from Egypt to Rome before the year 140, and passed some twenty years in that city. Throughout his whole system he borrows his terminology from the fourth Gospel. Irenæus expressly asserts that the sect used this Gospel to the fullest extent, and grounded their doctrines upon the proem. The Word, the Only Begotten, Life, Light, Fullness, Truth, Grace, were the train of hypostatized Æons which, with God, made up the famous octave of Valentine. That the author of the fourth Gospel borrowed from Valentine is fantastically absurd. That Gnosticism should try to get the fourth Gospel out of its way by taking it up into its omnivorous receptacle and translating it, somewhat as the ass translated Bottom the weaver, comports with its whole genius and history.

Hippolytus confirms Irenæus. He gives several instances where Valentine had quoted John's Gospel, always perverting it and trying to dovetail it into his own system.

The disciples of Valentine followed up the work. Ptolemæus was one of them who quotes Matthew several times, and once the fourth Gospel, naming it as the work of an apostle. "The *apostle* says, that all things were made by Him, — the Word, — and without Him nothing was made." Heracleon was another disciple and a distinguished one. He was contemporary with Valentine. He did not merely quote John, but wrote an entire commentary upon the fourth Gospel, fragments of which are preserved by Origen, in which it is plain that he sought ingeniously to *gnosticize* the whole book from beginning to end.

But Valentine's school had a still earlier founder in Basilides, who also comes from Alexandria in Egypt. He flourished as early as 125. He wrote twenty-four books on *the Gospels;* and that our four Gospels are the ones thus designated as a whole is nearly certain. He quotes Luke and John word for word, and tries to bring their expressions into accord with his system. He also refers to the star of the Magians in Matthew. Moreover the divine octave, named from the principal terms of John's Proem, is at the basis of Basilides' whole scheme, and Valentine must have found it there.[1]

Here then we have a false and fantastic theory of Christianity elaborated by its authors, all through the second quarter of the second century, appealing constantly to the four Gospels as authority, specially anxious to subsidize John and bend that to their purpose, and for that end writing a whole

[1] For these citations by the Gnostic heretics read Tischendorf's *Wen wurden*, etc., pp. 19–23. For other citations see Bunsen's *Hippolytus und seine zeit*, vol. i. pp. 63–66.

For quotations of Basilides, and of his heresy generally, see Eusebius, *H. E.* iv. 7.

commentary upon the book; involving so vitally the themes of that book, that sharp and bitter controversies took place between two parties in the Church, — the Orthodox and the heretics of that day, — and which continued down to the close of the century. Both parties appeal to one canon or rule of faith in which the Gospel of John is conspicuous, for in its interpretation its grand themes were vitally concerned. There are men who try to make us believe that right in the midst of this debate, when appeals were made by keen-eyed controversialists to canonical Christian Scriptures, a new and spurious book, involving more than all the others the very matter in dispute, was foisted upon the Christian public, received by everybody without a murmur of dissent, elevated to a place in the sacred Canon, and spread through various languages into all the Christian communions as of like authority.

We will put a parallel-case. We are separated by nearly one hundred years from the declaration of American independence, and the stirring events which led to the formation and adoption of the Constitution of the United States, the political canon of the country. After its adoption parties grew up, both appealing to its authority, both grounded on opposite interpretations. Suppose that just before our civil war broke out, the State Rights Party, not finding secession in the Constitution so plainly as they wished, got out a new chapter, added it to the old Constitution, and proclaimed it as a genuine portion of the fundamental law; and forthwith, and without dissent and simultaneously throughout the country, it is so regarded by all parties, quoted as such in Congress, cited in the courts of justice, and no trace of controversy about it was ever known or heard of. A more monstrous violation of all the laws of historical evidence and probability, and even of the first principles which determine human conduct, could not well be conceived. And yet the parallel fails in two particulars to give the argument in its unconquerable strength. We are one people, and speak and write in the main one language. The early Christian communions were separated by the barriers of dialect and nation which would render a simultaneous or general reception of a forgery a more violent impossibility. Our fundamental law concerns us only in our temporal affairs. Their fundamental law concerned them, so they thought, in their eternal well-being, and determined the conditions of heaven and hell.

V. We come to a species of evidence already indicated, which Tischendorf gives as the crowning portion of his argument for the New Testament canon. We have said that translations of the New Testament were made into other languages, for the use of the churches, and that these translations were the identical old Latin *Itala* and Syriac *Peschito* which have come down to us. They must have been made soon after the middle of the second century. This is certain from the quotations of Irenæus and Tertullian. How is this ascertained?

The manuscripts of the New Testament were copied and recopied for the hundredth time, and it was inevitable that some mistakes would creep in. The mistakes do not affect the main substance and doctrine of the New Testament, but they run down into countless minutiæ, such as the variation or omission of particles. Sometimes a word or a whole sentence has fallen out; sometimes a word or sentence, which might have been originally a gloss in the margin, has crept into the text. Not ten years would have elapsed after a manuscript had been dismissed from the hand of an apostle or his amanuensis to be copied and recopied, before these various readings would begin to appear. Of course the nearer we get towards the autograph of the writers the purer our text will be. Moreover it will be easy to see that this department of investigation furnishes the most absolutely certain of all circumstantial evidence to identify the received canon of any specified period, because the evidence branches into such delicate and interminable veins. The prince of scholars in this department is Tischendorf, who has made the exploration of it the main business of his life.

We have said that the Greek text which *preceded and formed the basis* of the translations of the second century is clearly identified in the Codex Sinaiticus, including our New Testament with its four Gospels.

We identify it, therefore, as the New Testament of the churches in the year 150; not of one church but of all; not alone at Rome but at Carthage, where Tertullian used the Latin translation made from it: at Lyons in Gaul where Irenæus used the same thirty years before him; at Antioch in Syria, where Theophilus must have used the old Syriac version or its basis in the year 170; at Alexandria in Egypt, where Origen wrote, whose quotations are in striking agreement therewith.

But the argument does not stop here. The Greek text in general use in the year 150, thus clearly identified, though the purest we have is not absolutely pure. It had already been a great while in use, for it is clearly demonstrable that A RICH TEXT-HISTORY LIES BEHIND IT. There is unmistakable evidence that it had already been copied and recopied and long passed from hand to hand. Tischendorf claims this as one of the most important and certain of the results of his labors. "If this is so," he says, "and there lies a long course of the text-history of our Gospels before the middle of the second century; before the time when canonical authority, along with a settled church order threw up a strong barrier against private modifications of the sacred text, — and I pledge myself to give complete proof of this in its proper place, — then we must demand for this history the space at least of half a century. Must we not date, then — I will not say the origin of the Gospels, — no; but the beginning of the evangelical canon about the end of the first century? And is not this result so much the more certain because all the historical facts of the second century which we have brought forward are in harmony therewith?"

We have exhibited in the two preceding chapters an outline of what is known as the historical or external evidence of the four Gospels. If the reader has imagined that it depends on uncertain traditions he will probably be surprised, if he has now surveyed it for the first time, at its cumulative and irresistible strength. He will ask, if there is not another side to the argument. There is undoubtedly another side, but there is none that we know of which can change the aspect of the case unless we say that all history is baseless and fabulous. We notice briefly two objections which may be supposed to break the force of the historical argument as we have stated it.

1. The Alogians, a small and obscure sect, appeared in Asia Minor soon after the middle of the second century, who rejected the fourth Gospel and the Apocalypse. Montanus and his followers who claimed the special gift of the Holy Spirit, and announced the coming of the millennium, had appealed to John's Gospel to support their fanaticism, claim-

ing for themselves the promise of the Paraclete and its realization. This extravagance the Alogians opposed. They met it with a denial that John wrote the fourth Gospel, asserted its inconsistency with the other three, and ascribed it to Cerinthus, the contemporary of John. Baur makes much of this fact. What does it really prove? Two things: —

First, that the Gospels were generally appealed to as canonical authority in the Church at the middle of the second century, and that the fourth was universally received as genuine, — a small sect who could not believe its doctrines because of their own rationalizing tendency being an exception to a general rule. Second, that the fourth Gospel as then known and received, was not a recent book, for the very men who seek to set aside its authority, assign its origin to the times of John, though most absurdly to Cerinthus, whom John opposed.

The fact argues not against the genuineness of the book, but strongly in its favor, and absolutely annihilates the pretension that it could have originated after the middle of the second century.

2. Another ground of objection is as follows: The verdict of the second century touching the genuineness of historical works, cannot be accepted as final, because the laws of historical evidence were not then understood. Learned men even were credulous and easily imposed upon. Works were then received which we know now to be forgeries, and quoted by

such men as Justin and Tertullian; and there are writings in our Canon at this time, such as the Epistle of Jude and the Second of Peter, which were not written by the men whose names they bear.

There are two plain answers to this. One may be as completely disqualified by skepticism as by credulity for applying the laws of historical evidence. The habit of doubting, caviling, perverting, and emptying words of their meaning, in order to suborn the facts of history to suit our theories, may even bring mist and darkness over a whole province of history which lies else in peaceful sunlight. We have no right to assume as a foregone conclusion, that the supernatural can only appear in the natural, as we have seen it, and then make our assumption an axiom of universal criticism. Yet this is what Strauss expressly and Baur impliedly have done. Allowing that there is a spiritual world, and therefore that the class of facts which the New Testament records, is possible, writers of the second century may be vastly better qualified to judge the record of them impartially, than those of the nineteenth, whose minds are darkened by a narrow or one-sided philosophy. Writers of the Alexandrian School, to name no others, such as Origen, Clement, and Pantænus so far as he is known to us, were learned men, not unskilled in historical criticism; and added to these qualifications were intuitions made quick and clear by the breathings of the Holy Spirit to discern the Scripture that throbbed freshly with its life.

But in addition to this, there was the *communis sensus* of the Christian Church when its glory was unstained by worldly ambitions or sectarian strifes. The Christ of Scripture then glowed warmly as the Christ of consciousness. Spurious documents might obtain temporary or local currency. But they would differ from the genuine as a daub from a landscape, and though individuals might be deceived, the Church Catholic would shed them off by the Power that reigned alike in its Bible and in the souls which it had redeemed and purified.

But the argument does not proceed solely under the authority of these writers of the second century, nor that of the church to which they belonged. It is various and cumulative, gathering strength and volume with every new investigation and every new discovery of documents. Our supposed better knowledge of the science of history, and more sure application of the rules which apply to it, do not bring the subject of the New Testament canon into greater doubt and difficulty, but bring it rather within the resolving power of a surer and more enlightened criticism.

CHAPTER VII.

CHRISTIANITY AS A NEW INFLUX OF POWER.[1]

FROM the close of the second century up to about the year 50 there is an order of phenomena not dwelt upon in profane history, nor much in popular histories of any kind; not because they are less authenticated than any other class of events, but because historians writing from the view-point of naturalism do not know what to make of them, and ignore them. They are not confined to the period above indicated. They belong in some sort to the more interior history of the Church in all ages. But during the period indicated they are marked and palpable, and unmixed with papal legends and impostures; for the hierarchy had not then arisen, and the Church was in her bridal robes. They were then new, taking the Church itself by surprise, unknown to the old effete religions as then existing, whether Jewish or Pagan.

This new order of phenomena may be described

[1] The principal authorities for this chapter beside the New Testament are Origen, Tertullian, and Justin. They are cited and enlarged upon by Neander in the first section of his *Church History*, and in his *Memorials of Christian Life*, Part I. ch. I.

as a disturbance everywhere of the old equilibrium of forces, social, moral, and spiritual. There were perturbations in the old system of statics like those which the astronomers observed among the planetary bodies, while yet the orbit of Uranus was supposed to be the boundary of our solar system. There must be the proximity, said Leverrier, of some body or system of bodies which we have never taken into the account; and so marked and decisive was the influence that he directed his telescope with the utmost confidence that the unknown disturber would swim into its field. The disturbance, however, in the field of history is so great as not only to produce irregularities of motion but to break up the old system of forces altogether and direct them anew.

We get a very poor and inadequate conception of the introduction of Christianity into this world when we imagine its Apostles going about and making an exhibition of miraculous performances as proofs of their message. The miracles did not cause the spread of Christianity, but were simply its outcome on the plane of nature. Christianity came only when the spiritual heavens were brought in closer and more naked contact with the human mind, and hence produced a NEW INFLUX OF POWER in human nature itself.

In comparing two coterminous periods of history, it is easy sometimes to see the second in the first, and to regard one as simply a development of the other. Thus the Protestant reformation was heralded a century before it came by signs which announced its approach, — to use the rhetoric of Coleridge, — as clearly as the purple clouds of the dawn announce the approach of morning. It is the past developing into the future. Let the historian scan the age of Augustus Cæsar and he will find there the science, the philosophy, the jurisprudence, the natural culture, and the religions, Hellenic, Jewish, and Roman, of the two centuries following ; to be modified as they might be by the ordinary forces of human development. The cause of the disturbances which we are about to notice he will not find; and unless he resorts to celestial observations he will set his glass in vain.

The new influx of power is traceable as one of the divine signatures of Christianity generally, but is found all through the second century, and always in connection with and within the circle of Christian ideas and the Christian communions. We mean by the influx of power, not the voluntary and normal forces of education and culture, but a new force, and one before unknown in the world, lying back of all human volition, producing a new creation out of the old chaos and transforming human nature itself. This is manifest in various ways.

1. First and on its lowest plane of operation, there is a new power of mind over matter, of the spirit over the body, found principally in a healing and

cleansing divine life, flowing downward and outward into its lowest forms. Of course this would be seen first in the cure of nervous diseases, because the nerves are the inmost texture of the physical body and join it with the spiritual, but it is seen in a restorative hand laid on all the diseases of the human form. This was called "miracle" in the language of the times, because it came as a surprise, but it was in conformity with universal spiritual laws operating within the natural as the heavens were pressing anew into the affairs of earth. For these phenomena we depend on no uncertain and private testimony, and they are altogether different in kind from the lying miracles of the monks of the middle ages. Origen appeals to them as matters of common experience. Grievous diseases and states of insanity, which had withstood all other means of the healing art, disappear when the subjects of them are brought within the circle of Christian truth and influence. No tricks of jugglery were used, but healing power ran down through the mind and the nerves and the whole physical frame, the entire outward man being recreated from within. Tertullian and Justin Martyr make the same appeal. They cite these facts as notorious. "That the kingdom of evil spirits," says the latter, "has been destroyed by Jesus, you may even at the present time convince yourselves by what passes before your own eyes; for many of our people, of us Christians, have healed and still continue to heal in every part of the world, and in your city of Rome, numbers possessed of evil spirits, such as could not be healed by other exorcists, simply by adjuring them in the name of Jesus Christ." Irenæus says the same, and declares that many came into the Christian profession because the evil influx which we call insanity, and which then held so many minds in baleful eclipse, receded and went out before the reviving glory of the inflowing Christ when the subjects came to themselves and rejoiced in their right minds.

So full and vital was this new influx of power that sometimes the apparent dead were brought back to life. We say *apparent* dead, for we will not assume as yet to know the exact line which divides the mysterious realms of life and death in putting off mortality, or that turning back and recrossing the line is a possibility within the supreme divine order. We only say that those who to the common apprehension had died, sometimes had a reviving consciousness within the sphere of Christian influx, and lived years afterwards as well known witnesses of it in the Christian Church. To this fact Irenæus bears unexceptionable testimony. But it is only one class of facts among others, notorious and well attested through the whole period in review, showing that the healing and restoring mercy was not only in first things but last things, not only ἐν ἀρχῇ, but in the ultimations of the natural world.

2. A quickening of the interior perceptions re-

sulting frequently in open spiritual vision, is another remarkable phenomenon of the period under review. It is found as late as the times of Origen, but it is continuous and more intense as we ascend the stream. As we find it in this period it has nothing in common with the visions of the monks, real or pretended, of a later age. It often came unsought, and to those outside the communion of the Christian Church, and ignorant of its system of faith, yet bearing in upon them gleams and intuitions of the same truths that lie at the centre of the Christian system. We mistake altogether when we suppose that a few unlettered men, merely by means of personal persuasion and eloquence, spread the Gospel laterally from Palestine throughout the Roman empire, as we find it in the second century. No wonder that Mr. Gibbon is nonplussed when he tries to account for its rapid, almost simultaneous diffusion, as if it had spread of itself. There is a large class of facts perfectly well attested, even while we keep within the track of common history, showing that the descending heavens were urging their transcendent realities into all receptive minds, sometimes with power so great that their scenery lay visibly upon the opening soul. Tertullian says the majority in his time came to a knowledge of the true God by visions (*e visionibus*); that is, they came into the Christian Church not because its truths had first been urged upon them from without, but because they had been borne in from above. Tertullian probably exaggerates, as he was wont to do, but Origen affirms the same class of facts not only as well known in the Christian communions, but as within his personal knowledge and experience, and calls God to witness the truth of what he says. These testimonies are important, not only as accounting to us for the rapid diffusion of Christianity in this early time, but for its invincible grasp upon the common mind, showing it a religion which prevailed, not so much by propagandism as by its outcome from the heart of God into the heart of humanity, prepared by some new agency for its reception.

3. Closely connected with the order of phenomena just named was another not less remarkable. The realities of a super-sensible world through all this period within the Christian communions are not so much matters of faith as of knowledge. Lying on the general face of society throughout the Roman empire there is darkness on this subject that might be felt. The philosophers did not believe their own speculations, nor the poets the creations of their imaginations, much less did the common mind have any intelligent convictions whatsoever. The Roman Senate might be said to represent the best culture and intelligence pertaining to religion, philosophy, science, and morals, which their times afforded. In the debate as to what disposition should be made of Catiline's conspirators, Julius Cæsar, then the High

Priest of the national religion, rose and opposed capital punishment, on the ground that death was the extinction of conscious existence, and therefore was not so much punishment as a release from it, thus publicly in the face of the Senate denying the immortality of the soul. Cato was there; and Cicero, who wrote the Tusculan Questions, was there. Both replied, and their replies are reported, but on this all important point they made no distinct issue with Cæsar, showing that even with the best minds the doctrine of immortality was only an airy hypothesis. There had been no change in this respect in the times which we have under review, except that they present the following remarkable phenomena. In the dense and general darkness we see little communions called churches, dotting the regions of night like spangles of gold and silver, gradually enlarging their circuit, while into each the heavens were open, and tidings of God and immortality were flowing free. Here was something which the age itself could not understand, and which we shall understand just as little if we suppose that this new faith subliming into knowledge was merely wrought by preachers who proved their assertions by miracles, or by reading the New Testament documents. Any one must see that such causes merely operating *ab extra*, were quite inadequate to produce such results.

4. But perhaps more remarkable yet was the new transforming power over human nature, everywhere

lifting it up and cleansing it. It is not merely the reformation of manners that now meets our observation. It is the new and original TYPES OF CHARACTER, and what is quite as remarkable, they were evolved out of the very material which a philosopher would have passed by as worthless. And more remarkable yet, they were evolved very often without the will, and even against the will of the subjects themselves, when those subjects were brought within the circle and operation of the new influence. There was some power lying behind all personal volition, and choice, transfusing the subject's whole being and bringing a new creation out of it which astonished himself as much as any one. Undoubtedly there was some preparation in the experience of such men, which made their natures ductile under the new supernatural influence; they were not made subjects of it by arbitrary selection; what we mean to say is, it came to them without their seeking; they did not go after it and find it, but it came and found them, and lifted them out of the grooves they had moved in, with a force they no more thought of resisting than the sea-weed torn up by the roots would resist the swellings of the tides.[1]

Celsus, who wrote against Christianity, evidently

[1] Origen says in his treatise, *Contra Celsus*, "Many, as it were, against their will, have been brought over to Christianity; since a certain Spirit suddenly turned their reason from hatred against Christianity into zealous attachment even at the cost of their lives, and presented certain images before the soul either awake or in vision."

with great subtlety and acumen, makes it one of his sharpest points of objection that it professes to accomplish impossibilities ; that the idea of changing *human nature,* and making it over is utterly absurd. "It is manifest to every one," says he, "that it lies within no man's power to produce an entire change in a person to whom sin has become a second nature, even by punishment, to say nothing of mercy, for to effect a complete change of *nature,* is the most difficult of things." To this the Christian apologists replied in substance : Come and learn for yourselves. Come into our assemblies and see what and who we are, and from what ranks and conditions we have been gathered. See how the old savagery and hate have been expelled from us, and how we can now love our neighbors as ourselves, and forgive our enemies and render good for evil, and blessing for cursing.

We have two scenes presented to us : one in Lyons, and one in Smyrna of lesser Asia, in which the new type of character is brought in vivid contrast with the depravity of the age out of which it had been won. We mean the persecutions and martyrdoms described in the letters sent out by those churches making known their calamity to sister churches. We make all due allowance for the enthusiasm inspired by Christian faith, but even then we witness virtues and graces of character and examples of a renewed and sanctified human nature wrought out of the lowest and roughest material, far more illustrious than any other miracles that we know of. It is magnanimity, faith, love, patience, heroism, and the sweetest spirit of forgiveness appearing like an "orb of tranquillity" in a general storm of hate, revenge, and cruelty. To their tortures by racks, by pincers, by faggots, by the tossings of wild beasts, by being seated in burning chairs that the fumes of their roasting flesh might come up about them, amid scoffs and jeers from the rabble and when a word of retraction would have saved them, "They went on joyful, much glory and grace being mixed in their faces, so that their bonds seemed to form noble ornaments, and like those of a bride adorned with various golden bracelets, and impregnated with the sweet odor of Christ, they appeared to some anointed with earthly perfumes." [1]

These great changes were not developments out of the age, but of a Power which was reversing its tides. They were wrought everywhere in the name of Christ, and within the influence of Christian ideas and the Christian communions; very often the new influx from within meeting the presentation of truth from without as by a stroke of God. Thus from the ruins of a reversed and degraded humanity as a background they bring out these portraitures of an-

[1] For an account of these martyrdoms given in the Letters of the Churches of Lyons and Smyrna, see Eusebius, lib. iv. c. 15; also lib. v. c. i.

gelic life and beauty. The change in these persons could not be better described than by saying "the Holy Ghost fell on them;" for not any voluntary agency had wrought the change, but a sudden income of power through the consciousness. These phenomena occur as you ascend along the second century into and towards the middle of the first, and they appear in the moral world like those you would witness in the natural if you went out at mid-winter when the ground was covered with snow and the forests tinkled with ice, amid which a few trees scattered here and there were appearing in the bloom and the greenness of their summer glories. Any mind of the least philosophical bent and untrammeled by false theories, ascending the stream of history, would conclude that "something had happened," and that this something was of a very extraordinary character thus to turn the stream out of its course.

Ascending through this series of phenomena we come to the times embraced in our New Testament canon. The reader will see that the earliest of our ecclesiastical history does not stand forth as exceptional; that the annals of the Church for more than a century afterward, to come down no further, give us a continuation of the same order of events described by Luke in the Acts of the Apostles, and of the dispensation of the Spirit inaugurated on the day of the Pentecost. The current of history as we ascend, prepares us for the events they record so that they break upon us without surprise. We ascend and note the perturbations with expectant minds, — like Dr. Kane's men travelling northward and watching the flight of summer birds and the growing evidence of some mysterious and warmer clime, till the open Polar Sea broke on their sight, its waters shimmering in the sun and its waves dashing at their feet.

Ascending this stream we come to a literature unquestionably genuine, bringing us into the very atmosphere of the warm open sea. There is one man who appears as the central figure of this literature; whose writings and personal history, while they are entirely congenerous with the history we have been now tracing, fling a light over the whole, disclosing the causes, and the only adequate ones, of these mysterious perturbations.

There was a man who started from Jerusalem towards Damascus on a mission of persecution, proud, cruel, and vindictive; he came from Damascus with a heart yearning towards all mankind, with the humility of a child, and with affections as tender as a woman's love. He went towards Damascus with an intellect narrowed down to a rapier's point and harder than its steel; he came from Damascus with an intellect broadened and fused with divine fire, and with a logic so invincible, and with its links so warm with the Holy Ghost, that it moulded the thought of the world for eighteen centuries. What does his change date from? Epileptic fits, says Dr. Strauss.[1] I met Jesus Christ on the way, says Paul, in a light from heaven which dimmed the Syrian noon.

We are brought to the earliest literature of the Church in the authentic letters of this most distinguished among the converts to the Christian faith. Some of them were written not more than twenty years after the death and ascension of Christ. Four of them, — and those the most important, — the most exacting criticism has never called in question. Nine of them are conceded as genuine in the criticism of Renan, who is sufficiently exacting and fastidious for the most refined scepticism. Thirteen we regard as genuine beyond all reasonable doubt or cavil; and only the Epistle to the Hebrews, so called, popularly ascribed to Paul, has been shown very clearly from evidence internal and external to have emanated from some other source.

Later than these letters, we have the history ascribed to Luke, — the Acts of the Apostles, about half of which is a record of Paul's life and labors. The first chapters Renan considers as legendary because of the supernatural events there narrated, which by his theory cannot come within the range of authentic history. The "tendency theory" of Baur makes the whole book a compilation of the second century. The critics of the anti-supernatural school

[1] In his last *Leben Jesu*, p. 302.

agree together as to the status of Paul. "The Christ," says Renan, who gives him personal revelations, "is his own phantom; it is himself he hears while thinking he hears Jesus."[1]

Their criticisms of the book of Acts are futile so far as designed to shut out and keep out the supernatural. Those letters which Renan concedes were written by Paul beyond all reasonable question, contain the essential elements of the book of Acts, include in their range the most important events which it records, while at the same time leading us up to the very spot where the gates open and the new influx of power comes in to sweep down the Christian ages and carry the old land-marks of history before it as drift wood upon the waves. If you tamper with the book of Acts you may just as well keep on and tamper with all the history that follows in continuous stream for more than three hundred years. It were as if Dr. Livingstone, in following up the Nile to its origin, should come to a thicket out of whose shadows a copious flood of waters is swelling free, and should say, Here, I think, we have found its source. We will go no farther, for the river has come to an end.

Paul had never seen the Lord Jesus Christ in the flesh. He tells us, too, that he conferred not with flesh and blood; he did not receive Christianity from any other persons who had seen the Lord Jesus in

[1] *Life of Saint Paul*, ch. xxi.

the flesh. How then did he receive it? He says that after his conversion he went into Arabia, and thence returned to Damascus, and only after three years went up to Jerusalem.[1] Meanwhile he gives us to understand that the Christianity he was to preach and expound he received by direct revelation from Jesus Christ, and in such completeness and integrity, and with such grasp on its interior truths, that some who had been with Christ all the days of his mission on earth were left far below him, sticking as yet in the mere letter, and only to be released from its scales as he had been, by the new influx of power from the risen and glorified. This Jew, imprisoned of late in the hardest Jewish shell, appears suddenly with the shell shattered in pieces under his feet, looking down upon it in triumphant scorn, much as we may suppose the immortal spirit new-risen in glory looks down on the body which lately incumbered it. Moreover, a whole system of truth, diviner and lovelier than he had ever dreamed of, he now holds and expounds as a concrete reality, involving a new doctrine of God, of man, of justification and redemption, of the resurrection, of the Church as a universal brotherhood, and the kingdom of Christ as the universal reign of righteousness on the earth. All this, he says, "I neither received of man, neither was I taught it but by the revelation of Jesus Christ." Not only so, but the ordinances of Chris-

[1] Gal. i. 11–24.

tianity which were to symbolize its truths forever, he says, were given him direct from the Lord Jesus, and the scene of the Last Supper is described, and the language repeated by which the ordinance was first established, coinciding substantially with the account which the synoptics gave some time afterwards from their own memory of the scene.[1]

Moreover, in times of perplexity and fierce opposition from unbelievers when difficulties seemed to close him round as a wall of adamant, he says the Lord Jesus stood by him to cheer him on, or his angels encircled him in bright array, and an open path was then made for him, or the prison doors opened and he went triumphant on his mission.[2] Not by seductive eloquence, not by human logic alone, often by simple prayer and the laying on of hands, came the influx of power involving all present in a sphere of new life and of transforming grace, and lifting up their interior minds to quick-coming conceptions of truth that shamed all the philosophies of the age. Moreover, this Paul, once so hard and bitter with theologic hate, becomes under the new influx as tender hearted as a child, and writes that chapter on charity which has been a sweet lyric of the heart, and tongued its highest inspiration to the present hour.

[1] Compare 1 Cor. xi. 23–26 and Matt. xxvi. 26–29; Mark xiv. 22–25; Luke xxii. 17–20.

[2] Compare Romans xv. 18, 19; 2 Cor. xii. 1–12; Gal. ii. 2; Acts xvi. 25, 26.

Those things in the book of Acts at which the skeptical critics boggle most, the speaking with new tongues, the visions of supernal realities, the miraculous healing, the incoming of the Holy Ghost at the name of Christ, are all found in Paul's unquestioned letters to the churches, and we are cornered up to two alternatives in tracing Christianity to its origin. The system of truth and influence which in its broadening course raised Europe out of barbarism, found England a horde of savages, and made it the England of to-day, shattered the Roman empire, and on the ruins of the old paganism to which the heavens were nearly closed, formed the Christian communions, into which tidings of immortality came full and free, — this system, followed up in history to the earliest literature which attempts to account for its origin, is found in the writings of a man who had epileptic fits, or swoons, in which he saw a phantom which he called Jesus, — or else to a real Jesus Christ, through whom the heavens were opened, and swept the inmost chords of our human nature with the sovereign grace and transforming power of Almighty God.

It has become fashionable of late to decry Paley and "the Paley men." His unpardonable sin is the perfect transparency of his style and thought. What he saw he saw in sunlight, though he did not see very deep and far; and he had the rare faculty of making his reader see exactly what he saw himself. He never pretended to tell what he did not see, and call his subjective fog-shapes the advanced thought of his age. Hence his offense to theology. He wrote a little book, which may still be found on the neglected shelves of old libraries, which is a masterly demonstration through internal circumstantial evidence and mutual corroboration of the authenticity of the book of Acts and the Pauline letters. It has never been answered, for the excellent reason that it does not admit of any answer. As respects the Epistles and the book of Acts, Mr. Andrews Norton very well says Paley has "put the matter at rest." [1]

[1] Paley's argument in the *Horæ Paulinæ*, and the kind of evidence which he exhibits, may be illustrated in this way, —

A piece of paper was once found which had served as the wadding of a musket. Unrolled, it was found to be part of a newspaper which had been torn in two. If the missing portion could be found in the possession of certain parties certain facts of great local interest could be established. Another piece was found, but how could it be identified as the missing one? Why, the torn edges fitted exactly together. Not only so, but the torn words also came together so as to make sense and meaning along the whole line of separation. Nobody doubted, of course, that the two pieces made originally one whole. This gives some idea of the way in which the facts and allusions of the book of Acts and the Pauline letters fit together and interpenetrate, as belonging to one historic whole. They run into minutiæ and delicate coincidence which no forger would have dreamed of and no mere compiler could have happened upon. Paley's argument must be read to be appreciated, and when read it gives the go-by to the boundless guessings of Baur's "tendency theory and" the critique of Renan on the four letters which he rejects as spurious.

CHAPTER VIII.

THE PAUSE IN HISTORY.

IN the last chapter we ascended the stream of Christian history through the two first centuries of the Christian era. Let us reverse this process. Let us come down from the other side and see what forces there were out of which Christianity could have been developed in the natural course of human progress.

The Greek culture and philosophy had their consummation in Plato four hundred years before Christ. We should anticipate were we to describe here that marvelous achievement of human genius. We will only say now that nowhere else do we find a system wrought out by the human intellect which anticipates so nearly the truths of Christianity. Nowhere before or since that we can discover has human culture advanced so far or caught brighter gleams of the higher realities. If humanity was to come by development into the open light of a spirit-world, it should have been from the Hellenic religious consciousness. Hence onward, however, its course in this line of development is ever downward.

At about 150 B. C. Greece was merged in the

Roman empire and became a part of it. In the wide-spread servility of the empire there is a dreary desert varied only by changes from unbelief to superstition, and from blank despair to a kindling hope that some divine interposition might be nigh. From the Academy to the Lyceum, from the Lyceum to the Porch, and from the Porch to the New Academy, the gravitation is sure and continuous towards Nihilism, — the crumbling away of all the foundations of faith and knowledge. Plato lived in the future; he was the child of hope and aspiration. He saw an interior way which led the soul upward to God, and to a personal immortality in her native star where once more she shall hear the music of the heavenly spheres. All this is fantasy to the intensely logical and practical mind of Aristotle. He scouted the ideals of Plato. He started from sensuous phenomena as the prime grounds of human knowledge, and from this the steps of his logic did not conduct him to the immortality of the soul. Aristotle acknowledges the Supreme Reason, the God of Plato; God and the World have had an eternal co-existence. But they have no such inexistence as Plato had taught. The Cosmos has a potentiality of its own, and God is in it only as a foreign element. Its changes are not a continuous progress from lower to higher towards some goal of ideal perfection, but oscillations back and forth within its own limitations. With Aristotle there is no ever-brightening future for the world or for humanity. The stoics who build upon him do not like him separate the world from God. They sink God in the world. They identify them as body and soul, as essence and form; God the essence being a divine fire, and matter being an evolution out of it, to undergo periodic involution, — that is, be consumed and taken back into the divine essence again. This periodic evolution and involution make up the grand æons of the universe, its conflagration and recreation. They are what always has been and always will be, the eternal round and round of the Divine activity, according to the laws of fate, which man can neither escape nor change. Man is the plaything of this eternal gyration, appearing one moment on the phenomenal surface, to disappear the next and be sucked back on his way to absorption in the eternal essence. This stoic fatalism inspired the patience of great minds, accepting the inevitable, putting on the pride of a godlike courage that could scorn alike the pains and pleasures of the hour, and like Lear meet the winds and the thunderbolts with kingly defiance. Nevertheless, in this amazing descent from Plato to Zeno it is remarkable how humanity, divested of immortal life, has retired into the background, and in the alternate rise and subsidence of the tides of being and non-being, man belongs ever to the latter division, and is the froth on the highest curl of the waves.

From Zeno to Arcesilaus, the founder of the New

Academy, the strenuous opponent of the stoic philosophy, the transition is natural and easy enough. It is natural, that is, to distrust the grounds of knowledge when knowledge leads to the brink of despair. Arcesilaus, planting himself on the doctrine of the old masters, Plato and Aristotle, denied the validity both of sensuous reason and intellectual intuition. For denial of the first he had abundant authority in Plato; for denial of the second he had abundant authority in Aristotle. They cancel each other like positive and negative; each is positive where the other is negative, and each is negative where the other is positive, and the result is NOTHING. The disciples of the New Academy can defend with equal eloquence any proposition and its opposite, and prove both sides true and false at the same time. Carneades, once a stoic himself, but afterwards a zealous convert of the New Academy, came to Rome with great affluence of learning and a most bewitching eloquence. He was sent thither by Athens as her ambassador because of his persuasive oratory. There he delivered his famous discourses for and against justice; speaking first in support and then in opposition to the same doctrines both in philosophy and morals. The young men were enchanted; and Cato insisted that the ambassadors from Greece should be dismissed with all possible despatch lest their prolonged stay should corrupt the youth of Rome.

But Rome was already corrupt, for faith was everywhere dead, and the flooring of all knowledge had fallen through. The Greek religion had spent its force. It had awakened aspirations which it could not satisfy. It had caught gleams of beautiful ideals which it could not incarnate. It had found rents through the mist into a golden age of the past and a golden age of the future. But that future was an enchanted island across stormy waves. It might be a dream and not a reality, and the darkness had come down again like a cover and shut it clean out. There was nothing in the Roman religion which could take the place of the Hellenic or was fit to supersede it. It had no prophets nor seers ; no openings upward or forward ; only a heavy ritual to be worked mechanically by priests and haruspices. Its mysteries were not those of Apollo and his choir, —

> " Who hymn the great Father
> Of all things ; and then
> The rest of Immortals,
> The actions of men ; "

but they consisted in the shape and appearance of the entrails of animals, in the flight of birds to right or left, or in the alternatives " whether the sacred chickens ate greedily or hung their heads ! " As religion sank down into sense the worship of the gods was superseded by the worship of the Emperor. Their statues were decapitated, and the head of the Emperor placed upon them. The Jupiter Olympus of Phidias ending with the bust of Caligula, represents pretty well the change of faith from its heavenly idealizations to the ugly features of the time. Of course sensible men had no faith in the fooleries of the haruspices, and only believed in them as having some influence over superstitious and vulgar minds. Cicero, who wrote the "Tusculan Questions" and "De Natura Deorum," accepts, nevertheless, the conclusions of the New Academy; and declaring it impossible to rise beyond the probable, and deploring the sad necessity of renouncing the discovery of truth, he cries out bitterly that he doubts of all, and of himself. Seneca relapses into the stoic pantheism, declares God inseparable from nature, and divinizes the sun. Cæsar we said, proclaimed from the Senate-house that death is the extinguishment of all conscious existence, and nobody seriously disputed him.[1]

[1] The Roman Senate were convened December 5, B. C. 63, in the Temple of Concord, to decide on the fate of the fellow conspirators of Catiline who had been arrested and were held in custody. At no time was the civil and religious character of the Senate more conspicuously represented. The proposition is before them to put the prisoners to death. Cæsar opposed the motion on the ground that death was an end of all consciousness and therefore too mild a punishment. Cato and Cicero were in favor of it. The debate constitutes one of the curious passages of history. Cæsar was Chief Pontiff, the highest functionary of the State Religion.

Sallust thus reports Cæsar: —

"De pœna possumus equidem dicere id quod res habet; in luctu atque miseris mortem ærumnarum requiem, non cruciatem esse; eam cuncta mortalium mala dissolvera; ultra neque curæ neque gaudii locum esse." — *Bell. Cat.*, ch. 51.

"In grief and misery death is not torture but a rest from troubles;

Magicians and fortune-tellers stroll about everywhere, and these mercenary vagabonds become the self-assumed interpreters of the mysteries of life. In the dumbness of the oracles and the awful hush on the minds of men, we can easily believe Plutarch where he says that a voice,—"Great Pan is dead!" seemed to come from the sea, articulate in the booming of its waves.

Two results follow inevitably the decay of faith and the paralysis of the religious faculty. Sorrow is without consolation, and cries into vacancy; morality is without support, and human nature relapses frightfully into its native savagery. How piteous are the plaints of bereavement and how barren the topics of

it dissolves all the ills of mortals; beyond there is no place either for sorrow or joy."

Cato replied, following closely and refuting generally all Cæsar's political arguments; but coming to this he bestows on it a single sentence which sounds very much like delicate satire of the popular faith. He says, —

"Bene et composite, C. Cæsar paulo ante in hoc ordine, de vita et morte disseruit; falsa, credo, existimans, quæ de inferis memorantur; diverso itinere malos a bonis loca tetra, inculta, fœda atque formidolosa habere." — Ch. 52.

"Very well and in good order Cæsar a little before in this connection, discourses about life and death; thinking, I really believe, those things to be false which they tell us about Hades; that the wicked go a different way from the good into places that are foul, rough, fetid, and fearful."

What Cato thought himself on this point he leaves us to doubt. Cicero, in his fourth oration against Catiline, refers to Cæsar's assertion without assent or dissent. The whole shows how little practical faith there was in the Hades of the poets.

consolation in this pause between the death of the old religions and the incoming of the new! Cicero has lost a lovely daughter, and his friend Sulpicius Severus writes from Greece thinking to soothe the anguish of the father's heart. The letter has often been quoted, and its import is, — Why bemoan the death of a girl, when she and all of us, together with cities and empires, are passing down the throat of everlasting oblivion?

This affectation of comfort in despair, indicates the want which uttered itself louder and louder from minds whose sensibilities had not been quenched in the wide-spread sensuality, or where the human had not merged in the brute. Clemens, a noble Roman who lived about the time of the first diffusion of the Gospel, thus gives voice to these wants of the heart, this very orphanage of human nature. "I was from my early youth exercised with doubts which had found entrance to my soul I hardly knew how. Will my existence terminate at death; and will no one hereafter be mindful of me, when infinite time sinks all human things in forgetfulness? It will be as well as if I had not been born. When was the world created and what existed before the world was? If it has always existed it will always continue to exist. If it had a beginning it will likewise have an end. And after the end of the world what will there be then? It may be the silence of death, or it may be something of which no conception can be formed.

Incessantly haunted by such thoughts, which came I know not whence, I was sorely troubled so that I grew pale and emaciated, — and what was most terrible, whenever I strove to banish this anxiety as foolish, I only experienced the renewal of my sufferings in an aggravated degree. I resorted to the schools of the philosophers, hoping to find some certain foundation on which I could repose ; and I saw nothing but the building up and pulling down of theories, nothing but endless dispute and contradiction ; sometimes, for example, the demonstration triumphed of the soul's immortality, then, again, that of its mortality. When the former prevailed I rejoiced ; when the latter, I was depressed. Then was I driven to and fro by the different representations ; and forced to conclude that things appear not as they are in themselves but as they happen to be presented on opposite sides. I was made more giddy than ever, and from the bottom of my heart sighed for deliverance." In this distress of mind Clement resolved to visit Egypt and hunt up a magician to summon a spirit from the other world, but some sensible philosopher dissuaded him.

Such was the hunger of human nature in this solemn pause of history. The wide spread decay of the moral sentiment and the frightful corruption of manners, were a necessary consequent of the paralysis of the spiritual faculties. The amusements of Roman ladies were the cruelties of the amphitheatre, and the shrieks from rows of crucified slaves fell on the iron ears of spectators with whom the throbs of pity were a childish weakness. If the moral sentiment found cheap utterance in poetry, or in moral codes, it was where the rights of humanity were trampled out without remorse. "I am a man and anything pertaining to man concerns me," brought down the applause of a Roman theatre, where the day after the groans of the dying gladiator might have been applauded with equal glee. Applauding noble sentiments in the theatre was the cheap commendation of virtues which only lived in history. A play of Atticus was brought out during the games, and some passages which expressed hatred of tyranny were loudly cheered. This was when the very spirit of liberty had departed and the gloom of despotism was thickening to its midnight; and Cicero remarked that it gave him sorrow that the people employed their hands in clapping at a theatre instead of defending the Republic. Seneca could write charmingly in praise of poverty and self-sacrifice. "What have you done with the tons of gold piled up in your cellars?" came back to him in the jeers of the multitude.

Tacitus, who saw only the ruin and desolation, stands as one under a midnight sky, whose darkness has fallen as a continuous blot upon the landscapes. Human nature itself is in decay; virtue has died out; servility and rapacity are universal; despotism has become a necessity; and he describes the face of things as if he were the last man who stood self-contained, wrapped in his mantle and surveying the ruins. "What is unknown," he says, "is thought grand and mighty; but no longer is there any tribe beyond us; nothing but waves and rocks, and Romans fiercer than they, whose unrelenting cruelty you would vainly escape by obedience and good behavior. Plunderers of the world, after the *land* fails from their ravage, they grope into the *sea*, being greedy of his wealth if the enemy be rich, imbibing his servility if he be poor; men whom neither East nor West can satiate. Alone of mankind they covet alike men's affluence and men's indigence. Theft, butchery, and robbery, they falsely name empire, and where they make a desert they call it peace."

On such a field as this Jesus Christ appeared, some say the product of his times. He must have been the product of the times, very much as a Lapland spring bursting from the bosom of an arctic winter, is the product of its ice and snow. Christianity appears in the next century in the form of little communions called churches, emerging as a thousand glittering islets out of this sea of blackness, the islets enlarging their area till they touched each other; very much as the geologists say Europe rose from the deep, first in spots of emerald that lay as scattered gems on a wilderness of waters, but which grew towards each other till they formed a great continent clothed in luxuriant green.

PART II.

HISTORIC MEMORIALS.

"We regard them as a child might regard the stars, as chance sparks of heavenly light, because we have not observed the law which rules their order. However far one evangelist might have been led by the laws of his own mind, it requires the introduction of a higher power that four should unconsciously combine to rear from different sides a harmonious and perfect fabric of Christian truth."—WESTCOTT.

CHAPTER I.

THE FOUR GOSPELS IN ORGANIC UNITY.

THE New Testament has four classes of writings which we must carefully distinguish: the biography of Jesus; the history of the churches founded on his life and word; letters to those churches formulating the Christian doctrine; and prophecy, which forecasts the final triumph of Christianity. Every one must see, however, that the biography contains the revelation. The history, the letters, and the vision of prophecy, are commentaries upon it, and illustrations of its divine power in its operation upon human nature. It is not necessary to suppose that the commentaries, however important, are final and exhaustive, or that its operation may not still be variant and progressive. Indeed, if the four Gospels embody a Divine Life, and the Divine Word made flesh, no exposition of their contents can be taken as final and exhaustive.

The relation of these four remarkable biographies to each other, and especially of the first three to the fourth, is a subject which has been investigated with a thoroughness worthy of its exceeding interest.

Before we speak of their connection we wish to say a few words of them separately.[1]

The order of time in which they were written, in the opinion of most critics is the order in which they stand in our Canon. Some place Mark first, but generally both in the ancient canon and the modern, not only the four Gospels but all the books of the New Testament fall into the order as we have them, or nearly so, as if by some intuitive discernment of their pervading and organic unity.[2]

We place the date of the Gospels of Matthew and Mark not far from each other, and not much before the year 60. We place Luke's Gospel later, and not far from the year 65. These dates are not merely conjectural. We can see no reason, after the most searching criticism, for adopting any statement essentially different from that of Irenæus (A. D. 170), which agrees in the main with that of Papias (A. D.

1 It is no part of our plan and purpose to exhibit at large the historical evidence for the synoptics. We give what we consider the fair results of investigation. For the process the reader who chooses may read Norton, Fisher, Tischendorf, and the popular work of Westcott on *The Study of the Gospels*, and on the skeptical side Davidson's *Introduction*, and the last *Leben Jesu* of Strauss. It will be seen, however, that to establish the genuineness of the fourth Gospel is to prove the genuineness of all the others, inasmuch as it supplements and so far indorses them. Lange's learned and exhaustive work gives the matured results of investigation from the orthodox point of view.

2 See this subject finely treated in Bernard's *Progress of Doctrine; Bampton Lectures*, pp. 231–236, *note*.

116), and with Clement (A. D. 200), and with Origen (A. D. 225). John's Gospel must be placed in the last quarter, and probably in the last decade of the first century. All its contents confirm the statements of Irenæus and Clement, that John wrote it at the solicitation of his friends to supply a growing want in the Church of a more full knowledge of the earlier life and miracles of Jesus, and of what pertained less to the "body" and more to the spirit of his religion.

That the original Matthew's Gospel was written in Hebrew, and that ours is a Greek translation of the same, is generally admitted in accordance with the early tradition, and with internal evidence in the Hebraisms which are found in it. Mr. Norton gives cogent reasons for believing that the first two chapters in the received version were no part of the original Hebrew Gospel, but were compiled from tradition, and given first as a preface to the Greek translation, to satisfy a natural craving of the reader for some knowledge of the birth and childhood of Jesus, and that the preface found its way afterward to the body of the narrative, as it inevitably would do. The flight into Egypt and return seem inconsistent with Luke; the intended return to Bethlehem as if that were His home and not Nazareth, seems out of keeping with both Gospels. The whole cast of the narrative up to the third chapter, has not the usual traces of Matthew's pen, which, as we read him, has a rare gift for historical narration. We cannot agree, however, with Mr. Norton, that the preface, even though not Matthew's, is to be set aside as of no value. We think it has very great value, and has just the authenticity which such a preface, if made soon after, would be likely to possess. The miraculous conception and birth agree with Luke's history, and with what seems to have been the uniform belief among the personal disciples of Jesus while his mother was yet alive. The story of the Magians might have been a variation of that of the shepherds mentioned by Luke, or it might have been real history; for numerous instances might be cited to show that angelophanies were described under the image of a guiding star. The alleged murder of the children by Herod might have had some ground of fact. It was preserved long afterwards in the traditions and even the histories of his bloody reign, for a pagan writer of later date plainly refers to it in a passage in which it is manifest that the writer had not found his authority in the New Testament but somewhere else.[1]

Assuming that Matthew's Gospel proper begins with the third chapter, and with the words, "In the days of

[1] The passage is from Macrobius, a writer whose date is not far from the close of the third century, and is as follows: "Cum audisset inter pueros quos in Syria Herodes, rex Judæorum, *intra bimatum jussit interfeci*, filium quoque ejus occisum, ait: Melius est Herodis porcum esse, quam filium." — *Saturnalia*, ii. 4.

Herod appeared John the Baptist,"[1] it proceeds with a unity and power swelling on to its close, unmatched in all literature for its simple majesty. We cannot understand the state of mind that genders such criticisms as those of Strauss and Schenkel. Nothing shall convince us that here is not an eye-witness of the events he describes, and an ear-witness of the discourses he reports; whose mind has been lifted up and greatened by the subject-matter beyond all ordinary inspiration. It is the highest inspiration where the writer entirely disappears in his theme, and such a theme as this. We do not remember a personal allusion or the expression of a personal feeling of grief or admiration thrown in by the writer himself, as if such things were profane in the awful hush of emotion produced by his narrative. The discourses are often reported at length, and generally in their natural connection with the events that are grouped so as to synchronize with them. The opening sermon on the mount inaugurates formally the public ministry of Jesus as the multitudes thronged about

[1] The third chapter of our version opens: "In those days came John the Baptist preaching in the wilderness of Judæa." In what days? The text just before relates to the infancy of Jesus. A writer like Matthew would hardly leap a chasm of thirty years in a single paragraph after that fashion. It ought to be said, however, that the Greek *ἐν δὲ ταῖς ἡμέραις* has in narrative more latitude of construction, and may only mean "in course of time." Supposing that Matthew compiled rather than composed the preface, and afterwards added it to his history, all difficulties would vanish.

him throbbing and swaying with excitement, expecting the first summons of the wonder-worker to battle for his temporal kingdom, when the words, "Blessed are the poor in spirit" broke on the ears of his disciples. The discourse that followed is plainly the report of an earwitness, and none of it could have been invented afterwards and put into the mouth of Jesus unless human wit had attainments then never reached before nor since. The hush of the soul becomes more profound, as the narrative moves on, with almost insupportable grandeur towards the consummation. It is plain that the order of events is here preserved, for one scene leads on to another and prepares the way. Who that did not hear the sentence of doom pronounced upon the "Scribes and Pharisees, hypocrites," in the last discourse of Jesus that rang through the temple courts, could ever have reported it as Matthew has done? And who that did hear it and have those words burned into his memory would ever forget it? And who that did not hear the discourse that followed on the slopes of Olivet, where the scene opens up to the eternal judgment, could ever have imagined it? And with what natural sequence do the scenes of Gethsemane, of the trial, and of Calvary hasten on! "The fragmentary character of these narratives!" If that means that they are fragments out of the whole life of Jesus, it is doubtless true, but we cannot imagine a work better arranged for unity of impression growing deeper to the end, producing without any art the effect of the highest art, than we find in Matthew's Gospel. There is a point where human passion and emotion, having gained their height, go down again and give place to the noon-day stillness inspired by the divine presence. That state must have been gained by Matthew when he wrote his description of the crucifixion. All of fear and agony that can wring human hearts he had experienced as an eye-witness of the scene; he totally disappears from it in his narrative. To call his history dramatic would be borrowing the language of the stage. It is dramatic only as nature is in those awful moods when man seems as nothing before the on-goings of Omnipotence.[1]

The Gospel of Mark we regard as in fact the Gospel of Peter, bearing the impress of what may well be supposed to have been the features of his mind. Papias, Clement, and Origen are excellent authority for ascribing the second Gospel virtually to this Apostle. Papias knew and conversed familiarly with the personal followers of Jesus. "I made it a point,"

[1] Mr. Norton rejects from Matthew's Gospel a passage in the description of the crucifixion found in chap. xxvii., verses 52, 53, but without a shadow of external authority. "Many bodies of the saints that slept arose." If, as was certainly the case at and after the resurrection of Christ and long after his ascension, the inner sight of his followers was touched, and opened, there would be appearances to them, not of Christ alone, but of some of his disciples lately deceased, not in their natural, but spiritual forms. In the darkened pneumatology of the times they would inevitably have been reported as "coming out of their graves."

he says, "to inquire what was said by Andrew, Peter, or Philip, what by Thomas, James, John, Matthew, or any other of the disciples of our Lord." He says he was informed by John the presbyter that Mark wrote as the interpreter of Peter; and Clement says further that, being the companion of Peter, he was moved by the hearers of the latter to write out the substance of Peter's sermons, and leave them a monument of the doctrine thus orally communicated. This agrees with the traditions of the Church so early, direct, and universal, that they would not be mistaken, and it agrees with the contents of the second Gospel. Papias says, "Mark wrote with great accuracy," but not "in the order in which it was spoken and done by our Lord;" and Clement says it had Peter's authority for being read in the churches.[1]

The second Gospel, then, is a faithful report of Peter's historical discourses. Of course, the first preaching would be fundamentally historical. Mark wrote down the most striking and important things he had heard in Peter's narratives, and strung them together separately without any single continuous historical thread. This we conceive is sufficient to account for the character of the book and for its abrupt close, without resorting to Mr. Norton's extraordinary and improbable hypothesis.[2] For there can be no

[1] Eusebius, *H. E.*, ii. 15; iii. 39.

[2] Mr. Norton imagines that Peter might have been preaching dur-

reasonable doubt, we think, that the best critics are right — among which are Norton and Tischendorf — in saying that the genuine Mark closes with the eighth verse of the sixteenth chapter, and that the following twelve verses are an appendix by some later hand.

Conformably to this early history of the second Gospel we find it a series of most vivid historical pictures, such as none but an eye-witness ever could have given. It has no such majestic sweep and flow as we find in Matthew, and while it gives fragments only of the discourses, and those often out of place, it details matters of fact with minute and graphic delineation, but with no subordination of parts to one great idea. Little details are often thrown in found nowhere else, which could not possibly have come from imagination, but from reality alone. Peter's narrative — for so we have a right to call the second Gospel — has two characteristics which are quite peculiar. It gives us glimpses, which are sometimes exceedingly vivid, of the personal manner of Jesus and the expression of his countenance. Again, incidents are thrown in, very homely and almost unseemly in their nature, which others leave out, and which no romancer would ever have inserted; for instance, the poor demoniac whom Jesus was to cure lay on the ground gnashing his teeth, and "wallowed, foaming at

ing the persecutions of Nero, and that Mark stopped short in his report when Peter was arrested.

the mouth." The whole seventh chapter is intensely Petrine, both in its report of what Jesus said to the Pharisees and in the explanatory passage concerning their customs in baptizing, cups, benches, pots, and kettles.[1] The second Gospel shows that the narrator had not the deepest spiritual insight of the meaning of his own story, but it gives us the most external life of our Saviour with every mark of downright and sturdy honesty. We say, with every chapter, these things were seen and heard on this earth, and are matters of fact, and not of imagination.

Luke was not an eye-witness of what he relates, but his narrative is doubly interesting from his having been the companion of Paul. There was an early tradition that he was one of the seventy, which is confirmed by the fact that he alone has recorded their mission and work. There is evidence, too, that he had the confidence of John, and that he relates things upon John's authority. This evidence is so strong, that we shall consider portions of his history as substantially that of John. We will state the evidence and the reader can judge.

1. No historian, of the rare qualifications which Luke certainly had, would be likely to undertake such a work as the third Gospel without availing himself of the best sources which he could command. But there are portions of his narrative, as we shall see, where John certainly was the only eye-witness,

[1] ix. 20; vii. 1–23.

and there are other portions where this was probably the case. It is tolerably certain that John had not left Palestine when the third Gospel was written, and we positively know that Paul met him at Jerusalem and found him a "pillar of the Church" very near the time when Luke became a companion of Paul.[1] It is hardly conceivable that Luke should not have been brought into personal intercourse with the disciple who had the most intimate relations with Jesus.

2. Luke in his preface, more than intimates that he wrote on the authority of eye-witnesses, and did not receive his facts at second hand. "Since many," he says, "have undertaken to arrange a narrative of the events accomplished among us, *conformably to the accounts given us by those who were eye-witnesses* from the beginning, and have become ministers of the Word, *I have determined also*, having accurately informed myself of all things from the beginning, to write a connected account that you may know the truth concerning the narrations which you have heard."[2] The conclusion is tolerably certain that he wrote on the testimony of men who heard and saw.

3. John heard and saw a great deal which the other writers did not. He was a disciple and intimate friend of Jesus, as we shall see, for a year or more before the twelve had been chosen. He trav-

[1] Gal. ii. 9, 10. [2] Luke i. 1–4.

elled with the Master, stayed with him at Nazareth, witnessed his miracles, went up with him to the Jewish festivals, and heard his conversations and parables, some time before Jesus took up his abode at Capernaum. Any writer who undertook "accurately to inform himself of all things from the beginning" and report thereon, would be strangely incompetent if he did not resort to John, a living witness close at hand.

4. Mary the mother of Jesus, was the adopted mother of John, and a member of his household from the day of the crucifixion. The main facts in the first chapter of Luke could come only from two possible sources: direct special revelation or the word of Mary. Luke's own statement precludes the former and necessitates the latter, and strongly implies his intercourse with John and his family. His entire introduction relative to the birth of Jesus and the Baptist has an air of historic certitude in details which Matthew's preface has not. The visit of Mary to Elizabeth, their conversation together with the whole subject-matter, are what women who had been mothers, and *such* mothers, would have fondly kept in memory and related afterward, but what would have originated in the head of no *man* to put into history. The chapter is intensely natural; the angelophanies, under all the circumstances, are not unnatural or incredible; and John in his introduction, gives the spiritual and divine side of the same series of facts

as if complementing what Luke had already written. Moreover, Luke's account of the childhood of Jesus, including his dispute with the doctors in the temple and the search for him by his parents, could only have come from his mother. Mary might have been living when Luke wrote; but whether so or not, John, adopted as her son under circumstances of bereavement unparalleled in any story of human sorrow, would be the person to whom she would have confided such facts as are detailed in Luke's first chapter; and any writer must have been strangely remiss and careless if writing on such subjects he would not eagerly avail himself of such authority.

5. Luke in portions of his narrative is intensely Johannean. Where he relates things in common with Matthew and Mark, there is a general indefiniteness, and except towards the close a want of historical order. The great discourses are broken up, and striking passages from them combined and distributed anew, and without any reference to the time and place of delivery. Important sayings are reported as being in "a certain place," or "a certain village," or "one day," or "one of those days," or "one day as he was teaching." Things are inserted in the forepart of his Gospel which belong to the latter part in the order of time.[1] But in one kind of narrative Luke is unrivalled. Those parables which search the inner life most thoroughly and go to the deeper

[1] See chap. ix. 44, 51.

hunger and thirst of the soul, are reported by Luke alone; and some of them plainly, all of them possibly, belong to that section of the ministry of Jesus which antedates the residence at Capernaum, but includes the sole discipleship of John and one or two others along with him. There are five of these parables preserved only by Luke: the Prodigal Son, the Unjust Steward, Dives and Lazarus, the Good Samaritan, the Pharisee and the Publican. They differ from the parables properly so-called and freely reported by Matthew, inasmuch as they are not drawn from the analogies of nature but from human life, sometimes in its dearest and sweetest relations, and touch a tenderer chord of sympathy and love. They symbolize a more intimate relation between the heavenly Father and the human child, and they represent the universal brotherhood of the race. The beggar in Hades resting in Abraham's bosom; the publican justified above the pharisee; the man robbed and half murdered in the city of priests, to be cared for by the despised Samaritan, show unmistakably the Saviour in conflict with Judaism in its own capital, where his ministry commenced with John and one or two others as his fellow disciples. They show Christianity thoroughly cleared of Judaism. These parables, where it is divinely embodied, could have come only through an eye and ear witness, and they are most congenial with the spirit of John.

6. There are events of which John of all the twelve was the sole spectator or presumptively so, and which Luke reports; and though elsewhere he is often vague and fragmentary he is wonderfully distinct and graphic here and has the scenic minuteness of an eye-witness. We cite two of these instances; one given by the other synoptics in more general terms, the other omitted altogether.[1] Again, there are cases where Peter, James, and John were the only spectators and where Luke's narrative is much more graphic and detailed than that of the two other synoptics and, twice at least, lets us more interiorly into the spirit of the scene in the very style and method of the favorite disciple.[2]

The relation of the first two Gospels to the third and the first three to the fourth, becomes a subject of exceeding interest and importance. It has been the common method to study these four biographies as parallel. How much we may be confused and nonplussed by any such attempt, those who have used the "Harmonies" can bear witness. The Harmonies leave us with a painful impression of fragments jumbled together, but not joined. The truth is, these narratives are not parallel, and cannot be made to appear such, and yet taken together they have a unity which is not fortuitous but providential and vital. It is like the unity between the body and

1 See Luke xxii. 63–71, and xxiii. 6–11, and 26–44.

2 See Luke ix. 28–36, and xxii. 41–46.

the soul that warms and inspires it. They are not parallel but introjacent, and the more we study them as such the more shall we see that organic completeness and correlation. One lies within another. We begin with the most external, — the sheer natural life of Jesus, — and we are carried successively to the heavenly and thence the divine heights of his being. Matthew and Mark dwell upon the ultimate facts, describe the outward life, the physical sufferings and death of Jesus. They do it with graphic power and more than Doric simplicity, as only an eye-witness could. It is true they do more than this. But the humanity of Jesus is put foremost and made intensely real, and the first two Gospels seldom tell us anything which an outside looker-on could not have reported.[1] Luke, on the other hand, relates with much detail his supernatural conception and birth; and he reports sayings of Christ without regard to chronological order, often with reference to some other series of doctrine or some other province of duty. And he gives us entire discourses and parables, as we have shown, which reflect the mind of Jesus in more spiritual hues, and the relation of all men to God in a more intimate and filial communion. But in the fourth Gospel we are carried up to the divine heights of the being of Jesus. We enter the "circle within the circles." Things are related

[1] The account of the temptation, and the agony in the garden, are exceptions, Matt. iv. 1–11, and xxvi. 39–45.

which serve to complement what had gone before, supplying from the divine side of his being, that which gives congruity to the whole. It is not credible that a child should be brought into this world without any human father, and the statement of Matthew's preface or Luke's genealogy standing alone is beyond the grasp of rational thought. John's Proem gives us, however, the same fact seen on the thither or divine side, and if one is true the other must inevitably be. One is only the basis or earth-side of a transcendent divine reality which alone can glorify it, and make it a perfect living whole, only to take on the ghastliness of death by being picked in pieces.

There is a wonderful Providence in the formation and development of the Christian canon of Scripture. What the nascent Church needed first of all things to know was the fundamental facts, the natural life, so to say, of the Lord Jesus Christ. This is what the earliest preachers would at first be at pains to present. Little else would then be likely to be understood. The Apostles would not begin the grand fabric of Christian doctrine at the top and build downward to the ground; they would begin at the ground and build upward into the skies. Hence the striking verbal coincidence between Matthew and Mark, as if the Apostles had been accustomed to recite to their hearers over and over again the fundamental facts in the biography of Christ, until the very words had become stereotyped in their memories. The new converts, whether Jewish or heathen, would need at the start to be thoroughly possessed with that biography as exhibited to the senses, "what the eyes had seen and the hands handled of the Word of Life." How absolutely necessary this was is shown by the baseless and fantastic speculations of Gnosticism which soon followed, which ignored the natural life of Jesus altogether, and which would have made Christianity only a gorgeous and ever-shifting cloud-castle floating in air. That the Church should have begun with the fourth Gospel, and ended with the first, is not conceivable. That it should have begun with the first, and from its secure foundations been drawn up to the celestial and divine heights of the third and fourth, accords with the facts of the case and the nature of things.

And it accords with our individual experience. We learn Christ after the flesh before we learn him spiritually and divinely. We must see him and know him on the side of his natural humanity, a partaker of our nature, a sharer of all our woes and sufferings, or he will not touch our human sympathies and our tenderest love. But we are not likely to rest here. That it is not merely the carpenter's son who has found us and melted the flint from our hearts by such friendship and philanthropy, and such self-abnegation as the world had not known, we begin already to perceive, and when the fourth Gospel draws us upward to a vision of his unveiled divinity, and oneness with the Godhead, we are made conscious of no incongruity in his life and character, but rather of their majestic proportions and harmony.

How utterly futile the objection becomes, that the fourth Gospel omits things which are contained in the first and second, and contains very important matters which we miss in the others, must be obvious from these considerations. Why should John repeat what he knew the churches already possessed, unless for the purpose of showing its relation to a higher series of truth and doctrine, which he sometimes does; or why should Matthew, or Peter through Mark his amanuensis, undertake to pour all the treasures of the new revelation upon minds just opening towards it out of Jewish formalism and heathen superstition? The objection too that each of the four Evangelists has his own peculiar style, and that the fourth Gospel throughout is chromatic with some mind and genius altogether foreign to the other three, not only is without validity, but suggests a most wonderful and providential guidance. Each writer, of course, would select and give forth that in the life of the Master which was most in adaptation to his own mind and capacity to receive and reproduce, — and Peter of all others would be the man to set forth the ultimate facts and physical environment; the life of Christ as addressed to the senses of men. Hence his Gospel has such an air of reality that Schenkel, who sees Christ only as a man of natural growth and development, receives only Mark as an authentic book, though the external evidence is not a whit stronger than that of the fourth Gospel. John of all others would be the man to set forth the inmost series both of fact and doctrine pertaining to the life of Jesus ; to describe the new temple of truth, not in its outer courts and granitic foundations, but in the holy of holies, where the glories of the Highest are without symbol and veil.

The writer just referred to, in his attempted "portraiture of Jesus," rejects the fourth Gospel as unhistoric. In that shuddering dread of supernatural light which characterizes minds of his class, he rules out this book as the work of some fabricator of the second century tinged with the Gnostic theosophy. Only Mark is authentic. But the writer becomes conscious that his portraiture must be incomplete from Mark alone. He sees even from his point of view that here is a foundation whose superstructure towers into the tranquil heavens beyond the clouds that hide it, and quite beyond his view, and he is compelled after all to resort to a book which he had rejected as unhistoric and spurious, in order to present the life he is depicting in its symmetrical and crowning perfections. He says of the writer of the fourth Gospel, "He has elevated into the region of eternal thought, and invested with the transfiguring glory of a later century, a selection of reminiscences from the Christian traditions, taken out of the framework of their history in time. He has done this with an understanding of the interior being, and the loftiest aim of the life of Jesus, as it could not have been done at an earlier, and morally considered, narrower time. The fourth Gospel, therefore, serves as a really historical authority, for the representation of the moral being of Jesus, but in a high and spiritual sense of the word. Without this Gospel, the unfathomable depth, the inaccessible height of the idea of the Saviour of the world, would be wanting to us, and his boundless influence, ever renewing our collective humanity, would ever remain a riddle. In the several particulars of his development, Jesus Christ was not what the fourth Evangelist paints him ; but he was that in the height and depth of his influence; he was not always that actualized, but he was that in truth. The first three Gospels have shown him to us still wrestling with earthly powers and forces. The fourth Gospel portrays the Saviour glorified in the victorious power of the spirit over his earthly nature. The former show us the son of Israel, struggling in his humanity up towards heaven ; the latter the King of Heaven, who descends full of grace from the throne of eternity into the world of men. Our portraiture of him must not disregard the natural, earthly foundation of the first three Gospels if it aims to be historically real ; but it can be an image of Jesus, eternally true only in the heavenly splendor of the light which streams from the fourth Gospel."

This writer will not believe that John, who leaned on the Saviour's breast, has described most perfectly "his interior being, and the loftiest aim of his life," but that some writer not yet released from heathen superstitions, living nearly a century afterward, has done this out of the legend and fable that came down to him. The Christ that changed the course of history, and that moves the heart of the world in its profoundest deeps, is not the Christ as he lived and acted in Palestine, but as an unknown writer of the second century has produced him from unveracious traditions and from his own ideals!

This is the miracle we are to believe in order to void the miracles of the New Testament. This undesigned and unconscious homage to the overwhelming internal evidence of the fourth Gospel, and to its essential place in a seamless whole, is vastly significant. We shall be relieved of much needless difficulty when we are willing to think that an interworking Providence had something to do in the canon of the New Testament, in the order of its formation, in the constitution and arrangement, especially of these four wonderful biographies, and their growth into organic unity in such wise that each demands and complements the others; one within another, like circles convergent towards an illuminated centre.

It is often said that the four Gospels do not contain any system of theology, and that Jesus never taught any. If this means only that he did not draw up a set of articles, it is certainly true. But the system is there, too vast for us to make a model of for exhibition, and all the more impressing us with a sense of the divine order that reigns through it. You might as well say that there is no system of nature, because the ocean-shores are not geometric curves; because the rivers are not canals; or because the constellations are not grouped in regular figures, which children can count off or copy in their diagrams. It is a fact exceedingly suggestive, that those who have attempted to make out a life of Christ and reduce him to our human proportions, sifting out everything which cannot be accounted for after the fashion of our common experience, or leaving out everything which cannot be defined in human creeds and propositions, make their readers painfully aware, if they do not become so themselves, that Christianity in its subtile and vital essence has eluded their analysis; that the Christ of their books is one of their own invention.

CHAPTER II.

JESUS OF MATTHEW IS THE LOGOS OF JOHN.

MATTHEW and Mark dwell primarily on the humanity of Jesus; but his natural life is not described as unfolding under conditions which are merely normal. It is described as the ground and the ultimate manifestation of a life which is more than human. Not only in what Jesus teaches but in his manner of teaching this is always to be observed. He speaks with that tone of command and authority which, with men giving their natural intuitions or the deductions of their private reason, would be intolerably offensive. The sermon on the mount amazed his hearers, not so much on account of its subject-matter, as on account of his method and tone, for he appealed not to the law and the prophets for his proof-texts, as the scribes were wont to do, but made his utterance out of that original divine sovereignty whence law and prophets derive their authority. What to him were Moses or Solomon,—"a greater than Solomon is here." Mark dwells less than either of the synoptics on the proper divinity of Christ; but all through his narrative there is an air and manner on the part of the subject of it which would be intolerable self-assumption for Moses or Solomon, or for any prophet or lawgiver, and which presuppose a divine epiphany in Jesus.[1] We can cool down these passages by a process of criticism into figure and rhetoric, but the whole air and method will remain, and they are such as fit in with the natural coursings of no human biography before or since.

But we come now to remark another of the boldest characteristics of Matthew's Gospel. If we imagine that because Matthew was concerned primarily with the humanity of Christ, he was forgetful of his divinity, and presents him to us as a fine specimen of the best culture of his times, we shall not read far before we find our imagination melting away. Not merely Jesus but the Christ — the Christ of authority from above — is presented with a sharpness and boldness made more uncompromising by the intense realism of the first Gospel. Many illustrations of this fact are crowding upon us, but we will select only three.

1. The doctrine of John's Proem is explicitly asserted in Matt. xi. 27. After rebuking the cities where his Word had been delivered and his works had been done, Jesus tells them that their guilt in rejecting him was greater than the guilt of Sodom, and that it would be more tolerable for Sodom in the day of

[1] Read, for instance, Mark i. 7–11; ii. 10, 28; viii. 38; xii. 35–37; xiii. 26, 27; xiv. 62; xv. 2.

judgment. Then falling into a strain of indescribable tenderness, he subjoins: "All things are delivered unto me of my Father, and no man knoweth the Son but the Father, NEITHER KNOWETH ANY MAN THE FATHER, SAVE THE SON, AND HE TO WHOMSOEVER THE SON WILL REVEAL HIM. Come unto ME all ye that labor and are heavy laden, and I will give you rest." It has been asserted that the Logos-doctrine is peculiar to John. We find it not so, but only its metaphysical form of statement. It is set forth here in Matthew, with a clearness which no human language can improve upon, coupled with invitations out of the very heart of the Divine mercy which no fabricator would invent or imagine.

2. Christ, as the judge of men, is unquestionably the burden of the fourth Gospel. But if found in John asserted in more metaphysical language, it is found in Matthew drawn out with more than dramatic power, and with a sublimity unsurpassed anywhere in the New Testament. And it is not found in Matthew as exceptional as if some interpolater had put it in. It is found at the conclusion of the discourse from the heights of Olivet, when, as the doomed city lay at his feet, the vast future opened to the eye of Jesus, even to the retributions of an eternal world. The discourse rises in grandeur to the final announcement, "When the Son of Man shall come in his glory and all the holy angels with him, then shall he sit upon the throne of his glory. And

before him shall be gathered all nations, and he shall separate them one from another as a shepherd divideth his sheep from the goats." There is no such passage as this in the fourth Gospel. The same doctrine is variously asserted. The incarnate Word is to be the Judge of men. "All who are in the graves shall hear his voice, and shall come forth." But it is stated in a more colloquial and supplementary way, and is no more than a commentary on the grand and sustained utterance from Mount Olivet reported in the first Gospel.

3. But there is another passage, if possible still more significant, in the first Gospel, asserting the Divinity of Christ with a power to which neither John nor any other writer has given any additional strength. It is the final charge of Jesus to his disciples, involving the formula of baptism. It was given as Matthew reports, at the last post-resurrection appearance of Jesus to his disciples. "All power is given unto me in heaven and in earth. Go ye therefore and teach all nations, baptizing them in the name of the Father and the Son and the Holy Ghost, teaching them to observe all things whatsoever I have commanded you: and lo! I am with you alway, even to the end of time." (τοῦ αἰῶνος.)

The passages we have cited are not exceptional in Matthew's Gospel, but with others of similar import they connect themselves organically with the whole narrative. The fact then stands thus: that the first

Gospel dwells primarily on the humanity of Jesus, for it comes first in the order of time. The whole doctrine of the incarnation is baseless without it, and would only be a Gnostic theosophy floating in air. But Matthew, in consequence of those very qualities of his mind and style which give his narrative this intense and uncompromising realism, has also made the Divinity of Christ stand out with corresponding distinctness of outline. John writes thirty years afterwards with the synoptics before him, professedly to complete them. He does complete them, not undertaking to lay the foundations anew, but telling us a great deal about the Divinity of Christ, which explains, illustrates, and enlarges what the others had reported, showing the sublime peaks of doctrine which they had left in rugged outline, bathed in a sweeter and softer splendor from the morning sky.

If the reader, however, is in any doubt as to whether the Jesus of the first Gospel is the Christ of the fourth, if he thinks the first may be a man developed like other men out of the culture of his times, while the other was the factitious invention of a later day, he can easily bring this matter to the test. Summon the best man you can find, the most advanced prophet of to-day, and let him stand in the position of this same Jesus, the *mere man* of the first Gospel. Let him see if he can grasp his thunders. Let some prophet of to-day who ought to have grown up to the stature of Jesus, — the mere human development, declare in the face of the world that no man knoweth the Father but himself, and those to whom *he* shall reveal him ; let him assume to sit on a throne of glory with all the holy angels around him, and part the nations to the right hand and the left, to everlasting punishment or to life eternal ; let him announce that all power is given to *him* both in heaven and earth ; let him put his own name into a formula of baptism, and charge his followers to make disciples, in the name of the Father and the Holy Ghost, and — himself. Would the world be converted by such preaching at the rate of three thousand in a day ; or would they regard it as self-conceit and self-assertion, passed into the stage of monomania, and fit only for an asylum for the insane ?

CHAPTER III.

THE MYSTERY OF BIRTH.

BIRTH, from any view we can take of it, is a profound mystery. There are two kinds. There is the birth of species, or ascent from a lower plane to a higher one ; and there is the propagation of the same species successively on the same plane of existence. In the former, the Divine power operates immediately through the matrices of nature ; in the latter, through finite parentage. That any new species or new style of life was started mechanically by the Creator, or "made out of nothing," not only shocks the reason, but lacks all confirmation in any known facts of natural history. Theology is strangely fearful lest the Darwinian hypothesis of development should sink us in atheism. Should it ever be verified it would only be to write out a chapter of a new book of Genesis, wonderfully confirming the old one, showing in succession the birth of species, and the ascent through six days of creation till man appeared upon the earth.

Nature only affords matrices for the all-fructifying spirit. If we attempt to trace to its beginning a new type of life we find, of necessity, that it abuts upon something both higher and lower than itself. On the natural side it has been produced from something lower; animal life, for instance, has been evolved from vegetable. But to suppose that the vegetable kingdom *mounted up of itself* into the animal, would be to shock the reason more violently than the most mechanical and potter-like theology has ever done. The same is to be said of the assumption that animals climbed up into manhood, the monkeys rubbing off their tails, and otherwise improving their condition, till they found themselves spiritual beings possessing immortal souls. But the idea that the human species at its origin abuts upon something both higher and lower than itself, seems almost a necessity of the reason; upon the matrices of a lower life in its selectest forms on the natural side, and on the paternal side on nothing less than the brooding Spirit of God. Development from lower to higher species is not self-evolution. Every creation of a new type of being is a conception and a birth, having only nature on the maternal side, and the immanent Deity on the paternal necessitating no finite fatherhood between. Suppose, then, it should turn out as one of the discoveries of natural science that man was not manufactured *de novo* by direct interposition of God, but that there is a vast system of evolution climbing upward, from the nebula to the mineral, from the mineral to the plant, from the plant to the animal, and from the animal to man, — the glorious flower of the whole opening upward into the light of immortality, for whom everything beneath serves only as root and stem, I can conceive of nothing more worthy of the Divine wisdom and omnipotence. And that wisdom is none the less adorable that its creation rises not through breaks and divisions where we can insert our dissecting knives, but in unfolding grace and order as the seed rises up into the palm tree, and then flowers forth towards the sunbeams.

Every new type of life draws up into itself the next lower one, including that and — SOMETHING MORE. The mineral is not the nebula, but it takes the nebula into its organic structure; the plant is not the mineral, but it draws up the mineral into its composition; the animal is not a vegetable, but he takes up the vegetable, and decomposes it in a higher vitality; man is not an animal, but he must take up and include the animal as the basis and background of spiritual existence. Each includes what is below it and something more, and that something more comes from above nature, unless the stream can mount higher than its source, and unless all our talk about the nexus of cause and effect is without meaning. And if it be true that man was not extemporized by his Creator, but that a million years were employed in making him, we do not see that the workmanship is any the less wonderful and superb on that account, for what are a million years but as the tick of a watch in the eternity of God?

Climbing up from these analogies we are ready to say that if a higher type of life than the human, including that and something more, is to be produced upon this earth, it will not probably descend externally out of heaven, and stand among us in its insulation. Neither again will it be manufactured. It will be born. And it will be born of the brooding Spirit of God on the paternal side and of our human nature on the maternal, with no finite fatherhood intervening, and the product of such conception and birth would be a style of DIVINE LIFE into which men do not develop by natural progress and self-improvement, but which would express to them more completely and openly the moral perfections and glories of the Godhead.

This is precisely what three of the New Testament writers affirm respecting the birth of Jesus Christ. Two of them affirm it mainly from the natural or maternal side, one of them from the supernatural and divine. It is easy to do this. Other writers had done like things before, putting in the claim of supernatural parentage and birth for the heroes of their narratives. But they do it at their peril. The progress and the ending of such a life must answer to its beginning, and be congenerous with it. He who puts up such a porch as this imposes upon himself the task of making the building correspond to it. If he resorts to invention and imagination at the beginning, so he must in the progress and the ending, and he is perfectly sure to overwhelm himself with confusion and disgrace. For a man can no more imagine and depict out of his own subjective state a style of life organically above it and divinely human than he could himself beget it or create it. To say that he could pre-determine and describe the hero of such a narrative, would be saying that he was himself the hero, or else that he occupied the same plane of existence with him. An elephant or a monkey could have just as easily imagined what was to be the style of human life before man existed on the earth. And so we find that before the birth of Jesus Christ all the stories of heroes with pretended superhuman birth and origin make their lives and characters more decidedly sub-human than those of common men. The very effort to make them more than human, or more than natural, renders them all the more inhuman, unnatural, fantastic, and absurd.

The commingling of the two streams of life, maternal and paternal, and the divine life within them both, is one of the inscrutable mysteries. The laws which govern it are as yet very imperfectly understood. The paternal life is wrapped within the maternal, the latter — the maternal — prevailing through the years of infancy and on into childhood, and serving to weave the garments of flesh and blood and the exterior qualities of mind and soul; all, in fine, that goes to make up the external man. The maternal life is sometimes vigorous and dominating to such an extent that the paternal never appears externally, or, if at all, only feebly and dimly. It is held within the other, and held in abeyance. Unless, however, it is dominated in this way, it appears, though later than the other; the paternal qualities coming forth with greater and greater fullness, while the maternal retire before them, and sometimes disappear altogether, having served as the scaffolding of the intellectual and spiritual man. Hence we often find that while the resemblance to the mother at first is very great, in mind, feature, and disposition, it grows less and less with increasing years, while the features and the mind and passions of forefathers, sometimes for generations back, break through and become envisaged in all their strength and brightness. Our paternal humanity is within our maternal, sometimes never invading the consciousness or shaping our exteriors till infancy and childhood have had their day, but nevertheless prevailing in the end, and descending through lines of ancestry for hundreds of years.

Within our entire humanity, deeper than all its wrappages and layers, is the immanent Deity himself. But He never invades our consciousness as God. He never is within us as any part of our proper selves. Behind and within our voluntary powers He is the inspiring energy on which we ever draw, and out of which we breathe the breath of life; but the limit of our self-consciousness is precisely the limit where humanity ends. When his life becomes our life it is no longer Divine but human, and within the reach of our voluntary agency, to give back to Him in self-renouncing service, or pervert to selfish and ignoble ends.

Supposing it possible, however, for a being to be born into our earthly degree of existence with a finite maternal humanity on one side and the Divine Spirit on the other, with no finite fatherhood between, then it is conceivable that as the maternal humanity waned and the paternal dawned and brightened through the consciousness, it would image forth to us the Divine perfections on a loftier plane of existence than man and nature had ever done. Such a person would not speak and teach and act merely from a finite and fallible intelligence, but as the inmost Divine waxed and the outward and finite waned, he would speak and teach and act from the Divine reason itself. Such would not be a case of mere prophetic inspiration which is temporary and vanishing, but of Divine incarnation, in which the voice of the Divine Reason is the normal dictate of the soul. It would not be right to say that such a being is God, if you mean that God is limited to any outward symbolization, but it would be true that the finite maternal humanity, waning and disappearing, God would be revealed to us in a higher degree of life, and in more perfect and unclouded glory than inanimate nature or sinful men could ever reveal Him. And though what is called "the hypostatic union" is beyond our comprehension and analysis, so also is any union of the infinite with finite natures. In man God is one degree nearer to us than in the animal, but in a Divine Humanity he would be nearer still, and with a personality more openly brought to view. In a person divinely human there would be nothing unnatural, but something more than natural; there would be nature transfigured and exalted. There would be nothing inhuman, but something more than human; humanity made divine, and therefore the most clear and spotless mirror through which the divine attributes shine forth upon the world. We can conceive that there might be a necessity in the course of human advancement for such a revelation of the Divine Perfections; that sinful men, however developed, are no adequate representatives of God; that there was an appropriate time for some knowledge of Him above the light of nature, above depraved human instincts, above legal codes and verbal declarations; that these instincts themselves might have been yearning forward in expectation of a nearer divine epiphany, as when men watch the reddening streaks of twilight; until God should appear as a new sunrise, to light up the dark annals of the earth with diviner glow.

We are assuming nothing here. We are only describing the rational possibilities and probabilities of the case. Men might find God partially in nature and in themselves, for He is immanent in both, but in such a divine epiphany He would be revealed in a higher DEGREE OF LIFE and illustrate both nature and man more perfectly from the divine side of all created things. By the immanence of God, in us, we might surely recognize such an advent of the Lord when it takes place. But we should not be likely to master its psychology, since we know it so little in the lower degrees of life, where infinite and finite interpenetrate in nature and in ourselves.

We have three narratives which describe the birth of Jesus Christ, those of Matthew, Luke, and John. The first, describe the human, the last the divine side of this one event, from which a long and marvelous history was to take its rise. Matthew, or whoever wrote his preface, says He was born of Mary, a Jewish virgin, and was begotten of the Holy Ghost without any intervening human paternity; and he shows the lineage of Joseph, afterwards her husband, in its descent through David from Abraham, the father of the Jewish nation. Mary's line, though not traced, runs into that of Joseph, as she belonged probably to the same tribe; so that although Jesus had no human father, yet on the side of his maternal humanity he would inherit the proclivities of the Jewish race from Abraham downward. Luke also gives the birth of Christ without any human or finite fatherhood, tracing the line inversely from Joseph to Abraham and beyond him to Adam, the son of God. Both these genealogies were probably copied from public records. The names in the two genealogies do not coincide, and much criticism has been brought to bear upon the supposed discrepancy. But there is no discrepancy that can be discovered. These names do not stand for individuals merely, but many of them for houses or families through a long lineage, the head of the line being preserved where it runs into another line, several intervening links being left out. Jewish genealogies were recorded in this way. Thus Matthew says,[1] Joram begat Ozias. But Joram was not the father of Ozias, but his ancestor removed four degrees from him, as any one will see by tracing the genealogy in the books of Kings and Chronicles. Three links are there recorded which Matthew leaves out. All that can be said is, the missing links of Luke's genealogy do not synchronize with the missing links of Matthew's. There might have been reasons which do not appear on the surface. The only reason for giving the genealogy at all was to represent the qualities in its several degrees upward of the humanity inherited and impersonated in Jesus Christ. So, too, the objection that Mary's genealogy, not Joseph's, ought rather to have been given, has no validity. Men, not women, represented tribes and lines of descent, and Joseph's name probably stood in the tribe to which Mary belonged and through which came all the ancestral blood that coursed through her veins.

Matthew's account, as we have said, has been chal-

[1] Chap. i. 8.

lenged as no part of the genuine first Gospel. But the genuineness of Luke's narrative is unquestioned. The most fastidious criticism does not attempt to mutilate the record. Still its story of the conception and birth of Christ is called "legendary" by easy assumption on the part of that class of writers who arbitrarily sift the record till the residuum leaves only a man of natural birth and endowment. We show elsewhere, as we think, excellent reasons for regarding Luke's account as coming direct from the lips of Mary, or at most with only one intervening witness, that of John her adopted son. John's testimony is at one with that of Matthew and Luke, and only rounds and complements it. His record assuredly of the birth of Jesus interpenetrates their's from the divine side of things. They had described from the earthly side and from Mary's point of view, the maternal humanity with all its inheritance of Jewish proclivities, and of human proclivities from Adam down. John supplements them by saying that the Word, which was ἐν ἀρκῇ with God, and in its first principle divine, descending into this world to subdue and save it, took this humanity for its clothing and was the soul of its soul and the life of its life.

Legendary! A legend is a cumulative accretion ot hearsays around a nucleus of common fact, clothing it in the garb of fable; and the common fact here was the birth of Jesus Christ, the son of Joseph and

Mary. Legendary! the story might appear so, if you isolate it and make it stand alone. But why do you isolate it? Read on, and at the farther end of the biography we come to the death of this person quite as exceptional as his birth. The flesh thus assumed as the investiture of a divine life did not become a corpse, like the bodies of other men to see corruption in the grave. It was extruded by a living process, through the abounding energy within, where the divine man it had served ascended to his place on high. If you make his ingress into this world as here given legendary, why not reduce his egress from it into the same category? If you shut the divine portal through which He came in, why not also the divine portal through which He went out? Then just sit down and scan the facts that lie between and see what can be made of them. The life between constantly forecasts just that exit from this world; it courses its way on planes of being far above those on which we walk, and subsumes just such a birth and death. You must run the legendary theory through that also, till all the history is disorganized and tumbles into chaos. And even then you have only just begun. This life of Christ on earth was preliminary and preparatory to a deeper and broader life in humanity, coursing through the history of eighteen hundred years. The record goes on to say that he appeared after his resurrection as the guardian of those communions called churches, and that the Holy Ghost through him "fell on them" and gave them their conquering power. The Christian Church ever since, conscious of his presence and inworking divine energy, has originated, led on, and inspired all the advanced civilizations of the world, and is leading them still. Legendary! Why not make all the after-history legendary too, and the world's progress starting from fiction and always proceeding under it! This life, dating from that birth at Bethlehem, has continued ever since, and it spans our lowly history and floods it with more than rainbow glories, one foot of its celestial arc resting at the manger where Mary lay, and the other on in the future, for aught we can tell at the end of time. Legendary! Is it necessary to abstract such a birth from its relations and reduce it to the conditions of our own babyhood? [1]

[1] See the Appendix B, on the Birth of Christ.

CHAPTER IV.

NAZARETH.

WE have only one chapter in the childhood of Jesus, and that is Nazareth. This, however, is an exceedingly important one, and better probably than any accounts which his mother or his teachers would have given us of his education. The only written statement which we have respecting his childhood is given by Luke, and seems to have come from Mary his mother, perhaps through John who became her foster-son. It is exceedingly general; and after relating the journey to Jerusalem and his staying behind to converse with the doctors of the law, we are told that He returned to Nazareth, was subject to Joseph and Mary, and that while he grew in wisdom and stature he grew also in those divine affections which won the favor of God and man. That Mary had much more to relate respecting the childhood of Jesus is an unavoidable inference from our knowledge of the instincts of maternal love; that the evangelists have treated it with a most severe reticence shows how providentially they were guided. They might have gratified our curiosity; but it is not likely the childhood of Jesus differed greatly from that of other children; and probably Luke tells us about all that is to be said when he implies this increasing grace of person and behavior with the increasing wisdom that shone through it.

But all about Nazareth lay the open book which He read, and it lies there yet. Paul went up from Tarsus to Jerusalem and studied Jewish lore at the feet of Gamaliel, in the most famous theological school of his times; and his writings bristle all through with Jewish terminologies. Jesus was soon to have the thick-coming thoughts, for which no human school could furnish adequate language, but only the types and images in the infinite treasuries of nature.

Nazareth, though a despised country town, was of all places the most propitious for an education of this kind. It lies in a small basin of northern Palestine imbosomed in hills. The basin extends about a mile from west to east, and about half as far at its greatest width from north to south, narrowing toward the east into a deep ravine, giving the basin the shape of a pear with a long stem. This ravine leads out into the noble plain of Esdraelon, which spreads out so far below that a transparent mantle of sky-blue is resting upon it. The hill at the west end of the basin rises abrupt and precipitous; along the northern side the ridge is depressed somewhat, and along the south and east it sinks still lower. The town itself lies at the western extremity of this basin, cowering under the bluffs or clinging to their feet and sides. It has three thousand inhabitants, about the same number probably as in the days of Joseph and Mary, and presenting a similar external appearance of low houses with flat roofs, looking like cubes of stone. As you enter the basin through the narrow opening on the east and come into the town, you are greeted at this day with a more friendly welcome even from the Jewish population than is usual in Palestine. A fountain, whose waters percolate through the veins of the western hills, is conducted into one of the streets of the village, and falls into a stone reservoir. Over the fountain itself stands now a Christian church consecrated to the Virgin, because monkish legends will have it that her house was near by. With more probability and with tolerable certainty, they might say that here she was wont to come, with the other women of the city, bearing their pitchers on their heads. You would see at this day a crowd of women around the reservoir each waiting for her turn, and you would notice among them a peculiar native beauty after the Syrian type, and a peculiar gracefulness and friendliness of manners, partly owing to the buoyant health they breathe in among the mountains.

But as you ascend "the brow of the hill whereon their city is built," and which in one place breaks off in a perpendicular wall forty or fifty feet in height; as you gain the summit of the ridge that curves round it on the west like a protecting arm, a most enchanting panorama is unrolled suddenly to your view, every fold in it being a rich historic page. On the west stretches the long line of Carmel, beginning far away south towards Samaria, but extending northwestward to where he seems to plunge suddenly into the sea. This ridge is not bald like some of the mountains of Judæa, but crowned with forest, over whose depressions the Mediterranean gleams here and there in silver curves. All the history of Elijah, the Tishbite, is given back to your memory as you gaze, up to the time when he disappeared in his chariot of fire. Look northward and the scene varies. Near by stretches one of the most beautiful plains of northern Palestine, watered by a stream which divides it like a glittering thread on its way to the Kishon, where Elijah slew the false prophets. Beyond this plain northward the ridges rise one beyond another like ascending stairs, each taking on a deeper tinge of blue. The mountains of Safed, twenty miles away, overtop all between, and there, lifted up into the sky, you see the place itself, "a city set upon a hill." But Safed is backed by still higher ridges, and they roll in ascending billows sixty miles away up to Mount Hermon himself, who looks down on the whole in cold and scornful majesty from under his crown of snow.

If you turn towards the east and southeast, another plain, the magnificent plain of Esdraelon, spreads out its long level floors of green, under their mantle of sky-color, sprinkled more sparsely with signs of population, with valleys winding like dissolving views among the hills. Out of this plain rises Tabor, rounded like a hemisphere, little Hermon, and Gilboa, where "the shield of Saul was vilely cast away;" and through a depression north of Tabor you look into the valley of the Jordan, and over the high plains away beyond to the hills of Peræa which shade off into the Orient. South towards Jerusalem rises a spur of the ridge of Carmel, and over it loom up Ebal and Gerizim, from which the curses and the blessings answered to each other. Nearer by, and forming the heart of Palestine, spreads out the vast plain of Esdraelon with its gentle undulations; fields covered over with corn, interminable flocks and herds ranging in luxuriant pastures; — the granary of the surrounding country, rich in natural productions and voluptuous beauty; rich, too, in historic memories, as the scene over which the most decisive battles had rolled back and forth. Such is the horizon of Nazareth, more crowded with life and industry when Joseph and Mary lived there, but whose paradisical enchantments have not yet faded out. To know all its loveliness and magnificence you should see it in the morning as the sky reddens beyond the hills of Peræa, till the sun crimsons the snows of Hermon and then lights up peak after peak below him as with a torch; or you should see it at even-tide, as the sun drops behind Carmel and dissolves in the sea, turning Kishon and its affluents into burning threads, turning the vapors of the Mediterranean into new "chariots of fire and horses of fire" for other ascending Elijahs, and thence diffusing over the broad panorama of the Galilean hills and valleys a purpling softness like the more tender and brooding mercy of the Lord.

And why do we open these beautiful pages? Because it is certain they were the study of Jesus for thirty years; because the infinite Word that was already dawning through his higher consciousness was here to find its language. This vast treasury of type and imagery was to be drawn up into discourse and parable, as the embodiment of truths for which no language of books could furnish an appropriate setting. Not only nature in all her lights and shadows, but human life in all its busy ongoings, was outspread within the horizon of Nazareth. The keepers of vineyards pruning their vines; the shepherds leading their flocks a-field; the husbandmen sowing their grain; the plains over which the breezes as they swept made waves in the fields of wheat and tare; the reapers at their work over the vast surfaces of Esdraelon and El Battauf; the prognostics of storm coming up from the sea, or of fair weather when the sky at evening reddens over the ridges of Carmel; the Light of the World coming out of the east to enlighten every man; — all these and much more were daily in sight over that "brow of the hill" whereon the city of Nazareth was built. Two processes were going on in preparing the Christ for his work, — one of Spirit and one of sense. Higher truth than men had received or known was coming down through the heaven of his mind; better and more universal types were drawn up from earth through the senses to meet it and body it forth. The Son of God was also the son of Mary; the Word was made flesh to find a dwelling-place in the midst of men.[1]

[1] Renan's description of the scenery of Palestine is picturesque, though distinctness of feature is often sacrificed for brilliancy. Robinson is both picturesque and exact as line and compass. After an excellent description of the horizon of Nazareth he thus indicates the associations of the place, looking from the plateau above the town: "Seating myself in the shade of the Wely, I remained for some hours upon this spot, lost in the contemplation of the wide prospect, and of the events connected with the scenes around. In the village below the Saviour of the world had passed his childhood; and although we have few particulars of his life during those early years, yet there are certain features of nature that meet our eyes now, just as they once met his. He must often have visited the fountain near which we had pitched our tent; his feet must frequently have wandered over the adjacent hills, and his eyes doubtless gazed upon the splendid prospect from this very spot. Here the Prince of Peace looked down upon the great plain, where the din of battles so often had rolled, and the garments of the warrior been dyed in blood; and He looked out, too, upon that sea over which the swift ships were to bear the tidings of his salvation to nations and to continents then unknown. How has the moral aspect of things been changed! Battles and bloodshed have indeed not ceased to desolate this unhappy country, and

gross darkness now covers the people; but from this region a light went forth which has enlightened the world and unveiled new climes; and now the rays of that light begin to be reflected back from distant isles and continents, to illuminate anew the darkened land, where it first sprung up." — *Researches*, vol. iii. pp. 190, 191.

CHAPTER V.

THE FORERUNNER.

THERE was nothing in the established ceremonies of the Jewish national religion which was worthy of the name of preaching. That religion was administered mainly in the temple, the synagogues, and the theological schools. The synagogues were the parochial churches. They existed in every town in Judæa. The most elevated sites which could be obtained were chosen for them, and it violated all sense of Jewish propriety and sacredness to see any other building overlook the synagogue. Ten men were considered a sufficient but indispensable number to organize a synagogue, which word, like our word "church" came at length to signify either the ecclesiastical organism, or the building in which they assembled for worship.

In any principal town or large city these buildings were multiplied indefinitely, all of them constructed after the same pattern. We may form some idea of their number when we consider that there were twelve in Tiberias ; and since the erecting of synagogues was a mark of piety and passport to heaven, we need not be surprised that there were no fewer than four hundred and sixty in Jerusalem alone. They were long rectangular structures, and always consisted of two parts. The ICEL, or sanctuary, by way of eminence, was in the most westerly part, corresponding to the most holy place in the temple, and in it was placed the ark or chest which contained the Book of the Law and the Sections of the Prophets. The other part was the body of the church, where the congregation assembled. At one extremity of this department was an elevated platform, on which sat the officers of the synagogue, facing the congregation, and on which was a desk or pulpit for the readers and the minister. The congregation sat facing the officers. They did not sit promiscuously, but the men were separated from the women by a screen which divided the body of the church lengthwise as far as the elevated platform.

The chief officers of the synagogue were three rulers, the readers, and the minister. The rulers had a general care and direction, told the readers when to begin and the people when to say amen. The readers were seven in number, and took turns in reading the lesson of the day. Any one in the congregation, however, could be called to this service. How important and laborious it was may be judged from the fact that the Law and the Prophets, comprising the bulk of our Old Testament Canon, were required to be read through once a year in the public ritual, and for this purpose were divided into fifty-two portions, one of which must be despatched every Sabbath-day. It must be read in the original Hebrew, and therefore there must be a translator to render it verse by verse into the language of the people, which in our Saviour's day was the Syro-Chaldee. Besides this, several prayers must be recited. If we may credit Buxtorff, there were not less than eighteen belonging to the regular service, which fact gives us a vivid apprehension of our Saviour's words denouncing the greater damnation against men who for show make long prayers. After the prayers came the repetition of their phylacteries, which was done mentally and individually, out of regard for the law of God and as a guard against evil thoughts and evil spirits. These were texts of Scripture attached to their garments and worn generally near the heart. The synagogues were opened not on the Sabbath alone but on two other days during the week, which were regarded as a kind of fast-days, but the same lesson which was droned on these week-days was repeated on the Sabbath following for the benefit of the laboring class who could only attend during holy time. The superlative merits of the young ruler who fasted twice a week, can hence be estimated. He despatched one fifty-second part of the Law and the Prophets three times during every seven days, to say nothing of his phylacteries and the eighteen prayers which swelled still further the amount of his meritorious works. The readers, who were selected for their devotion or intelligence, were at liberty to throw in running commentaries of their own, though the stated duty of expounding the Scripture devolved upon the minister, otherwise called the Angel of the Synagogue. This was done after the readers had got through, and with how much unction and enlargement may be judged from the fact that he generally spoke sitting in his seat.

What torpor and spiritual death must at length overtake a people buried under such a load of ritualism as this! We may well imagine how the startling news broke in upon the everlasting droning of the synagogue, when a man suddenly appeared of such fiery eloquence that he shook the whole valley of the Jordan from one mountain range to the other. Such was John the Baptist. The memorials of him, though few, bring him before us with great distinctness. The account given of him by Josephus, harmonizes remarkably with all that is said of him in the New Testament. His mother and the mother of Jesus were cousins-german, and John must have known something of his great kinsman by personal acquaintance; but they did not reside near each other, and there is no reason for supposing that his inspiration came from that intercourse. His education was mainly in the desert. That is to say, like the Essenes, he withdrew in disgust from the hollow ritualism of the synagogues and the pedantry which loaded down the theological schools, and away in the silent places of contemplation, the power of God came upon him in over-measure, and clothed him as with a robe of flame. He must have known the Essenes, as we said, for they were close by him on both sides of the Dead Sea, with the same doctrines of righteousness, the same disgust of Jewish hypocrisy, and the same baptism by immersion symbolizing repentance and newness of life. But John, in spirit and method, differed vastly from the Essenes, and did not belong to them. They were quietists aiming only to keep their own garments white, and to get to heaven by a secret way. John was aggressive, as the fire on a prairie swept by a mighty wind. Up and down the valley of the Jordan, where the desert skirted the line of cities and towns, he went in the power of the Lord, and poured his denunciations against hypocrisy and injustice. He was clothed in the coarse garb of the old prophets, with a leathern girdle about his loins. He lived in the very haunts where Elijah had lived, and ate the food of the desert. No greater man, said our Saviour, had been born of woman, and though the last of a long illustrious line of prophets, their moral power and grandeur culminated in him. The Jews of his day had seen and heard nothing like him. Of course it was not long before the sleepy synagogues waked up and emptied themselves into the desert. They came at first, doubtless out of curiosity, to see a seven-days' wonder, but the truth shivered through them like the lightning, and converts were multiplied. People came not only from Judæa, but from remote Galilee. "What shall we do?" said they, searched by the preacher's words. "Let him who has two tunics give one to him who has none, and let him who has food, do likewise," was the answer, rebuking the prevailing covetousness and rapacity. It was a time of war between Herod and Aretas, King of Arabia, and soldiers were quartered in the land. These, too, came under the strokes of the preacher, and asked, "What shall we do?" "Be satisfied with your wages, and stop plundering the people." Tax-gatherers came, a hated and pestilent class of men, to whom some patrician in his palace at Rome committed the farming of the revenue, with unlimited license to peel the people of his province. "And what are we to do?" "Exact nothing but what is your due." Jerusalem itself was shaken. The travelled road through Jericho from the capital was choked with a living stream emptying itself into the desert. John himself seems to have been surprised to see them. "Have you come, too, you brood of vipers, out of your serpent's nest? Bring forth fruits worthy of repentance. Boast not of your descent from Abraham, for I declare to you that God out of these stones could make better children of Abraham than ye are." His fiery rebukes, however, not only smote the heart, but melted it. He made disciples, and founded a school, which survived long after his death. He impressed his great and earnest mind upon the mind of his nation, and the whole people cherished his fame as theirs. He was more than prophet; as we shall see presently, he had the gift of seership beside. He was one of those great minds like the Grecian Demosthenes, in which the national life gathered intensity for a last effort, and flamed up with expiring brilliancy. Coming at the approach of a great crisis, and elevated far above the plodding interests of the hour, his ear heard distinctly the steps of the coming doom. Within the wider horizon which he swept with his eye, a great woe was in sight, and hourly drawing nearer. Hence his "cry in the wilderness" to repentance, as an escape from the wrath to come. But he belonged to the old dispensation and not the new. He was Hebrew through every fibre of his being. His call was to repentance, to the unchangeable morality, to the eternal justice which had been set aside for a pompous ecclesiasticism that filled itself with inhumanity and self-conceit, as a sponge imbibes water. But repentance and reformation were all he could preach. That opening of the heavens through which the Spirit was to come for a new creation and a new consciousness of God in human nature, was not given to him, and he knew it. But he knew that this, too, must come, and he watched for its prognostics in the faith that he was sent to prepare the way.

CHAPTER VI.

THE HOMES OF JESUS.

THE idea we get of Jesus from a cursory and superficial reading of the Evangelists, of a homeless wanderer, with no place of permanent abode, roaming about Palestine with twelve men, living by miracle, or claiming the hospitality of strangers, soon melts away on a more careful study of the records. He had his abiding-places, whence he went forth on his mission, and into whose shadows he ever returned either from the glare of notoriety, from the heat and burden of the day, or from the threats and persecutions of those who sought his life. Indeed, much of his time was passed in this retirement in preparation for his public work, which seems to be the reason of a common mistake, — that this work was all crowded into the last two or three years of his life.

The homes of Jesus were three. These are very distinctly traced. It is necessary always to keep them in mind if we would contemplate his life in its unity, and understand the coherence with which the Evangelists have described it. It is from want of attention to this subject that some writers talk of discrepancies, especially between John and the synoptics, where they only interlock each other in a consistent whole.

The home of his childhood and earliest manhood we have already described. That Joseph and Mary belonged neither to the highest nor the lowest rank, but to the robust and healthful middle class of Jewish society, is abundantly evident. There was a school attached to the synagogue, in which Jewish children were taught to read and write, and also instructed in the canonical writings of the Old Testament. Jesus must have been educated in this school. That he attended any higher one, is very improbable; indeed, it is implied in the narratives, that he did not. "Having never learned," means that he never had been a scholar in those higher schools of the Rabbins, where he would only have imbibed the intolerable pedantry embodied in the "Talmud" at a later day. The law and the prophets which he learned to read at the synagogue, and the great book of nature spread out gloriously from the plateau just above, must have been the sources of the lore which he acquired at his home in Nazareth.

There was another home which he occupied afterward, and during a part of his public ministry. It was at Capernaum, on the northwestern shore of the lake of Galilee, some seventeen miles from Nazareth. The narrative warrants the inference that acquaintances and kinsfolk of his mother's family resided there, as they went thither on a temporary visit before a final removal of residence.[1] It is certain that a married sister of his mother resided in Galilee, the wife of Alphæus, otherwise called Cleopas, two of whose sons, Jude and James the less, afterwards were numbered among the chosen twelve. She might have resided at Capernaum or its neighborhood, as she is found afterward associated with women who belonged there.

The Sea of Galilee has been called the Geneva of Palestine, on account of the picturesque beauty and sublimity of its scenery. It is about sixteen miles in length, and half as many in breadth, deep set within a cordon of lofty hills. Through these hills there are two openings, one on the north for the ingress of the waters of the Jordan, another on the south for their egress. They make a current through the middle of the lake, but elsewhere lie in their deep basin, still as glass, and giving back as truly the skies above them and the scenery around, except when some sudden gust finds its way over the hills, which is very seldom. The hills are now brown and stripped of forest ; but if we may trust Josephus, this region, in the times of our Saviour, was so luxuriant, that nature seemed to work here a perpetual miracle. Fruits which required a hot climate, and others which required a cold one, grew and flourished side by side." " One may call it," he says, " the ambition of Nature,

[1] John ii. 12.

where it forces those plants that are naturally enemies to each other, to agree together.[1] On the western side of the lake the hills trend away from the shores, and along its margin stood five cities, or towns, whose names have become immortal. Near the head of the lake stood Bethsaida and Capernaum, which had become noted stations for fisheries; farther south, probably, were Chorazin and Magdala, and farther still, Tiberias, built by Herod the Tetrarch, the murderer of John the Baptist, and often occupied by him as one of his capitals.

Along the shores of this peaceful lake, Jesus went forth from his home in Capernaum, on his heavenly errands. Here he found most of his twelve disciples. Here he wrought those wonderful cures which blazoned his name through the country, so that the crowds flocked about him whenever he appeared abroad. Galilee contained a mixed population, not Jews only, but people of heathen religions and of no religion, Greeks, Syrians, and Phœnicians, and though more ignorant and boorish than the pure orthodox of Judæa, they had much less of the flint of Jewish bigotry and pride. Almost the whole narrative of the synoptics is taken up with the work of Christ in Galilee, as it radiated from his home in Capernaum. There were personal reasons for this, as we shall see. Matthew and Peter, who were eye and ear witnesses of what they relate, resided at Capernaum,

[1] *Wars*, iii. x. 8.

and their own work as missionaries was mainly in Galilee.

But there was another locality which was also one of the homes of Jesus. It was such before he went to Capernaum. To understand this portion of our Saviour's life, we must divest ourselves at once of a good share of our occidental notions about religious culture. We are the least given to contemplation, solitude, and introversion, of any people on the face of the earth. We rush into crowds, hold meetings, din each other with sermons and exhortations, which sermons and exhortations are generally the common places of the sect we belong to; and the shallow draughts from each other's well-nigh empty pitchers, we call getting religion. It was not so in the East. They drew from deeper wells. All but the book-men and the pedants who only reproduced each other in geometrical progression till the traditions were too heavy to bear, drew their deepest draughts from the springs of divine grace in the meditative soul.

Long before Jesus appeared, what was best in religion, what was highest and purest in morality, was withdrawn from public view. The Essenes, if we may credit Josephus and Philo, — the former of whom dwelt among them three years to learn of their doctrine and manners, — preserved about the only cultus which existed in the East, purified from idolatry, superstition, and hypocrisy. Near the western shores of the Dead Sea, a community of these people existed in seclusion, disgusted with the knavery and petrified selfishness which lurked under all the forms of the popular religion, and there they maintained a lofty devotion, a pure doctrine of God, immortality, and retribution, with an unselfish morality and uncorrupted manners. They had all things in common. They had ramified into other communions of like faith which existed in the deserts and sometimes in the cities and towns, receiving the books of Moses, which they interpreted allegorically, never going up to the Jewish festivals, nor appearing in the temple, but "gazing on the bright countenance of Truth," in their own quiet contemplations. They dwelt on the love of God, denounced every kind of dishonesty, and insisted on justice, piety, and neighborly love. Baptism by immersion was a common practice among them, not only for keeping the body chaste and wholesome, but as the symbol of a clean heart. Their constancy was brought to the severest trial; for Herod put them to cruel tortures, which they would not only meet with serenity, but with a smile of triumph over pain and death, radiant with the hope of immortality.

There is no evidence that either Jesus or John the Baptist ever visited these people, but there is abundant evidence that both of them combined the rites, the morality, and some of the doctrine of the Essenes with their own. John must have known of them, for he preached and baptized in their immediate neighborhood, where he thundered forth their maxims of truth and justice.

Admitting that Luke's Gospel and Matthew's preface give us the true account respecting the conception and birth of Jesus, it must be obvious that there were twofold reasons for his withdrawment betimes from the disturbances of outward things. The Word that was to be given him was to come neither from human teachers nor from the external world. It was to come down through the opening heaven of his own mind as soon as the sensuous nature which he received through the maternal humanity had drawn up from earthly things the types and images which were to serve as the prints and copies of the heavenly. Necessity was, therefore, laid upon him by the constitution of his being, to pass away from the outward till the heavenly realities filled and possessed his consciousness. The whole nights spent in prayer, away from his disciples and on the lonely mountain heights, must not be understood as time occupied in verbal petitions to God. We shall see presently that nothing of the kind is signified.

The great Ghor, or valley of the Jordan, extends from the lake of Galilee to the Dead Sea, through some seventy miles. Throughout it presents the same phenomena. Two ranges of hills and bluffs bound it on either side, — that on the west skirting Galilee, Samaria, and a part of Judæa; that on the east skirting the land of Peræa, the country beyond the Jordan. From the summit of one of these ranges you look across to the other. Sometimes they approach each other to within five miles, sometimes they trend away to eight or ten. They are rocky and precipitous, and rise over two thousand feet above the bed of the river. This great valley is cut by the Jordan unequally. As it issues from the lake of Galilee it leaves most of the valley on the east, but before entering the Dead Sea it leaves two thirds of it on the side of Palestine, creeping nearer the Peræan hills.

The great valley itself is composed of two plains, an upper and lower one. The lower one is a mile in width, making the bed of the river itself, filled to the outer edge when the river is swollen, but offering quite a margin when, in times of drought, the river shrinks within its channel. This margin of the lower plane, therefore, being alternately wet and dry, is covered with reeds and bushes, and sometimes with tall trees, which harbor wild beasts of prey. Here lurked the lion who "came up at the swelling of Jordan" from his lair. The upper plain, extending from this reedy margin to the bluffs, is a barren waste of marl and ashy soil, presenting a scene of awful desolation. It is from two to four miles in breadth on either side. Sometimes, where the upper plane terminates with the bluffs, springs of water percolate through the rocks, making little oases, as is the case opposite Jericho. Sometimes the bluffs are rent by steep gorges which are the beds of rapid rivers in wet seasons, and in dry become cavernous and shaggy ravines.

What we have now described was known as the Desert or the Wilderness. The valley "on this side Jordan" from Samaria to the Dead Sea was "the Wilderness of Judæa," some twelve miles in length. As soon as you enter these profound solitudes you leave man behind, and the blandishments of his hypocrisy and the noise of his battles are heard no more.

The exceptions to this solitude are only found where springs and rivulets trickle through the mountains and make oases at their base. Most famous among these are "The Fountains of Jericho." Jericho is gone, and only dirty Arab hovels now occupy its site. But the fountains are still there; and what would be an oasis is there if it did not run to bushes and sedge. But here in our Saviour's day rose the goodly city itself, called sometimes the City of Palms. It stood within the great valley, but hugged the base of the mountain, commanding a fertile plain covered with groves and gardens which the fountains had rescued from the desert. Through a gorge of the mountain lay the road to Jerusalem twenty miles off, leading around splintered rocks and through gloomy and shaggy defiles, the haunt of thieves and robbers. Jericho was a city of priests and Levites, it being a favorite resort of the officials at Jerusalem when not on duty in the service of the temple.

Passing through this road from Jerusalem and entering the desert through Jericho, the traveller, in our Saviour's time, would soon leave the palm groves and gardens behind. As he travels towards the Jordan he passes over five miles of desert and comes to a ferry, by which the Jordan must be crossed. If he is in quest of a solitude still more profound, or an isolation from Jewish priestcraft still more perfect, he will cross over by this ferry into Peræa beyond the Jordan. There is no village on the opposite side, but only a ferry-house, with perhaps a few buildings. This is the place anciently called Bethabara, which means simply the ford, or place of passage, but which seems afterwards to have taken the name of Bethany-over-the-Jordan. Coming hither, the traveller has put both the Jordan and the wilderness of Judæa between himself and the busy Jewish world. But he has only come into a remoter solitude and into wilderness still. It is desert for two miles between the Jordan and the mountains of Peræa and all the way up and down the river. Opposite are the hills from whose summit the promised land broke on the rapt vision of Moses, and this Bethabara is the identical ford which his knights of the Ram's-horn crossed over to take Jericho.

And in this vicinity was one of the dwelling-places of Jesus for some time before he went to Capernaum, and to which he resorted again and again, both for the opening of the inner heavens and for escape from the snares of men.[1] He did not merely come hither to John's baptism; he was *dwelling* here while that great preacher was declaring his message. He came hither from Judæa when tired of Jewish bigotry and hypocrisy. He made this his abiding-place till replenished anew from the Divine armory, when he went forth for fresh strokes on the flint of Jewish malice and hate. Up to the time of John's arrest and imprisonment, when he left for Galilee, this was his most frequent place of retirement and abode, and this was his starting-place for new journeys into Judæa. His ministry began at Jerusalem agreeably to the theory of Scripture that salvation should come out of the heart of Judaism and thence extend over the world. After John's arrest, and his ministry had changed its circuit for Galilee, still he came hither to his retreat in the valley of the Jordan, as if its springs

[1] See John i. 38, 39; x. 40; xi. 54. Compare Matt. xix. 19; Mark x. 1, 46. In the passage (Matt. iv. 13) where Jesus is said to dwell in Capernaum, we read, κατῴκησεν, -- he *housed* there. But where he is said to dwell in the desert we have (John i. 39), μένει, — he *remained* there, suggesting a less fixed abode, perhaps in movable tents. The town called Ephraim, near the desert where Jesus went and dwelt (διετριβε, spent the time) to conceal himself from the Jews, is of uncertain locality. Perhaps it was the ancient city of that name near Jericho. It would seem that he spent the time, not in the city, which would be no place of concealment, but in the desert near by, and that in emerging from his concealment he passed through Jericho. See Mark x. 46.

and rocks and solitudes had been made sweet by angel ministries and the communings of sabbatic hours. In these solitudes the inner heavens first opened on his sight; and in these again they opened in yet more solemn grandeur, and over long reaches of prophecy just before he started on his last journey to Jerusalem; for it was from these retreats, where he had remained for some time, that he went up to the last Passover, knowing that he went as the Lamb of God for sacrifice. After finally breaking away from his home at Nazareth, Bethabara, or some spot near this ferry of the Jordan, was his point of departure for his mission into Judæa, as Capernaum was his point of departure for his mission in Galilee. Even when passing from Galilee into Judæa, his route often lay through these profound solitudes, and there he would abide for a time before committing himself anew to that hot-bed of sanctimonious iniquity at Jerusalem. Sometimes in these retreats the people followed him and sought him out to be cured of their diseases or to hang upon his speech.

CHAPTER VII.

JESUS IN THE DESERT.

JOHN had stationed himself by the ferry, beyond the Jordan, and near the great thoroughfare through the Desert. Thither the people streamed in crowds from both sides of the river to the scene of what in modern phrase would be called the Great Revival of the time. John's was the first word since the days of the old prophets which had thoroughly shattered the crust of the Jewish formalism, thrilling the masses with an agonizing consciousness of spiritual want. In the natural language of hyperbole used by the New Testament writers, "Jerusalem and *all* Judæa, and *all* the country adjacent to the Jordan," came to his preaching and were immersed by him in the waters of the river as the symbol of their repentance and reformation.

Jesus came also to Bethabara from his home in Nazareth, not, as we shall see, merely to receive baptism from John. The Divine Idea, for whose realization he came into the world, must have grown urgent within him by this time, and he must have seen that the word of John, which had shaken all the synagogues out of their sleep, was preparing the way for the new kingdom of God to be ushered in. Hence he gave his sanction to John's preparatory work, and his personal compliance with it, as if saying, "This is not the work of one who hath a demon and is mad, as some of your magnates affirm, but work which comes in the orderly course of Divine Providence." He left Nazareth and appeared at Bethabara.

It is necessary here to unfold a principle of interpretation, without which we shall find ourselves stumbling at every step, not only at the beginning here of our Saviour's public life, but through every stage of it to the close. We must forget here again and leave behind us our cold and sensuous occidentalism and enter largely into the thought and the faith of the Orient. Language which with us has sunk into the baldest materialism, or else has been frozen into the coldest and the hardest of philosophical abstractions, to the spiritualized Hebrew mind, much more to the mind of Jesus, was preserved from all such perversion. For instance, our words heaven, hell, angel, demon, Satan, and their correlates, mean with us localities in space and beings of material corporeity ; or if we say they cannot mean that, we proceed to discharge them of substantial realism, leaving nothing but a nominalism that floats vague and empty in the air. The New Testament writers and speakers fall into neither of these errors, but are clear alike of both.

We are to remember here — and we only restate

the principle of our opening chapter — that there are two orders of existence, — one natural and on a level with the senses; the other supernatural and beyond their sweep and range. Men hold commerce with the first through their material organism; they hold commerce with the second, if at all, through an interior and higher one. Death discharges immortal beings from their material coverings, but it does not extinguish their personality. They are men still, and not abstract ideas of men existing only in the generalizations of human thought, and the corruption of the sepulchres.

To understand the Realism of the New Testament, we must remember that its supernatural world is not one of abstractions. It is one of forms and substances not less than this; and for the very reason that it is not material and subject to hard material law, it is a more perfect symbolization of Divine truth, and more pliant to envisage the supreme excellence and beauty. The words "heaven" and "kingdom of heaven" describe, it is true, a state of the purified soul here in its earthly condition; but if we suppose that in the New Testament realism they mean nothing more, but therein are shriveled to an abstraction, there is a great gulf between its realm of thought and ours. Involved essentially in the conception is the idea of the supernal abodes, the angelic societies above us and yet near us when we become like them, and whether visible or invisible, imparting to us or sharing with us the shinings of the eternal peace.

"Heaven opened," therefore, does not mean merely, in the language of those times, a more vivid apprehension, mentally, of abstract truth. That may be included and implied; but a great deal more is also implied. It means that the inner sight has been so touched and clarified that the heavenly scenery lies objectively around it ; where the prints and copies of that truth itself image it forth more perfectly and divinely, just as they do to those who have passed out of time and space into the open prospect of the eternal realities. We may say that this is imagination, and we shall say so if we believe with the Sadducees that there are no tiers of substantial being above the flats of nature; but we must not project our philosophy into the New Testament and freeze down its language into figures of speech, when it is plain from its whole pneumatology, that the writers do not intend a mere play with rhetoric, but a description of things heard and seen.

There were two classes of Hebrew prophets. There were those who simply uttered the word which came to them with a "Thus saith the Lord," and there were those whose inspiration passed into seership or open vision. Elijah was not only prophet but seer. John, who came in the spirit and power of Elijah, but was greater than he, was also both prophet and seer. He was such, according to the narrative, by the divine gift which commissioned him for his work; but his ascetic and contemplative mode of life would tend inevitably to reveal it strongly and clearly to his consciousness.

The world was expecting a deliverer. Not the Jews only but the devout of all nations believed that a great crisis was near, and watched with aching eyes for the tokens of the coming man. The influx from the higher world of causes, prognostic of great changes, was urgent now. But in the mind of the Baptist it took voice distinct and articulate and came as the voice of the Lord. He knew Jesus well but he did not know him as the Messiah. He only knew him as a man wonderfully endowed, in whose presence he felt overshadowed and subdued. But he knew and felt that his own work was only external and provisional, and that a Power which wrought deeper and more universal than his baptism of water must melt down the heart of the world and shape it in heavenly moulds. The impression upon his mind, divinely given, had become so full and overpowering as to become languaged in the depths of his soul. It was in substance this, "The man for whom the nations wait will be signalized to your apprehension. You will know him, for to your vision the Holy Spirit will descend and abide upon him. Understand then that the person who will thus be designated is the expected Messiah, who will take up the work which you have only begun, and baptize the world with fire. He will not only reform its manners without, but purge it of evil within." Of course the

Holy Spirit working subjectively in the mind of Jesus would have been no token to John. What John was looking for was an open vision of that Divine Sphere above and within the sensuous and earthly, which would infold the Son of God, and in which the power of the Holy Spirit to give purity and peace would be imaged forth by appropriate signs.

John was burdened with this thought when Jesus appeared through the crowd before him on the banks of the Jordan. But Jesus, as we have said, had not travelled sixty miles from Nazareth merely to receive baptism from John. It is plain from the whole connection that his dwelling-place in the desert was near by; the Proseucha[1] to which he had already withdrawn amid the profound solitudes of the valley, where the din of human society was unheard and nature itself no longer wooed the soul outward through the senses; where "the weary weight of all this unintelligible world" was lightened or rolled away; and the higher world emerged through the rifted and scattering clouds. After such ascent into heaven as this, Jesus appeared before John. Evi-

[1] A Proseucha among the Hebrew people was simply an oratory, or place of retirement for thought and devotion. Sometimes they were on mountains; sometimes by the side of rivers. Sometimes they were artificial, simple structures open at the top to the sky; sometimes only an embowering shade. In Acts xvi. 13, we are told that Paul and his companions on the Sabbath "went out of the city by a river side where prayer was wont to be made" (οὗ ἐνομίζετο προσευχὴ εἶναι), literally, "where he understood that there was a Proseucha."

dently heaven itself was insphering Him and beaming from his face. John is overcome with reverent emotion: "I have more need to be baptized by thee." Jesus replies, "It becomes us to fulfill all righteousness." Your baptism of reformation comes first in the Divine order and has its rightful place.

"And while all the people were receiving baptism, Jesus also being baptized and praying, the heaven was opened, and the Holy Spirit in a bodily form, descended upon him like a dove, and a voice came from heaven saying, 'Thou art my beloved Son, with thee I am well pleased.'" Luke iii. 21, 22.

"Being baptized and *praying*," the heaven was opened. Let us not mistake. Prayer with Jesus was not simply a verbal petition. It was passing inward and upward out of the realm of sense into the broad disclosure of eternal things. He has described it as "ascending into heaven," and his teachings and revelations out of that high state as "coming down from heaven," and the normal elevation of his soul amid the eternal serenities and perspectives of immortality as being or dwelling "in heaven." The heaven was opened, to whom? Clearly to the mind of Jesus into which the Divine influx came with such fullness and power as to take voice and articulation, and over whom the white wings hovering dove-like symbolized its all-cleansing and peace-giving work through a Saviour's mediation; and to the mind of John brought into this open vision and communion where the promised tokens were disclosed to him. "I saw and I bear witness that this is the Son of God." He knew him not *as the Messiah* until then. Now his tone changes towards his own followers. I am not the coming Deliverer, but He is already among you. I have seen Him though you cannot. He must wax and I must wane. Once in his lonely prison hours, weary with what seemed the long delay, doubts flitted over the mind of John and he sent to Jesus for further evidence. It may be hoped that the answer he received reassured him of the divine authentication in the heavenly vision by the waters of the Jordan.

The Spirit remanded Jesus to his solitude. A great conflict was inevitable. Such incoming of the Divine truth, glory, and power through the inmost consciousness towards their ultimations in the outward life could not be without meeting and waking into armed resistance all the hereditary tendencies of the Jewish mind. All these had been subsumed in the maternal humanity received through Mary. They had grown with the growth and strengthened with the strength of the sensuous nature which for thirty years had drank in the glories of this lower world. The hereditary proclivities of a long line of ancestry running away up through Jewish kings and priests yearning for worldly empire and ecclesiastical rule, looking towards a Messianic kingdom, which, beginning at Jerusalem, should overspread the earth and absorb all other kingdoms into itself, all these were waked up as if by a voice sweeping down into the soul as the cumulative urgencies of a thousand years. The possession of superhuman power had now come to Jesus, no longer in the dim twilight of consciousness, but in its noonday brightness. It was power, compared with which that of David and Solomon, the pride and boast of the Jewish annals, was contemptible. We do not know of any chapter in history more true to nature and bearing more indubitable marks of reality than that of the temptation of Jesus. It never could have come within the experience of feeble and shallow natures, but only those which are deeply and broadly representative, and which take up and compress vast provinces and ages of history into their own. In such as these the influx of heaven becomes strong as it meets and conquers the efflux of hell.

Let us pause a moment at the words "devil" and "satan." They never mean, in any canonical Scripture, a fallen angel. Nor again do they mean "the abstract principle of moral evil." Neither Jesus nor his biographers know anything of these philosophical nonentities. To them the demon-world, no less than the angel, was real, active, and personal, imbreathing through the souls of men and projecting infernal sorceries through their minds and imaginations. It was composed of the spirits of bad men who had lived in the flesh, and were, therefore, human, like ourselves, but unregenerate. Like the angel world, it lay proximate to this, but on the side of our lusts and evils, which it breathed upon and fanned into flame. The words devil and satan described originally the supposed prince of this kingdom of evil; but they ceased to become mere proper names, and stood simply for the impersonation of all the seductive influence from the realm of darkness; and on the other hand such proper names as Gabriel and Michael might denote perhaps the influx of the angel-world itself. But the New Testament writers give no sanction to the childish superstition of devils assuming material bodies, and in that shape set free on the earth for temptation and mischief.

The Spirit remanded Jesus to his solitudes. Heights of exaltation and depths of depression and trial are unavoidable in minds whose range is large enough to include the profoundest workings of God. Having just now become conscious of most divine endowments, the whole spirit of Judaism, from Abraham down to Mary, rose up in his soul to clutch these celestial weapons, and wield them only for Jewish ends. Yes, farther, the awakened selfhood of human nature, including its hereditary proclivities from Adam down, sought to bring these endowments into the service of self alone, and so place the son of Mary in conflict with the Son of God, and, if possible, subject the latter to his will.

We follow Matthew's order. The first temptation came in this form: "Turn these stones into loaves and live by them alone." Or, dropping the language of parable, Be satisfied with the lowest and most external life of sense, and with that alone, for stones are the lowest grade of external things. What visions of ease and self-gratification are here comprehensively described! all of which could pass at once to their realization if the divine power newly-awakened could be subsidized to such an end. Such a course were compatible with all the pride of life, including the pride of knowledge, the pride of philanthropy, all tending, however, to exalt self and surround it with worldly decorations. Such was the tempting path now obvious, and it led to no cross, no conflict, and no sacrifice.

The next temptation was deeper and more subtle. It placed Jesus in the Holy City and on the pinnacle of its temple; in other words, at the very summit of the Jewish ecclesiasticism. The highest exaltation to which the Jewish religious system could elevate him now rose upon his view. All the honors of its high priesthood, enlarged beyond its ancient pomp and splendor, were within his grasp. Already he had confounded the Doctors in the temple by his precocious wisdom, and now a wisdom more pervasive and comprehending than that of the whole Sanhedrim, or all the scholars of Hillel, was his. It lay in his power to raise Judaism to a fame which would outshine its brightest days in the past, if, instead of breaking its forms in pieces, he would throw his Spirit into them and make them more glorious than ever. Its priesthood would renew its fading lustre, and all its honors would cluster around his person. No conception of ours at this day is adequate to the fact which is here tersely set forth; a temptation that winds into the most hidden recesses of human nature. Ecclesiastical ambition is the most devilish of all, for it perverts a more interior and more sacred principle than any other, appears always in sanctimonious guises, and secretes a more specious and deadly poison. But Jewish ecclesiasticism excelled all others in this respect; and now the pride and conceit of a long and splendid priestly line, swelling and gathering force with every new generation, was sending its last efflux into the mind of Jesus. Had it prevailed it would have placed him in Moses' seat, the most authoritative, the most accomplished, the most honored of all the Pharisees.

The remaining temptation, though not so subtle, appealed to an instinct more universally dangerous. It placed Jesus at the summit of Jewish national renown. It showed him all the kingdoms of the world, and he at their head as the long looked-for temporal Messiah. The magnificent national dream could now be made actual. It had become an essential of Jewish faith engrained in the heart of every loyal man and woman, that the boundaries of Judæa were to widen and widen over the earth, and over the isles of the sea, and over all peoples, till Jerusalem should be the capital of the world, till "the Gentiles should come to its light, and kings to the brightness of its rising." The grand old spiritual promises had sunk from their meaning into the grossest literalism, and pampered the national pride with the expectation of unbounded empire. It was kept alive continually as they answered "Amen" in the synagogues to the ancient prophecies. "The sons of thine oppressors shall come bending before thee: they that despised thee shall fall down at thy feet."[1] How this vision flamed up to its highest grandeur as it took body and shape in a mind like that of Jesus, till "all the kingdoms of the world in a moment of time" were seen crowding to his standard in endless ranks; how the stream of national pride pouring through the hearts of all the Jewish kings into his was urgent to grasp the divine weapons now fairly in his hands, subjugate the Roman oppressor, and inaugurate the universal reign which all the prophets had foretold, — all this we may faintly imagine from our knowledge of hereditary proclivities, which set in strongest and swiftest tides through the largest and most receptive natures.

Forty days, say the records, these temptations continued, or, as Luke says, till the devil, "having come to an end of every temptation," left Him. Forty days, in Scripture usage, is an indefinite number, and means simply, as Luke intimates, a time, whether longer or shorter, during which the thing

[1] Isaiah lx. 14.

appointed to it is accomplished and complete. "The forty days' temptations," as we understand, are the terse and graphic summing up of the whole conflict up to the time of the public ministry of Jesus, — the conflict in which the descending heavens met and subdued the principles of earth and hell, and thus found their unobstructed ultimation in his mind and in his life. The abounding peace which followed, where, we are told, that as Satan left him, angels came and ministered unto him, is also strictly accordant with all our human experience. Those blessed ministries come like tranquillity after storms, consequent on all our moral and spiritual victories. They come to us in the mellow sunshine of the heart, flung from the face of God and the invisible presence of those who reflect his beams; they came to him not only in the peace within, but in the "heavens opened," amid whose visible serenities he won his abiding-place.

It is plain that the narration of these conflicts comes originally from the lips of Jesus in that comprehensive language of parable which he was wont to employ. They have the air of most intense reality; they were witnessed by no mortal eye, and they are the last things which his disciples afterwards would have invented or imagined with the intent of glorifying their Master. Mark puts the whole in, but very concisely, evidently not knowing what to make of it. John omits it, for the plain reason that he wrote with a full knowledge that the other three Gospels were in possession of all the churches, and that this history already had been thrice told. John, of all the others, would have entered most profoundly into its vast spiritual import. Luke seems to have done this more than either Matthew or Mark, and Luke was probably in communication with John. Portions of Luke's Gospel are essentially the narrative of the beloved disciple.

Up to this time we have been following Jesus in the common and blending light which the four evangelists have thrown upon his path. We now come to a point where the synoptics leave us, and where for some time, and for the most part always in his more private walks, John is our only guide. We ask the reader's attention now to the following points, which, if carefully observed, will verify to him as he reads on how these biographies interlace each other with most remarkable congruity.

1. The distinctive Messianic work of Jesus begins at the close of the temptation scene. The Word had not merely glimmered in his consciousness; it had not merely emerged into full intellectual brightness, but it had "become flesh." It had cleared off all the hindrances of hereditary and Jewish selfhood, and now not only in the inmost but the outermost life, in mind and will and action so far as concerns his mission, Jesus is the Wisdom and the Power of God. From this complete Messianic consciousness, his

special work begins, and it divides itself into two portions: into his ministry, which was more private and personal, and his ministry, which was more public and organized.

2. His private and personal ministry began first, as of course it would. It was for some time informal and tentative. It was mainly in Jerusalem and its environs, in that yearning toward his own people to save them first from the wrath impending over the nation. This personal ministry covers, at least, the first year of his Messianic work. During this time he had no *organized* band of followers. A few intimate friends who believed in him, were generally with him, and travelled with him, and among them and most cherished of all, was the beloved John. In this personal and mere informal ministry in and about Jerusalem he encountered always the bigotry of the ruling ecclesiastical power, and acted under threats against his life. There was no possibility here of any organized public work. His home, thus far, was partly at Nazareth, partly in the desert, whither he would withdraw for concealment.

3. Soon after the arrest and imprisonment of the Baptist, he removed to Capernaum. There *his public ministry* commenced. He was thronged by the multitudes, and out of these he selected and organized two separate bands of disciples, the Twelve and the Seventy, whom he indoctrinated more thoroughly, and on whom he conferred miraculous pow-

ers. Through these he evangelized the whole of Galilee. But even here we must not imagine him travelling about with twelve men. They dispersed over the whole province, appearing generally in the synagogues. The Twelve went, it would seem, individually; the Seventy, two and two. The latter was a temporary, the former a permanent organization. Both would return to Jesus and report the fruits of their mission, but only on special occasions were the Twelve together with Jesus. So much we gather clearly from the account given of this organized work without knowing the minute details. Two of the synoptics confine their narrative almost entirely to the public ministry in Galilee, till they come to the tragic consummation at the last Passover, for the simple reason that here, with his public ministry, they were personally concerned, and here only were eye and ear witnesses.

4. But we must not imagine that while his organized missionaries were at work, Jesus was idle at Capernaum. His work in and around Capernaum was notorious, and the synoptics have detailed it. But this was not all. He did not abandon Judæa, but his private personal ministry he prosecuted there still. People were there who believed in him, whom his first ministry had deeply moved, who had clung to him with devoted love, and several times from his home at Capernaum, as before from his home at Nazareth, he went up to the capital. But he always

went privately and cautiously, often withdrawing of a sudden either to the desert or back into Galilee. He went up to the festivals, but except at the last and fatal Passover, he went after the crowds had gone, and followed on with the least possible demonstration. We must not imagine him marching up to Jerusalem with the Twelve, but appearing with one or two friends, among whom always was the beloved John. These were episodes in his public ministry in Galilee, grateful to the heart of Jesus, and doubly grateful to some homes in and about Jerusalem, which received and welcomed him with blissful and tender recollections of his first private and personal ministry there.

5. These points, carefully kept in mind, will reveal an organic unity in the narratives, and in the life of Jesus: and they will demonstrate a design which runs through the whole of the fourth Gospel. They will plainly show that the author of it wrote with the other three open before him, and with the intent always to complement them. The fourth Gospel thus becomes an indorsement of the other three. Any fabricator would have drawn upon the synoptics, or imitated them in some way. But there is not an instance, as we shall see, where this has been done, and the early tradition of the Church — hardly a tradition, for it is so early and fresh that it amounts almost to personal testimony — has the fullest internal evidence of its truth running sometimes into delicate threads

of circumstantial proof — that John, seeing what the synoptics had written, approved of it, but wrote a fourth Gospel to supply what they had left out of the early ministry of Jesus, and what pertained more exclusively to his Divinity.

CHAPTER VIII.

THE LAST MEETING BY THE JORDAN.

THE conflict was over. The forty days of temptation were accomplished, and the first dawning heaven had broken through his soul with its angelic peace, and with the clearness and the fervors of noonday. Now that the victory of the inward over the outward was accomplished, the Word was in last things as well as first, and the Messianic consciousness was plenary and complete. It is easy to imagine what peaceful majesty and command this must have given to his personal bearing.

The "forty days" of conflict may have been many months, for aught we know, of high communings and victories. They denote the closing period, "the end of every temptation," when Jesus reappeared on the banks of the Jordan where John was still prosecuting his ministry with a school of disciples gathered about him. Some of them evidently had become temporary dwellers in the desert, with their tents pitched along the shores of the Jordan; for men were there from remote Galilee, seventy miles away, drawn and subdued by the electric power of the Baptist, and numbered among his personal followers. Among them were two brothers, Simon and Andrew, and two other brothers, James and John, the fathers of whom were partners in the fisheries at Bethsaida, on the north-eastern shore of the Galilean lake. Philip also was there from the same place, also a disciple of the Baptist.

John had stirred the country so deeply, that when he was organizing a school of followers, some anxiety was felt at Jerusalem by the proper authorities as to what the issue would be. Who was this wild prophet of the Desert, and was he going to subvert the old order of things? A delegation was appointed, probably by the Sanhedrim, to go and sift the matter and report. They appeared before John, and put him under examination.

John remembers the descending vision which a few months before had illumined the desert: but the delegation of Pharisees could not have been much enlightened by the final answer: —

"I baptize in water unto repentance, for whether Jew or Gentile, you all need it alike; but there is One among you whom you do not know; who is coming after me, and whose sandals I am not worthy to unbind, and who will baptize you in the fires of the Holy Spirit."

The day after this interview, Jesus, emerging from his solitude, appears a second time before the Baptist. We infer that the delegation from Jerusalem were still present. John sees Jesus coming, and says to them: "There is the man I spoke of yesterday — the Lamb of God who takes away the sin of the world. I know this by tokens which cannot deceive. He who sent me to preach and baptize, had said to me: 'The Man on whom thou shalt see the Spirit descending and resting, is he who will baptize in the Holy Spirit.' And I have seen it and bear testimony that this man is the Son of God."

The delegation have gone home with their report to the Sanhedrim. Jesus reappears the next day, from which we infer that his home in the desert was not far off. The Baptist, with two of his disciples, John and Andrew, are standing together as Jesus approaches. "And looking at Jesus *as he was walking*, he said: 'See the Lamb of God!' And the two disciples heard what he said, and followed Jesus. And Jesus, turning about and seeing them following him, said: 'What do you desire? And they said to him, 'Rabbi (which means teacher), where do you dwell?' He said to them, 'Come and see.' So they went and saw where he dwelt, and remained with him that day. *It was about the tenth hour.*"

What marks of truth and nature do we find in this description, so very brief and elliptical! Any romancer, at least of these times, would have employed pages of rhetoric to express what is here only implied. The personal appearance of Jesus, the divine life flowing in like a peaceful river after temptation overcome, making the sphere about him radiant therewith, his majesty of mien in the newly awakened consciousness of divine power, giving grace to his motions as he walked along, the attractive spiritual force which drew the two disciples irresistibly after him, so that they followed him to his home in the desert, — all this we are left to infer; but any writer at pains to exalt the subject of his story, would have described it in full. How the words, "Lamb of God," with the imagery which they evoked, clung ever after to the mind of John, we have already seen, and it shows how beyond any power of description was his first impression of Jesus.

"It was about the tenth hour." What if it was? Why record a fact sixty years after it had transpired, of so little consequence as that they arrived at the dwelling-place of Jesus at four o'clock in the afternoon? Here is one of the inevitable touches of nature. Great and pregnant moments which seem the turning points of destiny, or in which the life of years seems gathered up, we fix instinctively as a date to start from, and such was the meeting of John with Jesus. The light of memory thrown back over this auspicious hour, was so concentrated and unfading, that the smallest things stand out on its canvas sixty years afterward, and especially that hour of the day when they entered the dwelling-place of Jesus.

In the meeting of Jesus at this time with three of the other disciples of the Baptist, Peter, Philip, and

Nathanael, we remark that mysterious gift which appears frequently afterwards; the power not only of discerning character but of reading individual history and turning backward its pages, even the secret record of mind and heart which the subject supposed locked up in his own bosom. Nathanael, known afterwards among the twelve as Bartholomew, was now a disciple of John. His home was in Cana of Galilee only a few miles from Nazareth. He knew nothing of Jesus; but he had come up to John's baptism. He had his place of retirement and secret prayer. Such places were furnished by the hand of nature in the embowering shades on the lower banks of the Jordan.

> "The fig-tree — not that kind for fruit renowned,
> But such as at this day to Indians known
> In Malabar or Decan — spread her arms
> Branching so broad and long, that in the ground
> The bended twigs take root, and daughters grow
> About the mother tree, a pillared shade
> High over-arched, and echoing walks between."

Philip had been drawn to Jesus, and he hastens to find Nathanael and tell him, We have found the promised Messiah in Jesus from Nazareth. Nathanael lived in the neighborhood of Nazareth and knew it as a poor town of no repute. That he had never heard of Jesus shows that the childhood and youth of the latter had been retired and noiseless. Very naturally he is slow to believe that any one of great fame is to come out of Nazareth. In the interview with Jesus it is evident that we have only brief hints or topics of the conversation. Nathanael finds to his amazement that Jesus already discerns him and reads him through, and he asks, " How came you to know me ? " And when Jesus replies, " I saw you under the fig-tree, I knew your place of prayer, and the thoughts and aspirations and purposes that have hallowed it," recounting to him we know not how much of his secret history, Nathanael confesses himself convinced, and exclaims, " Thou art indeed the Son of God and the expected King of Israel." Jesus promises evidence to him still more complete: " Hereafter you will have prophetic vision of my mission from above, in which, as to John at my baptism, its divine agencies and attestations will be openly revealed."

Soon after this Jesus returns to Nazareth, in company with three disciples. We infer at least that John, Philip, and Nathanael, whose minds had now been freshly opened to the evidence of his Messiahship, went with him to Galilee. John keeps himself out of sight here as elsewhere, but he writes afterwards as an eye-witness. That Philip went is plainly implied; and that Nathanael went with them is also implied, his home being in Cana only nine miles from Nazareth.

The relation of the Baptist to Jesus and the nature of the mission of both, are shown in the alacrity with which the former gave up his disciples to the latter. No founder of a sect, no theologian ever did the same before or since. Unless their mission had been from heaven and not from men, we should have seen some tinge of earthly ambition, or disappointed hope. There is not the slightest, but a burst of gladness as the Baptist sees his light flickering and going out in the glories of the new day.

PART III.

THE PRIVATE MINISTRY OF JESUS.

"The soft evening cloud, and behind the cloud the great full moon bodily! Something so contemplative, so sublime, and so full of presage that one can never weary of it! Every time I read John it seems as if I could see him before me at the Last Supper, leaning on his Master's breast; as if his angel at certain passages held a light in his hand, embraced me, and spake something in my ear. There is much which I do not understand as I read, and John's meaning floats away before me in the distance; but even then when I look into a place altogether dark, I have a prescension of a grand royal meaning which some day will be revealed to me. Therefore I grasp eagerly at every new exposition of the Gospel of John. Alas! most of them only ruffle the evening clouds and the moon behind them is left in peace."

CLAUDIUS OF WANDSBECK.

CHAPTER I.

THE WEDDING AT CANA.

WE have distinguished between the private and public ministry of our Saviour. The distinction must be steadily kept in view if we would understand the unity of the four Gospels and see how John's lies within the other three. Jesus returned from the Jordan to Nazareth in his full Messianic consciousness. But he did not proclaim this publicly nor organize a school of followers.

His first private ministry was an exploration of the mind and heart of Judaism to see if it had any place for the reception of the new faith. It is a most interesting feature in the philanthropy of Jesus that its universality, the absorption of his love for the whole race, took nothing from the fervor and tenderness of his private friendships or his love of his own people and nation. The hereditary proclivities which made him susceptible of temptation from the passions and ambitions of the Jewish mind would at the same time give to that passion which we call patriotism an intenser glow. How intense it was we shall see not only from his persistent efforts to save his own people first of all, but the depths of anguish when the

Jewish mind had been fully explored and revealed, and the final disappointment came. In this respect John, even more than the synoptics, reveals the full humanity of Jesus ; humanity, that is, in the entire range of its affections.

It will be obvious at once that this private ministry, as revealing the heart, mind, and life of the Saviour, is quite as important to us and as full of interest as his public proclamations of his mission. It will be obvious too, that in his private walk and intercourse he would not be seen with a band of followers. We should rather find him with one or two men, the sharers of his most familiar thoughts and tenderest personal love. That this was the case, and that John was the companion of this private ministry, there is most unquestionable internal evidence. The presumption is very strong of the truth of a very early tradition, that the family of John on the mother's side had kindred relations with that of Jesus.

It will be seen at once why the fourth Gospel should differ so much from the first and second both in matter and style. It abounds in reports of colloquial intercourse, sometimes of intercourse so confidential and sacred that the report of it could not have been placed on public record without manifest indelicacy and impropriety until some of the parties had passed away. These serve as delicate finger-marks in determining the date of the fourth Gospel.

John, therefore, not only complements, but interlaces

the synoptics, generally with a clear and beautiful consistency. He never in a single instance relates what they had reported except to show its essential connection with something which they had omitted. A special as well as general purpose is evinced in the narrative from beginning to end. It must have been written by one familiar already with the synoptics, and by an eye-witness of what he relates, for no one else could have so dovetailed the narrative as to make it fit into theirs so delicately and with such marks of reality.

Jesus returns to Galilee with three disciples, and now his private ministry begins. There was a wedding in Cana, nine miles from Nazareth, and the mother of Jesus was there. She would not probably have been there unless she had kindred relations with the bridegroom or the bride. That the bridegroom was John himself cannot be affirmed with absolute certainty; but if any one will take pains to group all the facts which bear upon the subject he will hardly escape the conviction that this was so; that Salome, the mother of John, was the sister of Mary, and that the early tradition is right which makes John the bridegroom of this marriage feast.

Immediately after the wedding Jesus with his mother and brethren went to Capernaum on a visit of a few days, at or near which place the family of Zebedee lived and where John subsequently resided. Recall the scene at the cross where Mary and Salome stood side by side, and from which time John took Mary to his own home ; recall, too, the special intimacy which ever subsisted between Jesus and Salome and her two sons, and the family connection becomes still more probable. And if John was the bridegroom at the wedding he describes, the manner in which he has kept himself in the shade is highly characteristic of his whole style and method.

Jesus and his disciples were invited to the festival; that is to say, Philip and Nathanael who came with him from the Jordan, the latter of whom was already at his home in Cana. John is at pains to tell us that here was the first miracle which Jesus wrought. The whole scene is of vast significance. What Jesus would do when the complete Messianic power had come into his consciousness to be ultimated in his works, would give shape and color to the new religion now descending upon the world. He comes from the desert, from long fastings and solitudes, from the baptism of John the hermit, bringing three of the hermit's disciples with him, and in the natural course of human development his religion would have taken a tinge of moroseness and gloom. But its first office was to fling light and gayety over the common paths of life and a charm and consecration over its most delightful joys. The "beginning of miracles" was an entire breaking away from the asceticism of John ; and Christianity at her very inauguration has no leathern girdle, nor raiment of camel's hair, nor food of locusts, but comes garlanded with festal flowers and with cups of innocent pleasure in her hands. The miracle which changed the water into wine was not more wonderful as the exercise of new-given power than for its beautiful significance.

The details of the narrative are such as no fabricator would be likely to invent. The ideals of the next age began to have a coloring of asceticism, and would not probably have made Jesus the chief figure and purveyor at a marriage scene, and such a marriage scene as was made conformable to the ideas and customs of Palestine. We have nothing like it in the marriage customs of our freezing occidentalism. It was a prolonged festival of eight days with gay processions and rejoicings. Marriage was held by the Hebrews in supreme honor. The espousals were made early, generally in childhood, that the mind and imagination might be kept pure and loyal, and the marriage scene was the consummation of the fond hopes and aspirations of years. The bride in her chamber was decked by her maids and veiled, like Rebecca, amid festal songs. When the hour of marriage arrived, a procession came with the bridegroom, usually in the night and by torchlight, and under a canopy supported by four attendants, the bride's party exclaiming as they approach, "Blessed is he who cometh!" The marriage was consummated amid the pouring and drinking of wine If the home of the bridegroom was near, the procession returned to his house with the bride and her maidens, the latter conveying nuptial lamps while their rich attire reflected the dazzling lustre. They walked under a silken canopy, hence the figure, "Thy banner over us is love." Arrived at the bridegroom's house, the festivities were continued with dance and song. Amid a festal scene like this Jesus appears in the first miracle which signalized his divine mission to mankind. There was no return procession, however, in this case, if our conjecture is right, the home of the bridegroom being, not in Cana, but in Capernaum, whither his friends attended him with his bride, as indicated in the sentence following, "After this, Jesus and his mother and his kinsmen, his disciples (guests at the wedding), went down to Capernaum, but continued there not many days."

The spontaneous touches of truth and nature contained in the narrative are inimitable. How much is unconsciously implied in the conversation of Jesus with his mother! Mary must have long seen and felt the growing and overshadowing power of Jesus, and now more than ever on his return from the Jordan after the new immersion into the depths of the Divine Love from which he comes beaming forth. Mary is no such person as the Catholic Church would make her. She has a mother's fondness, with all its foolish pride. She importunes Jesus to make a display of his astonishing power. The wine failed, and she said to him, "They have no wine." She said a good deal more, as the reply indicates. The reply is not harsh and cold, as our common rendering would make it, though it contains a mild rebuke. The rebuke is not in the address, "Woman," which was one of honor and reverence, but in what follows, and whose sense is, "Do not be troublesome; the time has not come for me to make a public proclamation of myself." She would have had him make such a blazon of his miraculous power as to fill the guests with admiration, and he refuses. The way in which its beneficent exercise is veiled and the miracle wrought, through private directions to the servants, is in keeping with the whole bearing of Jesus during his private ministry. Any forger would have shown it paraded foremost, and not held in reserve. The way, too, in which Mary is introduced upon the scene, and a delicate veil thrown over her weakness, so as to hide it as much as possible, has the spirit of John in every line and word, and his tender regard for the adopted mother of his household. Mariolatry began very early, but we have no trace of it in her own family, and the record herein has one of the plainest marks of genuineness.

The *rationale* of what we call miracles will elude our philosophies, but no more than the whole power of spirit over mind and matter, or of the will over the body, which we exercise every day and hour. The theory, from the stand-point of supernaturalism, assumes that, from this time forth, Jesus was in open communication with both the spirit world and natural, and in larger and more vital communication with them both than any other person before or since; in more ample endowment of that Creative Word, out of which all things were evolved, and of which nature itself is only the leaf and flower. That being so, the control of his will not only over his own bodily motions, but over natural processes beyond his immediate personality, is not to be reckoned as belonging to magic or prodigy any more than ours is when it controls the muscles of our frames. One is as mysterious as the other, and the "Word made flesh" being once assumed, one is as credible as the other, since both are through the influx from the higher planes of being into the lower ones, the former, however, under conditions more enlarged and comprehending. This "beginning of miracles" attests the newly opened divine consciousness in Jesus, and the proof thereof is to be found afterward, when in him and through him the heavens are nearing the earth, and the spirit-world pressing into the natural to make the latter more entirely its healthful and beneficent body and robe.[1]

[1] The six water-jars mentioned in this narrative were vessels kept in a back room for the washing of hands before meals. The urgent importance of this will be seen from the fact that the Jews in those days used at their meals neither spoons nor knives and forks, but only their hands and fingers. Dr. Clark writes: "It is worthy of note that,

walking among the ruins of Cana, we saw large mossy stone water-pots, answering the description given of the ancient vessels of that country; not preserved nor exhibited as relics, but lying about disregarded by the present inhabitants as antiquities with whose original use they were unacquainted. From their appearance and the number of them it was quite evident that a practice of keeping water in large stone pots, each holding from eighteen to twenty-seven gallons was once common in the country." *Travels*, vol. iii. part ii. ch. 14. It will be seen how the miracle at Cana was performed in a retired part of the house where only the servants could be witnesses of it, and where display could be carefully avoided.

CHAPTER II.

THE FIRST VISIT AT JERUSALEM.

NOT a great while after the wedding at Cana, occurred the annual Passover festival at Jerusalem. It appealed with stirring associations to every Hebrew family, for it was the day of national deliverance from Egyptian bondage. It occurred in the new moon of the month Nisan, answering in part to our month of March. Great care was taken by the Sanhedrim at Jerusalem to proclaim the exact moment of its commencement through all the tribes of Israel. They watched for the first beam of the silver crescent in the sky, and the moment it appeared a man went to the top of Mount Olivet, kindled a torch, and waved it aloft, backward and forward through the air. It was answered forthwith by torch-lights from the immediately surrounding hills. These again were answered from the hills farther outward, and so the wave of fire enlarged and extended on and on till every Hebrew family had greeted the summons. It went south towards Egypt till it touched the desert; westward, till the range of Carmel flung it to the sea; northward, till it blazed from Libanus and Antilibanus; eastward, even into

Babylonia, till it gleamed on the waters of the Euphrates. Subsequently, after hostile Samaria had broken the wave by false signals, or perhaps by refusing to give any at all, the torch-lights were superseded by swift messengers, who went forth to proclaim the festival.

Every Hebrew male, circumcised, of adult age and able-bodied, was bound to go up to Jerusalem at the Passover festival, either in person or by some representative of the family to which he belonged, and offer sacrifice. Women and children were not required to go, though they often did; and so the ways converging to the capital were thronged with people, generally travelling in groups, and chanting select psalms of David. They crowded into the capital by the hundred thousand, and it was one of the beautiful features of the occasion that private houses now became public, and sacred to its hospitalities. Not every individual of this great multitude was required to offer sacrifice in the temple. They organized in groups or companies, each company offering its lamb or its bullock, for which purpose they were admitted into the court of the priests, three companies at a time. Vast numbers of animals were required for sacrifice, and the festival was the grand market time for the shepherds and graziers of Judæa. They had their pens and stalls about the temple, and those more eager and unscrupulous pushed them into its sacred precinct, and invaded its outer court. The court of the Gentiles covered about fourteen acres of ground, and it now became thronged with great crowds, speaking in various provincialisms, with the obscene spectacle of bleating sheep and lowing herds; the herdsmen at the stalls chaffering for the best bargain; Jewish avarice making the most out of Jewish piety. A very lively and promiscuous scene!

We must suppose that Jesus had often attended these festivals, but John describes his presence at the first after his Messianic consciousness had changed from twilight into noonday. That John was with him seems certain. That Nathanael and Philip were also with him seems probable. His first act on entering the temple was to purge it of the unclean nuisances, —the sheep-pens, the cattle stalls, and the traffickers. The wonder is not that they were driven out in confusion and dismay, but that they had ever been permitted to come in, and that the police regulations had become so lax and sleepy under a decay of reverence for sacred places and the ideas which they represent. To enter into the spirit of the scene we must remember that the men knew they had no business there, that the crowds knew it and were glad to have them driven out, but had not sufficient command to effect it. Jesus assumed the command in that conscious power of control over men which had now become clearly his. To understand how intolerable was the nuisance, it must be remembered that the temple in all its courts had a representative significance. It was regarded as copied from the courts of heaven, and so again represented humanity itself regenerated and made the shekinah of the living God. Hence, when the spectators asked him why he assumed this lordship over the temple, he made immediate reference to the temple of his body about to be glorified as the fullness of the indwelling Godhead, — a reference which, of course, they could not understand.

Skeptical writers stumble at the fact that a similar transaction is related by the synoptics, but by them at the last Passover of his ministry instead of the first; that is to say, two years later. There is no discrepancy. Almost inevitably the nuisance would be repeated at subsequent Passovers in the absence of police regulations to prevent it, and if repeated it would be likely again to be abated under the same authority with severer denunciations against the traffickers as a pack of thieves driving their business in a house of prayer.

Many believed on Jesus at this festival from "seeing his miracles." The evangelist does not specify them, and the inference is that they were now his familiar and spontaneous actions in his walk amongst men, and especially amongst the sick, who became well in the radiant sphere of his life and under his healing hand. His ministry was altogether personal and conversational, and the most important and significant incident related was, —

THE INTERVIEW WITH NICODEMUS.

John reports the conversation as if he were present and heard it. The first remarkable fact connected with it is one which we shall find evermore repeated and which characterized our Saviour's intercourse with men. Nicodemus begins with a remark which he intends shall be introductory to further inquiries. Jesus does not reply to anything he had said or was going to say, but directly to his inmost thought and state of mind. He searches him with a glance and knows that his whole conception concerning the Kingdon of God now approaching, is sensuous and worldly, and no more corresponds to the truth of things than that of the babe before birth corresponds to the world of light and colors. A new range of senses must be touched and opened ; he must be born into a new world before he can know what the Kingdom of God is. Jesus wastes no words in exhibiting his credentials or appealing to his miracles to authenticate his claims, which were sure to be misunderstood. He describes the change from a natural to a spiritual state of mind as a first essential condition. Nicodemus sits bewildered and suffers the heavenly discourse to flow on. We shall fail to enter fully into its import unless we construe it in the light of the scene a few weeks before on the banks of the Jordan. When Jesus avers that he speaks what he knows and testifies to what he has seen, he means plainly that he holds the truth which he teaches not as opinions, and reasonings about them, but as seen in the higher range of existence out of time and mortality and above their sphere. "If I tell you of those heavenly things you will not believe them, for you do not understand the earthly things that represent and image them forth. You stick in the letter and you cannot rise out of it. And no man hath ascended up to heaven but him that came down from heaven, even the son of man who is in heaven." Let us not sink the strain of this high utterance to a lower key, for only by rising to its level we get an adequate idea of that state of mind out of which Jesus spake, taught, and acted from the first opening of his ministry; which made him speak, not from tradition, but from original and inexhaustible fountains, when he surprised his hearers by his commanding tone, or smote his enemies as by electric power. In the language quoted, he is not claiming a separate, personal pre-existence and personal descent from heaven, — conceptions we think entirely foreign to the New Testament, nor yet is he using an extravagant oriental style which we must freeze down into mere rhetoric to find the meaning of. By "ascending up to heaven" he means, as the scene at the Jordan shows, the opening of his mind through all its ascending degrees even up to the central Light and Life of all, so that the heavenly worlds as they exist beyond sense and mortality lay on his perceptions more unerringly than this world of matter lies obvious to the senses of men. By "coming down out of heaven," he means passing from these high frames into conditions which were earthly and mortal, that those immortal realities might have clothings and representations on the plane of sense and matter. By dwelling *in heaven*, he means that these high states were normal and not exceptional, so that while he had intercourse with men through these bodily organs, in his inmost being he had open cognizance of the heavenly orders of existence, and lived amid their eternal serenities. To fail of following Jesus in thought to these celestial heights, is to fail of understanding both his character and message. But hearing and seeing him as thus "coming down from heaven," we shall appreciate in some measure his tone of authority; shall see why he never reasons out the truths of his religion but simply reveals them; why he says nothing about "the evidences" of immortality, since he lived amid its scenery and had only to announce it; why he often speaks of future events as if already transpiring, including his own death and resurrection, and the passing away of the Jewish Church and nation, since he lived in the realm of causes whence he saw into the heart of things and the germs of all history.

JESUS RETIRES FROM JUDÆA.

He saw the state of the Jewish mind, and that here there could be no general reception of his message, but that it would provoke open and intense opposition and hate. Many believed in him seeing his miracles. "But he did not trust himself to them for he knew them all, and had no need that any one should tell him what men are, for he knew what was in man."[1] He withdrew, at first, into the country of Judæa, away from the glare and notoriety of the city, and many resorted to him, were taught by him and were baptized by his disciples. This excited the jealousy of John's disciples. The Baptist had come over from Bethany, beyond Jordan, and was preaching and baptizing near Salem on the border of the desert. By the laws of mere human growth and development, the schools of Jesus and of the Baptist should now have become rival sects, with the usual envyings and recriminations of ecclesiastical strife. That they did not, affords a strong confirmation of the averment of the Baptist, that he had seen Jesus from a higher than a mere earthly point of view. His answer to his own jealous disciples who came to him with manifest alarm, is one of the sublime passages of history, — "Lo, Jesus is baptizing, and all men are going to him," say they. The answer of John is found in chapter third, from verse 27 to the end of the

[1] Chapter iii. 23-25.

chapter. Expositors have been in doubt where the words of the Baptist end and where those of the Evangelist are resumed. We understand this whole passage to be the utterance of the Baptist, showing the heighth and breadth and clearness of his illumination. That alone accounts to us for the grace and even exultation, with which a man of his wonderful power, with converts flocking to him from every side, was content to see himself superseded in the breaking glories of a new day.

Jesus was making disciples now more rapidly than the Baptist. The authorities knew it, and Jesus was aware that the eye of the Sanhedrim was bent keenly upon him. He knew that his own doctrine was to be tenfold more revolutionary than that of the Baptist, and that his immediate arrest would follow if he remained in Judæa. He returned to Nazareth by the shortest route, which was through the heart of Samaria. The "disciples" who were now with him, were probably the same men who followed him from the Jordan, and who went up with him to the Passover festival, — John, Nathanael, and Philip. It was a quiet and private journey on foot, made for the purpose of avoiding publicity or getting away from it. It was with two or three intimate personal friends.

CONVERSATION AT THE WELL.

They passed through Sychar, the ancient Shechem of the tribe of Ephraim, lying between Mount Gerizim on the left and Mount Ebal on the right, both of them clothed to the Hebrew mind with the most sublime historic memories ; facing each other with a sort of grim horror which contrasts with the rich valley between, where the city lies embedded in green gardens and olive-grounds, rendered more verdant by the lengthened shade which they enjoy from the mountains. The city is in the heart of Samaria, being forty miles from Jerusalem, and as many more from Nazareth. This journey of eighty miles, travelled on foot by Jesus and two or three intimate friends, holding converse by the way with persons whom they met or with whom they tarried, gives us a very distinct and vivid idea of the private ministry of our Saviour. Jacob's well was near the city, just outside its walls as you approach from Jerusalem. It is there yet, near the point where the narrow valley of Shechem, which is the modern Neapolis, opens into the wider field. It is a permanent landmark, being an excavation thirty-five feet deep out of the solid rock. The wells were places of public resort, and this one was peculiarly so, being near the city walls and on one of the thoroughfares, where women morning and evening would be seen coming from the city gates, waiting their turn and filing away with their pitchers on their head.

We know of no composition pervaded more thickly with threads of historic reality than the fourth chapter of John. The air, the scenery, the manners, and prejudices of the people, are before us in the spontaneous allusions of the narrative. Every word is fragrant with them and with the spirit of history running back more than a thousand years. All that can be gathered from Josephus is only a verification of this chapter. "The journey of our Lord from Judæa to Galilee" says a traveller writing from the spot, "the cause of it, his passage through the territory of Samaria, his approach to the metropolis of this country, its name, his arrival at the Amorite field which terminates the narrow valley of Shechem, the ancient custom of halting at a well, the female employment of drawing water, the disciples sent into the city for food, by which its situation out of the town is obviously implied, the question of the woman referring to existing prejudices, which separated the Jews from the Samaritans; the depth of the well, the Oriental allusion contained in the expression 'living water,' the history of the well and the customs thereby illustrated; the worship upon Mount Gerizim,—all these occur within the space of twenty verses."[1] The incidental and cumulative evidence becomes well-nigh irresistible that the writer of the fourth Gospel is an eye-witness of what he records, as none else would catch with such precision and spontaneity the minute features of his pictures.

[1] Dr. Clarke's *Travels*, p. 517. Robinson's *Calmet*, p. 845.

"It was about noon," an attention to precision of date purely incidental, and a further indication of historic reality. More than all, the conversation with the woman is in striking accord with what the writer had previously told us concerning the methods of Jesus, and his power over the minds of others. The woman understands not a word of the discourse about "living water," sinking the spirit in the letter all the while; but when she finds not only her own mind and soul laid bare under a perfect diagnosis of her spiritual condition, but the pages of her memory read backward through all her personal history, she springs to the conclusion that not only a prophet but the very Messiah has come. It seems probable that John has only given us here the heads of conversation, and that when the woman said he told her all she ever did, it was not such sheer exaggeration as might at first appear. She runs back to the city, forgetting her pitcher and leaving it, and brings out her acquaintances to see the wonderful man. He converses with them in turn, enters the city along with them, and remains there two days engaged in personal intercourse with these people, many of whom believed "through his own teaching." No "miracle" is recorded of him here, nor are we led to suppose that these Samaritans were initiated very far into a knowledge of the mysteries of the new kingdom of God. But the power of Jesus in sounding the depths of the human consciousness, and reproducing the past on the living canvas of the soul, and thence speaking to its condition, is here brought freshly into view as it characterizes his method through all his subsequent ministry. It was a power higher in degree than that over outward nature or over the physical body, for it involved such a knowledge of the hidden past and present, that the future about to be evolved therefrom lay before him already as in sunlight.

THE SECOND MIRACLE IN CANA.

Jesus returned to his home in Nazareth. Before his arrival, reports of what he did at Jerusalem had preceded him. Of course a great many persons from Nazareth and its vicinity were at the Passover festival, witnessing, not without some complacent pride, the wonder and admiration produced there, by one from their own humble and despised town. They welcome him home. He remains at Nazareth now nearly two months, or until the next Jewish festival, evidently in the exercise of the offices of his private ministry. He revisits Cana, where his miracle at the wedding-feast had become known and had placed the minds of the people in receptive attitude towards him. Herod Antipas was now tetrarch of Galilee, with his residence at Tiberias, on the shore of the lake, a few miles south of Capernaum. An officer of his court was at Cana, who had a son sick at Capernaum. He had heard of the mysterious power of Jesus, and besought him to go down to Capernaum and heal his son who was dying. "Go," said Jesus, "your son is well." Capernaum was fifteen miles from Cana. This case in some of its features resembles so much that of the servant of the centurion narrated by Matthew that skeptical writers assume that Matthew and John give contradictory accounts of the same transaction. It is sheer assumption. They both belong to a class of miracles distinct from those of ordinary healing by the touch of the hand, but no more difficult to account for under the action of spiritual laws. In all these instances of the restoration of vital power, it is the mind of Jesus flowing into the mind of the sufferer, and thence throbbing by a new influx of life through the whole physical frame. The only essential condition was that Jesus should be brought into such relation to the sufferer, that the latter could be ensphered within that restoring love and mercy. Personal presence, or physical contact with words surcharged with electric sympathy, we know from common experience are sometimes worth more to the patient than any medicine in the world to make the languid or freezing currents of life to start anew. There was no other magic in the hem of Jesus' garment or the touch of his hand, than the magic of this creative and healing sympathy. But who of us shall say that there is no access of mind to mind and of soul to soul except through these fleshly, clumsy instrumentalities? Who shall say this, especially of one who "dwelt in heaven" while yet in the flesh, and thence came down with the divine restoratives among the woes and agonies that flesh is heir to? The Spirit knows nothing of space and distance as we measure them, and we can well conceive of it in such power and fullness that distance vanishes before it, so that the feeble partitions of sense and matter are no hindrance to the healing balm of mind over mind, and thence over all the functions of the body in which it dwells.

CHAPTER III.

THE SECOND VISIT AT JERUSALEM.

FIFTY days after the festival described in the last chapter there was another, called the Feast of Weeks, or Pentecost. This also summoned every adult male to Jerusalem, and Jesus went up thither from Nazareth.[1] The inference is that the intervening seven weeks had been spent in the discharge of the benign offices of his private ministry, and that the second miracle at Cana was only one of them. It is not likely that John was with him during the whole of this interval. He would naturally return to his home on the lake of Galilee. But he would be

[1] It is a question, however, among commentators whether this second visit related by John was the Feast of Pentecost. Many of them make it another feast of the Passover. This is highly improbable for many reasons. It would make a whole year interspace the events of chapter fifth and those of the preceding ones, with the exception that we are told "He remained in Judæa baptizing" after the first Passover. But the whole connection indicates that this was a short sojourn. Again, the Passover festival continued eight days, and, being the principal one, is always elsewhere mentioned by name. The Feast of Weeks was a shorter one, and would be less likely to be specially designated. For these and other reasons, we take this second visit at Jerusalem to have been at the Feast of Weeks, conformably with the opinions of the earliest fathers, though, it must be confessed, the whole question can be decided only conjecturally.

likely, on going up to the Feast of Pentecost, to take Nazareth in his way, and go in company with Jesus, with whom the most intimate of friendships had been formed ; and that he did so we have confirmatory evidence in the fact that he alone has told us what Jesus said and did at this second visit to the capital, and told it with the air and the detail of an eye and ear witness.

The Feast of Weeks commemorated the giving of the law from Mount Sinai. It was also a feast of prayer and praise, in acknowledgment of the God of the harvest, the people bearing the first fruits to the temple as an earnest of the looked-for bounty of the season. Unlike the Passover festival, this lasted only a single day, and required only one night in Jerusalem. Nothing could be more picturesque than their journeyings to the city. Neighbors and friends would form into companies of twenty-four each. They lodged in the streets or the open field the night before starting, for fear of pollution. This, under the soft vernal skies of Judæa, was attended with no exposure. On the morning of the following day the president of each company called them betimes with the salutation, "Arise, and let us go up to Zion!" They set out on the journey preceded by a bullock intended for sacrifice, whose horns were gilded and whose head was garlanded with olive-branches. A person playing on a pipe went before them to cheer them on their journey, while bursts of religious fervor were frequently heard from the people, chanting from the Psalms, "I was glad when they said unto me, Let us go up to the house of the Lord." They avoided fatigue, travelling only morning and evening, and when nearing the city they sent a messenger to announce their arrival, whereupon some of the priesthood went out to meet them. Each carried his basket of wheat, grapes, figs, apricots, olives, or dates, waving it anon as his offering to the Lord. The baskets of the rich were of gold or silver; those of the poor, of wicker work, fancifully adorned with flowers. As they entered the city the artificers in the shops rose to salute them while they passed, and the inhabitants of the city cheered them from the house-tops. Some of the Psalms seem to have been written expressly for these occasions, and to have been chanted in responses between the people of the city and the companies of the tribes crowding through its streets towards the temple.

Such was the Feast of Weeks, which occurred in the season answering to our month of May. Jesus went up to these festivals, as we learn elsewhere, not in one of these companies, but in a private way, and now especially during his private ministry would he avoid the glare of notoriety. But he would find the city alive with the pilgrims, and the courts of the temple and the ways leading thereto densely crowded with people.

Only a single incident is related of this visit, which

is remarkable as having led on to the colloquy with the Jews, and that utterance of more than human eloquence contained in the fifth chapter of the fourth Gospel, whose single annunciation, says Paley, is worthy of all the splendid apparatus of miracle which the New Testament records.

Near one of the gates of the temple was a reservoir, probably fed by a stream which ran near the temple-walls, and was imagined, for that reason, to have some mysterious power of healing. This virtue was supposed to be intermittent, owing, perhaps, to the intermittent flow of the waters. Very naturally, porticoes had been built around the spot for the reception of the sick. Hither the blind, the lame, and the paralytic were in the habit of resorting, each waiting his turn to try the virtue of the waters.[1] Hither our Saviour bent his footsteps. A crowd of diseased persons, blind and cripple, were here before him. That he did not work at once a wholesale miracle, and restore all this withered humanity, and cover it with the bloom of health, is sufficient evidence that his power was that of mind over mind, and not arbitrary and magical, as we are too apt to imagine. He walks among these wrecks of men, and selects one who

[1] We understand the last clause of the third verse and the whole of the fourth verse to be a gloss, placed originally in the margin, and that the original text gives no sanction to the popular superstition respecting these waters. The passage thus included lacks support from the best manuscripts, and has the air of a commentary.

answers to him with gleams of intelligence and confidence. He enters familiarly into conversation with him, evidently for the purpose of bringing the man within his own interblending and life-giving sphere. Through the man's own mind and memory Jesus read backward the history of the long thirty-eight years of disease and suffering. It was not that this case was milder than the others, and easier to cure, physically. It was one of the most obstinate, but easier to take hold of spiritually, because Jesus found somewhat responsive in the spirit of the patient, so that when he tells him, "Rise, take up your couch, and go home with it," the deep fountains of life gushed forth afresh, flowing from within outward, and with instant creative energy through the whole physical man.

Other cures might have been performed, but this evidently was selected because it served as the text of a conversation on the Sabbath, and of an all-revealing discourse on death, life, and resurrection. Fancy the long, hard faces of the puritans of the law as they meet the man with his couch thrown over his shoulder walking with the rejoicing step of his freshly flowing energy. "It is the Sabbath-day: it is not lawful for you to be carrying your bed!" When they sought out the author of the cure, and laid a snare for his life as a Sabbath-breaker, the answer of Jesus bears us, though with few words, into the very heart of the Divine Beneficence: "My Father works con-

TINUOUSLY,[1] and so do I." He does not stop his work on the Sabbath; for life every moment is a fresh gift from his hands; in the hearts of men that beat on that day as on all days, and in all nature, that blossoms as brightly on the seventh day as on any other. If the Sabbath does not interrupt his mercy, why should it mine? This is the meaning of the reply, and nothing could illustrate more benignly the new religion now coming direct from the heart of God.

"MY Father works continuously, and so do I." The possessive pronoun is emphatic. Jesus means to say that now, in his plenary Messianic consciousness, his words and deeds are no longer his own, but the unbroken outflow of the Divine wisdom, power, and love. This is what offended the Jews. It was not that he asserted in general the Divine Fatherhood, but that Fatherhood was impersonated in himself so unreservedly that it spake directly as of old from Sinai, overriding all other authority and sweeping it clean away. It was not that he, the finite human being, was "making himself equal with God," but that in him the finite was being held in such complete stillness and abeyance that the Divine wisdom and truth were coming forth with unmingled clearness. "Verily I say unto you, the Son does nothing of himself,

[1] So the words ἕως ἄρτι should be rendered. They mean the unremitting exertion of the Divine governance and preservation for the safety and welfare of the creation.

but only what he sees his Father doing, for what the Father does the Son does likewise. For the Father loves the Son, and shows him all that He does, and will show him greater works than these, to your astonishment." If you are surprised — such is the burden of his meaning — that my Word, through my complete oneness with the Father, has sent life through the mind and the limbs of this cripple, much more will you be surprised at the wider and profounder miracles about to be wrought by it. I see the wrecks of humanity strewn all about me, the death and ruin of which these blind and withered specimens give only the outward form and semblance. And the Father commits all judgment unto the Son to discern and distinguish this spiritual death and ruin; — how much of it is the sad inheritance of the past, and how much of it comes of individual guilt and voluntary depravity? Verily I say unto you, the hour is coming, yea, is now come, when those who have gone down into this death shall hear the voice of the Son of Man, and they who will listen to it shall live. For the Father has self-subsisting life, and that life flows through the Son, unchanged and continuous, into these places of decay and death. Marvel not at this, for the hour is coming when not those only who are willing to hear my Word shall awake, but when all who are in these sepulchres of spiritual death shall hear it also; the grace hardened and impenitent to have their quality searched out and shown, and their guilt made blacker in the light of a more intolerable day. There is to be both a resurrection of life and a resurrection of condemnation. That this last passage was a denunciation of the Jewish state of mind, is evident both from what is before and after, — a state in which spiritual death, ruin, and darkness come upon men not as an involuntary inheritance, but under light and privilege, on whom therefore the light will break, not to save, but to condemn.

This was the last visit of Jesus to Judæa previous to the opening of his public ministry. If he had once entertained the desire or the thought of inaugurating the new kingdom of God at the capital its impossibility was now fully demonstrated. Twice had he come there after his Messianic consciousness had grown to its noon-day power and clearness, and twice had they reviled him, rejected him and sought to put him to death. At this last visit they charge him capitally, first as a Sabbath-breaker and then as a blasphemer. With that divine vision through which he saw into the heart of things he now reads them through and through, and then leaves them to themselves. It must have been an enterprise congenial with his fondest desires, perhaps with early cherished hopes and imaginations, to begin at Jerusalem, and let the light of the new revelation spread in successive waves, till his own people and nation were first involved in it and saved by it, and thence the outer heathen darkness penetrated by it and at last completely illumined. We know, indeed, that all the urgencies of a tender and brooding patriotism had kindled these desires, and hopes of inaugurating his ministry at Jerusalem and first gathering its people, as a hen gathers her brood under her wings. But this was not to be. His first ministry there was tentative and personal, and proved that this was not to be. And now in the full opening of his Messianic vision the whole future lies before him. The path of triumph is not less sure, but it lies across Calvary. Henceforth the cross was never out of sight. The closing words at this Feast of Weeks are a farewell to Jerusalem, as far as these first hopes and purposes may have been concerned. There is, even in his denunciation, an undertone of deeply grieved and disappointed love: "I know you that you have not the love of God in you. I have come in the name of my Father and ye receive me not; if another shall come in his own name, him ye will receive. Think not that I shall accuse you to the Father. There is one who is accusing you, even Moses in whom ye have trusted. For if ye had faith in Moses ye would have faith in me, for he wrote concerning me. But if ye believe not his writings how should ye believe my words?"

CHAPTER IV.

REMOVAL TO CAPERNAUM.

THE people of Galilee differed vastly in character and susceptibility from those of Judæa. They were not such simple children of nature as Renan describes them, but bold, hardy, and brave, and with the inspiration of liberty thrilling through their veins. The best soldiers came from Galilee, and the most dangerous insurrections had their origin among its hills. In our Saviour's day it had a dense population, but the Jewish element was not the principal nor dominant one. Though there were Jewish synagogues in all the cities and larger towns where native Jews and proselytes worshipped together, yet Phœnicians, Syrians, and other pagan Asiatics, mingled largely in the population. The northern portion of the province was called specially, " Galilee of the Gentiles." Rough and primitive in their manners, in mind, character, and religion they were yet fluid under any hand strong enough to impress them with the divine signature.

Towards the northeastern border of this province the river Jordan on its course southward, spreads out into the Lake of Galilee, described on a preceding page. On the western side of the lake the hills trend away from it, leaving a plain which curves round the water's edge the distance of about eight miles. Along this plain and creeping sometimes up the hill-slopes, were the five towns already named, humble and obscure, but soon to become famous. Their names are preserved, but their locality now is in part only conjectural. Bethsaida and Capernaum were situated towards the northern head of the lake, and were fishing villages of considerable thrift. Capernaum was not at the water's edge, but climbed up the bank and looked away over a prospect of mingled life and beauty, and especially over the lake itself, whose surface, except when broken by storms, was rippled only by fishing-boats and flocks of swimming birds ; or, touched and changed by the magic light of even-tide, the water seemed to lie on the bottom of a cup of gold.[1]

All hope of inaugurating the new religion at Jerusalem was at an end. Jesus removed from Nazareth and came to Capernaum, making that place his home. It is only a conjecture, but under all the circumstances the conjecture rises to strong probability that his home was with John or with Salome, John's mother, the sister of Mary, the mother of Jesus.

Here, among these protecting hills and among a ruder population, largely heathen, and when Jewish,

[1] The figure of Renan. We follow principally Josephus and Calmet.

yet sometimes without the iron encasings of Jewish bigotry, the new kingdom of God was to have its first public proclamation. Jesus proclaimed it to the populace till they were shaken by it as the leaves of a forest in a mighty wind. He proclaimed it on the mountains, by the sea-side to the fishermen in their boats, in the synagogues, and to the multitudes who pressed around him in throngs. His Word went to spiritual natures which were starving, and which were born into a new consciousness of life, that thence had its outflowing into the lower sphere of sense. Paralytics, maniacs, cripples, and blind men were restored under his hand, and the dead came back to life. Though his home was at Capernaum, to which he ever returned, he went through the neighboring towns and cities, crossed over the lake into Peræa, and made journeys beyond Galilee into Phœnicia. None opposed him, except here and there a few Pharisees who came as spies and informers. "Truly," he exclaimed, on seeing these multitudes ready to perish with spiritual hunger, "the harvest is abundant, but the laborers are few."

He organized two select bands or companies, one of them permanent, the other temporary, and made them the heralds of the new kingdom of grace. They could not have entered fully into his thought, but his mantle of power rested upon them as they spake and acted in his name. The first need was not so much truth in the understanding as a quickening power over the will and such cleaving through the encasings of sense as to reach the spiritual nature and bring its wants distinctly and urgently into the consciousness. The company of twelve was soon found and organized. Six of them had been the disciples of the Baptist, and Jesus had met them at Bethabara. Two, and probably three of them, as we have already seen, had been his personal followers; had been with him in his private ministry in Judæa and around Nazareth, and been drawn into the tender intimacies of personal friendship. Most of them dwelt on the shores of the lake, were fishermen, unlettered and rude, but with natures earnest, hardy, and glowing with health. Matthew and the sons of Zebedee seem to have been men of more education and culture than the rest. John, already the companion of Jesus, had friends and acquaintances at the capital. It is remarkable that all the twelve were Galileans except one, and that was Judas, who was a Jew and who betrayed his Lord.

Taking into account the time and the occasion, the charge of Jesus to these twelve men after they had been gathered and organized for their work, is most wonderful, and seems more than the language of inspiration. The synagogues had become places where much freedom of exhortation was allowed. Any one who had a word to say was at liberty to say it, provided, of course, it did not break the decorum of the place; and it must have been a great relief sometimes from the monotonous droning of the readers. Into the synagogues Jesus often went to speak, and into these he charged his missionaries first to go. It shows how deep and persistent was his yearning towards his own countrymen and people that, notwithstanding his recent rejection at Jerusalem, where his words fell on their hearts like strokes upon an anvil, he will not yet give them up. Still, up there in Galilee, *they* shall have the first offers of the divine mercy: "Go not away to the Gentiles nor enter any town of the Samaritans, but go rather to the wandering sheep of the house of Israel." And yet he knows what commotion this will make in the synagogues; and that while a few will welcome his heralds and believe, the many will drive them away with cursings and buffetings; and he forewarns and forearms them against the whole. "Lo, I send you out as sheep into the midst of wolves: be ye therefore wise as serpents and harmless as doves."

The other company consisted of seventy men, and they went out in pairs. These were not directed to go first to the synagogues. They went wherever there were ears open to hear them. It is evident that these two bands of missionaries evangelized the whole of Galilee, and that its stagnant sea of spiritual death was shaken into surging waves.[1]

1 Luke, in all probability, was one of the seventy. So say the early traditions, and he alone gives the history of their mission, with the charge given to them as they were going forth, and he gives it with the graphic details of a personal witness.

The public ministry of Jesus in Galilee, has been described by the synoptics; for Matthew and Peter were eye-witnesses of it, and their personal experience was mainly with it. We should hardly know from their narrative that Jesus had been much out of Galilee. They were not with him ordinarily in his private walks. They were abroad on their journeyings doing the work which had been committed to them, though at stated times "they gathered themselves together unto Jesus, and told him all things, both what they had done and what they had taught." Mark vi. 30.

It does not come within our plan to follow the course of this public ministry, but rather the private ministry, as John has described it. The evidence is constantly cumulative that the fourth Gospel was written by an eye-witness with the synoptics before him.

We will give an instance which comes appropriately in this place, where the fourth evangelist has repeated the first two, plainly to supply something in close connection which they had left out entirely. Soon after the execution of John the Baptist, the people were pressing after Jesus in throngs, some of them bent on making him a temporal prince. Herod had already taken the alarm. Jesus retires from the scene by taking a boat with his disciples and crossing over into Peræa, seeking concealment in an uninhabited place on the sides of a mountain, probably at that time covered with forest. But the people see the boat put off from Capernaum, and they follow on to the number of five thousand, walking on the shore, and keeping the boat in sight. They seek out the place of retreat, and Jesus, soon after coming to the spot, finds again a multitude around him. He does not repulse or rebuke them, but teaches them still. They hang upon his lips till towards evening, when the disciples remind him that they are in a desert place and without food. The disciples had taken food only for themselves. Now follows the narrative of Matthew and Peter, of the miracle of the loaves ; of recrossing the lake by night, leaving Jesus behind ; of the storm which overtook them ; of Jesus coming to their relief, walking on the sea ; of Peter rushing out to meet him on the water, and sinking in it ; of the calming of the storm, and the safe landing again on the shore near Capernaum ; of the people bringing their sick on beds, when they heard that Jesus had returned ; and of the multitude who recrossed the lake and sought him again. All this is detailed by Matthew and Peter (through Mark), the latter with lively and graphic touches, for he was telling his own strange experience. But we never should have known from either of these writers that all this was only the external setting and frame-work of the highest truths, serving merely to embody and preserve them for all ages. We never should have known that the miracle of the loaves was merely the text and the occasion of one of the most heavenly discourses that ever fell from human lips. All that teaching which comprises most of the sixth chapter of the fourth Gospel, respecting "the bread which came down from heaven," whereof if one eat he shall never hunger, and which rises and flows on till it unfolds the doctrine of atonement, of resurrection from the dead, of a blissful immortality, of an interworking providence assuring them that all whom the Father gives to the Christ, shall come to him, since he will raise them up at the last day,— all this was the sermon for which the miracle of the loaves furnished the text and the imagery. It flowed on until Jesus merged his own personality in the truth which he revealed to the world. The scene of the cross ever before him, is now transfigured and the body to be rent upon it, and the blood to be poured out, are taken up and transfused in the glowing language of analogy. So completely is he identified with his cause, that he acknowledges no personal existence, except as the very form and body of the truth he brings. "I am the living bread which comes down from heaven. Let men break my body and eat my flesh and drink my blood. Whoever does this hath eternal life, and I will raise him up at the last day."

All this was preached to those people who ate of the loaves and were filled, partly on the shore after recrossing the lake, and partly in the synagogue at Capernaum, close by. Matthew and Peter make no report of it, for the obvious reason that they did not understand it, and it did not live in their memories. They were "hard sayings" to most of the twelve; and many of the other disciples "fell away" after hearing it, for they stuck in the letter and could not ascend so high. Matthew and Peter were greatly impressed with the miracles and all the external phenomena, and were rapt in wonder by them at the time. These they describe with scenic power and vividness. But the doctrine of which all else was only the type and symbol, and which, in the mind of Jesus transcended all the rest in importance, was congruous with the very mind and genius of the favorite disciple who had long shared the familiar thoughts of the Teacher, and been drawn up towards the heaven in which he lived. John makes mention of the miracle of the loaves, but goes on straightway to report the divine discoursings, for which the miracle served only to furnish the text and the imagery. It is another illustration of a fact which will meet us continually, that the four Gospels are not parallel, but convergent, and that the fourth lies at the very heart of Christianity. That Matthew and Peter should have been impressed mainly with the miracles and the physical concomitants, accords with all that we know of the character of their minds especially, at this stage of discipleship; that John alone, who had now been in intimate communion with Jesus for a whole year, should have been drawn up into its spiritual significance, is most natural. It entered deeply into his thought, so that he not only reports the discourse at length, as if that were more important than anything else, but its imagery glows afterwards in the scenery of the Apocalypse. Other disciples thought such discourse fanatical, and fell off. "How can this Man give us his flesh to eat?" Some of the twelve wavered. "Will ye also go away?" Only John drank in the whole of it, and has given a full report.

CHAPTER V.

THE THIRD VISIT TO JERUSALEM.

WHILE Galilee was moved through its breadth and depth, and Jesus was drawing the gaze of all ranks upon himself, another festival supervened which summoned all the Jewish adult males to Jerusalem. The Feast of Tabernacles occurred in September, and was attended with much peaceful pomp and ceremony. It commemorated the sojourn of the children of Israel in the desert where they encamped in movable tents and tabernacles. It was also a festival of thanksgiving for the ingathering harvest. It lasted eight days. The streets of Jerusalem and all the environs were crowded with arbors woven of evergreen boughs. These were reared, too, on the flat roofs of the houses, so that the city presented the appearance of being almost buried in a mighty forest, gleaming out here and there through the darkly embowering foliage. In these arbors the people lodged during the festival; every loyal Jew deserting his house for these temporary dwellings. The people formed processions, when each held in his hand branches of palm, myrtle, and willow, waving them and singing hosannas to the Lord of the harvest.

The eighth day of the festival was called "the grand day," because the rites were specially imposing. Close by the temple walls was the fountain of Siloam, a spring which bubbled up and became a little brook that channeled its way into the Cedron. A procession was formed, reaching continuously from the fountain into the temple courts, carrying pitchers of water, winding round the altar, waving their palms and shouting hosannas, pouring the contents of their pitchers down at the foot of the altar, and singing, "With joy we draw water from the wells of salvation." The rite was attended with dancing, and the festival closed with an illumination of the courts and porches of the temple. It was celebrated with so much of picturesque pomp that it drew the admiring notice of heathen nations.

There was a pause in the public ministry of Jesus, as the people of Galilee were wending their way towards Jerusalem to attend this Feast of Tabernacles. Some of his kinsmen urged him to go up to the capital, and there proclaim himself, not believing that the Messiah was to break upon the world from an obscure corner of Galilee. Go, they said, to this great feast and publish your claims. Jesus replied to them as we construe his words: "You can go without me. I am not to celebrate this feast,[1] for

[1] John vii. 8. There is some doubt as to the true reading of this text, and whether οὐκ or οὔπω should be preferred, *i. e.*, whether Jesus said, "I am not going," or "I am not going *now*." Griesbach adopts

the time is not yet come for me to be sacrificed. You can go in safety; I cannot. The world does not hate you as it hates me." He means, "I am not going to keep this festival." Its legal observance would have required him to be at Jerusalem at its beginning, to go up in one of the processions and in a public manner. So he says, I am not going to observe this feast; and he waited till the crowds had gone up, and the public ways were still, and Jerusalem was in the midst of its rejoicings, before he started. He knew that in that city he stood charged with two capital crimes: Sabbath-breaking and blasphemy. He knew that the stir in Galilee had alarmed the Sanhedrim, and that if he appeared now in his public character at the capital his arrest and execution were certain. So he tells his kinsmen: "Go up yourselves, I am not going to celebrate this festival." And yet with what unspeakable tenderness does he yearn towards the devoted city! There are his own people and they of his own lineage; there too he has made many disciples during his private ministry and among its humbler classes, and they will look with longing eyes for him at the festival. The crowds gone, and the ways still, he goes up in a private manner, though he comes into the very jaws of danger and death.

Of course he would not appear there as in Galilee,

the former, and we think rightly. Either way there is no room here, as Porphyry pretends, for impeaching our Lord's veracity.

at the head of twelve organized followers. The festival was half over when he arrived. There is evidence, as we have said, that John had friends and acquaintances in the city, and we infer that during this third visit he was there with his Master, as he reports minutely the incidents and conversations of which he must have been an eye and ear witness.

True enough, the old charge of Sabbath-breaking comes up again. The case of the cripple cured at the pool of Bethesda is remembered, and there are whisperings among the crowd, "Where is He?" He ventures into the temple and teaches by personal intercourse and conversation, and he is making converts from among the common people. The Sanhedrim are eagle-eyed, and watch all that is going on. They appoint police-officers to arrest him as a Sabbath-breaker, which under Jewish law was punishable with death by stoning. These police-officers lurk among the crowd, and wait their opportunity, but Jesus discerns the fact, and is acquainted with all their wiles.

Chapters seventh, eighth, ninth, and tenth, as far as verse twenty-second, of the fourth Gospel, describe what took place at this festival and soon after, in the intercourse of Jesus with the Jews at the capital. He remained after the festival was over, holding colloquies with the groups that gathered about him; mixed companies, some of whom scoffed and caviled;

some of whom were receptive under his teachings, but timid and reticent, knowing that an overwhelming odium from the ecclesiastical authorities was resting upon him. No less than seven of these personal colloquies are described by John, who evidently kept with Jesus both in his retirement at night and in his walks by day. These conversations are exceedingly characteristic. They are not given evidently in the order of time, but they are photographs of the temper of the times, of the Spirit of Jesus, and of well-known traits of human nature; and have that air of reality which no romance ever succeeds in imitating to entire perfection. Sometimes the hearrers and spectators are charmed, and half convinced by the speech and bearing of the wonderful man. Then they bethink themselves. The Messiah of their imaginations was to come in some supernatural and unaccountable way: "We know whence this man is. When the Messiah comes no one will know whence he is." "The Messiah was to break upon us out of some splendid supernatural halo; but we know all about this man, and just the place he comes from up there in Galilee, and there is no great mystery about him." John would not have reported such talk as this unless he had heard it. No romancer would have done it, bent on glorifying his hero.

That Jesus, after the full opening of his Messianic consciousness, foresaw and forecalculated his own death and resurrection, is not inferred from any obscure intimations which might have been afterwards exaggerated and misapplied by his fondly mistaken disciples. These form the burden of discourse, conversation, and prophecy, and his forecast of these events shapes the whole plan of his ministry. Leave out the discourses, conversations, and plans of action in which his death and resurrection are presupposed and necessarily involved, and there is nothing left in the life of Jesus which has any coherence or significance. In this third visit to the capital, his own death, and the manner of it which he forecasts so persistently and clearly, is a subject of constant reference, his mind being full of it, and the minds of his hearers being of course utterly incapable of taking in the meaning of it. To the men who he knew were plotting for his arrest and execution, he said, "I shall be with you but a little while longer. You will seek me, but you will not find me, and where I shall be you cannot come." They thought he was planning an escape out of their hands. "What can he mean? Will he go to the Greeks and teach the Greeks?" But again afterward he speaks more openly and explicitly, "I lay down my life to receive it again. No one takes it from me, but I lay it down of my own accord. I am commissioned to lay it down and I am commissioned to receive it again. This charge I received from my Father." Some, very naturally, thought him insane. "He is mad, why do you listen to him." Others, charmed by his words and amazed by his miracles, are simply perplexed and bewildered. "Can a maniac speak like him and cure cripples and blind men?" To suppose that Jesus had not this clear supernatural forecast, is to assume that these details of conversation were invented afterwards; and this is to assume that some dishonest forger, a century after the events, photographed the living manners of Jerusalem and the inmost life of Judaism with a subtle genius transcending that of Scott or Dickens; and in addition to this put into the mouth of one of his characters discourses so much more divine than any which ever fell from human lips, that they have been bread from heaven to our hungering humanity for eighteen hundred years!

CURE OF THE BLIND MAN.

The cure of the blind man, and the incidents and conversations which followed thereupon, are transactions as full of nature as they can hold. Here was a miracle right under the eye of the Sanhedrim, and in the temple-court, and the people have seen it. It will not do to arrest and execute this man unless the fact can be accounted for or explained away. They appeal to the parents, hoping the parents will deny that there was any blindness in the case. They evade most ingeniously, and are non-committal: "All we know about it is that he was born blind and that now he sees."

"Who opened his eyes?"

"He is of age, ask *him?*"

Then follow the cross-examination of the young man himself, and his excommunication and the rebuke of Jesus to the Pharisees for their own incurable blindness, ascending as usual from natural things to spiritual. The miracle is only the nucleus of a whole texture of natural events, and the discoursings which proceed from them, which are indissolubly bound together with the plainest marks of historic certainty, and the most subtile shadings of human character.

SERMON AT THE POURING OF THE WATER.

Once, however, at this festival, Jesus broke from his reserve and proclaimed himself in tones that pierced the crowd and held them in the stillness of profoundest awe. It was under circumstances where it is hard to conceive it possible that his divine eloquence should have been either repressed or resisted. On the last day of the feast, "the grand day," the long procession was streaming up from the spring of Siloam, winding through the courts and circling the altar, pouring out their pitchers of water, waving their palm-boughs, and chanting, "With joy we draw water from the wells of salvation." The court of the Gentiles would be thronged with sympathizing crowds through which the procession would wend its way. The rite commemorated the miracle in the desert, when Moses smote the rock with his rod and the water gushed out of it. The people must have had some perception of the spiritual significance of the event they were celebrating with joyous hosannas. The police-officers were in the crowd, watching for what they might deem the last opportunity to arrest the Sabbath-breaker and blasphemer. But Jesus knew the men, and in his hour of divine exaltation was conscious that he held them and the crowd at his command. The rock, smitten by the prophet's rod and turned to a spring for the thirsting travellers ; Siloam, gushing forth and flowing on into the Cedron, become the text and imagery of his discourse. "He stood and cried," says the record ; implying that his voice broke on the crowd above the murmurs and the hosannas with such startling power and clearness that it arrested them and held them. "If any man thirst let him come unto *me* and drink. Verily I say unto you if any one have faith in me his heart shall be a spring out of which shall flow rivers of living water." It is plain that John only reports the topic and heads of discourse, and that it flowed on till it unfolded the truths of the new reign of God, and a new dispensation of the Holy Spirit.

The Evangelists do not describe our Saviour's manner, from which we infer that he had none which drew attention to it. They describe his power by the effect his words produced in searching out the secret of the soul, and subduing it under a supernatıral awe. This convinced and conquered more than ıny external miracles could do which were only incidental to it, for it struck on the deeper chords that thrilled through the more mysterious realms of consciousness. So now many believed simply from hearing his discourse, and only because his words smote them as with supernatural power. " Surely," they said, " this is the Prophet."

The seventy judges, which constituted the Sanhedrim, held their session in a room at a corner of one of the courts of the temple, and it was not far off. The police-officers slink away from the crowd and report themselves to the judges.

" Why have ye not arrested him and brought him hither ? "

" Never man spake like this man."

HIS EXISTENCE BEFORE ABRAHAM.

At another of the seven colloquies which John has reported on this occasion, they attempted again to take his life. It was also in one of the temple courts, probably in the court of the Gentiles, under whose open porticoes the devotees of the temple were accustomed to assemble and hold converse, as in a kind of theological exchange. Here Jesus had gathered around him a group of sympathizing friends and believers, and was exhorting them to be steadfast. "My truth shall make you free," — referring to the Roman subjection under which the Jews were chafing, and the higher than civil freedom which was now within their reach. But the cavillers were present, and Jesus sees the eyes of the police-officers gleaming through the crowd. The cavillers boast of their descent from Abraham as conferring a higher freedom and nobler pedigree than Jesus could give. Jesus charges them with their murderous intent: "Ye are seeking to kill me, which Abraham would not have done. Your father is the Devil, for you are ready to execute his purposes, and he was a murderer from the beginning." Then alluding to the eternal life which was beyond their reach, he says, "Verily I say unto you, whoever obeys my teaching will never see death;" meaning, though you kill the body, you cannot touch the life within. This they cannot understand. "Abraham died, and the prophets died, whom do you make yourself?" Jesus replies, "Your father Abraham exulted that he might see my day, and he saw it and rejoiced." Sticking in the letter they rejoin, "You have not yet reached the fifty years which is the average length of human life, and have you seen Abraham?" Jesus replies, in a passage which has been made famous by the controversies which have proceeded from it: "Before Abraham was born I AM." Notwithstanding the controversies, we can find but one meaning to it: Jesus is claiming that God in a peculiar sense is his Father; and for this reason they are charging him with blasphemy. We must remember that his Messianic consciousness is now at its meridian fullness and power, and that he claims that he is not speaking from himself, nor from any dictates of finite intelligence; but that the Word, or the Eternal Reason, is speaking continuously through him, as much so as when it spoke from Sinai. He claims that his own finite personality is lost in these revealing annunciations, or is held in perfect abeyance. It is not a mortal man that is speaking to you, he would say, but the Logos himself. It is one with me and my Father. Passing into this divine consciousness and speaking from it, he uses the first person singular, claiming that the Logos has become incorporate with his own being and substance. On any other theory the language of these discourses is very often utterly unwarrantable, and would have furnished the Jews with just ground for their charges of blasphemy.

When he declares, then, "before Abraham was I am," he means to say, the Eternal Word from which I speak is not like Abraham and the prophets, who grow old, or to whom you can apply the measure of your mortal years. It has no past, and no future, for it is without beginning or end or succession of days. To these cavillers, boasting of their ancient and honorable descent, comes the annunciation: The Being who is speaking to you is the Eternal Now, who is timeless, — cutting short their driveling logic; and it could not, as we conceive, have been more concisely and sublimely done.

They understand him, evidently now, for they regard this as blasphemy. They take up stones to cast at him, and would have murdered him, but Jesus suddenly withdrew and concealed himself, and passed out of the temple by a private way.[1]

THE FAMILY AT BETHANY.

Whither did he go? Luke — who as we have seen, must have obtained much that he has written from John and his household — has told us of one place where Jesus went at this time; and the fact indicates what were his resorts and private communings when he withdrew from the strife of men. He sought the soothing intercourse of personal friendship in the retreats of social and domestic love. How many of these friendships must have been formed among the families in and around Jerusalem who had become receptive of his Word and believers in his Messiahship! They would be mostly if not entirely among the common people, who would conceal the fact from the respectable dignitaries at the capital.

[1] So we read the passage, John viii. 59, which has been variously interpreted. Some render ἐκρύβη, "made himself invisible," by which the advocates of the genuineness of the fourth Gospel understand a miracle; the opposers a trace of Gnosticism. Neither is found in the passage, unless by being first put into it by the expositor. The latter clause διελθὼν . . . . οὕτως, "going through the midst of them and so passed by," is rejected by Griesbach on external grounds as a gloss, as also by some of the best expositors. It probably got into the text as a gloss copied from Luke iv. 30. The whole passage would read, fairly rendered, "He concealed himself from them and passed out of the temple."

About two miles east of Jerusalem, beyond the Mount of Olives, near the foot of the mount, and on the road to Jericho, was one of these families, evidently in middle or humble life, to which Jesus resorted for safety, repose, and the intercourse of personal love. Lazarus and his two sisters not only had faith in him, but had become endeared to him by offices of hospitality and affection. They must have been among his earlier converts and disciples, for when Luke introduces them to our notice at this time, we find their intercourse to be of the most sacred and confidential nature. The characters are individualized by a few unconscious strokes of the pen. Mary sits at his feet, lost to everything beside, as she drinks the wisdom from his lips. Martha is the more anxious and careful, lest the comfort of a guest so honored and beloved will not be attended to. Jesus puts them both at ease by a few words characteristic of his religion and of himself. A delightful picture of tranquillity and rest after the stormy controversies at the temple!

So ended the third visit to Jerusalem. These journeys to the capital were plainly episodes during his more public ministry in Galilee, and while his organized followers there were achieving their great success. Thither he would return, and at his quiet home in Capernaum, and amid a people receptive of his Word, receive the reports of his evangelists as they came back with tidings of their mission.

CHAPTER VI.

FOURTH VISIT TO JERUSALEM.

ALL this while both the Seventy and the twelve were evangelizing Galilee, and probably regions beyond its limits. They were amenable only to the Roman power, and not immediately under the shadowing and oppressive authority of the Jewish Sanhedrim. We have no intimations that as a body, either of these organizations attended upon the Jewish festivals, or that their work extended within the limits of Judæa. But they were to return to Jesus at Capernaum, and bring to him a report of what they had done. The Seventy did so, it would seem, about this time, when Jesus returned again from Jerusalem and its vicinity, and escaped from the snares which were there involving him, to this quiet spot among the sheltering hills of Galilee. The Twelve, ere this, had reported to him; but the mission of the Seventy was more general and more remote.[1]

The whole province of Galilee had been shaken as

[1] "And the apostles gathered themselves together unto Jesus, and told him all things, both what they had done and what they had taught." Mark vi. 30. "And the seventy returned again with joy, saying, Lord, even the devils are subject unto us through thy name." Luke x. 18.

from the slumbers of death. The words of Jesus to the Jews when he cured the cripple, had become verified, — "The time is coming, and is now come, when the dead shall hear the voice of the Son of God, and they that will listen shall live."

There was a class of men very common in those days, called demoniacs. They were not ordinary cases of insanity, but cases in which men's voluntary powers had been overlaid and possessed, even to the bodily organs, as if the unseen world of evil was breaking visibly into the world of matter. They were the most difficult of all cases to cure, requiring a stronger and more pervading influx of power through the whole organism of mind and body, and the disciples were not always equal to the work. But the Seventy returned with the joyful report of their success: "Even the demons are subject to us through thy name." Jesus is rapt into the highest ecstasy on finding the success of his Word so widespread and complete. "I see Satan falling from heaven like lightning." "I see the Evil Power, so long enthroned over the minds of men, vanish like a meteor trailing down the sky." And then contrasting his repulse at Jerusalem with his reception among these rude and simple-hearted Galileans, he breaks out in a glad strain of thanksgiving: "I glorify thee, Father, Lord of heaven and earth, because though thou hast hidden these things from the wise and prudent, thou hast revealed them unto babes." It is impossible to understand this lofty and exultant strain, except as we figure to ourselves the Saviour escaping barely with his life, from his personal ministry at the capital, and seeing the result of his public ministry at Capernaum, which shook all Galilee from the slumbers of spiritual death.

Within two years after the removal to Capernaum, the change had become so great in Galilee, that the authorities at Jerusalem saw the revolution rolling up to the capital, and they saw that unless it could be arrested, they must inevitably go down before it. Unquestionably they were so far right. From any possible view which the ecclesiastical powers were capable of entertaining, there was now nothing for them to do but to put out of the way the author of the new movement, which was already shaking the ground beneath them. How insecure they were in their seats, we shall readily imagine when we call to mind the triumphal entry of Jesus into Jerusalem at the last Passover festival, with a throng of people, many of them from Galilee, shouting hosannas and strewing his way with palms.

He must have remained several months in Galilee, seeing and hearing the results of his organized ministry and inspiring it with his presence. His next visit to Jerusalem was at the "Feast of Dedication," which took place in December. This festival did not claim any divine authority, nor did it require the presence of Jewish believers at Jerusalem. It was appointed by Judas Maccabæus as a new dedication of the temple and altar after they had been polluted by Antiochus Epiphanes; and the festival down to the time of our Saviour had been kept with rejoicings and illuminations. Jesus is drawn again from his work in Galilee. It is apparent, too, that only John, his most intimate disciple, went with him from Capernaum.

JESUS WITHDRAWS TO BETHABARA.

He appears again in one of the porticoes of the temple, and holds conversation with the people who gather there. But he is more reticent than at his last visit, for he knows that the plottings are thickening and ripening, and he will not surrender his life till his work in Galilee is complete. He comes to the capital now, evidently not so much to make new converts there as to hold communings with those who already believe on him, and make them strong for the trial hour. Observing this reticence and caution, the Jews came around him, and said, "How long will you hold us in suspense? If you *are* the Messiah, tell us plainly?" He reminds them that they are not of his fold and will not believe; that he has come to find his own, and does find them; that no robber can pluck them out of his hands, because they were given him by the Father, and he and the Father are one. This revives the old charge of blasphemy, and kindles, as with a spark, the rage which since the last encounter had been gathering strength and determination. They take measures for his immediate arrest, and he withdraws both from the temple and the city. His purpose in coming hither to strengthen those who secretly believe on him, cannot be accomplished in the neighborhood of Jerusalem, and he retires to the desert, away beyond Jordan, drawing them after him into those profound solitudes. It was the old familiar place where John had first baptized, where Jesus had made his desert home while his Messianic consciousness was coming on with power, and where, emerging from the water at John's baptism, the heavens up to the central throne, had opened upon his mind. Hither he came now, and abode for some time; and how consecrated must the spot have been! And here his own people came to him, and gathered around him for those communings which could not be had under the scowl of Jewish authority. John implies that they continued for some time in this delightful intercourse, in those far-off solitudes. "And many came to him who said, John, indeed, performed no miracle, but all which John said of this man is true. And many believed in him there."[1] They were choice Sabbatic hours where no police-officers were watching in the crowd. It was across the desert, some twenty-five miles from Jerusalem.

[1] John x. 40-42.

LAZARUS DIES AT BETHANY.

But a family of these disciples whom Jesus had left Galilee to strengthen and support, was in affliction. Lazarus was sick. The sisters know the place of Jesus' retreat, and disciples of the neighborhood of Jerusalem were going over to Bethabara and returning. By some of these they sent word to Jesus, confident that the news would bring him at once to the friend whom he loved. He was not ready to leave his retirement at once, but lingered there till after Lazarus had died.

It is impossible to enter into this scene, if we regard the "miracle" which restored Lazarus, an arbitrary display of divine power. It is none the less a miracle for being in accord through all its processes with the highest and inmost laws of our human nature, but whose action is here sublimed and intensified by a love such as never throbbed before through the heart of man.

Bear in mind that our knowledge of the process of death is for the most part a very superficial and outside knowledge. Swedenborg says, that the final extrication of our immortal being from its mortal envelopments, does not generally take place till the third day after death has transpired. That it does not take place instantaneously, is reasonable in itself, and facts are abundant which go to prove it. We ought to infer from all the analogies and all the divine dealings with us, that death is no such change as the frightened imaginations of our childhood have made it; that it is not a sudden and violent wrenching of the soul from the clasp of the flesh to the giant wonders of eternity. Not so did we come into this world; not so shall we go out of it; not so are the births of nature when in all her embryonic cells she feels the troubled life that calls for a new stage of development, when the tender germ is breaking from its capsula into bud and flower. Death is birth in its ultimation, the final unclasping of the bands of nature that held us. There is an interval, longer or shorter, between the last streak of our earthly twilight and the first gleam of the new morning sky. We know this, for hundreds have passed into it without touching finally the shore beyond, and come back to this natural life again. It is longer or shorter, according to precedent conditions physical and spiritual. It is a total suspension of all the voluntary and involuntary powers. It is where our whole being is bathed in the most soothing of Lethean waters. Instances are reported where this interval has been prolonged through several days. In what we call death the spell of total silence is laid on all our fluttering pulses, lest any of our struggles and outcries might hinder the divine process of resurrection. The mother's caress, when she stills the wailings of her infant on her breast, represents but poorly the unequaled tenderness of the Divine Father when He hushes his babes to sleep, that their waking in the air of immortality may be orderly and serene.

It is also true that the process of death is prolonged and even postponed by the clinging sympathies of friends. This law of sympathy sometimes acts disastrously, lengthening out the last agonies when those we love ought to be given up on their part and on ours, with an unreserved resignation to the Divine Will. That there may be a sympathy so divinely strong as to postpone the final extrication of the spiritual body from the natural, is certainly conceivable under the same law of mental and spiritual action.

Bear in mind, too, that the sympathies of Jesus were so pervasive and strong that space and distance often vanish, and the sorrows and pains of those who were miles away, are drawn up into his heart, and healing power sent forth to restore them. Analogous cases have been known where hearts, sundered by wide spaces and even by ocean waves, have so throbbed into each other as not only to beat consciously together, but to impart some knowledge of their mutual joys and sufferings.[1] We get hereby some dim intimations of what our mysterious nature might be without the clogs and limitations of sense, and of what the nature of Jesus actually was when sense was becoming the transparency of the spirit within.

[1] The case of the Buckminsters, father and son, will occur to some of our readers in this connection.

HE IS RAISED TO LIFE.

In conceiving the resurrection scene which now follows, the English reader must carefully eliminate from it the idea suggested by our word "grave." The tombs in the vicinity of Jerusalem were chambers excavated in the sides of limestone rocks. Around the sides of the chamber were placed stone tables, and back of these were niches, or narrow cells, sunk farther into the rock. The tables were first occupied with the corpses, and when the tables were full, the bodies were laid away in the cells beyond. We must dismiss the notion of coffins and of our modern funeral paraphernalia. The bodies were embalmed, but the balming varied according to the rank or vanity of the deceased. The usual way was to anoint the body with odoriferous drugs, and swathe it with linen bands; and so prepared, it was laid tenderly away upon one of the tables at the side of the sepulchral chamber, the door closed which opened laterally into the recess, and a stone rolled against it.

We are now prepared to understand the resurrection scene at the tomb of Lazarus. The friendship of a soul like that of Jesus, the personal ties that held others in the embrace of his love, are a most essential element in the interpretation of this whole chapter, — a chapter which quivers with a pathos, as fresh, when we read it now the thousandth time, as if the whole scene were enacted but yesterday. We must think of the mighty power, even of our poor human affection over those who are near to us when struggling in the grasp of death ; how it holds them in the body and will not let them go ; how sometimes, after the eyes are closed and the pulses are all still, and the shroud has been put on, affection will hold them in ties that cannot break, and in some cases well certified, has divined the fact that the spirit was still there, and called it back to life. Think, then, what the power of the Saviour's love must have been when acting under like conditions! The miracle began two days before, and it was a miracle of all-knowing and all-conquering sympathy. Jesus was twenty-five miles off beyond the Jordan, when Lazarus sickened and died. He was so rapt in communings with his followers, and so intent in preparing his flock against the wolves that would scatter them, that he remained there two days after the afflicted family sent for him. But in heart and spirit he is at Bethany also, and knows the progress of the disease by those throbs and disturbances, which a heart both great and tender, feels along its hidden chords, and which draws up the sufferings of others into itself. How naturally he discerned, or rather *felt* the hour when all was over! "Our friend Lazarus sleepeth and I go to wake him." He would not call it death, for he was still conscious that he held him in his power and held him to this world in the mighty embraces of his love, and only for the dull perceptions of his disciples he says, "Lazarus is dead." When all this is kept in mind, the scene at the tomb almost ceases to be a wonder, for it is hardly strange that the spirit came back to its consciousness in the flesh, when it had been held to this world and within its fleshly organism by sympathies so divinely strong. We cannot read patiently the sermons of the commentators on the words "Jesus wept," as if here was something unaccountable. How perfectly do they bring him before us, burdened with the feelings caused by drawing all the pains and sorrows of the family, and the dying man into himself, pent up before, but now convulsing his breast and brimming over in drops of tenderness! And how entirely in keeping is the scene that follows, which we are let into in a way that no forger would ever have thought of! As the tenant of the tomb rises from the stone table on which he had been lying, and struggles with the linen bands that impede his movements, and the lookers-on are fixed in wonder and awe with no offer of assistance, Jesus, who alone was self-possessed, says to them with a wave of the hand toward Lazarus, "Loose him and let him go."

Then the characterization of the narrative is so plainly unstudied and undesigned as to render it morally certain that the whole scene is real and not imaginary. How perfectly, though incidentally, are the two sisters individualized! It is Mary and not

Martha who sits in the most retired part of the house, given up to tender sorrow, and does not know that Jesus is coming. It is Martha and not Mary, still "cumbered with much serving," who sees his approach and rushes out to meet him. One repeats after the other, the same words which they must have said over and over together. It is Martha and not Mary who makes the coarse remark respecting the state of the body. Any forger or romancer could have imagined a resurrection scene, and we have abundance of them in the legends of the saints. No forger or romancer of these times, or of any times, could have made the central fact the heart of a narrative like this, threading the whole body of it with veins into which beats the finest life-blood of our human nature.

A late writer objects to the prayer at the tomb as dramatic, in the clause "because of the people that stand by I said it, that they may believe that thou hast sent me." If it was dramatic, then all prayer is except secret prayer, for all other prayer is specially "for the sake of the people that stand by," they being supposed either to join in it or be brought more directly under its influence. It is to be presumed that John has here given only the summary of what Jesus prayed for, and which was mainly for faith on the part of the people who were with him. His desire was that they might not stupidly wonder at the miracle he was about to work, but be helped by it to an apprehension of the Divine doctrines which he taught.

On a careful study and review of this resurrection scene, I want language to express the conviction of its historic certitude in all its particulars. The narrative is beyond the highest reach of art, in those delicate touches of nature which are plainly unconscious, and therefore the indelible marks of reality. A forger would not have brought Jesus to the grave "weeping," nor would he have described a scene of such thrilling import without betraying some effort to be dramatic, nor without weaving in elements in disharmony with the naturalness and tenderness of the scene. It is objected that such a miracle as this could not possibly have been omitted by the synoptics. The objection is futile. Whenever Jesus approached Jerusalem he came under the frowns and threatenings of the authorities. To come up with twelve organized followers, would have been madness. He never did, except at the fatal Passover, foreseen and intended to be the last. But he knew how many hearts and homes were yearning towards him in and about Jerusalem, how much they needed strength, and how soon they would need consolation. These more private visitations give us gleams far into the more interior life of Jesus; and whoever reads the fourth Gospel with care, must see that they are described by an eye-witness who keeps himself out of sight. Let the reader note carefully the *time* of the resurrection scene at Bethany. Jesus had come up privately to Jerusalem for the last time before the fatal Passover; he had escaped for his life and gone over the Jordan into the desert; he had drawn after him disciples from the city, and was communing with them there; he goes back to Bethany to raise up his dead friend, though against the remonstrance of those disciples who fear he will be arrested; he leaves immediately after, and returns to Galilee by an unfrequented way, where we find him again with the twelve. It is pretty certain that the twelve were *not* with him at Bethany; it is exceedingly probable that John would be there, and taking the whole evidence, we think it morally certain that he *was* there, and that his pen has described the scene.

JOHN INTERLACES THE SYNOPTICS.

We have observed how constantly he supplements the synoptics and fits into them. Sometimes the interlacings are exceedingly delicate, and where he disagrees with them in details, the disagreements are confirmatory evidence of genuineness. We cannot avoid the conclusion, that we have an instance of this in the history of the resurrection scene at Bethany, and one of a very remarkable kind. The characters are introduced in this way:—

"Now a certain man was sick named Lazarus of Bethany, the town of Mary and her sister Martha."

Then we have this explanatory sentence, thrown

in parenthetically: "It was the same Mary which anointed the Lord with ointment, and wiped his feet with her hair, whose brother Lazarus was sick."

Why this reference to Mary as one whose deed was already famous? We cannot mistake the prominence here given to her. Martha is only known as Mary's sister, and Lazarus as Mary's brother, and she is spoken of as if her good deed had somewhere else been described without being credited to her by name. "This Mary was the person who anointed the Lord with precious oil." Turning to the synoptics we find this deed of tender friendship described by Matthew and Mark in a strain of the highest commendation, with the assurance of Jesus that its fragrance should yet fill the whole world.[1] But the name of the woman thus highly praised is kept back, for when Peter preached, and Mark and Matthew wrote, she was probably living. How natural for John writing later, when he came to speak of Mary to say, "This is that person who anointed the Lord with precious oil," in tacit reference to the well-known and remarkable eulogium which the first two evangelists had recorded.

But this fragrant deed of Mary, John himself describes afterwards; and as we are persuaded, with a delicate reference to the narratives of Matthew and Mark. We have it in the fourth Gospel on this wise:—

[1] Matt. xxvi. 6–13. Mark xvi. 3–9.

"Then Jesus six days before the Passover came to Bethany, where Lazarus was whom he had raised from the dead. And supper was made for him there, and Martha served, and Lazarus was one of those at table with him. Then Mary, taking a pound of pure oil of spikenard, very precious, anointed the feet of Jesus and wiped them with her hair, and the house was filled with the perfume of the oil. Then said one of the disciples, Judas Iscariot, the son of Simon, he who was about to betray him: 'Why was not this oil sold for three hundred denarii, and given to the poor.' This he said, not because he cared for the poor, but because he was a thief, and had the money-box and what was put in it was in his hands. Then Jesus said, 'Let her alone; she has kept it for the day of my burial. The poor ye have always with you, but me ye have not always.'" [1]

This is the same scene which Matthew and Mark describe. The details and the language ascribed to the interlocutors are such, that it cannot possibly be any other. The time is the same, it being just before the last Passover, when all the disciples attended him, and when his nearing death so filled his contemplations, that the ointment had the odor of the tomb. The place is the same. Why then has John here departed from his rule, and told over again the story of the synoptics. Plainly, because their narrative had inaccuracies which John would naturally wish to set

[1] John xii. 1–8.

right. John's memory would be more minutely accurate than Peter's or Matthew's, for John had intimate relations with the family at Bethany; had been there again and again with Jesus, while Peter and Matthew had not. They tell us vaguely that it was at the house of "one Simon." How fondly does John recall the scene, in order to name the guests and put in the names of Lazarus, Mary, and Martha! But Matthew had said "*the disciples*," and Mark still more generally "*they*" rebuked the woman for wasting the ointment, and that it was poured upon the *head* of Jesus. John says with indignant accuracy, that it was *Judas Iscariot* who uttered the rebuke, and that, not because he cared for the poor, but *because he was a thief* and kept the money-box, and wanted to put something into it; thus exonerating the other disciples. He is careful even to give all the additions of Judas, and make him stand out from all the rest, —"the son of Simon, who was about to betray him." He also says with more minuteness and as a more interested observer, that it was the *feet* of Jesus which Mary balmed,—the feet of the weary traveller, —and that she wiped them with her hair, thus giving to the incident all its touching significance.

These corrections of the other narratives so delicately done are indubitable marks of truth and genuineness. No fabricator would have thought of supplementing the synoptics in this way. He would have dealt in generalities, instead of going down into details which photograph the scene with such sharpness of outline as to correct the more vague and inaccurate statements of observers, who must have witnessed it with an interest not near so tender. He would have had no motive to depart at all from the synoptics in such matters as these, but every motive to keep in harmony with them. But how fondly has John supplied these details in scenes over which his memory was brooding, putting in all the names of the dear family which the others had left out! And while he corrects them with sharpened accuracy he puts in the hated name of Judas with a tone of his ancient anger and scorn. The evidence is irresistible, because so perfectly artless, that the author of the fourth Gospel is writing of scenes and characters endeared and long familiar, and to which Matthew and Peter were comparative strangers.

CHAPTER VII.

FIFTH AND LAST VISIT TO JERUSALEM.

HE went back to Galilee, not publicly, but by way of the desert, lingering for awhile at a town called Ephraim, on the borders of the desert, there drawing his Judæan disciples to him in his last private ministry. Returning again to Galilee, his intercourse with the twelve from this time forward seems toned with an indescribable pathos in a constant endeavor to prepare their minds for the impending blow. The synoptics describe the teachings and events of this interval with graphic detail. We have them in Matthew, from chapter xvi. to xx. 28. Now Jesus speaks constantly of his death at Jerusalem, for he knows that the plot there for his destruction is fully prepared and ripened. Now occurred the scene of the transfiguration, which drew up his most intimate disciples to a vision of immortality and of the spiritual body, which was above the power of Roman crucifixion. Now were given the most urgent lessons of self-sacrifice, to cutting off the right hand or plucking out the right eye, that the spiritual body might be kept whole and not perish in hell. Now come the most impressive rebukes of all their sensuous ideas and ambitions, telling them again and again that the baptism in his kingdom is one of blood, and the cup to be drank is the cup of trembling. The next festival is that of the Passover. He is going up to it, not privately, but with his whole organized band, and he knows what the result will be.

A question will naturally arise here. Why did Jesus go up this last time to the capital, when he knew he was walking into the jaws of death? The vicarious theology, of course, has a ready answer; but it is too technical, and it does not satisfy us. And yet it is the husk of a truth most profound and comprehending. Jesus might have avoided this martyrdom, but it could only have been by the abandonment of his work, and by escape from Palestine. He was no longer safe within its borders. The revolution beginning in Galilee had rolled up to Jerusalem, and under it, pervading the minds of the masses, till the Sanhedrim felt that the whole ground was tremulous beneath them. And yet it is plain, from any human point of view, that the movement, left to itself at this stage, would soon have subsided, and nothing would have come of it. Neither the twelve nor the masses which they had moved upon, had as yet any adequate conceptions of its nature. One of two things was inevitable now, — failure or martyrdom. Even on the well-known principles of human nature these had become the fatal alternatives. Death at Jerusalem, in the lowest view that could be taken of it, was a sublime testimony to the doctrines of self-abnegation and sacrifice which had made up the very body and substance of our Saviour's discoursings. To escape out of Palestine would have been to turn them into empty words; to "go up to Jerusalem" now, was to render them fragrant through all ages with the inspirations of a Life which for the first time was to make the most splendid visions of moral perfection a fixed reality on the earth. Therefore when Peter remonstrated, saying, "This shall not be unto thee," Jesus turned upon him with what seems at first a sharp rebuke, "Go from my sight, thou Satan! thou wouldst cause me to fall, for thou carest not for the purposes of God, but for that which pleases men."[1]

But from a point of view vastly higher than this, death had now become an adamantine necessity. He had taught his disciples the highest truths of heaven, but they had entered scarcely deeper than their memories. Jesus saw what none of his disciples could, that death was only the reverse side of resurrection; and, that accomplished, he should have access to their minds on the purely spiritual and immortal side, with an influx of power that would

[1] This, however, was not a rebuke of Peter, or even addressed to him. Jesus evidently felt a temptation assailing his own mind, suggested by Peter's words, — a temptation to avoid death and abandon his cause. The words are aimed directly against the tempter, as they were in the early scenes of temptation, "Get thee hence, Satan," and Peter, unconscious of blame, is lost sight of.

stream through their memories and thence through their whole being, making the truth which now lay cold and dead to burn like fire, and melt them down and purge their dross away. It *was* necessary, then, that Jesus should now die, in order that "the law might be satisfied," if we mean by law not an abstract or arbitrary rule, but those eternal principles of being through whose fulfillment alone our fallen humanity could be laid hold of, and renewed, and lifted up to the Divine embrace.

This interval, apparently of about three months, seems to have been passed in Galilee in these communings with the twelve, who had accomplished their mission in that province, and returned to Jesus with its tidings for the last time. Matthew and Peter, through Mark, make full reports of these last months in Galilee, for they were conspicuous actors in them. John says nothing about them, for the good reason that they had already been narrated. The Passover at hand, they go up now in company, and there is no longer any effort on the part of Jesus to elude the toils of his enemies. The hour has come, and it would be talking very tamely to say that he meets it with courage. Courage is required when we walk partly blindfold into danger. Jesus, from his height of transfiguration to which the three disciples were drawn up for an hour, but where Jesus was standing serenely all the while, has a forecast of the track of history, including his death and resurrection and the destruction of the Jewish state, and the new kingdom of God rising on its ruins and radiating to the end of the earth. All this was before him, and must account to us for the entire change of tone and manner, now that "the hour is come," and which are a challenge flung down from aloft to the authorities at Jerusalem to do their worst, and fulfill their hour of darkness.

The Passover festival took place from four to five months after "the Feast of Dedication" at which we last saw Jesus in the temple, soon to be driven from it and from the neighborhood of Jerusalem. Not then was he ready to die. His followers were to be strengthened for coming events, his organized twelve were to be gathered around him again in Galilee for a similar purpose. All this has been done, and Jesus makes ready to go up to Jerusalem openly and eat the Passover with the twelve. They seem to have gone, not through the heart of Samaria, but through the desert, or near it, skirting its western border, and entering Judæa by way of Jericho. At the beginning of the journey, Jesus took the twelve apart, telling them explicitly that he was going up for the last time, and was now to be crucified. They fell behind him in that perplexing dread produced partly by his words and partly by the coming calamity whose shadow already involved them. Before reaching Jerusalem, however, his way was thronged with people. Doctors of the law came to dispute with him. Mothers came with infants in their arms to get his blessing upon them, making their way through the ring of doctors for this purpose, showing how deeply and fondly the heart of the masses had been stirred, and how it throbbed at his approach. Blind men stationed themselves by the way, and cried for his healing power as he passed. As he neared Jerusalem, he applied for an ass, and rode upon it, probably to prevent the crowd from thronging him.[1] He makes no effort to repress the enthusiasm which breaks spontaneously from the lower ranks of people, and comes up around him in shouts. They strew his path with palm-branches, and throw down their garments for him to

[1] Strauss has this criticism on this passage, as near as we can quote it from memory. Matthew mistook the passage in Zechariah, which really speaks of only one animal, and should be rendered, " Behold, thy King cometh sitting upon an ass, even a colt the foal of an ass." Matthew thought there were both an ass and her colt in the case, and so he makes the disciples bring two, and makes Jesus ride on both, — showing that the whole is a myth put in to fill out a Jewish preconception. The writers of the second and fourth Gospels, not falling into Matthew's blunder, mention only one animal, — the colt. This is a very subtle and ingenious criticism. But the author of the first Gospel, who probably wrote it in Hebrew, would be quite as likely to understand Zechariah, either in the Hebrew or Septuagint version, as Dr. Strauss would. The inference most natural to our minds is, that Matthew mentions two animals because he describes the fact *as he saw it*, albeit the prophecy names but one. They found the colt with the dam, and so both were brought; but as Jesus rode only one of them, the garments being placed upon the other, Mark and John only mention the colt. Matthew does not necessarily imply that Jesus rode both, and one reading of Matthew of considerable authority (ἐπ' αὐτὸν) makes him ride only one.

ride over. Little children even join in the throng, and cry, "Hosanna in the highest!" and he enters Jerusalem, not as a malefactor under sentence of death, but as a hero returning from his conquests. He must have known what all this portended. He must have known how these acclamations would strike on the ears of the ecclesiastical authorities. "All the world has gone after him," they said. The conclusion, in their logic, could not be avoided.

This entry of Jesus into Jerusalem, strikes us at first as having an air of eccentricity, and it is just one of those incidents which, when narrowly scanned, are found in such close and logical connection with other events and circumstances, that its first apparent singularity avouches its reality the more. The evangelists put it forward as if it were solely from a predetermination to fulfill an old prophecy, but incidentally and unwittingly they disclose quite other reasons, and reasons which show that it was the wisest and most natural thing which Jesus could have done. Remember that all Galilee had been deeply moved, and was crowding in long procession after him to the capital. Another throng comes out from the city to join it. What was the thought which ran through the crowd from mouth to mouth? Luke has indicated it: "Because he was near Jerusalem they thought that the kingdom of God would immediately appear." They thought he would put himself at the head of his followers, as the temporal Messiah, commence his reign with Jerusalem for his capital, and subdue the world to himself by miraculous physical power. He must ride, into the city, or be overrun by the throng. But he chooses the humblest way. He comes not with horses and chariots, but sends for a beast of burden never used in war. The ass, though of more spirit and mettle in Oriental countries than the one which goes by the same name amongst us, was nevertheless used only in peaceful industry. The act was plainly intended to proclaim distinctly to the Jewish authorities, and his own followers as well, that he was no insurrectionist, and that his kingdom was to extend only by peaceful methods. He was really fulfilling the prophetic words quoted by Matthew from Zechariah.

Why does John repeat the story? Because he alone sees its connection with the miracle at Bethany. The raising of Lazarus some months before must have excited curiosity and wonder in and around Jerusalem. Any writer bent on making a sensation with his readers, would have enlarged upon this, and brought multitudes to see the risen Lazarus, and talk with him, and see the man who had called him back from the tomb. There must have been much of this kind of excitement, supposing the event to be real; but John gives us an idea of it naively, and in a few lines. Jesus enters Jerusalem riding upon the ass; and John too makes prominent the prophecy which was fulfilled, charging himself and the other disciples with stupidity for not understanding it sooner, while rather incidentally he tells us that a throng went out of the city to meet the throng coming in, "because they had heard that he performed this miracle." Thus while the evangelists make the entry to Jerusalem appear like an eccentricity by their mystic theory concerning it, they supply incidents unconsciously which show its natural connections, and give it the indubitable marks of reality.

It is remarkable that while the synoptics up to this time tell us little or nothing of what occurred at Jerusalem during the ministry of Jesus, they now become very full, and report minutely and with graphic power, showing that while before this they had only been eye-witnesses of the work of Christ in Galilee, after this they are eye-witnesses of the events at the capital. All the twelve are now there. John's narrative and that of the synoptics now flow on together. Still the narratives are not parallel. Though John narrates much in common with them, he is supplementing them all the while, and introducing us to an interior range of fact and of experience to which they were partial or total strangers. Still the disciple nearest to the Lord was a sharer of his thoughts, his works, and his perils, to an extent which they were not; and we shall find that while Jesus now had his public work to do, and his messages to deliver, among which was the denunciation of woes against the enemies of his truth, he had also his private and personal ministries, and that they belonged to the inmost ranges of his tenderest love.

CHAPTER VIII.

THE NIGHT OF THE LAST SUPPER.[1]

WHEN we read of the private communings of Jesus with his disciples, at the home of the sisters in Bethany, or in the depths of the desert beyond the Jordan, or again in the secluded places "near Ephraim," the heart naturally yearns to be drawn into the confidence of those quiet sabbatic hours. What did Jesus say to them to strengthen their souls and bring them out of the shadows of doubt, distress, and fear which were falling upon them from the clouds which thickened and grew black around them? What did he say to them to prepare them for the impending woe? We know tolerably well what he said. The topics of discourse at the Last Supper, in which he sought to draw his disciples upward towards the serene heights on which he stood, must have been those which he urged repeatedly upon his followers in his last personal ministry with them, whether near Jerusalem or in the seclusion of the desert. His oneness with the Father that they may be one in Him, and with each other; his promise of the Comforter; his exhortations to steadfastness as he described the trials that

[1] See the Appendix A.

awaited them; his prayers to the Father in those states of exaltation in which "the Son of man was glorified," that is, when the Spirit within so irradiated the whole outward man that the body lay upon the soul as a garment of light; his rebukes of all personal ambition and rivalry with lessons of self-forgetfulness and self-sacrifice; these are the topics of the strain at the Last Supper which runs through five consecutive chapters, unparalelled for its celestial beauty. John must have heard it often, varied in its adaptations, as he attended Jesus privately in those personal ministries on the approach of the final catastrophe; and this doubtless is another reason why he was the sole reporter of it. He had heard it so often that it dwelt in his soul as a strain of heavenly music, one note of which called up all the rest.

In his narrative of the tender scenes of the Last Supper, John supplements the synoptics, and in one instance fits into Luke's account with such delicate connections and shadings that they become the strongest of circumstantial evidence. Apart, there are things not easily understood. Compare them, and we have the interblendings of a picture recognized at once as a perfect copy of nature and reality.

The washing of the disciples' feet, mentioned by John alone, seems in his narrative to be ill-timed and out of place, and a piece of downright eccentricity. Jesus in the midst of the Supper, rises from the table, girds himself as a menial, takes a basin of water, goes round and washes their feet, and that done returns to finish the meal. No wonder they were surprised, and remonstrated. Turn to Luke, and we find the reason of it. The disciples were engaged at table in a most unseemly dispute of personal rivalry, and the symbolical act of Jesus was an interruption and hushing of this noise of tongues. They were immediately shamed into silence and humility, and it was to the state of mind thus prepared and made receptive that the discourse of those five wonderful chapters was addressed, immediately afterward, and out of which the prayer must have been breathed: "I in them and thou in me that they may be made perfect in one, that the world may believe that thou hast sent me."

Some one has undertaken to criticize the prayers reported in these chapters, as partial and lacking the comprehensiveness of humanity, because Jesus included principally his own disciples. "I am praying for them; I pray not for the world." But his whole purpose in gathering them about him was to create an organism to receive and embody his Spirit, and which after he had passed from sight should embody it with progressive power and be the fulcrum on which Omnipotence would raise humanity itself to the Divine embrace. "As thou hast sent me into the world, so I send them into the world. Nor do I pray for these only, but for those who may believe on me through their teaching, that they all may be one, as thou, Father, art in me and I in thee." Never was prayer more comprehending and efficacious, for it requires the breadth of the world and the remaining ages for its fulfillment.

The discoursings and colloquies of these five chapters were not all at the Last Supper. Chapter xiv. closes with the words, "I shall not talk much more with you. The prince of this world is coming, and in me he has nothing in common with him. . . . . Arise, let us be going hence!" He knew that the police of the Sanhedrim were on his track, and to prolong his intercourse with his disciples somewhat farther he walks with them to the Garden of Gethsemane. On the way the contents of the three following chapters, commencing with the beautiful figure of the Vine and its Branches, seem to have been uttered familiarly in the ears of the eleven, with short prayers and communings with the Father as he saw the great crisis at hand.

As we come to the closing scenes, three very general facts are most strikingly manifest: that the third and fourth Gospels give us a whole congeries of events running into graphic detail chromatic with the inmost life of Jesus, which the first two Gospels leave out altogether; that John is an eye-witness of what the others were not, and that Luke reports things upon John's authority.

The open triumphal entry into the capital, with the retinue from Galilee shouting hosannas, hastened the catastrophe. But it was finally precipitated by that discourse of Jesus in the temple courts, reported by Matthew alone, where members of the Jewish priesthood had gathered as usual around him to question and cavil. The style of speech, on the part of Jesus, is no longer colloquial and reserved. It rises to sustained and continuous discourse, and though inspired with tones of grieving mercy, is nevertheless the most awful denunciation that ever rang on the iron casings of the human heart and conscience. As he closed with the words, "Lo! your house is left you deserted!" and went out of the temple, knowing he was never to enter it again, it must have sounded like the last sentence of doom through its corridors. The quick determination of the plot, the brutality and maddening rage at the mock trial and the crucifixion, follow in natural sequence, but else were hard to understand.

The scene in Gethsemane is given by each of the Evangelists. But Luke and John become minute and graphic in the extreme. In the last grievous temptation, when the flood of agony became overwhelming, they alone unveil to us the inner sanctuary. Luke, elsewhere vague, here becomes exact, telling us that in the terrible wrestling, when Jesus took the three disciples apart to watch with him, he had withdrawn from them "about a stone's throw;" that is, he was still within sight and hearing. He alone describes the sweat falling thick and heavy like drops of gore, and the appearance of the strengthening angel.[1] The contrast between the exaltations of the Last Supper, and the abyss of woe in Gethsemane, is striking indeed, and it is alleged by objectors that other martyrs have exhibited a greater measure of fortitude. Such critics lose sight of the fact that fortitude does not consist in meeting suffering without sensibility, but in spite of it, and that the largest and the deepest natures rise the highest and sink the lowest through the ranges of bliss and woe. Susceptibility to pain is in exact proportion to the wealth, abundance, and fineness of the material it consumes. An American savage would meet death by slow torture almost without emotion, because his nature lies proximate to the animal; but he would judge very poorly of the anguish whose nerves run not through the animal tissues alone but through the textures of a humanity so angelic and divine that its sympathies drew up into itself the sufferings of a race. The alternative is now upon Jesus in more awful force than in the temptations of the desert, — the sacrifice on the morrow, or escape out of Judæa. The latter is still within his choice, for the twelve legions of angels, if invoked, will guard him invisibly through the danger and out of it. But the sacrifice

[1] We do not understand Luke to say that the sweat itself was blood. The word ὡσεὶ, "as it were," implies the contrary, so that Mr. Norton's objection to the passage vanishes, for the external evidence against it is inconsiderable.

is already chosen, and the anguish of it is not physical merely. It is heart-anguish the most terrible, for his own people and nation are to put him to death, whom he has yearned to gather under the wings of Mercy, as a bird gathers her brood, but whose sun has now sunk behind the thunder-clouds soon to go down in a sea of blood.

It is one of the beneficent and compensating laws of suffering, that it becomes shorter as it becomes intense, and hastens the sufferer into the sweet refuge of death. The death of the cross was a prolonged agony of days and weeks in ordinary cases. The robbers crucified with Jesus were alive on Friday evening, and unless the execution had been hastened by other means, would have lived much longer, whereas Jesus expired at the end of three hours. It astonished the insensate soldiers, even as the agony in the garden does the commentators; but both the sufferings of Gethsemane and Calvary come under that great and merciful law which governs all suffering, that Life, which is the highest and most finely organized, is most fiercely rent and lacerated by it, and for that very reason its organism soonest gives way and refuses to be the inlet of pain, but shuts it off through the insensibility of death. The process began in the garden, where the sufferer exclaimed as he fell under it, My soul is exceedingly sorrowful even to the verge of death, — and only three hours of agony remained for the cross.

It would appear that while Jesus fell prone under this load of anguish, only a stone's throw from Peter, James, and John, they were heavy with sleep.[1] This should not surprise us when we remember that it was now far into the night. It is not implied, however, that none of them were witnesses of this last and most overwhelming of all the Saviour's temptations. The sleep seems to have been fitful and broken, and heaviest on the part of Peter. John, who describes the scene most vividly, if Luke's narrative be his, entered most fully into its meaning, and knew the influx of Almighty strength represented by the helping angel. John alone tells us of the awe which came over the minds of the police, who at first fell back as Jesus appeared before them, declining to arrest him as once before, till he told them to do so and let his disciples go.

1 It will be observed, that when Jesus returns to rouse the disciples, he addresses Peter only.

CHAPTER IX.

CALVARY.

THE place of crucifixion must have been just north or northwest of Jerusalem, not far beyond the city walls, on one of the mounds which rise up from the undulating surface, and which probably on account of its shape was called the " Skull." A throng of spectators followed the cohort of soldiers who had the prisoners in charge. Each, according to Roman custom, was compelled to carry his own cross. While the two robbers were bearing theirs, Jesus fainted under the burden, because the sufferings already endured had prostrated his strength, and the soldiers compelled a man from the crowd to carry it after him.

In this crowd two classes of persons are to be distinguished. There were the enemies of Jesus whose rage was now to be glutted in full. These followed near at hand and gathered close around the cross, feasting their revenge upon sight of its agonies. But the personal friends and disciples of Jesus followed afar off, keeping in sight but hovering at a distance, probably on some neighboring mound that commanded a view of the scene. In this far-off group were friends which had come from Galilee. Among these are four devout women, — Mary the mother of Jesus; Mary her sister, the wife of Cleopas; Salome, the mother of James and John and a kinswoman of these sisters; and Mary of Magdala. Probably most of the twelve were also in this far-off group. They dispersed and fled when Jesus was arrested, but we infer are included among the friends now hovering cautiously and tremblingly within distant view of the crucifixion. Close about him Jesus sees only the brutal soldiers, now leisurely sitting down by the cross as a guard, and the more cruel men who pass by with scoffings and gibes. But there is one exception. John is there. He was the only one who did *not* "forsake and flee" at the arrest in Gethsemane, except to follow close on the heels of the police and come in with them at the mock-trial. He was in the procession that kept close to the soldiers when Jesus was led to execution, and now he stands alone under the cross where the storm of hate is fiercest raging, and he gives us again an inside view; the lines of light athwart the blackness, the undertones of mercy within the storm. He alone of the disciples hears the prayer of the sufferer: "Father, forgive them for they know not what they are doing." We do not think this refers any more to the savage soldiers who drove the nails, but could not understand how piercing was the torture they made, than to the men who set them on, passing to and fro with fiendish glee. But John does not long continue there as a solitary disciple. Three persons of that group looking on afar off, break away from it and come nigh, drawn by the awful fascination of the scene. These are the mother of Jesus and her sister, the former leaning upon the latter and clinging to her with maternal anguish. The third is one who had been healed of disease, Mary of Magdala. She, too, ventures nigh, and all three find their way to the cross and come up and stand with John. Jesus looks down upon them ; and now follows the tender colloquy in which He commits his mother to the care of the favorite disciple. There are writers who discredit this account, because they think the women could not have endured such a sight. Strange that any man who ever had a mother could write such a criticism ; could believe that one mother in ten thousand would have kept afar off and not come nigh for the last benedictions and farewells, or could be ignorant of the fact that in such hours as these the gentlest natures are the strongest, and that woman's affection is the mightiest power on earth, and inspires her courage after it has failed from the souls of men. The alleged discrepancy here between John and the synoptics is altogether specious, for it is only another instance where John interlaces them with such touches of nature as to make the harmony more pervading and complete.

There is another colloquy at the cross, which is

reported by Luke alone, but which, without reasonable doubt, comes originally from John, who stood by the cross and heard it. Two men called "thieves" were crucified with Jesus, and to one of them Jesus gives the assurance, "This day shalt thou be with me in Paradise." This passage, we think, has been signally misinterpreted; and a supposed discrepancy has been alleged between Luke's (John's) narrative and Matthew's.

We get a very inadequate notion of these men called "thieves," if we are thinking only of those who steal their neighbor's goods in peaceful and civilized communities. The word is rendered well enough, though it includes, further, the idea of robbery or violent seizure of the property of another. Who these men were, or to what class they belonged, there is not much doubt from the circumstances of the case. Josephus describes them. The Roman provinces, of which Judæa was one, were placed, as we have said, under proconsuls and governors, whose main object was to gather a revenue from the people from which to enrich themselves, and then return to Rome and live in luxury and splendor. These exactions were sometimes exceedingly oppressive, — were excitements to insurrections, concealments, and reprisals. Some of the more daring and reckless among the oppressed would band together and seek the fastnesses of the mountains. There they would conceal their goods, and thence issue by stealth and make reprisals on the power that oppressed them, — perhaps make assaults on the unwary traveller. They sought the wild coverts of Judæa, leading a life of irregular warfare, always objects of dread to the Roman governors, and subject, when arrested, to execution under Roman law. They answered in part to the clans of the Highlands, the Dreds of the Great Swamp, or the John Browns of our border warfare. Probably Barabbas was one of these men, for whose release in the place of Jesus the Jews clamored at the trial. They might include men of a vast range of character, from the very worst to men of natural humanity, pursuing a good end by unlawful means, and roughened and made grim in the irregular strife. They would be very likely to come from the rude heathen population of Galilee.

Two of these men have been arrested, and are to be executed under Roman law. Amid the darkness and convulsion, Matthew describes the demeanor of *both* the robbers, — how, in the frenzy of pain, both joined with the Jewish scoffers, and taunted the Divine sufferer with the invitation to come down from the cross. But when we open Luke and see the spectacle from John's point of view, a new scene opens upon us, and one of so much moral beauty that it flings a gleam of sunshine across the horrors of Calvary. It is a scene of penitence, forgiveness, and triumph over death. One of the malefactors, Luke says, railed on him, but the *other* rebuked him, saying, "Dost thou not fear God, seeing thou art in the same condemnation; and we justly, for we receive the due reward of our deeds, but this man hath done nothing amiss?"

On the surface there is a discrepancy between Matthew and Luke. It is only apparent, and because the harmony is so profound and complete.

When the crucifixion *commenced*, the two robbers, thinking Christ was a malefactor, joined the Jewish rabble, and reviled him. Matthew tells us so much, and leaves us. But John takes us farther inward. The crucifixion proceeds through the weary hours from morning till afternoon. Within the sphere of grosser vision, within the tumult around and the anguish of mortality, one of the malefactors sees Christ as he is, himself as he is, hears him and understands him, and turns to him for salvation and pardon. How all-revealing is the hour! — passed the sphere of carnal perception, passed the maddening paroxysms and the torture of the nails, passed the sound of passion and hate that were raging around the cross into that still haven where all is calm and clear, under the nearing immortality and the subduing spirit of the Lord. In that undertone of indescribable tenderness, which few could have heard who stood amid the storm of rage and the wagging of heads, he says, "Lord, remember me when thou comest into thy kingdom." And Jesus replies, "To-day shalt thou be with me in Paradise."

This narrative affords no ground for the belief that a prevailingly bad life can terminate in a happy and triumphant death. But the narrative does give us some prevision of the inversions of the spiritual world, where judgment is not according to appearances, but according to intrinsic realities. What a contrast have we here between this wild bandit from the mountains and the Jewish Sanhedrim, which condemned and crucified the Lord! — they the most outwardly religious men, grace-hardened in long years of light and privilege; he garbed in the grimness of strife, but preserving a more honest heart and more susceptibility to the Divine mercy: they the heirs of all God's revelations, whose light they never followed; he the heir of small light and privilege, following, very possibly, righteous ends by unlawful means. We get some idea of that state of being to which this tends, and in which it consummates, where splendid externals and grim and horrid coverings are both removed, and man's hidden and intrinsic life is brought out and robed anew. How much susceptibility to the Divine mercy is preserved under heathen darkness, to be awakened under the dawning light and grace of immortality, and how much of impenitence and inhumanity have been confirmed under church privilege, till the Divine grace rebounds from it as from a rock of flint!

CHAPTER X.

THE REAPPEARINGS OF JESUS.

THAT Jesus reappeared to his disciples after his crucifixion, and that his ministry was continued to them with tokens of yet more searching and irresistible power, we may regard as the fundamental fact of the New Testament history. The language and the very life-plan of Jesus prophesied of his resurrection, and the whole subsequent history refers back to it and takes its significance therefrom. Leave this out and the whole record falls into an inexplicable jumble and loses its unity, and Christianity, as a transforming power in human affairs, is a most unaccountable phenomenon.

But it is not strange that a fact of such vast significance should have been apprehended by the first disciples with considerable variations, and that after a short time had elapsed there should have been traditions and rumors concerning it which were very imperfect reflections, if not absolute refractions of the great reality itself. It was a fact partly natural and partly spiritual, partly that is in both worlds, and liable to be misapprehended. We should distinguish the statements of eye-witnesses whose testimony is first hand, or nearly so, from those which are plainly legendary; and we should distinguish the pre-ascension appearances, or those of the "forty days," from the post-ascension which continued for some time afterwards.

There are reasons, as we have shown above, for regarding the twenty-first chapter of the fourth Gospel as an appendix not written by the same hand, but subjoined after John's death.

We have two other witnesses at first hand beside John, — Matthew and Paul. The genuine Mark closes with the eighth verse of the sixteenth chapter, the last twelve verses having been proved by the best evidence, external and internal, to be additions made by a later hand. So that the genuine Mark only gives us the second-hand reports of the women. Luke is a second-hand witness, though nearly the same as first hand if, as we believe, he writes from John's authority.

Paul testifies to a general fact of the utmost significance. According to him, the reappearings of Jesus to his disciples were of a very frequent and familiar character, and a subject of common remark with each other. He appeared to Peter and James individually, and twice to the twelve together, as John has related: facts which Paul must have derived from the Apostles themselves in his intercourse with them; and he appeared to five hundred brethren at once, most of whom were alive when he wrote. Elsewhere Paul refers familiarly to the same general fact. Not long after the vision from whose overpowering glory he was led blind into Damascus, a man came to him on an errand of love, saying that Jesus had appeared to him and given him the message. Paul says nothing of the women who saw the angels, but appeals to Apostles and to living men too multitudinous to call by name. The genuineness of Paul's record the most skeptical have never called in question, and it enables us to understand why the evangelists have not dwelt more at length upon a fact which must have been of universal notoriety among the early believers in Palestine, and therefore did not need repetition.

Among all the witnesses at first hand there is entire agreement, some supplying what others omit; but the general fact rises and rounds upward in congruity, and in its stupendous import under that blending testimony, both on the natural and the spiritual side. None of them tell us that Jesus ate with his disciples after his resurrection. All those accounts are legendary, and they might easily date from the fact that he appeared to them, as he most naturally would, at those sacred social hours when they ate together with tender memorials of his love. None of them tell us that they saw angels; these accounts all come at second hand from the women, and we believe them to have been true, with just such variations as would be made under the excitement of fear and surprise, and which the evangelists have most faithfully recorded as they heard them. All of the accounts are totally inconsistent with the idea that Jesus rose in the unchanged natural body, for then he would have lived over with them the natural life as Lazarus did with his family at Bethany and been subject to death again.[1] He only appeared at intervals of time, never to the Jews who had crucified him, always to his friends and followers when their minds were held under a supernal influence and awe. But up to the time of his ascension he appeared to them in natural form, as one who had been crucified, and showed them his hands and his side, as if in accommodation to their carnal conceptions and sensuous faith. Two of these reappearings are recorded by John, an additional one by Matthew; all three were to the eleven assembled privately together, Thomas only being absent from one of them. This is the sum of the direct testimony. Paul supplies the added information that the reappearings were not confined to the eleven, but were vouchsafed to multitudes who were living when he wrote.

Such were the pre-ascension appearances. But after forty days and after the ascension, there were other reappearings, and they were made with a more overwhelming power and from amid insufferable splen-

[1] We say the *unchanged* natural body without denying that Jesus rose in the natural body. What the change is, from natural body to spiritual, is a subject beyond our grasp till we know better what matter itself is. On this point read the chapter on the "Transparencies of Nature," in Part IV.

dors. All the communications to Paul were of this kind. They were not from one who wore a body which had been crucified, but from a glory above the brightness of the sun at noon-day. He reminds us again and again that his intercourse and communion with this glorified Being was so frequent and of such a nature, that he received from him direct the whole body of Gospel truth which he was to preach, so that he had no need to consult the other Apostles or confer in any way with flesh and blood. He was their peer as much as he would have been by following Jesus through the track of his earthly life. He gives the best evidence of what he says in the broad Catholic Christianity, replete with the life and inspiration of its author which glows through his pages.

John's record, in the Apocalypse is similar. The post-ascension appearances were from amid the same overwhelming glory out of the midst of which he received his message to the constellated churches. The reappearing which Matthew describes, though not post-ascension, was yet, as we infer, near the close of the forty days, and as one period was melting into the other. Not now as at the first two meetings does he stand among them showing them his wounds. He appears far above them and they fall on their faces doubting and afraid, till he comes near and assures them, giving them his final charge with the declaration, "All power is given me in heaven and on the earth."

Such is the report of the eye-witnesses, made with some variations, but the variations are mutually and strongly corroborative. But there is evidence of another kind. It is the common consciousness of the first Christian Church and the first Christian age of the new Power moving upon human nature and rapidly transforming it, as the risen Christ, both in his truth and his spirit, was melting through its depravities and errors. It will not do to ascribe this consciousness to fanatical imagination and allow to it no objective reality. Neither fanatical imaginations nor epileptic swoons change men from the dominion of lust, hatred, deceit, and demoniacal passion to that of love, purity, meekness, and the peace of God ; and from narrow and selfish ends to the most heroic self-sacrifice and the highest moral energy the world had ever known. Dreams and visions which are generated of morbid conditions, and are only subjective, never bring new clearness and vigor to the wasted faculties, never evolve a more perfect manhood from under the old decay. But all this was done, and it was done with the common consciousness that the risen and glorified Christ was in the work as its inspiring life, and again and again was this corroborated by a parting of the clouds, between which he appeared to them from his nearing heavens to guide them. The inauguration of a new era of history in connection with this common consciousness is the complete confirmatory evidence of the resurrection of Jesus Christ.

We should apply our philosophies with great modesty and reserve to such facts as are reported by these witnesses. Difficulties occur. Deny the facts and the epoch which dates from them is wholly inexplicable and the greatest life ever lived on the earth is without unity. Admit the facts and there are difficulties still, but they are of another kind. They are such as are resolvable into our ignorance, into our crude and clumsy pneumatologies or our very superficial knowledge of laws which are subtile and all pervasive, and which we only see as fragmentary now. Touching the resurrection of Christ we look from below upward. We stand gazing into heaven, and so we look at the clouds on the darker side; when we look from heaven downward the same clouds will be illumined wreaths lying off on the world below.

In the death and resurrection of Christ the natural body saw no corruption. In this mainly is his transition distinguishable from ours. But there are considerations connected with it of vast significance. The transforming power of our own interior life over the natural body which is its clothing and exfiguration continues up to the moment of death. There it ceases, and the immortal being must be extricated from his mortal coverings. He has no power to extrude them and return them uncorrupted to their native elements and so he leaves a corpse as his legacy to the earth. But the Life made flesh in Jesus Christ is not to be measured by the weak and languid pulses of ours. It was nearer the infinite source and was the fullness of the Godhead bodily. That a Spirit like his should not need extrication from the bonds of death but should rapidly transform them and turn them by a living process into their native ethers, leaving no corpse to see corruption, is consonant with all that is told us of his birth, of his Divine Life transfiguring the natural form that invested it as that Life was growing deep and full and too resplendent for its earthly foliage.

What is the change signified by the ascension of Christ? A higher and more perfect pneumatology will show, we doubt not, that death is something very different from what our childish imaginations have made it; that there are no breaks and chasms in our continuous being; that, therefore, the first condition after death is in some sort of congruity with the condition before death; that the spiritual body evolved from the natural does not put off at once all its natural appearances and adaptations.[1] Hence the pre-ascension appearances of the "forty days," when Jesus showed his disciples his hands and his side, saying, "A spirit hath not flesh and bones as ye see me to have." But when the Divine Life from

[1] Swedenborg in his very rational pneumatology illustrates this at large, showing that the changes from an earthly to a heavenly condition through death are not made by crossing over chasms, but by the life within, unfolding in an orderly way and robing itself anew, so that the natural appearances just before death and just after may be similar.

within was ultimated in its full power and brightness, all the remnants of the natural life disappeared, and Jesus was only ensphered with the celestial glories. And this was the ascension of Christ! Type and representation of our own transition, if we follow humbly through his upward and radiant pathway! After the ascension his disciples only saw him in their more heavenly frames and beholdings.

There are those who talk of intuition as the surest and highest evidence, but who do not seem to be aware of the application of the truth which they invoke. All other intuitions pale into dimness before those which attest the resurrection of Jesus Christ. All other revelations of God in humanity compared with this are as starlight which precedes the dawn. Not the vision of apostles alone, not the word of eyewitnesses on the great morning and during the "forty days;" but the *consensus* of Christendom for eighteen hundred years is cumulative evidence for the reappearings of Jesus. The highest experiences and profoundest introversions of the purest and healthiest minds along this whole track of the centuries bring them into correspondency with the risen and glorified Saviour; not by open vision, but by signs and tokens quite as trustworthy. When men have been turned from darkness to light, from the slavery of lust and sin to the joyous service of the living God; when the Divine Voice has come down upon the stormy seas of passion in the soul commanding audience, "still as night or summer's noon-tide air;" when all its higher powers have been waked into life; faith, sympathy, disinterested love, tenderness towards God and towards everything that breathes; when the peace has come at last where storms and conflicts are no more; it has all been with the profoundest consciousness of a risen Saviour near at hand, with his assurance, "All power is given me both in heaven and upon the earth." If the intuitions of the soul are to be appealed to, what are its shadowy gropings compared with these sun-bright beholdings of so many of the best and healthiest minds through a period of eighteen hundred years?

CHAPTER XI.

THE PERSON OF JESUS CHRIST.

THE four biographers of Jesus have given no description of his person, such as his form, figure, features, expression of countenance, walk, gesture, tones of voice and style of speech or eloquence. The reason is partly that moral painting after the modern style was remote from their thought and purpose, simple narrative being all they aim at; and there was a further reason, for the subject-matter of the divine message so controlled and subordinated the manner as to blend with it and become a part of it, and they never thought of separating one from the other.

In reading these biographies, however, it must occur to any one that such things could not have been done nor such words spoken in a way comporting with our ordinary methods of utterance. There is a class of writers who, looking at Jesus only from the natural side, and ignoring or denying a large portion of the record, find in him an amiable young man, of sweet and winning manners, almost feminine, which endeared him to his followers, and gained the affections of little children and Syrian maids;—a remarkable and promising youth cut off by an untimely death. Herein they discern those traits of moral beauty which cannot be mistaken, and which beam forth along the whole pathway of Jesus of Nazareth. But let any one take this portraiture as expressing his entire character, and go through his history with it, and he will find a whole range of facts which are utterly inexplicable, and that he has not yet seen the person of Jesus Christ. Though his biographers attempt no such portraiture, it comes of itself, and gathers consistence, clearness, and brightness in the imagination, as we read their story. It is that of supernal power and majesty, always in reserve under these lineaments of moral beauty and gentleness. This comes to us from casual expressions which they let fall here and there, and more yet from the impression which his person and manner made upon their minds, and the minds of the multitudes. We are to remember that they seldom understood the import of his doctrine, while their sensibilities were stirred sometimes to their lowest depths; and that this effect, therefore, must be ascribed to the tone and manner of its utterance. At the close of the Sermon on the Mount, crowds were struck with astonishment because he taught as one having authority, not as the teachers of the law. To get the whole meaning of this, we must reproduce the scene to ourselves. Moses was the supreme authority in all the teaching of that day; as binding and as sacred as if they heard it audibly from Mount Sinai. Here is a man who quotes no precedent, acknowledges no authority, but standing up before the people, pushes Moses and all his special code clean out of the way, and with only the formula, "I say unto you," legislates to the world from the immediate conceptions and revelations of his own mind. What amiable young Jew could have done this? What man of ordinary presence could have done it, without raising a shout of derision from the multitude? This man did it in such wise as to fill them with a sense of wonder. And it shows that they had some vision, however dim, of a moral power and majesty towering above Sinai itself.

It is no explanation of the authority of Jesus over the crowds that came to him, to ascribe it to the miracles which he wrought. If the miraculous power was merely something adjoined to him as a common man, he would have excited the same curiosity as the wonder-workers and jugglers of his day. His miraculous works were plainly the emanations of his own being, the forthgoing of that Divine force which gave command to his words. Not merely the works themselves, but the mind and grace beaming through them so as to determine their manner and adaptation, impressed the multitude and held them as with a spell. Hence people approach him as one clothed with royalty. They come "worshipping," that is, bowing in adoration, or they come "kneeling," or they come "falling at his feet," or "trembling and falling down to him."[1] Remembering the air of command and authority, felt always in his presence, and its subduing power over the minds of men, many passages in his biography otherwise inexplicable need no explanation, — the money-changers vacating the temple courts at his word; the police officers going to arrest him, but cowering before him as they come into his presence; his walking unharmed among the enraged multitude, as at Nazareth, where they were prompted to throw him down a precipice but did not dare to lay hands on his person; the fear and vacillation of Pilate in the palace at his final examination. Often he speaks to the people and holds them by the power of his words when it is plain that his meaning is quite above their range, and that it is the manner not the subject-matter that amazes and even convinces them. On the great day of the Feast of the Tabernacles, for instance, when they were pouring out water around the altar, Jesus arrests the ceremony, standing above it and calling aloud, "If any man thirst let him come unto me and drink." "He that believeth on me, out of his breast shall flow rivers of living water." Not a word of this could his hearers have understood as to its interior meaning. But many of the crowd said to one another on hearing it, "This is certainly the Prophet." "This is the

Matt. xv. 25, xvii. 14, xx. 20; Mark i. 40, x. 17; Luke viii. 41, 47.

Christ." And his enemies present, and wishing to arrest him, did not dare to lift a hand against him.

Even after his arrest there was a lingering fear in the minds of his enemies, lest some supernatural agency should take him out of their hands, for even at the cross when the drugs were brought to him to drink, some of them said, "Hold! let us see whether Elijah is coming to take him down."

Though his biographers do not describe to us the expression of his eye and countenance, they more than intimate their efficacy and influence. Sometimes when his hearers were astounded at his words the Evangelist says he spake "looking around" or "looking at them;" or again, when the cavillers came to ensnare him, he "looked at them with anger;" or again, when the young ruler came kneeling to him, he loved him, "looking upon him," — passages which plainly imply that power and grace went out from him, not merely in his words, but in the beamings and flashings of his countenance.[1]

In the walk of Jesus with his disciples, we find none of that kind of intercourse which they had with each other. There is confidence, love, tenderness; none of that entire interchange of mind and lighter sentiment which we find among familiars. True they stand with him on the common ground of humanity and friendship, but they are conscious all

[1] Mark x. 23-27, iii. 5.

the while of a Divine sphere of Being rising above them and beyond their sight and comprehension, beneath which they are held in mysterious awe. This feeling seems to have grown deeper and stronger after his transfiguration. It was their sense of his power and majesty, always felt but never understood, which drew them to him at the first in the bonds of discipleship, made them forsake their business at once and follow him, and held their minds in daily expectation that, in some way unknown to themselves, he was to break upon the world as the conqueror of the Roman power. No personal attractions or amiability of deportment could have thus wrought upon the minds of the people; no power of working miracles could have invested an obscure peasant of Galilee in those attributes which so separated him from all other men as to inspire a reverence and fear more profound and pervading than any inspired by the glare of earthly royalties.

The tones of voice in which a man's words are spoken, generally measure the extent and the depth of his moral power and influence. They are the soul of all speech. The grandest speech without them may fall frigid and powerless, whereas truths which had seemed commonplace and worn out, may be so reinspired with them as not only to become new, but pierce the soul with depths of meaning never before dreamed of, and fill it with tremblings of hope and fear. Tones can neither be assumed nor imitated;

nor can they be reported. Their power can only be represented by the effect which they produce. Whitefield's preaching which so shook the crowds and swayed them, owed its power primarily to the tones that inspired it, for his printed sermons contain nothing but the commonplaces of the received Christianity.

We may faintly conceive, but we cannot adequately represent how truths new-born in such a nature as that of Jesus would be toned and uttered; nay, how the most common and familiar speech of a nature so inspired would vibrate through the hearts of his hearers. If we take into full account this element of moral and spiritual power, we shall be saved a great deal of futile criticism pertaining to the miracles wrought by "the voice of the Son of Man." His manner evidently was simple and undemonstrative, but the tones of his voice searched the very centres of being, melted their frozen springs of life, and set them free. How careful the evangelists are to preserve the very words he spoke, to which such wonderful effects were traced; rather how the words clung to the memory, and would not go out of it, and though common words were untranslatable into any other language! The little girl who had expired, he takes by the hand, with the words, "*Talitha cumi*," and the little girl came back to life and rose up. To the deaf man he says, "*Ephatha*," and his ears are opened. These were Syriac words; the language spoken by our Saviour in his intercourse with men. They were common words. Why does the Evangelist retain them when writing in Greek? Because, as Dr. Furness has said, "they were severed as by a stroke of lightning from all other words," not merely, however, because the disciples saw the effect which they produced, but because the tones in which they were uttered made them untranslatable; tones which so searched the very life-centres as to touch the fountains of existence, and make them flow with healing power through the physical frame. These tones, not because of their loudness, but because a divine compassion more pervading and far-reaching than ever vibrated in a human voice was thrilling through them, found Lazarus in his death-sleep. Jesus "cried with a loud voice," says the Evangelist; literally with a great voice (φονῇ μεγάλῃ), great because of its power to reach the seat of consciousness and make the frozen currents of life to melt and start anew. And in that cry upon the cross, "Eloi, Eloi, lama sabachthani," there seems no other reason for preserving the original words, unless it be that the tones, not the words, shivered through the hearts of the standers-by, and startled them with thoughts of a suffering that was more than mortal, as if the heart then breaking had drawn into its divine recesses the woes of a whole race, which found utterance in its expiring wail.

With these conceptions of the power and majesty

of Jesus, we cannot look with satisfaction, or even patience, on those paintings and engravings designed to represent his person, and which are put into so many picture-frames, and so many "Lives of Christ." The features of some of them are feminine, some of them Jewish, all of them the feeble conceptions of artists who ought to keep their poor ideals out of sight. The only portraiture, it seems to us, which any earnest believer can regard with satisfaction, is the one which dawns upon his rising faith ; nor will that satisfy him as anything which he can fix and frame, for it will change as he changes, and as the Christ of consciousness grows into the image and likeness of the living God.

PART IV.

THE JOHANNEAN THEOLOGY.

"It breathes the air of peace, yet sounds at times like a peal of thunder from the other world; it soars majestically like the eagle towards the uncreated source of light, and yet hovers as gently as a dove over the earth ; it is sublime as a seraph, yet simple as a child ; high and serene as the heaven, deep as the unfathomable sea."

SCHAFF.

CHAPTER I.

THE COSMOLOGY OF PLATO.

THEOLOGY is the knowledge of God. Religion is that knowledge so used and applied, and so entering into human experience and the personal life that it draws man to God and binds him in loving fealty to the throne. There may be theology without religion, for God may be apprehended by the intellect alone, and then the idea of Him floats idle as a speculation and is never converted into conduct. There cannot be any true religion without theology, for where there is no knowledge of God there is either atheism or blind superstition. And just in that degree that the knowledge of the Divine becomes clear and sufficing is human nature swayed and renovated by it and drawn upward into the Divine communion.

The Christology of the New Testament and that of the fourth Gospel preëminently, has for eighteen centuries brought men into conscious relations with God, more filial and tender than any other work has done. This undoubtedly is the highest and the ultimate evidence both of its authenticity and genuineness; for any work which opens in human nature the deepest fountains of devotion and joy comes to it with the most authentic tidings of the divine nature and name. But what is to be said if there are very good and capable persons, and very keen critics withal, whom the book does not affect in this way? Why, there is nothing to be said. But it is an urgent motive to study a book with expectant minds, when men like Clement, Origen, Augustine, Chrysostom, Neander, and Schleiermacher have found in its theology the key-note of all the harmonies divine and human, and the open entrance to the knowledge and fruition of God.

After all, however, let us confess that none of our statements are likely to be exhaustive. None of our creeds have crystallized the whole Johannean theology, or probably ever will. When we have put every thing visible and tangible to us into our formulas, there is still a divine atmosphere which infolds us, and which we breathe and live in though unseen, and there are clefts in the heavens still higher, suggesting fields of truth not yet open to our gaze.

The theology of the New Testament, and of the fourth Gospel especially, took peculiar form and determination, because it collided with preceding or contemporaneous systems of belief. There are in the New Testament traces of Platonism, and of systems into which Platonism developed, and which, in the time of Christ and for more than a century afterward, were in constant flower and fruitage. No exposition of the Johannean theology can be made tolerably intelligible without some clear apprehension of the leading features of the philosophy and the cosmology to which it stands contrasted, and which consciously or not determined the moulds in which it was cast.

It is not necessary to reproduce the whole system of Plato; and the best scholars who have attempted it have found it no easy task. It is to be gathered from the Platonic dialogues whose interlocutors conflict with each other, and which of them are personating Plato himself it is very difficult sometimes to decide. But two of his latest and most elaborate productions were the "Republic" and the "Timæus," and there is no doubt they give us the ripened wisdom of the master-mind of antiquity. They were written after he had completed his travels, and gathered and compacted the highest truths of the Grecian and Oriental philosophies, and fused them into a system of his own; and the workings of his genius in their reproduction come the nearest to divine inspiration of anything we know of within the compass of what is absurdly called profane literature. True, he leaves the inductive method and breaks away from sense altogether, and his science would provoke the derision of any sophomore; but his undazzled imagination quickened by a pure moral instinct gives him a vision of divine truths which science had groped after in vain.

Timæus, the chief speaker in the dialogue that bears his name, is a Pythagorean; but he is giving the thought of Plato colored deeply with the Pythagorean philosophy. We may leave out the physiology, as not necessary to our purpose. Its cosmology becomes important, and with collateral lights of interpretation from the other dialogues is capable of being clearly evolved and described. It is the highest utterance that comes to us from the ante-christian ages, and has been called, not inaptly, "The Hymn of the Universe." It did not claim to be the absolute truth, but the most rational probability which the human intellect was able to achieve.

Three postulates are assumed. First a Demiurgus, or divine artificer. This is not an unconscious force, but a being of personal attributes. He is the Supremely Good. But lest the Good should be mistaken for an abstract quality, or a mere dynamic force, it is described also as a Divine Intelligence. It is the *Nous*, or Supreme Intellect; under which designation the Good is conceived as determined by an infinite REASON, and so giving its impress upon all things where it operates, of the highest order and beauty. Thus the Agathon and the Nous are names which are used interchangeably. It is important to bear in mind this two-fold designation and to remember that in the Platonic hypothesis not the Good merely, but INTELLIGENCE or MIND was in the beginning of things and was the presiding and constructive force in the architecture of the universe.

The second postulate of the Platonic cosmology is the ideals or archetypes, after the model of which all things were to be made. They were co-eternal with the Demiurgus, existing not within his mind but objective to it, apart in their own heavenly locality. They were the patterns of all beauty and perfection. They were timeless, for time implies succession and change; but since the archetypes were unchangeably perfect, they had no past and no future, and so were without time. Some writers, it is true, have tried to make these ideals to exist only within the divine intellect, its ideas or subjective states. Herein they modernize Plato, for he makes them separate entities occupying their own intelligible world, no more existing within the divine mind than the stereotype plates of the printer exist within his mind. The ideals are objectively things of the divine contemplation though subject to the divine control. They correspond in some sort to Kant's things-in-themselves, — primal essences, that is, which exist within and beyond phenomena, and which remain after phenomena have passed off and left them bare. Only Kant denied that we could ever shake hands with them, or know the least about them in this life, and across the gulf of phenomena. Plato, we shall see, contrived wings on which to cross the chasm and soar, with his All-hail, into the midst of them. These archetypes existed as both general and special; as one perfect eternal whole, subject to no increase or diminution, but comprehending in itself all possibilities of class, order, genera, and species.

The third postulate of the Platonic cosmology is a primitive chaos which had existed from the beginning. It is first described as wild and disorderly matter, containing the prime elements of earth, air, fire, and water, subject to no beneficent law, but eternally discordant and surging only by indeterminate chance. But in the latter portion of the Timæus Plato corrects himself, and renders this primitive chaos not as visible and disorderly matter, but a wild *fundamentum* of existence, the womb of some *prima mater*, dark and evil, but still an outlying chaos of indeterminate chance.

Such being the postulates and antecedent possibilities, the Demiurgus proceeds to the architecture of the universe. He constructs the best possible from the material at hand. He takes the eternal and perfect patterns, the ideal earth, air, fire, and water, and dips them down into chaos, where they become clothed in visible and tangible body, — become material, earth, air, fire, and water, — and hence arose this Cosmos of beauty and order. The whole realm of ideals thus became incarnate or clothed upon, and so to the primal chaos succeeded the vast system of sun, moon, and stars, with the earth at the centre of the whole. In this constructive process all the contents of the primal chaos were used up, so that nothing was left outside to act upon the new order of things. The primal chaos, however, though wrought into the Cosmos, was never entirely subdued, but was always a disturbing element. The Demiurgus did the best he could with it by incarnating the ideals within it, but it still remained an evil and deceptive covering, so that phenomena or sensuous appearances are not realities, but ever-changing phantasms, not the perfect envisagement of the eternal ideals, and therefore not the ground of knowledge but of opinion only.

So the Cosmos arose. But as yet it was only a beautiful corpse. It must have a soul and be alive. This soul the Demiurgus proceeded to generate. It was constituted in a threefold proportion. It consisted of the harmonic, pure and simple; the discordant, pure and simple; and the harmonic and discordant mingled together. The soul thus constituted he infused through the Cosmos, stretching it from the centre through all its remotest parts, giving to the whole a *communis sensus* running throughout as on living nerves. Thus endowed the Cosmos became an animated being, though of many members; a visible god, the most beautiful image of the invisible, having the impress of the Nous, the Divine Reason itself. Then began its motions and revolutions and the endless processions of Time.

The Cosmos was constituted a perfect sphere, and with the exception of the earth, which is fixed near the centre, it turns perpetually on an axis or spindle that passes through it, and sweeps round in one circular motion the planets and the stars, which are portions of it. But though the Cosmos itself was an animated being and a visible god, the Demiurgus constituted within it other gods, the Cosmos being the genera of which the others were species. The earth, the planets, the sun and moon and the fixed stars, were endowed severally and specially, each with a soul and consciousness of its own, so that each of them became an animated being eternal and divine. Let not the reader be puzzled with this Platonic conception of gods special, existing within another god which is generic and all-comprehensive. Plato conceived of it, we presume, somewhat as we conceive the life of the plant determined from that of nature in general, or as we represent to ourselves angels and men existing within the all-pervading Deity, their consciousness flowering out individually from one broader and more generic, which is the ground of them all and underlies them all.

The earth was the first-born of these gods individually constituted; was placed stationary at the centre of the Cosmos to preside over its axial motions, and thus made the ruler of Night and Day.[1] Next were

[1] We generally follow Mr. Grote's exposition of the difficult passages in Plato, but here we cannot. It is a question whether Plato teaches that the earth rotates on a common axis with the planets, the sun, and the stars, that is, on the spindle on which the whole Cosmos turns ; or whether it is fixed at the centre while the others move round it. Grote thinks that in the Platonic astronomy it ro-

the fixed stars or stellar gods, which were placed on the extreme circle of the Cosmos; and last, the planetary, which constitute our solar system with its revolving orbs. But in the bodies of our solar and planetary system the discordant soul was largely infused. Hence their irregular motions. Besides their revolution on the cosmic axis towards the right, they have a counter revolution of their own towards the left, though not rapid enough to overcome the other in which they are always borne along. But in the sidereal circle the harmonic soul inspires

tates with the rest. How then could it be the ruler of night and day, since it would always expose the same hemisphere to the sun, while the other hemisphere would be in perpetual night? Grote thinks Plato did not see the inconsistency. The following is the passage in the Timæus: *Γῆν δὲ τρόφον ἡμετέραν, εἰλλομένην δὲ περὶ τὸν διὰ παντὸς πόλον τεταμένον, φυλακα καὶ δημιουργὸν νυκτὸς τε καὶ ἡμέρας ἐμηκανήσατο, πρώτην καὶ πρεσβυτάτην θεῶν ὅσοι ἐντὸς οὐρανοῦ γεγόνασι.* "Then he made the earth our common nourisher, which being *crowded* round the axis which extends through all things, is the keeper and artificer of night and day, as well as the first and eldest of the gods that have been generated in the universe."

Mr. Grote understands *εἰλλομένην* to mean "*packed round*," so as to be fixed fast to the axis and move with it. It is not necessary to suppose this. The axis was like a spindle through a series of spools, some of which might be stationary while the others rotate. But Plato must be held no way responsible for our laws of gravitation, nor any of our modern physics. His worlds are all gods alive and conscious, and the earth is the elder born, ruling from the centre like the commander of an army, not by physical laws but by moral, so that under this ruler they dispense night and day by moving in majestic order and with rhythmic melodies. Even the spindle at the centre we imagine was an ideal one.

every motion; hence the stars of the upper firmament move with the most perfect rhythmic order, discourse the most heavenly sphere-music, and sing together their everlasting song.

Thus the gods were generated by the Demiurgus, the only gods towards which Plato seems to have had any faith or reverence. For the polytheism of his times, copied from Hesiod and commonly received, he has evidently a profound contempt, thinly veiled, however, and insinuated rather than expressed, as the fate of Socrates warned him of the consequences.

Having formed the Cosmos, and all the stellar and planetary gods that live within it and make a part of it, the Demiurgus next proceeded to the formation of man. But man was to be mortal; therefore the Demiurgus, who was essentially immortal, does not create man directly and in his own name, but he commits the work to other and inferior hands. The gods whom he had formed are assembled, and to them is confided the construction of the species next below them. He tells them that they (the gods) will be immortal, not in their own nature but by his appointment; that the Cosmos, however, is not complete; that other and lower races are to be constituted; that *he* cannot undertake their construction, because they would thereby be rendered immortal; but that they (the gods) are to undertake the work in imitation of the power which had just been exercised in the formation of themselves. The Demiurgus supplies an immortal element, to which the gods are to join bodily and mortal elements to be drawn from the body of the Cosmos.

There was a remnant left of the cosmical soul, an over-soul which had not been used up, but greatly inferior in excellence and purity. This remnant the Demiurgus compounds anew, and then divides and distributes into a number of souls equal to the number of the fixed stars. Each soul previous to its mortal incarnation was to be sent to its own congenial star, there to be carried round in the cosmic revolutions, and enjoy the contemplation of supernal wisdom, and hear the sweet music of the harmonic spheres. In this pre-natal state the destiny of each soul in the long future was to be unrolled to it, the mysteries of the universe explained, and the heavenly knowledge drank in, afterwards to be overlaid and buried under the swathings of mortality. In this pre-natal state it was to learn that at an appointed hour it must be joined with a mortal body, and with two inferior and mortal souls along with it; that it must descend into this earthly incarnation, be subject to pleasure and pain, and fear and anger; encounter the irrational enemies of the lower souls and the mortal body; that these enemies must be overcome and subdued as a condition after death of reascending to its native star. But if it was itself overcome and failed in the combat, it would descend after death into lower conditions ; into the body of some inferior animal, would continue to sink into lower and lower animal natures, until its victory had been achieved. That done and not before, it could reascend to the enjoyment of the supernal wisdom and the music of the harmonic spheres.

The gods having received these instructions, proceeded to carry out this plan of the Demiurgus. The human souls were first distributed each to its congenial star, and then born into bodies which the gods constructed from the body of the Cosmos, that is, from the four elements, of fire, air, earth, and water, to be returned to the Cosmos again. But into this body they placed also two mortal souls, there to be the accompaniment of the immortal soul descending from its star, and to antagonize it in the combat of life. The immortal soul they placed in the head ; one of the mortal souls they placed in the thorax, and made it the seat of passion, anger, and rage ; the other and still baser one they placed below the diaphragm, and made the seat of sensual and beastly appetites. Such in the Platonic philosophy was to be the conflict between the higher and lower natures of man.

At birth, and for some time afterward, the celestial nature — the soul descended from its star, — is completely dulled and muffled, and does not report itself in the consciousness. Gradually, however, it makes itself to be felt and heard ; and when its behests are obeyed, gleams of its pre-natal condition and knowledge, and murmurs of the sphere-melodies like snatches of far-off music, come over the inward sense and draw it upward. By contemplation of the glories of the Cosmos, not through sight alone, but through the rational and immortal soul, passion and appetite are held subordinate and become its lackeys; the celestial nature triumphs in the conflict, and the soul reascends at death to its congenial star. Not so if it basely yields and the battle goes against it. Then it descends by a series of degradations through lower and lower natures, — the Pythagorean doctrine of the transmigration of souls.

Plato reverses the steps of modern naturalism. It develops man out of the polypus or the oyster through all the ascending grades of reptile and quadruped, till the human form rises erect and looks into the skies. Plato sees in all animal natures a reversed and degraded human nature, where the victory had been lost in the triumph of the mortal and bestial souls over the celestial, or of sense over reason. Originally, at the first formation of man, there was no division of sex. Pure manhood was the primitive shape of our unfallen humanity. But men who became cowards transmigrated after death into the forms of women, and thereafter the race was bisexual. Men whose minds were only speculative, light, and fantastic, transmigrated in the form of birds that flit through the air. Men who became enslaved to bestial appetites, in whom the star-soul was overlaid and lost, bent earthward lower and lower, their heads elongated downward till they were prepared for the bodies of quadrupeds, in which they walk on all-fours and look earthward and feed from the ground alone. Some become still more bestial, cleave closer to the earth and become reptiles. Those who are buried still deeper in sense, become too stupid to live in air, and transmigrate as fishes of the sea, or as oysters that live in mud. Thus the range of animal existence is not an original creation. It is man fallen from his primitive state into forms of degradation of remoter and remoter resemblance to the form of his celestial manhood till it is almost lost and disappears. It is the mirror in which man may read in the long and ever-darkening imagery the effect of the slavery of the celestial nature to the irrational and the bestial.

This is Plato's Book of Genesis. Its darker pages he hurries over, charmed with its brighter ones; and he ends in a strain of exultation and delight: "Our discourse about the universe is ended. It has received its complement of animation, mortal and immortal; it has become greatest, best, most beautiful and most perfect: a visible animated Being comprehending all things visible, a manifest God, the image of the cogitable God; this Uranus, one and only-begotten."

CHAPTER II.

CHARACTER AND INFLUENCE OF THE PLATONIC COSMOLOGY.

THE Platonic Cosmology was prophetic of some of the highest truths of Christianity. All the Greek and oriental religions which had preceded it, not grossly polytheistic, broke down in materialism, pantheism, or atheism. Plato's system may have found its root and stem among them, but it rises out of them and above them into a clear and positive monotheism. It anticipates the first grand annunciation of the Christian revelation, by placing the Word at the beginning and not at the end of creation. Reason and intelligence were coeval with primal being. At the end was the Word, says Pantheism. Reason and intelligence are the last evolution of natural forces, whose beginnings were unintelligent and unconscious matter quick with life at some unknown centre; developing outward into the various forms of vegetable and animal, and last of all developing a human brain. This fine secretion, deposited in a skull, is the last and best organized essence, and out of this come reason and thought. Reason first appears at the outermost limit of the Cosmos, and flashes forth as a pale fringe of light on the circumference. That is the logos of pantheism. And such with insignificant variations were the antecedent Greek Cosmologies, not polytheistic, from Thales to Plato. The only apparent exception is found in Anaxagoras, and this is hardly more than apparent, for the Nous, says Mr. Grote, which figures in his philosophy, scarcely rises above the rank of material agencies.

In the beginning was the Word, says the cosmology of Plato, postulating the prime truth of the highest theism. The Nous, or Divine Reason, was at the origin of things. It preceded all development, presided over it and gave to the Cosmos its own divine beauty and order. His system clears itself alike of polytheism and pantheism. He sees the infinite mind in its unity; differenced from the universe, yet ruling over it and through it and constructing all its forms after the patterns of the supreme perfection. Except in the Mosaic writings there was no higher and purer theism.

Plato does not grasp the Christian doctrine of Providence, but he approximates and foreshadows it. The Cosmos is all alive. The smallest part is related to every other part and to the whole. It has a conscious soul that pervades every atom, and brings tidings from its outmost limit to its centre. The smallest star, as it goes round in its radiant circle, adores its Maker, and like an angel sings. The highest soarings of modern poetry, in Plato, are sober prose. What in Shakespeare and Coleridge are momentary flights of imagination, in Plato are symmetrical truths wrought by splendid mosaic in a system of the universe. The mere scientist can afford to laugh over the Platonic physiology and astronomy; but his analysis accomplished, dead matter is all which he has left. He cannot join the severed members again so as to make a living whole. He is like the boy who hacks the bird in pieces, but thereby loses its warble forever. Plato, with all his mistakes of analysis, more than atones for them in his majestic synthesis, which gives us not a dead but a living universe.

His doctrine of human nature on one side is not only beautiful but divinely true. The immortal soul that is in man opens by an internal way towards the soul of the Cosmos, and through that towards its divine Maker. It never loses the first imprints of the supreme perfection stamped upon it from the ideals. They may be obscured and overlaid by mortality and corruption; they may recede from the consciousness altogether, but they are never lost. Some day they may come out again in radiant outline. Some day the star-music of a pre-existent state may wake in the soul its sweetest memories, and breathe through it the lost harmonies again. Even on its downward course through the animal degradations, it is possibly careering towards its aphelion, where it may turn and on a brightening pathway regain the heaven it started from.

Plato's doctrine of the animal kingdom, though false in form, has yet substantial truths, truths which even under the light of the Christian revelation sometimes get loosed from our grasp. The meanest animal has not an isolated and altogether forlorn existence. The brutes are kith and kin to the human beings that rule over them. They are not original creations, but the outcome of our fallen humanity in lower forms. They reflect back upon us its woes and sorrows, and touch a chord of tenderness, like the human grove in Dante's hell, which must not be rent too rudely. At the same time they hold up to man the mirror in which he sees, in the long and ever darkening perspective, the penalties of subordinating his higher nature to the lower, and suffering the celestial soul to be trodden down out of sight under cruel passions or swinish appetites.

The defects and the inhering vice of the system seen under the light of Christianity must already be obvious to the reader. Its dualism works mischief from centre to circumference, and is destructive of any real unity between God, the world, and humanity. The divine *Nous* was not alone in the beginning. An outlying chaos was also in the beginning; a ὕλη of disorder, essentially evil, coeval with God and co-eternal. This with the ideals is the material already at hand out of which the Demiurgus must build the universe. Hence he is never a creator but only an architect. He builds as best he can, but some of his material is bad and continues bad when wrought into the building, an element of unsoundness and destruction. Matter, the element drawn from the ὕλη, is essentially evil, but forms the outward body and enrobement of the visible Cosmos and all which it contains. Though compelled to an external and apparent order, it is the corrupt and poisonous garment of the soul and the lying element in all material phenomena. Hence nothing is as it seems to be. External nature only presents to us a troop of apparitions, always coming and vanishing. but giving no solid foundation for human knowledge. The perfect ideals are behind them and in them as their soul and essence, but they get no adequate expression or incarnation. The Nous, or Divine Mind, is in first things, but never in last. He is the Alpha but never the Omega ; in the beginning but never in the ultimation. God is at the centre, but the hylic covering of matter is on the circumference, — the evil garment in which all essences are enveloped. Hence there is no pathway through Nature up to God. The universe can never be known through the senses. The immortal soul in man must ascend by an internal way to the soul of the Cosmos, quitting sense as much as possible, which is always dragging it towards the brute and the reptile. The Demiurgus affords no direct access to himself from his human subjects, but one indirect and circuitous through the Cosmos, — his first and best image and manifestation.

In the Platonic philosophy sin is not an intrinsic, but an extrinsic evil. It comes from without, not from within. It belongs to the sensuous coat, which the soul, descending from its native star, is compelled to put on and wear through its earthly existence. Moral evil is removed not by an inward divine cleansing, but by being shelled off through the long and dreary process of transmigration. Why the soul was not kept in its native star, there to move through its celestial circle forever, instead of being muffled and smothered in these poisonous coverings, Plato does not tell us, for it was evidently an ugly mystery in his own contemplations.

Since the Platonic theology does not bring man into direct relations with God, it could not search the deeper mysteries of human nature, and reveal them to its own consciousness. This is nowhere more manifest than in Plato's estimate of woman. The feminine element in humanity, which is the interior, higher, and more divine, Plato makes exterior, lower, and more bestial. The masculine element, which is exterior, coarser, and lower down, he makes first and highest. By this indecent inversion of the two essentials of humanity he makes woman only a degradation of the species, a connecting link between man and the animals, drawing him down towards the reptiles, not between men and gods, drawing him upwards towards the celestial abodes.

Platonism could be a religion for the philosophic

and contemplative few, but offered no boon to the toiling multitude buried under hylic coverings too deep to become conscious of their celestial lineage. The parting of the ways right and left satisfied no principle of divine justice, for on the right were only a few men of æsthetic culture and civil and social privilege, who drawing inward and upward from all mundane things and all sensuous influence sought communion with the soul of the Cosmos and thereby found pictured within them the ideals of the First Perfect and First Fair; while on the left were the mass of mankind immersed in sense and in affairs on their way downward through the dreary road of transmigration. The inevitable result of the Platonic cultus was ascetic communions, separated from the world to the solitary and lazy intuitions of their own souls.

It had a twofold development, in both directions sinking down from the high level of Plato. In one direction it sank to the Nihilism of the New Academy.[1] In the other direction it sank into Gnosticism, which was only saved from Nihilism by coming in contact with the Jewish and Christian religions, which it sought to take up and transform in its omnivorous receptivity. It furnished Gnosticism with the prime material out of which all its systems arose and flourished. We have already displayed the outline of these systems. In the present chapter we will show

[1] See Part I., chapter viii.

the historic connection between them and Christianity, and especially with the Johannean theology as formulated in the fourth Gospel.

Alexandria in Egypt, at the advent of Christ, was next after Rome the most flourishing city in the Roman Empire. It was the centre of commercial intercourse between the east and the west. Moreover, it was the centre whence learning and philosophy were diffused throughout the then civilized world. Its population was largely composed of Jews and Greeks, not the Jews of a despised race, as they subsequently became, but a people distinguished for wealth, learning, and refinement. Philo, writing at or near the Christian era, says that two out of the five divisions of the city were occupied by Jews; and that in Alexandria and the other cities of Egypt they numbered one million inhabitants. The Greek language had become the language both of learning and commerce, and was spoken in the principal cities of the east and the west. It was the language of Alexandria, and opened to the Jewish population the treasures of Greek literature. The city became a second Athens, from whose schools and libraries the Greek philosophy had a vastly wider reach and influence than in the times of Plato four hundred years before. Here Plato lived again, and for more than one hundred and fifty years had been moulding the thought of the most enlightened and contemplative minds. His works were studied and commented upon as a divine fountain of truth. His language became the language of the Jewish Scriptures in the famous Septuagint version, and it was the language of worship in the synagogues of Alexandria. Jewish writers endeavored to adapt Judaism to the Greek mind by making Moses talk like Plato. They imported the Genesis of the Timæus into that of the Pentateuch, and then charged Plato with borrowing from Moses. Philo breaks away from the rugged and narrow literalism of Judaism by assuming that the letter, like the hylic covering of the Platonic cosmology, is only for ignorant and sensuous men, who can only be governed through their fears; that God is far within and above, whose true sons find Him by an internal road away from the letter and from sense into the heart of the Divine love. There are two Jehovahs, he says in the Old Testament; one of them is presented as a man with human form and passions as the governor of ignorant masses; the other is not a man, and is only to be known by the wise and virtuous few. The Logos, or Creative Word of the Jewish Scriptures, he subordinates to the Supreme Deity. He calls it a second god, king, angel, high-priest, first-born son of the Highest, and to this sub-deity he ascribes the creation of the visible universe and the promulgation of the law from Mount Sinai. In this Logos he says the ideals, or patterns of visible things, preëxisted, a perfect intelligible world from which the visible was copied out. We agree entirely with

Mosheim and Dorner that Philo in his own thought did not herein make the Logos a second person in the Godhead, and that he only lugged in Plato and made Moses talk like him as much as possible in order to recommend Judaism to the Greek mind. But the Jewish Hellenizers went farther than Philo. The dualism of Plato they imported completely into Judaism. The Jehovah of the Old Testament was not the Supreme God at all. Philo's rhetoric hardens into dogma. The all-pure and perfect one did not create this bad world, and never comes in contact with it. The Word which created the world and governs it was only one of his angels. In this milder form of Gnosticism we have Plato's dualism over again with very insignificant modifications.

The development did not stop here. Platonism, by borrowing an element from the Parsee religion, made the God of Judaism and the creator of this world not one of the higher angels, but an evil demon; so that Judaism becomes not angel worship but devil worship. The dualism is still more fatal and hopeless, and the chasm between God and the world yawns wider and deeper than ever.

How Platonism garbed as Gnosticism collided with Christianity at its earliest formulation, and sought to absorb it, we have already described.[1] The Christ, it said, comes into this world not through Judaism but from above it. He is a higher angel

[1] See Part I., chapters i. and ii.

than the Demiurgus, the best and most immaculate of that celestial hierarchy which they call the Pleroma. His ingress was at the scene of the baptism, and his egress was just before the crucifixion, so that the Christ was never born nor crucified. This was the Christology of Cerinthus, who was now at Ephesus. The Syrian Gnostics went farther than Cerinthus, and turned the whole Jesus Christ into an apparition. The scandal of the cross, the prime difficulty, as it was thought, in commending the Gospel to the cultivated Greek mind, was hereby removed out of the way. The most devoted disciple of Plato could find room for Christianity in the unbounded hospitality of the Academy.

That the Apostles, during the first half century after the ascension of Christ, were well acquainted with both these forms of Gnosticism, the Alexandrian and the Syrian, we regard as an established fact of Christian history. To assume that Gnosticism was a heresy which dates from the second century, is preposterous. True, it was then first known by this name, and had crystallized into a perfect system. But for one hundred and fifty years before Christ, that is, from Aristobulus down to Philo, Judaism in its cross with Platonism had been giving birth to these forms of thought. They were as widely diffused as the Jewish-Greek literature ; that is, through the principal cities of the Roman Empire. The pages of Philo are colored with it. A community existed in his day which had cleared itself of the hard rind of the Jewish ritual, and found their way, as they thought, directly to the heart of the Divine Love. There was every shade of hellenizing Judaism between the rugged literalists and this offshoot from them at Alexandria.[1]

That Paul would know the Gnostic tendencies of the Jewish religion, which he had professed in its most rigid ceremonials, is more than probable, even if we had found no indications of this knowledge in his writings. Apollos his fellow worker, had been a Jewish Hellenist, and was fresh from Alexandria. Paul quotes the Alexandrian version of the Old Testament, in which the Apocrypha was included, a work full of Hellenisms, and in which the Logos as Wisdom was strongly personified, if not already hypostatized. There was a Hellenist synagogue at Jerusalem, of Alexandrians and Jews from the Egyptian province of Cyrene. It must have been crowded with wor-

[1] Aristobulus was an Alexandrian Jew, and peripatetic philosopher, who lived B. C. 170, and undertook to interject the Greek philosophy into Judaism, pretending that it was borrowed from Moses. Commentaries on the Pentateuch were forged in his name for the purpose of commending Moses to the Greeks. Some account of him may be found in Cudworth's *Intellectual System*, i. 504. The Egyptian Therapeutæ, once regarded by some writers by an absurd anachronism as Christian monks, were, as later writers have shown, contemplative Jews of the Philo-platonic school. They only indicate a general tendency here run to its extreme. Philo himself refers to them in his book *De Vita Contempliva.* They tried to find God after the Platonic and Gnostic method, by withdrawing from sense through an interior and secret way. They formed a community on the shores of Lake Mœris near Alexandria.

shippers during the days of the Jewish festivals when the Jews, scattered abroad, came up thither through all the thoroughfares of the Roman Empire. Hence on the day of Pentecost we find among the multitude who composed the audience of Peter, "Jews from Egypt and in the parts of Libya about Cyrene."

Basilides, one of the early systematizers of Platonic Gnosticism, pretends he borrowed his doctrine from Matthias the Apostle. Hippolytus is authority for this.[1] Moreover, Basilides produced an elaborate exposition of his system, a refutation of which was made by Agrippa Castor in the reign of Hadrian (117–138). It is certain then that one of the distinguished apostles of Gnosticism had published his principal work soon after the close of the first century. He was in the flower of his age when John died, and was for some thirty or forty years a contemporary of that Apostle.

That John met the Gnostics at Ephesus, that they were there in considerable numbers and influence when he wrote, the evidence both external and internal, is abundant and convincing.[2] That the fourth Gospel, the Catholic Epistle, and the Apocalypse, set forth a cosmology and Christology calculated to disperse its shadows in a warmer and clearer illumination, in the Epistle with a direct and conscious purpose, will we think, be apparent.

[1] See Bünsen's *Hippolytus und Seine Zeit*, i. p. 65.

[2] Eusebius, H. E. iii. 26. Read also in this connection, Polycarp's Epistle.

CHAPTER III.

THE JOHANNEAN COSMOLOGY.

THE Logos or Word, the term used by Philo and his Gnosticizing successors to designate the creative power, is found in the Septuagint. It corresponds in part to the Nous of Plato, though it has a more full significance. The Nous of Plato is reason, simple and self-contained; the Logos is reason in the process of self-revelation. The former may or may not, according to its connection, involve the idea of manifestation; the latter necessarily implies a Being of whose mind it is the utterance and disclosure.

"IN THE BEGINNING WAS THE WORD," is the first postulate of the fourth Gospel. Reason was at the origin of things, and intelligence was coördinate with being. "And the Word was with God." There never was a time when God was inclosed within himself; never any epoch of silent eternities when God was in repose; never a state of inaction, or mere self-contemplation, out of which He had to rise and break silence. "And God was the Word." He could not be God except as one speaking, or imparting himself, and lavishing the wealth and glory of his own nature.

A God silent or self-inclosed were no God at all. He is only God as He is the Word, or in self-revelation. "The same was in the beginning with God." The writer evidently reiterates this truth to give it emphasis, as if it had been travestied or denied. If Reason were a co-essential of primal being, then the first evolution from the central life was not through an unconscious force, but a self-conscious Divine Intelligence. "All things were made by him," that is, by the Word. The Greek term, here rendered "made," does not mean constructed out of preëxisting material. It involves the idea of original creation. All things by Him came into existence (ἐγένετο). The Cosmos is the language of God speaking. Nature through her infinitely varied forms is the forthgoing and exfiguration of the Divine reason in self-manifestation. "And without him nothing was made that was made." The Greek is still more emphatic. Without Him not one thing (οὐδὲ ἓν) existed that came into existence. The same was asserted in the foregoing clause affirmatively. Here it is declared negatively, and the notion of an outlying chaos is repudiated and thrust off by a double emphasis. Christianity at its inauguration rises pure from the least taint of dualism. "And the Word was made flesh." It was not only in the beginning or in highest and first things, but in last and lowest things It was in nature and in humanity, yea in humanity as its outermost form, here on the earth, where we gazed on its glory full of grace and truth.

The introduction to the fourth Gospel, comprising what Chrysostom calls the Golden Proem, announces the prime doctrines which the narrative following is designed to establish and illustrate. They interpret the whole book, which keeps up to the high level of the introduction. Forms of speech are constantly occurring which would be entirely dark and enigmatical, were they not held steadily in the resolving light of the opening chapter. We do not believe this chapter was written with any *direct* reference to Gnosticism, or that it had any polemic purpose whatever. That would have given it the coloring of the place and the time, whereas it formulates a cosmology which clears itself of all places and times, and of difficulties which baffle the wit of men in all ages of the world. We only say that these difficulties were rife when the fourth Gospel was written; that the air was burdened with the fog of human speculation on these very themes; that John must have known it; that indirectly the whole Johannean theology stands negatively related to those speculations, and is more clearly understood when compared with them; for they were the earliest mist which Christianity cleared from its way as its first beams shot through its morning sky. Let us now endeavor to bring out, and place in comparison with them, the features of this divine Cosmogony.

I. The Supreme Divinity is here declared as never hidden, but always manifest. There is no secret way into the divine love which only a few choice spirits can find by introversion, painful and difficult. It belongs to his essential nature to go out from himself, and there was no antemundane period when He was not a creator. Hegel's doctrine that a God not creating is no God, was eighteen hundred years old when he announced it. The idea of a God existing alone through the cycles of revolving eternities, till, tired of the awful solitude, He rose out of it and produced something which He could love, is one of the dismal conceptions of our finite understanding. In the beginning, at the point beyond which human thought is barred from going, the Divine was not separated from his Word; He is not to be conceived except as going out of himself in creative speech replete with creative love. A being, employed through unimaginable years in the selfish pastime of inspecting his interior glories, is excluded from Christian thought, and a being who never was without his self-revealing Logos, is the first affirmation of Christianity.[1]

II. As clearly, we conceive, does it affirm that this Logos is not a second god or sub-deity, but co-essential with the One Divine Nature. There is no Demiurgus to whom the work of world-making is delegated. That was the heresy of the time, de-

[1] It does not follow that God from eternity was creating human beings, or that the present system is coeval with Him, — a doctrine which Dr. Bushnell has pretty thoroughly refuted.

signed to relieve God of being contaminated with the contact of matter, and at a later day the heresy of Arius, leaving God on the further side of an unknown gulf and making nature stop short of Him as leading upward only to a finite intelligence. God was himself the Word — or, if we choose to make the subject and predicate change places, the Word was God. There is good authority, exegetical and grammatical, for reading the sentence either way. Either way it affirms the same thing, — that the divine Reason, which is essentially creative, is no inferior Demiurgus, but the Supreme Divinity. This same disciple says, in another connection, God is love. He means plainly that love is his essential nature; He cannot exist without loving, for if He could He would not be God. He means here, we think, just as plainly, that Reason in self-manifestation is also his essential nature. He would not be God without his Logos. He is not bare goodness. He is not a mere fountain of life that flows blindly on and on. He is Reason as well, that guides it to ends supremely wise, and determines it in moulds of infinite beauty and order.

III. The notion of a divine carpenter or architect, an essential feature of Platonism, is excluded from the Johannean Cosmogony. God does not build nor manufacture. He creates. There is no preëxistent material which He works into his universe. It is all the forthgoing of his own nature. The Cosmos is a divine speech that never breaks off into silence, and so nature is the daily thought of God in concrete forms, the print and copy of the eternal mind. By making the *Nous*, or mere Intellect, the author of nature, God is only a contriver, a master-builder, whose plans are executed by inferior agents; and the Platonic theism never gets out of this clumsy carpenter-work in constructing the universe. The first word of the Christian theism, the Logos, gets us rid of it, for the universe is now the language of God speaking; and the old psalm only rounds out into a sublimer strain, "Day unto day uttereth speech, and night unto night showeth knowledge of thee."

IV. Hence dualism is an impossibility. It had been the besetting vice, not alone of the Platonic system and of those which were built out of its material, but of every religion which had not swamped in Pantheism and found its unity there. Here it is announced that everything was spoken forth out of the Logos, which is none other than God himself in the act of speaking, and otherwise than by this process not one thing ever came into existence. Hence nature is sweet and clean, for it is God's thought in visible and concrete form, and it can have no taint unless man taints it with his own moral evil. The coverings of matter are not corrupt nor poisonous, but swathings that come fresh from the hand of the All-pure. Sense does not lure away from God, but wins us toward Him through avenues that open upward into the wealth of his own being. The flesh is no corrupt envelopment of the soul to smother and extinguish its divine ideals ; the Logos itself assumed it as its material clothing, and in it, and through it, the divine glory most truly and gracefully appeared. All this is involved in the propositions of the Golden Proem which the history following is to demonstrate. God is in Last things as well as First ; in the End as in the Beginning ; on the outermost limits as at the divine centre, filling all things ; and the unity of God, nature, and man is to be consummated in Christianity.

V. NO MAN HAS EVER SEEN GOD. The infinite depths of divine Being are not merely beyond our comprehension, they are beyond the reach of objective thought. God as the absolute, as sheer Noumenon, is a word that presents no image to any finite mind. He is only to be apprehended through his attributes, for by these alone He comes into personality. Inevitably, by the laws of thought and of speech these attributes must become personified when we think and speak of God. Qualities or attributes are what alone personify anything. Think away these attributes one by one, Love, Justice, Mercy, Wisdom, Truth, Beneficence, and the idea of God shades off till it vanishes from thought altogether, and only a vast vacuity remains. You may believe it contains something, and you may call it the Absolute, but the word answers to nothing in your own mind. The vacuity there has become complete. Hegel is right, therefore, so far as our own minds stand affected; when after thinking away all the qualities of Divine Being to find the essence within them, he comes at last to nothing, and makes zero the ground of all existence. Only we should have the grace to acknowledge, after this process is accomplished, that we are the vacuum, and that the zero is only in ourselves.

Hence there is not an attribute which in the Bible is not made to image forth the divine nature, and which for the time being is not made to stand for the person of God. It is God himself, as if for the end in view the whole Deity were there. He is Wisdom. It is not enough to say He is wise, for Wisdom is his eternal essence. But again, Wisdom is his daughter; she was with Him when He prepared the heavens, she was "as one brought up with him, his daily delight rejoicing always before him."[1] As the daughter of God, she is described at large in the apocryphal writings as doing what elsewhere God is declared to have done himself. But again, God is Light.[2] Because all our illumination is in Him, Light for this end expresses the whole Deity, as we say the sun is the light of the world. Again, He is Love;[3] for to say only that He loves, does not affirm sufficiently his eternal essence. And yet again as to his retributive justice, he is a "consuming fire."[4]

[1] Proverbs viii. 30. [2] 1 John i. 5. [3] Ib. iv. 16.
[4] Heb. xii. 29 quoted from Deut. iv. 24.

But when it is said that God is the Word, or the infinite Mind, in the act of revelation all the other personifications are comprehended in one. For everything that can be known of Him comes through the Logos, — God speaking, — the Divine Reason in manifestation. All the riches of his nature, love, justice, truth, tenderness, grace, beneficence, must come through his Word, for it stands as the forthgoing of all that is known or knowable of the Divine perfections. Hence it is described as "dwelling on the bosom of the Father" and alone revealing Him, just as the photosphere on the sun's disc, ever generated from its unknowable deeps, floods our universe and warms it with solar day. Hence the Word is the only-begotten of the Father, and it was no paradox of the Christian fathers when they called it *eternally* begotten; for they only say over again in different phrase that it was "in the beginning," and that God never insulated himself in dreary solitude. Hence in the New Testament the word is *the* son of God and in the fourth Gospel the only son. He is never spoken of as made, or created; he is always born or begotten; not born in time, but born eternally and always out of the infinite deeps of divine Being, and thus ever becoming to our finite minds the resplendent Person of the Godhead.

A question here very naturally occurs: How came these divine metaphysics to be first enunciated by a fisherman of Galilee? All that has been told us of the Platonism or the Gnosticism of the fourth Gospel turns out the most baseless of all assumptions. If you except Plato's monotheism, the fourth Gospel sets aside those systems as to their distinguishing features, cuts its way through the fog which they had diffused, and rises above them into the clear sky like one of those peaks of light, that first catch the day-spring and fling it down on the shadows below. A distinguishing feature of Platonism is its dualism, and this became more hopeless the longer it developed, till finally it turned God out of his universe, and shut the door. Take dualism out of Plato and he is no longer Plato. His carpenter-work falls in pieces and vanishes from sight, and leaves the Demiurgus without a stone or a timber to build with. Put it never so slightly into the Johannean cosmology and the whole system would be changed and corrupted as if poison had been diffused through a living organism to dissolve its tissues. There never was the least color of it in any of those theologies which were wrought from the fourth Gospel, not even in the Alexandrian school, which was thought to Platonize the most; for neither Clement nor Justin nor Origen have the least smell of it upon their garments.

If we turn to the opening chapter of the Apocalypse, we shall be at no loss in ascertaining the source of the Johannean cosmology. It is all there, but in different form, given not in metaphysical propositions, but in the glowing symbols of an objective world. Here the disciple who had leaned on the breast of the Master says he was *in spirit*, as the old prophets were when they saw truth in its representative imagery; that he heard a voice saying "I am the Beginning and the End, the Alpha and the Omega, the First and the Last—not only ἐν ἀρκῇ, that is, in the prime principles of being, but in their lowest and outermost ultimations. At the divine centre as at the utmost circuit of a living universe, I fill all things with myself." The writer says he turned and looked and saw what afterward he called the Logos represented as a human form entirely glorified; "his hairs as white as wool and his feet as if they burned in a furnace"—glorified, that is, even to its ultimations. The unity of God nature and humanity is the one comprehensive truth, given in one case as divine metaphysics, given in the other by prophetic vision and symbol, whose overwhelming brightness was as the sun shining in his strength.

The Logos-doctrine was not first enunciated in the fourth Gospel. It only received here its final and most perfect formulation. The substance of it under different phraseology was evidently in possession of the earliest Christian communions, and they grasped it as the prime essential of Christianity itself. It is implied, as we have shown, though not given in its completeness, in the discourse of Christ, as reported by Matthew, where instead of the Word "the Son," is the phraseology employed.

Paul was in full possession of the doctrine twenty-five years at least before the fourth Gospel was written. His letter to the Colossians, whose genuineness is admitted even by the doubting and fastidious Renan, and asserted by all the ancient authorities without exception, must have been produced not far from the year 65. It is so full of nerve and so robust with the Pauline spirit, that Baur's reasons for setting it aside we must regard as entirely baseless. It was written to chide the heresies which were plaguing the church at Colosse, among which were angel-worship and false asceticism — the doctrines of which had long been gendered in the cross between Judaism and Platonism, and which entered so largely into the Gnostic systems of a later day. It is plain that he alludes to their celestial hierarchies and world-makers, when at the name of the "well beloved Son" the mind of the Apostle takes fire in this burst of inspiration — "Who is the image of the invisible God, the first-born of the whole creation; for in him were all things created; things in the heavens and things on the earth; things visible and things invisible; whether they be thrones or dominations, or principalities or powers; in him and for him were all created. And he is before all things, and in him all things hold together (συνέστηκέ). And he is the head of the body, the church, for he is the beginning, the first born from the dead, that in all things he may be preëminent. For the Father was pleased that in him the whole pleroma should dwell."

To say that the Apostle is here only describing a moral creation would be to sink the passage far away from its full meaning. It is plain that he had obtained some vision of the truth which John saw in serener light. The Christ represents to his mind not merely a man born in time, but the creative Word, the divine Reason in manifestation, and as such he opposes it to the angel-worship of an incipient Gnosticism which made the creative Word one of the pleroma, an angel of the heavenly hierarchies. There is no reason to doubt that before Paul's day Jewish Platonism had ripened into just that result.

We waive for the present the question of identity between the Christ and the Word, and why these two terms became perfectly interchangeable. Such certainly is the fact which meets us in the earliest symbolization which sets forth the sublime theism of Christianity. Paul perfectly anticipates the theogony of the Golden Proem. The Word here called "the well-beloved Son" is the first born of the whole creation, the primal emanation or offspring of the Eternal Mind to image forth its invisible deeps; through whom the heavens in all their ranks were constituted, and all things of time and sense — all things visible and invisible. And in him all things stand together, or are held in order. Not only the universe visible and invisible is created in and through the Word, but all its parts are held to each other in harmonious relations. It is the same as if the Apostle had said — All things visible and invisible are instinct with the living mind out of which they came, and they are held to one divine purpose and end. The all-creating Word is behind and within the shifting panorama of nature and of history, making all things and all events stand together as held in unity.

The Epistle to the Hebrews is beyond all reasonable question a production of the apostolic age, and probably written by a cotemporary of Paul. We think it antedates the fourth Gospel by nearly a quarter of a century. Its introductory chapter asserts the Logos doctrine with the clearest emphasis, and as we read it is exactly parallel with the utterance of Paul just quoted. "The Son" is above all angels, and by him God "made the worlds."[1] And the Father addresses the Son in the words, "Thy throne, O God, is forever and ever," and again "Thou Lord in the beginning hast laid the foundation of the earth (τῆν γῆν) and the heavens (οὐρανοί) are the works of thy hands." The Word here called "the Son" is invested with the same attributes as in the proem of John.

[1] That τοὺς αἰῶνας, here rendered "the worlds," means the whole creation, may be seen by reference to Heb. xi. 3, where the same word is used. It may mean "the ages" or the whole flow of time. But see as decisive the tenth verse of Chapter first. We are perfectly aware of a different application of these texts made by one class of expositors, but it strikes us as entirely arbitrary.

CHAPTER IV.

THE TRANSPARENCIES OF NATURE.

NATURE, as we have defined it, is the material plane of being which we apprehend by the organs of sense, and the order of sequence in its endless changes and recombinations we call natural laws. To ascertain these laws and group them is the business of natural science. And it is only science pretending to knowledge beyond its discovery that antagonizes the truths of revelation. The best scientific research and progress do not tend downward towards a grosser materialism, but away from it towards the highest spiritual philosophy, and the line becomes almost tremulous, which distinguishes the discoveries of science from the disclosures of revelation, where the light of the one is merging in the clear blaze of the other.

No such elements of nature exist as the ancient philosophers built their systems with; none such as entered into the cosmology of Plato; no such fixed primordial elements as earth, air, fire, and water; no ultimate particles of matter, out of which Leibnitz and others of a later day wrought their atomic theories of the universe. Nature presents to us her ever shifting phenomena; a new phasis every day and every hour, through which something benign and lovely is looking out upon us; and what that something is becomes a question, in answering which religion and science were never so much in accord as now.

Our text books told us not many years since that material substances were classified as those which could be weighed, and those which could not be. The imponderable substances were light, heat, electricity and magnetism, whose particles were exceedingly subtile, and travelled with immense velocity. It is now perfectly well demonstrated, that no such substances exist in nature. They are only the equivalents of *forces producing motion;* and the light, the heat, the electricity, and the magnetism measure by their degrees of intensity the amount of force which has been resisted and deflected. If you stir the atmosphere by the vibratory motion of your vocal organs, or of a stringed instrument, or by the concussion of bodies with each other, you produce wavelets of air, which striking the ear produce the sensation of sound. Sound is not a material substance, but motion resisted. The subtile ethers pervading all the spaces between us and the sun are acted upon by some force in that central orb, and the motion touching our eye-balls produces the sensation of light, or touching the surface of our bodies the sensation of heat. Light and heat are not material substances, but motion resisted.

Or let the resisting medium be varied according to laws well ascertained, and the heat becomes electricity. This change in the resisting medium may be effected by an artificial electric battery, or by states of the atmosphere which is one of the electric batteries of nature. Or vary the resisting medium yet again, and the electricity changes back into light, shown either by sparks from the electric wires, or by flashes of lightning through the air. The impact of homogeneous bodies by friction produces heat, that of heterogeneous bodies produces electricity, and two currents of electricity meeting at right angles, produce magnetism. What were once called imponderable substances therefore are simply motion resisted ; or force changing its form of manifestation according to the method or medium by which the resistance is made. So much heat, or so much light, or so much electricity are the equivalents of so much force arrested ; and so subtile and exact have been the experiments, that the equivalents are weighed and noted down. Joule, an English chemist, by a series of exceedingly delicate experiments, tells us by his calorimeter what quantity of heat is produced by a given mechanical action ; and he demonstrates he thinks that the fall of 772 pounds through the space of one foot is able to raise the temperature of one pound of water through one degree of Fahrenheit's thermometer.

The analysis does not stop here. The heat, electricity and magnetism of our own bodies, all, in fine, that we call the vital force, are resolvable into the same general law. So much bodily temperature is so much force whose motion has been arrested; so much nerve-power or brain-power is so much electricity or magnetism, the equivalent of so much motion converted into the *vis vitæ* of our physical organism. Our activities either of mind or body are just so much heat, electricity, or magnetism converted back into motion. Touch the nerves of a corpse with the galvanic wires, and you produce the same motions of the body that the will produced in the living man. The difference is, that the brain of the living man, which was the electric battery before, has now failed of its supply, and an artificial battery has been substituted in its place. The emotions and passions of the living man moved the muscles of the face so as to express fear, anger, or rage, and this was done by the electric action of the corresponding nerves: touch the same nerves of the corpse with the electric wires, and the same muscles will move again into the same expression. Vital heat like all other heat is the exact equivalent of so much motion; nerve power and brain power are the same equivalent converted to electricity or magnetism, the power on which we draw in all our thoughts, emotions, intellections, and imaginations. Organic life is the equilibrium of these equivalents, and to break down and destroy the equilibrium is — death.

So, therefore, what were called the imponderable substances, are not substances at all, but simply force changing its mode of manifestation ; first into motion, then into the equivalents of motion, heat, light, electricity, magnetism, vital power. These in turn change back severally into motion again. The evolution of force by heat and electricity converted again into motion by the telegraph, the steam engine, muscular action, or on the more magnificent scale of nature, is only the illustration of a general law which science now holds to be perfectly demonstrated — *that force once exerted never ceases and is never lost.* In some of its equivalents it is always preserved, and produces the endless phases in the cycle of life that ever returns into itself, and constitutes the activities of a living universe. This is THE CORRELATION AND CONSERVATION OF FORCES ; in other words, their equivalence and eternal continuance, whose discovery and demonstration is the auspicious achievement of modern science.

So much of what were called imponderable substances. But what are called the ponderable or solid substances, the rocks, the minerals, the earths and the flora that grow out of them — are resolvable in the last analysis into FORCE changing the form of its manifestation. That is the last boundary of science, and beyond this as mere physicists, we cannot go. Matter has no ultimate units, but is divisible to the point where it vanishes from human perception. All the properties of matter, primary and secondary, are but the manifestations of force, and we know of no such entity as the essence of matter. The most solid and ponderable substances are resolvable, the solids into fluids, the fluids into vapor, the vapor into gases, and the gases into ethers, and the ethers into those more simple and elementary, and very possibly a finer and more complete analysis will some day resolve all the ponderable substances into the imponderable. What we have called matter, is composed of no fixed and final atoms that we know of; it is a coördination of forces which may be recombined or changed into their equivalents. Thus the most enlightened materialism tends to spiritualism and almost merges in it.

But come to the last analysis. These coördinate forces are resolvable one into another and all of them abut upon a Prime Force which lies within and behind them all; of which they are only the ever changing phases and out of which all phenomena are evolved. The single question, which now concerns us is — What is the nature and quality of this Prime Force, towards which all the others are resolvable as only the forms and methods of its activity? Herbert Spencer says it is unknowable, and that Science is here brought up to its impassable boundary. But why unknowable? The question is, does it act unintelligently, like brute matter, or does it not? The answer is — it acts as a vast and all pervading INTELLIGENCE, so comprehending and stupendous that we must call it infinite. Take as an illustration the planetary motions. It is demonstrable that if the force which holds the planets toward a common centre and the force which projects them from it, were not kept in equipoise within assignable limits, the whole system would tumble into chaos. It is demonstrable that if their periodic revolutions had been coincident, so as to arrange them on the same side of the sun, that is to bring them in conjunction, the whole system would break up in a common disaster. It is demonstrable that the whole system is one of the most delicate balances and compensations, so that seeming temporal disturbance preserves an intrinsic and eternal harmony. Some of their compensations and balances forecast periods of thousands of years. For example the orbits and periodic times of Jupiter and Saturn are such that they may be in conjunction and send disturbance through the whole planetary system. But every third conjunction falls in advance of a former one and the conjunction point is carried round the entire orbit in 2,648 years, at the end of which time the exact condition will be restored and all the perturbations will have completely neutralized each other. Such illustrations might be multiplied indefinitely, so as to show how this Prime Force into which all other forces resolve themselves, is an all-seeing intelligence.[1] It answers precisely to the Logos of Scripture, the Divine Reason in the act of manifestation. The light of science tending upward meets that of revelation streaming downward and they blend together. Matter, the more we analyze it, loses its grossness and becomes transparent, showing the motions uncovered of Him who works in us and around us; and nature is only the veil with which we cover our eyes, that we be not too much dazzled or overawed under the open face of the Godhead.

Consider one moment another point. Science, we said, demonstrates the conservation, or, as Herbert Spencer calls it, the PERSISTENCE of force. This means that, so far as science knows, the same amount of force now in the universe always has been and always must be. It is constantly changing in form but never in quantity.[2] Motion arrested changes into heat; but if you could utilize all the heat you could produce precisely the same degree of motion again.

[1] See Mitchell's *Popular Astronomy*, especially chap. xv.

[2] Professor Yeomans thus states concisely the same law: "The movements we see around us are not spontaneous, or independent occurrences, but links in an eternal chain of forces. When bodies are put in motion it is at the expense of some previously existing energy; and when they come to rest, their force is not destroyed but lives on in other forms. Every motion we see has its thermal value, and when it ceases its equivalent of heat is an invariable result. Should the motion of the heavenly bodies be arrested, it would produce a conflagration of the universe." — *Chemistry*, p. 174.

Solid matter changes into gases and ethers; but condense the gases and the same amount of matter returns and nothing has been lost. There is the same now, no more no less, that there was when the morning stars first sang together; and the same would continue though the world should be "burned up." The only changes have been in the combinations, each combination offering a new phasis of the vast primal force of all. The annihilation of matter is impossible, for no such substance *in se* exists or was ever created. The destruction of the world is both scientifically unthinkable and theologically monstrous. It is saying, to state it otherwise, that the ground force which comprehends all the others, and from which phenomena are evolved, could cease, or is not "*persistent*," and that is saying theologically, that the Logos was not in the Beginning, or is not born eternally, but is only finite and temporal; that it began to be, once on a time, and that it can cease to be or can die out again; that God could be without it; that the essential divine attributes, those which make him God, could be abolished; that the Divine Mind could introvert within itself in the lonely and selfish contemplation of its interior glories; nay, farther, that its interior glories could themselves be quenched, for it is precisely their lavishment that makes them beneficent and therefore essentially divine.

Such, then, are the symphonic affirmations of

Theology and Science. Theology declares that God is essentially the WORD, was ever in self-manifestation that is, and always must be; that there was no primordial material outside of him, but that all things came into being by the Word; or in other phrase, that the Prime Force of Nature is God in the act of speaking. So John announces from above. Science begins from below, and reasons up towards the same truth. Nature is some vast Power in action; its phases change constantly, but it is only a change of equivalents, the sum total is the same yesterday, to-day, and forever. Nothing can be taken away. Creation was not an act which was accomplished centuries ago, but is an ever fresh evolution of the central power of the Universe, acting not blindly, but as the utterance of an Eternal Reason. Creation is a grand epopee, a song which has no beginning and no languishing, but whose notes, running through an infinite range of keys, make the harmonies of the universe. "The discoveries and generalizations of modern Science," says Professor Tyndall, "constitute a poem more sublime than has ever yet been addressed to the imagination," and he sums up his conclusions in a noble passage which we quote as a fitting close to this chapter: —

"We pass to other systems and other suns, each pouring forth energy like our own, but still without infringement of the law which reveals immutability in the midst of change, which recognizes incessant transference or conversion, but neither final gain nor loss. The law generalizes the aphorism of Solomon that 'there is nothing new under the sun,' by teaching us to detect everywhere, under its infinite variety of appearances, the same primeval force. To Nature nothing can be added ; from Nature nothing can be taken away ; the sum of her energies is constant, and the utmost man can do in the pursuit of physical truth, or in the applications of physical knowledge, is to shift the constituents of the never-varying total. The law of conservation rigidly excludes both creation (temporal beginning) and annihilation. Waters may change to ripples, and ripples to waves ; magnitude may be substituted for number and number for magnitude ; asteroids may aggregate to suns ; suns may resolve themselves into flora and fauna, and flora and fauna melt into air, — the flux of power is eternally the same. It rolls in music through the ages ; and all terrestrial energy — the manifestations of life, as well as the display of phenomena — are but modulations of its rhythm."

CHAPTER V.

THE WORD MADE FLESH.

THAT Jesus Christ was a man, finite, tempted, suffering, having the same propensities and weaknesses, the same wants and sympathies that other men have, is manifest through the whole evangelic narrative. He was more of a man than any other person of whom we have any history; for nowhere else do we read of a humanity where the compass of its powers and attributes was so full and complete. Its sublimest heights of moral grandeur, and its most delicate shades of moral beauty are all here. The manhood of other men, even the best of them, is somewhat distorted or defective. There is strength without tenderness, there is breadth without depth; there is intensity without catholicity; there is clear intellection without the sweet and fervent sympathies of the heart. The peculiarity of the manhood of Jesus consists in the union of qualities found elsewhere incongruous and in separation; union in such majestic and delicate proportion as to give the impression of perfect symmetry and harmony. It requires not only a life-long study, but a heart open to all that is grand and lovely in nature and in man, to be brought into full correspondency with the humanity of Jesus. This constitutes the charm of the writings of Dr. Furness, through whom the natural life and character of Jesus become to us a new revelation of moral beauty and perfection. Some of the critics have assumed that the fourth Gospel denies, or at least ignores the humanity of Jesus; that it has a Gnostic tinge, and imports that his relations to space and time, to sense and matter, were apparent and not real. Every candid and careful reader we are persuaded will come to just the opposite conclusion. More plainly and persistently than the synoptics, do the fourth Gospel and all the Johannean writings, set forth the Incarnation as a stubborn and fundamental fact, for the plain reason that when John wrote, the fact had been denied; and in the Gnostic metaphysics, the essential humanity of Jesus had exhaled in gilded mist and become spectral. In the proem the fact is made prominent; and John even goes out of his way to put in his own personal attestations as an eye-witness. "The Word was made flesh and dwelt among us and WE BEHELD HIS GLORY." He puts this in the foreground as a postulate which the entire history following was to establish. When he comes to narrate the sufferings and death of Jesus, he purposely gives his readers to understand, that he of all the twelve was an eye-witness, standing under the cross while the others were standing afar off. Hence he supplies facts which they had left out; and he not only supplies them, but interlines his personal affirmation, as if making oath to what somebody had denied. "One of the soldiers pierced his side with a spear, and immediately blood and water came out. And he who saw bears testimony, and his testimony is true *and he knows that he speaks the truth.*"[1] He seeks to confirm this in his description of the post-resurrection appearances, when Jesus came among his disciples, and showed them his hands and his side. The Catholic epistle opens with the same attestations, and it is one of the proofs of identity of authorship, that all the Johannean writings lay special emphasis upon the proper humanity of Jesus down to its outermost clothings of flesh and sense. The ears, the eyes, and the touch are the threefold witness summoned to bear testimony to the fact that the incarnation was not spectral, but actual. "That which we have heard, which we have seen with our eyes, which we have looked upon, and our hands have handled we announce to you." He denounces as antichrist those who deny that "Jesus Christ has come in the flesh," and he makes acknowledgment of this truth a test of genuine discipleship.[2] The "liars" who denied that Jesus was the Christ, or who called themselves apostles and were not,[3] were, in all probability, the followers of Cerinthus, who made Jesus one person,

[1] 1 John xix. 34, 35. [2] 1 John iv. 1–3.
[3] 1 John ii. 22; Rev. ii. 2.

and the Christ another person that merely spoke through him as a higher angel, but whose immaculate garments of light had never been soiled by the overlayings of mortal and corruptible flesh. If the Johannean spirit rises, on the one hand, into the more celestial ethers, it descends on the other hand, into a realism as crass and solid as we find anywhere in the New Testament history. Jesus Christ on the side of his humanity, is a partaker of flesh and blood, and through that of the weaknesses, the temptations, and the woes, which beset the race of Adam, even to its humblest and most forlorn child of sorrow.

In the fourth Gospel, as nowhere else, Jesus is described as in constant peril of his life, and evading the snares that would bring it to a close before his time had come. He begins his ministry at Jerusalem, evidently in the expectation that his own people would be the first to receive the new revelation, and that the light of the New Jerusalem would radiate from the old, and thence roll back the pagan darkness. But he is opposed, thwarted and threatened, and a plot laid for his life, which he is obliged continually to evade; and he finally leaves Jerusalem, ceases to make it the centre of his plans and operations, retires to the obscure province of Galilee for personal safety, organizes his ministry there, and only goes up privately to Jerusalem, the focus of danger. All this we have in the fourth Gospel with fullness of detail; while in the synoptics we only have it in hints and fragments. How baseless is the theory which regards it as a Gnostic production designed to show that Christ was not really incarnate and subject to suffering and death, when the whole narrative represents that the plan of his ministry was constantly varied lest he should meet death prematurely! Then the assertion, that in the fourth Gospel he breaks suddenly upon the reader as superhuman or superangelic, is entirely unfounded, for no Scripture shows more plainly and constantly than this book, that his Messianic consciousness came like the dawn of the morning, that it had to break through clouds of temptation and of ignorance; through alternations of doubt, of hope and of fear; through all the limitations of the finite understanding, before the unfluctuating noontide flooded his consciousness with the wisdom and the peace of God. The fourth Gospel shows preëminently and in the lowest degree the human phasis in the life and character of Jesus Christ.

But it contains also another range of fact and doctrine pertaining to that life and character which we cannot reduce within the dimensions of our finite nature. The synoptics rise sometimes to the same height, but they only rise to it occasionally. It appears with them in solitary peaks, far off beyond the clouds; whereas in John it is a continuous range, always bathed in the mellowing glories of the heavens. In the proem, Jesus Christ is the Word, and the Word is God himself. He is not an angel or æon, but the Being who creates the universe. This might perhaps be explained as a rhetorical figure, were it not that a whole range of fact and doctrine, through the fourth Gospel, and through all the Johannean writings, keeps up to the same level, showing plainly that the proem was given as a key for the interpretation of the whole. Jesus asserts repeatedly his preexistence. "I came down from heaven" is the annunciation which startles his hearers and excites the Jews to anger and charges of blasphemy; but he repeats it in its sharp significance, and will not explain it as metaphor. He asserts an existence of his own before that of Abraham; and the connection shows that he does not mean merely that he was the Messiah in the counsel and foreknowledge of God, but that he had an existence which was without time, and therefore was before Abraham. In those communings with God, which Jesus had at the last supper, communings of indescribable tenderness, where no factitious self-assertion is even conceivable, he speaks of his preëxistence as a familiar fact, but now glowing more vividly and gratefully in his consciousness, "I have glorified thee on the earth, I have finished the work which thou gavest me to do, and now, O Father, glorify thou me with thyself, with the glory which I had with thee before the world was."[1] "Father, I would that those which

[1] John xvii. 5.

thou hast given me be with me where I am, that they may behold my glory, which thou hast given me, for thou lovedst me before the foundation of the world."[1] To say that an order of events was established from all eternity in the decrees of God, is only to assert the common dogma of predestination. Jesus does more than this, unless he asserts the baldest truism, for every Jew who took up the stones to stone him for blasphemy, might have claimed such preëxistence as that. That which he calls repeatedly *himself*, — which was so far forth his own being, that he applies to it the personal pronoun, — I, he says, was with the Father before time was; and when death was near, he said he was going back to merge again in the glory from which he emerged when he took on the clothings of our finite humanity. "I have come forth from the Father, and come into the world: again I leave the world and go to the Father;" and his disciples said on hearing this, "Now speakest thou plainly, and art speaking no parable."[2] Passages may be quoted which fall upon the ear at first as like forms of speech, such as "the Lamb slain from the foundation of the world." Even there, other preëxistence is supposed than one merely in the foreknowledge of God.[3] But the pas-

[1] John xvii. 24. [2] John xvi. 28-29.

[3] This passage imports as we interpret it, that God did not merely provide a sacrifice in time and once for all, but that eternally, he sacrifices himself for his creatures; that such is his nature always, and the cross only symbolizes it in time.

sages are not parallel. When Jesus persistently asserted his preëxistence, and was charged with blasphemy, and his life was imperiled because he put forth so hard a doctrine, he yet refused to retract it, but asserted it over and over till the last. Coming forth from the Father into the world he places in antithesis with leaving the world and going to the Father. One member of the antithesis is placed in balance with the other; preëxistence is asserted in the same sense as his post-existence, and if one was real, the other must also be.

But why go into any verbal interpretations? The egoism of the Johannean writings is so stupendous and persistent, that we are shut off to the conclusion that if Christ was a "mere man" though a sage or prophet, he was a man whose self-assertion transcended all the bounds of reason and modesty. For what is the bearing of sage or prophet who have any just apprehension of their function and calling? According to the depth and fullness of their wisdom and inspiration, so will the entireness of their self-abnegation be. As the divine mind and message roll in upon them, their own nothingness becomes more complete; they keep themselves out of the way lest they sink under the awful burden of the Divine Word. "Woe is me for I am undone; because I am a man of unclean lips, and I dwell in the midst of a people of unclean lips, for mine eyes have seen the King, the Lord of hosts." No mere man can bear the weight of the infinite without being crushed and consumed under it. Even the sage who comes into a larger discourse of reason bows before it in profound acknowledgment that it is not *his* reason, but a loftier and diviner intelligence, and he shrinks from projecting his little ego into it, to darken its lustre. But much more will the seer keep himself out of sight before the incoming of the Lord, for he sees and speaks from a more profound and irrepressible spontaneity, and he is more ready to "fall as dead" than to see his own fantastic figure outlined on the heavenly vision.

Nor would it make any difference in this respect, though the messenger who speaks in the name of God, were angelic or superangelic. If greater and wiser than men, so much more perfect would his self-abnegation be. The highest angels (so we interpret the Saviour's words), those who are nearest the Lord and reflect most brightly the glories of his face, are the guardians of little children, because they are most childlike and are brought more directly and entirely into sympathy and correspondency with the little ones. And so to become great or greatly angelic is not to rise into greater self-assertion, but to rise to such a consciousness of God, that when made the minister of his truth and will, all selfhood — the I — vanishes and disappears.

But what have we here as we open the Johannean writings? We have an egoism for which the synoptics had in some sort prepared us, but which is consummated in the book of John. Matthew reports Jesus as saying: "No one knoweth the Son but the Father, neither knoweth any man the Father save the Son, and he to whom the Son shall reveal him." "Come unto *me* all ye that labor and are heavy laden." But in the fourth Gospel the proem is pitched to this high strain, and the discourse of Jesus rises up to it even to the close. He tells his disciples that to see him is the same as seeing God, and instead of abnegating himself he puts himself in the foreground continually. He does not tell his hearers that simply to receive his message will be enough. He tells them that "all men should honor the Son even as they honor the Father," for "he that honoreth not the Son honoreth not the Father who hath sent him." He does not say, I bring you the true doctrine which is bread from heaven, but rather "I am the bread which came down from heaven." "I am the bread of life." He does not bring news merely that there is to be a resurrection of the dead. He proclaims rather "I am the resurrection and the life." He does not tell his disciples as any mere preacher would have told them, — If you are obedient to the truth, God will vouchsafe to you a resurrection among the glorified; he tells them as to every man who is a true believer, "I will raise him up at the last day." He does not say in prophetic style, — I proclaim truth which is to enlighten mankind; he proclaims rather

"I am the light of the world." Instead of withdrawing his own personality, that the light may shine unbroken from the mind of God, he interposes his person as if there alone the light was inorbed, and became the sun of the moral universe.

These stupendous claims are made not in exceptional and rhetorical phraseology, but they are based on the alleged prime facts of the gospel history. The last festal discourses abound in promises of the Holy Spirit that was to comfort, enlighten, and sanctify the disciples of Christ. But who is this man who claims that *he* is the dispenser of this sovereign agency of God, and that its coming depends on his own personal agency? "If I go not away the Comforter will not come, but if I depart *I will send him.*" Yet again the Father is to send him, but it is to be only through the intervention of Christ, and in his name. What these promises imported, and how the disciples understood them, we learn by the subsequent fulfillment. The time and place where the new dispensation was to be inaugurated was Jerusalem, at the feast of Pentecost—and there it came, the imbreathing of heavenly airs transforming the whole inward and outward man, and creating him anew in the radiant image of his Lord. And Peter, standing up to explain the new phenomena, rehearses the facts pertaining to the death, resurrection, and ascension of Christ, and says, "HE hath shed forth this which ye now see and hear." Saul, the hardest of the Pharisees, fell under the same influence. The steel of the Pharisee melted, and was moulded in gentler forms, and he tells us that when he had open vision of the source of the power that subdued him, he found himself ensphered in light from the face of Jesus Christ, above the brightness of the sun. The whole history of the primitive church only repeats these facts in fulfillment of the promise of the Comforter, and in full explanation of the nature of the promise. The primitive church, do we say? We might just as well say the whole church for eighteen hundred years. For ever and everywhere under the administration of Christianity, when the Holy Spirit comes with the most of its cleansing, subduing, and transforming power, though not with the open vision of Christ, it is with the unquenchable consciousness of his presence and his insphering light and love; and where this is denied, the power of Christianity wanes, its ordinances become meaningless, and the Holy Spirit pales its ineffectual fires.

Such self-assertion was never heard of before nor since except among men of disordered intellect. Why do we read it in the evangelic narratives without being shocked with it? Plainly because of its place and setting in a biography which is unlike any other, and which none of our scales of human grandeur are competent to measure; and the entire harmony and proportion are not broken but preserved. But take out this egoism and try to fit it into the life of any other great man, prophet, apostle, or sage. Isaiah, as we have seen, when the vision of God broke upon him and the burden of his message was laid upon him, did not challenge his adversaries. "Which of you convinceth me of sin?" "Ye are from beneath — I am from above," but cried aloud from a profounder consciousness of mortal infirmity and weakness. Nor did John and his fellow apostles when a like mission was given them, and the "Woe is me if I preach not the gospel" came upon them. They resolve themselves into nothingness as fast as possible, and are more conscious than ever of an uncleansed selfhood which must not fling its shadow across the sunlight of God. If we think this was owing to any usages of speech peculiar to the men themselves, we have only to take any of our modern apostles of truth and try to fit such egoism into the frame of their history.

I do not know of any man whose message to this age has been of more deep and solemn import, than that of William Ellery Channing. His word, probably more than that of any other man, has broken the fetters of the body and the mind, and prepared the way for a new coming of the Lord. In the delivery of his message he uses very freely the first person singular, not in the way of self-assertion, but rather to set forth his individual convictions in such wise as not to invade the freedom of other minds. But if this great prophet of modern freedom had announced himself as "the Light of the world," as "come down from heaven," as the Judge of the earth who was to sit on a throne of glory, summon the nations to his bar and part them to the right hand and to the left, to eternal punishment or eternal life ; if when his hearers had asked the way to the Father, he had said to them — Look upon me, that is the same as looking upon God ; if he had promised when dying to send them the Holy Spirit, or if he had told his followers to put his name into a formula of baptism along with that of God and the Holy Ghost to be used in proselyting to the end of time, who does not see that he would have been answered with a universal shout of derision, and that the report of his hearers would have been "No man ever spake like this man, because no man's ravings were ever half so wild ?" Put any other great historic name in the same connection and you have the same result : their genuine manhood forthwith is sifted out of them and the only residuum is human pretense and vanity puffed out to their least attenuation.

If the argument of the foregoing chapters has failed to convince any reader that John wrote the fourth Gospel, and if there is any lingering suspicion that its theories of Christ belong to the second century, let him turn to the Apocalypse, the conceded and undoubted production of the beloved disciple.

We have shown in a preceding chapter that the imagery of the discourses of Jesus as deposited in the mind and memory of John, are in the Apocalypse unrolled as the heavenly landscapes, and so representative of the angelic life and worship. All that we have described as the stupendous egoism of Jesus in the fourth Gospel appears in the Apocalypse in another form. What Jesus had asserted of himself in his discourses, as John reports them, what the Golden Proem had claimed for him as the eternal Word, appears in the Apocalypse as conceded to him by the ascending ranks of the heavenly world. In the Apocalypse the metaphysics of the Proem and the discourses that follow and illustrate it, are seen objectively as concrete forms and personalities. Like the diagrams of the mathematicians who put abstract reasonings into shapes palpable to sense; or like the chromos of the traveller which translate his words into scenery that glows upon the canvas, the Apocalypse translates the doctrines and theories about Christ found in the Gospels and in Paul's epistles into the ritual of heaven, heard and seen. "I heard behind me a loud voice," says the seer; and turning he saw one like unto the Son of man — Jesus Christ in glorified form, who said, "I am the First and the Last and he that liveth; and I was dead and behold I am alive forevermore and have the keys of death and the underworld."[1] Jesus Christ, in the fourth Gospel, is the Lamb of God that taketh away the sin of the world. In the Apocalypse the Lamb is coupled

[1] Revelations i. 10, 17, 18.

with the name of God as designating the object of supreme adoration and love. "The twenty-four elders fell down before the Lamb, having each one a harp and golden bowl full of incense, which are the prayers of the saints. And they sing a new song saying, Thou art worthy to take the book and to open its seals, for thou wast slain and hast redeemed to God by thy blood, men out of every tribe and tongue and people and nation, and hast made them a kingdom and priests and they reign on the earth. And I saw and I heard the voice of many angels around the throne and the living creatures and the elders, and the number of them was ten thousand times ten thousand and thousands of thousands: saying with a loud voice, Worthy is the Lamb that was slain, to receive the power and riches and wisdom and strength and honor and glory and blessing. And every creature which is in heaven and those who are on the earth and under the earth and on the sea and the things in them, I heard them all saying, To Him that sitteth upon the throne and to the Lamb be the blessing and the honor and the glory and the dominion forever and ever. And the four living creatures said Amen, and the elders fell down and worshipped."[1]

Not any man however great, or greatly inspired, could be thus exalted so as to receive joint honors and worship with the Supreme, in any system of

[1] Revelation v. 8–14.

pure theism. Not any angel or archangel could be thus exalted; nay, the higher his exaltation the farther away would he be from such homage, for the lower down and the farthest from sight would be all that is himself when ascriptions of glory and dominion were ascending "to Him that sitteth on the throne." And if Christianity has thus exalted a mere man, however great and good, if it has thus exalted any created being whatever, it is as gross a system of idolatry as can be found among any of the religions of the earth.

Is there any other range of fact and statement, complementary of that which we have here given, whereby a pure monotheism is preserved to us, and the Johannean Christology along with it, and made bread from heaven for the hunger of the soul?

CHAPTER VI.

THE LOGOS DOCTRINE.

TO void this idolatry from the cultus of Christianity, two ways are open to us. One is, to apply to the record such destructive criticism as will cut out from it all that asserts the essential divinity of Jesus Christ. Such criticism assumes that this supposed divinity is a factitious halo which has been thrown about him from the warm and idolatrous imaginations of his followers. Take all this away, and we should find a remarkable preacher and reformer, a man developed probably from the best spirit of his times, who was born and who died like other men, but who like some other men received an apotheosis after death. He was divine, says Baur, speaking from the stand-point of his Hegelian theosophy, only as all human nature is divine; and the doctrine of the incarnation is passed over to the interest of the race, serving only as a type of the divine incarnation in all humanity, evolving the Christs of every age, according to the nature and fullness of its inspiration.

Try this theory and see how it applies. Beginning with Matthew and ending with the Apocalypse, go through and sift out from the record everything which imports the superhumanity of Jesus Christ. Go over those passages which we cited in the last chapter, and all the Scripture essentially involved with them, including the discourses of Jesus, which put forth claims such as no prophet or sage could do; go over these and eliminate them all, and what have we left? We have not a "mere man" left, nor the ghost of a man which can be outlined to any rational criticism, however microscopic and keen. The Johannean writings must be voided almost entire, as the German critics very well see. So much of the synoptics as constitute the very frame of their history, must be ignored (for example, Matt. i. 8–25, xi. 27, xxv. 31–46, xxviii. 18–20). The Apocalypse must be rejected, — a book whose genuineness is past all reasonable question, — as a vision which has no objective reality answering to it. Whatever is merely natural and human in the life of Jesus as given in the New Testament, so interblends with the supernatural and superhuman, and makes so complete a whole, that if you pull away the latter, the former comes with it, or else gives a remainder of shreds which belong to no history human or divine. For instance, the birth accords with the resurrection and ascension; the incarnation with the excarnation, the ingress into the world with the egress from it. These mutually explain each other, and explain the miracles as well. Again, the discourses of Jesus constantly forecast just such a death and coming again, and imply their necessity, and they give tone to his divine eloquence and to that inimitable and tender pathos that swells through every sentence of his later utterances. And those are the very utterances which a forger could no more have invented and put into his mouth, than Titian could have invented the landscapes which he copied upon his canvas. Then the history of the Church, and that especially of the first two centuries, as already shown, grounds itself on just such facts as the New Testament records, such a birth, life, death, resurrection, and second coming in the Comforter.

We must seek some other and more rational method to clear away this supposed idolatry from the cultus of Christianity. We must find it in the key of interpretation offered to us freely and constantly in its own unmutilated records. The proem taken as the grand postulate of Christianity, and not resolved into mere rhetoric, gives us an open way into the heart of the divine revelations, and justifies the egoism of the fourth Gospel. The Word, the Divine Reason itself, which is God in the act of utterance, God coming into personal manifestation, was incarnate in the Lord Jesus Christ. It was not an inspiration merely, it was not a vision of God like that of Isaiah or of St. John. It was a more interior union of natures, the divine within the human. By conception and birth the divine was nearer in degree to the human, and dawned through the consciousness more clearly until Jesus speaks from it and acts from it as the normal condition of his own being. Then it is not the finite, tempted, suffering man who speaks; it is the Divine Logos itself, God revealing himself with no admixture of our mortal fallibility and infirmity. Jesus in his full Messiahship has passed into this consciousness of the divine and speaks from it, and the I is no longer the man Jesus, but the Word that existed before Abraham was, which was always with God, which always was God in the act of self-revelation. Even so would the Word ever speak of himself as derived from the Father, as less than the Father, as begotten of the Father, and his only Son. Because the Father is the infinite deeps of Divine Being; in its infinitude unrevealed and unrevealable to any finite mind. The Word is God so far forth as He is revealed; forthgoing from the depths of his infinitude; eternally born of the divine nature, and bringing God into personality and into blissful relations with the creatures He has made.

Let no one say that this is Sabellianism or Arianism, or Trinitarianism, if that means the worship of three persons. The well-informed reader knows it is neither. It is THE LOGOS-DOCTRINE of the primitive church, found roughly in the synoptics and in Paul's fervent metaphysics, but found in the Johannean writings in a continuous blaze of light, the central sun of the whole system of Christian doctrine whence all its other truths are harmonized. It affirms an essential distinction in the divine nature of Father and Son; that these are not merely modes of manifestation in time, but were "in the beginning," and therefore timeless and eternal. God as the Father is the infinite deep of divine being, beyond finite apprehension, beyond the reach of human thought; what "no man hath seen or can see." But left here we are in blind worship, and can only build an altar to the Unknown. Left here we should not know God as a self-conscious intelligence, or as a being who felt the yearnings of an unchanging and tender affection. But the Word is God speaking, the divine Reason in self-revelation, ever on the bosom of the infinite deeps, and bringing forth their treasures of truth and love. This is the Logos-doctrine. We grope towards it in nature, for nature, the more its forces are analyzed, resolves itself into one primal force, a supreme intelligence with unknown depths beyond. The nature-religions groped after it and sometimes saw it in dim twilight. But not till the Word was made flesh, and dwelt among us in Jesus Christ, full of grace and truth, did this benign personality of God appear in its unclouded splendor and break as a new sunrise upon the world.

We see no possibility of missing the doctrine the moment we listen to Jesus as his own interpreter. When the Jews charge him with making himself

God, he meets their accusation by saying, "Believe the works, that ye may know and believe that the Father is in me and I in him;" and to one of his own disciples, as if guarding him from a like misconception of making the Christ a God exterior to another or a higher one, he says, "He that hath seen me hath seen the Father. Believest thou not that I AM IN THE FATHER, AND THE FATHER IN ME? The words that I speak unto you I speak not of myself, but the Father that DWELLETH IN ME he doeth the works." The preëxistent sub-deity of Arianism, we do not find here. The coeternal second person in the Tritheism of the modern church, we find not here nor anywhere. Personal preëxistence, claimed by Jesus, construed as of another person exterior to the Father, is a doctrine rigidly excluded by his own explanations of his own language. But the church-doctrine, ancient and modern, of "the hypostatic union," an interior UNION AND INEXISTENCE OF NATURES, we do find such as justifies language on the lips of Jesus, which on any other lips, angelic or human, would be insufferable, and would be blasphemy indeed. And so, in his full Messianic consciousness, the Divine Word so possessed his being, that he could identify himself with it and say, "I came down from heaven,— I *am* the Word." Or again, the Absolute Truth was inorbed within him so complete, the truth that was to feed the world forever, that he could speak as the absolute Truth itself, and say, "I am the bread that came down from heaven." Tri-personality, we do not find. But the three central doctrines of Christianity, — the uncomprised Oneness of God, the essential divinity of his Christ consubstantial with Him, and the complete humanity of Jesus, making all humanity sacred, — we do find in their full consistency and harmony.[1]

The Eternal Word, which was in the beginning and in which God ever is, was so embodied and impersonated in the Christ that in his full Messianic consciousness he calls it himself. As such he came forth from the Father, and returned to the Father; as such he comes down from heaven, ascends to heaven, and is the Son of Man in heaven; as such he created the world, and judges the world; as such he raises the dead; as such he was before Abraham, and as such he promises, "Lo! I am with you always." This we understand to be the doctrine of the Logos which, carried through the Johannean writings, and the whole New Testament as well, makes a continuous line of light.

There are two objections to the Logos-doctrine. One is metaphysical, the other practical. The first is the *argumentum ab ignorantia.* We cannot understand how there could be two natures in Christ, the divine within the human. What is human is finite; what is divine is infinite, and they cannot be conjoined in one person. It is a self contradiction. The answer is, it may be a mystery; it is so more or less,

[1] See the Appendix C.

but it is no self-contradiction. And it is just the same mystery, which we find in ourselves and in all nature, — the union of the infinite with the finite, in such wise, that the latter is not abolished and lost, but ever remains. The objection sounds strange enough on the lips of a philosophy which asserts the essential divinity of all humanity; which has no trouble about the deification of every child of Adam, and sees no self-contradiction there. How God can be in man, how man can be his absolute subject, a fresh creation of omnipotence every hour, and yet be a self-conscious responsible moral agent, is a mystery which has not yet been resolved. How God can be in nature, where the infinite is ever becoming finite, is a mystery which has never yet been resolved. The line where one passes over into the other eludes our clumsy analysis. Pantheism denies the fact, and resolves the finite in the infinite. Atheism denies the fact, and resolves the infinite in the finite. Herein they rush into mysteries just as inscrutable, and make the verdict of the human consciousness a lie. In the humanity of Jesus Christ, a humanity sinless and complete, there is also the union of the infinite and the finite, but a union in such degree as brings God vastly nearer to ourselves than in a human nature depraved and darkened by sin, and vastly nearer than in dumb nature around us; a union in which the finite is so turned into living transparencies that herein the Word becomes the perfect image and manifestation of the Godhead. In the Johannean speech and imagery it is God not only in first things but in last things; not only in the centres of infinite being, but in the lowest degree of the finite, even to the material clothings of our human nature which were lighted up with the transfigurations of his glory. God in nature, is power, majesty, beneficence; God in our sinful humanity is conscience with trembling apprehensions of the divine justice. God in Christ is Fatherhood, justice, mercy, love, tenderness, forgiveness, sacrifice, the inmost heart of God lavished on the creatures of his hand. It is a revelation which the world waited for and needed to be prepared for. It unitizes its history and lights up its annals to-day. It meets science in its gropings upward at the vanishing point of its discoveries, and transfigures nature in a light which is above nature, turning it into living types of the same spiritual realities which revelation had brought into more open view.

But there is a more practical objection often urged against the Logos-doctrine. It takes Christ out of our human sympathies and loves. He ceases to be our example, our brother whom we may follow through like temptations and victories. Make him like one of ourselves, a development of our own human nature, under like conditions of trial, suffering, and help from God, and how encouraging to follow in his steps! Make him divine, as no other human being ever was or can be, and how vain must all our efforts be to imitate his virtues and put on his perfections and graces!

We should be very sorry to abate the admiration of any one who has been smitten with the loveliness of the character of Jesus, seen merely on his human side. That it has vastly exalted the ideals of the world, as to what constitutes the worth and glory of a perfected manhood, and the direction toward which we must strive for its attainment, is certainly true. That class of the virtues which are hardest to practice, and which, in the world's estimate, were scarcely reckoned as virtues at all, — forgiveness, meekness, love of enemies, love of man as man, complete self-consecration in the service of the race, — are manifest in Jesus Christ, not only as the loftiest ideals, but as the most concrete realities, clothed in flesh and blood like our own, and as such, flinging perpetual rebuke on all our selfish strifes, angers, and enmities, and in some degree charming them into silence and peace.

But if Christ is our pattern, so is God in precisely the same sense, and as He is revealed in the Christ himself: "Be ye perfect, as your Father in heaven is perfect." "Be ye followers of God, as dear children." Must God, too, be brought down within our finite proportions, in order that we may follow Him? Or shall we not gratefully acknowledge, rather, that the ideals which shine down upon us from the

Divine Perfections, are all the more worthy of our aspiration and love because no dimness has come over them from our corrupt earthly exhalations? And how true it is, that these ideals never would have been furnished us through sheer development, and that they come down to us out of heaven, as imaged in a humanity in which dwelt the fullness of the Godhead bodily! And if eighteen hundred years of culture and progress, with all the added appliances of education and philosophy, still leave those ideals burning far above us in their solitary splendor and beauty, away in the depths of infinite space, Christ as a *mere* example which I am to follow and overtake, is no such vast encouragement after all. There it shines,— a star in the heavens of royal brightness and magnitude, but I cannot reach it.

If Jesus Christ, as he beams upon me from the only biographies which we have of him, taken in the whole range of his nature, and the whole height of his excellency, is a model which I am expected to imitate and translate into my daily life, then he is no encouragement to me, but condemnation and blank despair. How long must I attain before, standing up to challenge the world, I can say, "Which of you convinceth me of sin?" How long before I can tell my hearers, "Ye are from beneath; I am from above?" How long before I can announce to them, "All that the Father hath is mine," or "No man knoweth God but me, and he to whom I shall reveal Him?"

At what stage of my moral progress may I become so at one with Almighty God, that I may consider myself his purely embodied reason, and speak in my own name, and from my own self-consciousness as from God himself, and bend his bow and launch his thunders? "The hour is coming when all who are in the graves shall hear my voice, and shall come forth — they that have done good to a resurrection of life, and they that have done evil, to a resurrection of condemnation." Or when from my super-angelic acquirements may I announce — "I am the Alpha and the Omega, the beginning and the end, the first and the last, and I hold the keys of hades and death?" To make Jesus Christ my model throughout, would not crown me with all human graces and excellences. but would place me a fantastic figure on the heights of heaven, gesticulating in its lightnings and outlined for a moment on its thunderclouds, the next moment to disappear in its consuming fires.

And if this majestic and beautiful life is not to be taken as the biographers have made it, if they have interjected imaginary facts and discourses, and I must carve it and reconstruct it in order to make it sheerly human, and bring it so near to my own condition as to make it easy for me to copy, what becomes of its value to me as an example? I can make it then just what I please. I shall leave out what I think unattainable, very likely the excellences and graces after which I ought to strive with prayers and self-denials, and the model of perfection which I shall construct will not be an ideal let down to me complete out of heaven, but one which I have made out of my own preconceptions, and which, in some sort, will be a pattern of my own contrivance. Jesus Christ as the perfect example, subjected to such a process as this, is not the humanity ever shining above us, but constructed after our own notions, and brought near to a level with ourselves.

An example to imitate is not my primary and sorest need. I can find plenty of good examples when I want them, scattered along the ages, much nearer to me and more easy of imitation than the example of Jesus Christ. I can find enough of them which are not altogether out of my reach, and I should doubtless apply myself to copy them, if the main business of life consisted in plagiarising the virtues of dead men. Indeed I have altogether too many good examples already for my peace of mind. They are all about me, flinging a lustre across my path at every step and rebuking my low attainment. They are in my own community, in my own household; examples of royal men and women, the beauty of whose daily lives makes us ugly. Thank God for these, but our deepest necessities are not in this direction. Models of behavior for one man, will not serve for another; his environment, his duties, and the sweep of his inward life being altogether different. We want God. Our deepest hunger and thirst reach thitherward. We want Him both within and from above. Within He comes to all, but with a vast difference as to distinctness and clearness, as the shinings of his presence struggle through the chaos of our evils and passions. We want Him from above also, in the unclouded glory of his attributes, across whose serene disk no spots from our own depravity are passing to bewilder and darken our judgment. We want Him from above to flood our consciousness with light, uncolored by our own passions and false conceptions, to make clear our inward beholdings, and bring the subjective consciousness into correspondency with the eternal objective Reality. For want of this, what deities have men conceived out of their own lusts and fears, and then grovelled before them — the reflex image of themselves! For want of this how have men sought out of their own emptiness deities shadowy and unthinkable — the reflex image of themselves! We want God revealed from above, not less than from within, that his image within, overlaid and darkened with corruption, both hereditary and actual, may be cleared and made bright. We want God from above, unobscured by the guessings of any human theosophies, to melt the ice out of us, to warm our frozen affections, and enlarge them to universal love. And with this the true ideals of manhood will come also; come to every man according to the sphere of duty he is to act in, with inspirations and impulsions to follow them, and fill that sphere with a fragrancy and light which are the breathings and shinings of the Lord. Then the ideals we are to follow will not be some good example of sainthood, after the pattern of which we must be stretched or trimmed ; they will be given every hour to our clarified reason ; the pillar of flame that always goes before us, the heavenly vision that always leads us on.

The strictly human virtues of the man Jesus Christ are not more valuable to us as examples of a full-orbed humanity, than as revelations of the Divine attributes. Nature reveals God only on the lower and outer planes of existence. Man, sinful and unregenerate, is at best his distorted and broken image. But a humanity perfected under his hand, and in which He dwells in fullness, is the complete thought of God as to what moral perfection truly is. Whether God's justice, mercy, tenderness, forgiveness, compassion and love, are the same in kind with those qualities as we find them in the characters of the best men, or whether as Mr. Mansel says, they stand like algebraic signs for unknown quantities when we talk of the awful and infinite One, are questions which are painfully oppressive, till the Deity shines upon us in the face of Jesus Christ. Herein we know that God is not only divine but human as well. Because all the virtues of Jesus are human virtues, we know that the attributes of God are human attributes, for the former are the unobstructed creation of the latter and therefore their direct and resplendent image, and so the open revelation of a Divine humanity. Thus the union between God and all his human children as they become one in Christ is intimate and full; they are partakers each of the other's nature; the Divine of the human, and the human of the Divine, and the relation is all-sufficing and indescribably sweet and tender. "I am the Vine, ye are the branches," unfolds all its beautiful significance.

We want God not alone in our darkened intuitions, but from the cloven heavens. Other religions abound in both precept and example. There have been good men, thank God, under all forms of faith and codes of morals that have anticipated some of the divine sayings of the Sermon on the Mount. The best men of all nations and ages have seen in some degree, at least in their most lucid hours, what they ought to do and what they ought to be. Buddhism, Parseeism, and Judaism, as the Essenes received it, had their lofty ideals of moral perfection, and their strivings after it. God has never been without a witness, for the Word has ever knocked at the door of the human heart, and sought to enlighten every man that cometh into the world. But in the Lord Jesus Christ the heavens indeed are cloven, and not only our ideals of perfection are exalted and purified, but God is yielded to us with transforming power to cleanse from evil, to energize, to create anew, to bring the ideals which He gives more rapidly to their realization, and to glorify himself in a human nature redeemed and sanctified. Do you say that after eighteen hundred years the work is not yet done, and very imperfectly done in Christendom itself? But what are eighteen centuries in the cycles of God, for bringing such a world as this to such a pitch of glory and of experimental knowledge of himself? It was longer than that before the world discovered that the nearest fixed star was any thing but a twinkling point in the firmament. But Herschell says that when he turned his glass in that direction, the star changed to a sun and came on like the dawn of the morning, and he had to turn away from the beautiful sight. What wonder that God, revealed in Jesus Christ, should not be seen at once and alike by all; yea, that He only seems far off like a shimmering star! What mercy is it that this is even so! and that only so far forth as the heart is renewed and the vision clarified and enlarged thereby, He comes nearer and nearer, till He warms and fertilizes our whole being, and fills our whole life with the day-spring.

CHAPTER VII.

THE JOHANNEAN ATONEMENT.

THE Christian atonement may be contemplated from two very different points of view. It is a doctrine of philosophy, or it is a doctrine of the Christian experience. The former we grasp with the understanding only, as we attempt to fathom the reasons and methods of the Divine government; the latter we know, as its manifest results are achieved and as they glow in the consciousness of the believer. As a question of the understanding, it is a matter of indefinite controversy, inasmuch as all the reasons of the Divine government involve the knowledge of all the laws both of the spiritual and the natural world. As a question of consciousness it admits of no controversy, for the atonement of the Christian experience is the believer himself brought into harmony with the Divine mind, purpose and will, through the Mediator; and it involves a knowledge of the love of Christ, and its exceeding and abounding peace. This is the atonement as a doctrine of individual faith. Stated at large and as the final achievement of God in this world, the atonement is the union of

God, man, and nature ; so that disharmony between man and nature, and between both and God, shall cease altogether, and God become all in all ; or in Johannean phrase, He shall be not only ἐν ἀρκῇ, in beginnings, but ὁ ἔσχατος, the consummation ; glorified in lowest forms of nature and humanity.

The Pauline writings treat this doctrine as one of the understanding. But they do this almost exclusively, as regards Jews and Jewish converts, and to silence objections which come from that quarter, and which were temporary and local. When Paul leaves them he rises to the heart of the doctrine. But John did not write for Jews. Jerusalem had fallen, and with it Judaism was passing away, and Christianity, as the New Jerusalem, had come in its place. John throughout gives the atonement purely as a doctrine of the Christian consciousness, and as it came from the lips of Jesus in those Sabbatic hours, when his disciples were drawn nearest to him, and his heart opened out to them its inmost treasures of truth and love. How this doctrine of his religion was then declared and explicated, becomes a question of supreme interest, for we shall be sure to have its essential contents as concerns the salvation of the Christian believer.

In one of his latest discourses, which seems to have been uttered in colloquial intercourse with the disciples on their way from the last supper to Gethsemane, the oneness of the disciple with his Lord, and the means of it, are set forth by imagery of great significance and beauty.

"I am the true Vine and my Father is the husbandman. Every branch in me that beareth not fruit he taketh away: and every branch that beareth fruit he cleanseth, that it may bear more fruit. Ye are clean already by reason of the word which I have spoken unto you. Abide in me and I will abide in you. As the branch cannot bear fruit of itself, unless it abide in the Vine, so neither can ye unless ye abide in me. I am the Vine, ye are the branches. He that abideth in me and I in him, the same beareth much fruit; for separated from me ye can do nothing. If any one abide not in me, he is cast forth as a branch, and is withered; and men gather it, and cast it into the fire, and it is burned. If ye abide in me and my words abide in you, ask whatever ye will and it shall be done for you. Herein is my Father glorified, that ye bear much fruit. So shall ye be my disciples."

Neither man nor angel could avow himself an original fountain of life unto others, so as to tell them, "Separated from me ye can do nothing;" or "ye are cast forth as a branch cut from its parent stem, to wither and die." Least of all, could any man say this on the eve of his death, when the total and final separation was to take place. Jesus plainly is speaking here as the Word; God revealing himself in all his human attributes, so that the believer could lay hold of Him by a clear and living faith, and thereby the Divine Life flow down through all his nature, as the juices of the Vine flow down through the branches, till the grapes hang in clusters on the stems. This is the true oneness with Christ. Salvation in him is not by an imputed righteousness, but by a righteousness imparted and inwrought; manifested in the fruits of righteous living; in the clustering charities of a life always replenished and flavored from its Divine fountain. It will be seen by this that the Johannean theology is the farthest possible from any form of Antinomianism, and the farthest possible from teaching a dreamy and lazy devotion. True, it is profoundly contemplative; but to the end of being more intensely practical, and producing fruit more abundantly, and of more heavenly quality; and any member of the Christian organism that is not thus receptive of the Christ, both in faith and in practice, is a withered branch to be pruned away, cast into the fire and burned.

How the believer is to abide in Christ and receive life from him as the eternal fountain, we learn more fully and further on in these last divine colloquies with the disciples. The Holy Spirit as Teacher, Comforter and Guide, is promised as the gift of Christ, as coming through faith in him, and obedience to his word. The Holy Spirit is the forthgoing sphere of the Divine light and love, finding the believer and infolding him in its celestial airs; hence the Father and the Son — God through his revealing Word — coming to him and making their abode with him. It is the opening down of the Divine Nature to transform the human, and take up the burden of its sins and sorrows, and bring man into fellowship with God. But this could not be unless man was first brought into true fellowship with man. It would not have availed to reveal God unless states of reception had been wrought in men fitted to receive Him. Oneness with the neighbor is a prime condition of oneness with the heavenly Father. Man must stand right towards his brother, or he never can stand right towards his God, and be receptive of Him, and a partaker of his nature. Hence the new code of human fellowship which Jesus labored to inaugurate and exemplify in his own life on the earth. Every man is a part of every other man — this is the sum of the new doctrine, and on this was founded the society of believers called a church. Until that were done, there was no organic form for God's reception and indwelling amongst men. Until that were done, men individually were so many repellent forces, every man's life antagonizing the life of God. But Jesus left eleven disciples, recipients of his word, and the first organized form of his kingdom of universal love. What followed? The God who had been revealed, had now a place to come in. As soon as man was put right towards his fellows and towards his God, the Divine love and blessing came and swept his soul like a lyre. THE PROCESSION OF THE HOLY SPIRIT followed in the logical sequence of events. God newly revealed as divinely human, began to flood our wasted nature with his life and power, and hence the new dispensation of the Spirit as the inheritance of after ages. Bear this in mind, and we shall have a full explication of the atonement, or the doctrine of man made at one with God in Christ as enunciated in the following language: —

"And now I am coming to thee; and these things I speak in the world, that they may have thy joy complete in themselves. I have given them thy word; and the world hated them, because they are not of the world, as I am not of the world. I ask not that thou take them out of the world, but that thou keep them out of the evil. They are not of the world as I am not of the world. Consecrate them in the service of thy truth; thy word is truth. Since thou didst send me into the world, I also sent them into the world. And in their behalf I consecrate myself, that they also may be consecrated in the service of truth. Yet not for these only do I pray, but also for those who believe in me through their word; that they all may be one, as thou Father art in me and I in thee, that they may be in us, that the world may believe that thou didst send me. And the glory which thou hast given me I have given them, that they may be one because we are one.[1] I in them and thou in me, that they may be made perfect in one, that the world may know that thou hast sent me, and hast loved them as thou hast loved me. Father! as to those whom thou hast given me, I desire that they also be with me where I am, that they may behold my glory which thou hast given me; for thou lovedst me before the foundation of the world. Righteous Father!

[1] Καθώς has considerable range of meaning, and is used either in a comparative or causal sense; and when in the latter means *according as*, or *because that*. So it is used in this same chapter (verse 2), and in the passage cited we understand Jesus to be setting forth his oneness with the Father as the ground, or procuring cause of oneness with the disciples.

though the world knew thee not, I knew thee, and these knew that thou didst send me. And I made known to them thy name and will make it known; that the love wherewith thou hast loved me may be in them and I in them." [1]

Such is the Christian atonement, as set forth in the divinest language that ever fell upon human ears. It is God in Christ, and Christ in the disciple, so far forth as he yields himself to Christ, and is brought into union with him in obedient and childlike faith. The Church in formulating the same doctrine, emphasizes the requirements of the Divine Law, which Jesus came to cancel and satisfy, and hence dwells primarily, and sometimes too grossly and exclusively on his sufferings and death. Let us not ignore or undervalue the great truth involved in this formulation, which even in its grosser apprehension has brought to so many minds a sense of the divine forgiveness. It is all true that the sufferings and death of Christ were necessary to satisfy the requirements of the Divine Law. Who can follow on through Gethsemane to Calvary, and believe that such a sacrifice is merely to pay the debt of our common mortality; that there was not demanded in fundamental reasons of the Divine government, "the Lamb slain from the foundation of the world?" It is not, going beyond the letter or the spirit of Scripture to say that the death of Christ was an irreversible condition of human redemption and salvation. In this sense his sufferings and death were vicarious.

[1] John xvii. 13-26.

But what do we mean by the laws of God, which this great sacrifice was to satisfy? Not any written statutes or parchment regulations, except so far forth as these are transcripts of the eternal principles of being. The laws of God are the inherent conditions of the supreme order of the universe, as they pervade all worlds and all ranks of existence. That order is such arrangement and such subordination of lower to higher, of special to general, of evil to good, of the less good to the greater, of natural to spiritual, as shall insure the highest and widest beneficence. If any jot or tittle of these laws of the supreme order were to fail, no one can tell the consequent ruin and suffering, for the universe is conjoined part to part, the whole to each, and each to all, by sympathies and relations finer and more pervasive than any analysis of ours can show. *These* laws — not any police regulations of Moses — Jesus came not to destroy but to fulfill. The sighs of the creation, and the deepest undertones of nature, and if we may believe the record, the urgencies of the angelic worlds themselves, forecast an epiphany of God in humanity at the time it came, and they felt when they could not articulate the exigencies of the hour. The benefits of that coming, for aught we know, might extend to other worlds as well as this. It might have been necessary in order to subordinate hell, in order to preserve the heavens and keep them clean, not less than to redeem the earth, which is the substructure and support of the heavens themselves, that God should be in Last things as well as First things, and so become all in all. The Word become man in Jesus Christ. His life on the earth, his death, resurrection, ascension, and coming again in the Paraclete, with new regenerating power, were alike the fulfillment of these laws of the supreme order, through which alone God could yield himself to his creation, and redeem it and glorify himself in it, while the essential principles of our manhood are still preserved. An angel might have descended and proclaimed the abstract truths of the Gospel from the tops of the mountains, and then disappeared with dissolving views into heaven ; but who does not see that the truths, like the lovely vision, would have melted away. God must come into this world in such wise as to take hold of it and save it, the elements of human nature and the laws of action upon it being such as we find them ; and this could not be unless He made himself a partaker of our nature, drawing up into his consciousness by divine sympathies the wants and sufferings of ours.

All this we get gleams of as this great subject of the atonement unfolds its mysteries, and we learn it in all its relations. Undoubtedly my intellect would be gratified if I could see those relations all complete, and know the Lamb as "slain from the foundation of the world." Here, however, is not where this subject touches me savingly and vitally. That is through my relations to the Christ, received not as a mere man but as God with us, so as to make me a branch of the Vine into which the Divine Life perennially flows. When I have this I have the daily fulfillment of the promise, "Thou Father art in me and I in thee, that they may be in us, that the world may believe that thou didst send me." By this I may be brought into such daily communion with God, and fellowship of his Spirit, that it shows me what I am and what I need; shows all my sins in contrast with his own dazzling purity, helps me to acknowledge and repudiate them, and lay their whole burden upon Him as his care and no longer mine. Then comes the assurance of forgiveness, and the peace of God flows in like a river clear and tranquil. For it is one of the paradoxes of the Christian experience that the more fully our sins are revealed within us, the more perfect and well assured is the peace that comes; and when they loom blackest and most sharply defined against the clear blue of the heavens beyond them, we know that a power mightier than they is working in us and taking up our burden for us, that they may not trouble us any more. What multitudes have found not only rest but everlasting joy at the feet of Jesus Christ, simply by giving themselves away to him in an unbounded trust, who never tried to excogitate the methods of the atonement, or those eternal laws of being which it fulfills! In spiritual things, as in natural, the law of demand and supply is sure in its operations and its last results. What we want in Christ we always find in him. When we want nothing we find nothing. When we want little we find little. When we want much we find much. But when we want everything, and get reduced to complete nakedness and beggary, we find in him God's complete treasure-house, out of which come gold and jewels and garments to clothe us, wavy in the richness and glory of the Lord.

CHAPTER VIII.

CONVERGING LINES.

MORE than fifty years of controversy have been waged in New England between Trinitarianism and Unitarianism, as if they were two conflicting forms of Christianity. In this warfare Trinitarianism has been opposed as if it were both tritheism and idolatry; and Unitarianism has been opposed as if it were a denial of Jesus Christ and a rejection of his authority. That these mutual charges and imputations are both true and false, could be proved abundantly by citations from the writings on both sides. Trinitarianism may be held and explicated as the worship of three gods, or it may be held as the purest theism. We believe it has been held as both. Unitarianism may be held as conserving both the unity of God and the divinity of Christ, or it may merge both these doctrines in sheer pantheism, and lose the historical Christ altogether. It has had all this range, and has it to-day.

At the same time Christianity, as God's all-revealing Word and his final achievement in human nature, has a unitizing power more manifest from age to age. The Paraclete which it promised and which it ever brings, ought to melt down artificial distinctions, and develop amid all this diversity an increasing and controlling Catholicity. Christianity was given to mankind in a state not much removed from barbarism; and to say that clouds gathered about it, drawn from human conceit and earthliness, is only saying that it did not turn the earth by magic into Paradise. At the same time we should expect the obscuring clouds to grow lighter, and finally dissolve. And so they do. Two great facts are noteworthy. Jesus Christ, as given in the New Testament, and in the consciousness of the Church, ever growing deeper and clearer, is the guide of the nations to-day. The statistics show it. The denominations which receive Christ, not as the self-development of human nature, eighteen hundred years ago, but as the opening down of God to man, and of heaven to earth, at this hour, are spreading and growing, and their ratio of increase is higher than that of the population. Faith in Christ, as the great want of man and the renewing power of a fallen world, waxes but never wanes. This is one fact, we say, which the statistics of the denominations carefuly collated clearly reveal. And there is another, which may not be within the reach of statistics, but concerning which we presume the reader will have no shadow of doubt. It is this: — the denominations are becoming more fully possessed with the mind and spirit of Christ. If you doubt it compare the present century with the last, or compare the modern with the mediæval ages as pertains to the golden fruits of a true faith, righteousness, charity, brotherhood, and universal love. The beatitudes of the Sermon on the Mount, the humanities of the sermon on Mount Olivet, and the love that breathes through the Johannean discourses, never beat with more tender pulses than now, to move and inspire all the ecclesiasticisms of the Christian world. Worthier and lovelier views of the divine character and attributes; zeal for Christ purged of all bitterness from the gall of the unregenerate heart; tolerance of error in opinion; intolerance of wrong to any child of God, or of cruelty to any creature He has made; better theories of human nature and destiny; and better feelings of human fellowship that make every man, not only the image of God but the image of every other man, — these mark the advent of Christ, as John foresaw it, — Christianity displacing at length the old Judaism and heathenism, as the New Jerusalem coming down from God out of heaven. The unbelievers who assail Christianity now must go back into the centuries, where they find it as corrupted and overlaid by the Judaism or Paganism, through which it was melting its way, not as it breaks through them from the face of the Christ himself. True, it is not yet entirely cleared of them, for they are "the old man with his lusts" that lurks in all our hearts, but the missions, the charities, the self-sacrifice, the faith in God, the hope of man, and the deeper tenderness that beats through them all, are the inspiration of the Christ always coming in his kingdom. If you doubt this, strike out that name and the faiths organically connected with it; faiths which make man an immortal being, to be cared for as such, and not an animal, to be fed and dressed for this world only ; faiths which give the Paraclete as the inspiration of our work-day songs and our visions of heaven at the dying hour, — strike these out and leave every man to his own guessings and intuitions, and how speedily would our beneficent Christian enterprises collapse and die! The living Christ, we say, leads and inspires the thought of all our advancement to-day. Any reform that meets with tolerable success, succeeds, because the Christ is in it, showing the worth of man as an immortal being, the child of a universal Father and the member of a universal brotherhood, his fellowship being not of earth and time only, but of the glorified in heaven as well, whose sympathies draw us mightily upward, and whose "Come up hither!" ever falls down to cheer us. There is not a denomination of Christendom, whose literature we are acquainted with, which does not show that the Spirit is coming within them with greater fullness and tenderness, making their theologies fluid in the love of Christ, as they reflect from his face in softer light the Beatitudes which he spake and lived.

All this being so, another consequence inevitably

follows. We cannot move towards the Christ without coming closer to each other. Leave out him and his unitizing Word, and let every man strike out for himself, and we tend to a crumbling individualism, to endless distraction and confusion. But those who acknowledge Jesus Christ as the supreme authority and guide, and enter more into his all-revealing mind, are making progress towards the harmonizing truths which he represents. However wide apart they may be at the start, their progress is ever on converging lines. Essential truth becomes more and more central and manifest, the non-essential falls away to its subordinate place, and orthodox and unorthodox move alike towards a higher and higher unity. It is not that any one sect is making a conquest of the others, but Jesus Christ is making a conquest of us all.

Some time ago Professor Stuart declared in the name of Trinitarian orthodoxy, that it did not teach three persons in the Godhead, in the sense in which Unitarians interpret that phraseology; that Trinitarians did not use the word *person* in its modern acceptation, but to indicate a distinction in the Divine Nature, which they did not pretend to understand, and that the word "person" was only employed on account of the poverty of language. And because of this liability to misconstruction, the word has been dropped from many declarations of faith. Several orthodox creeds are before us, some of them of large representative churches, which read, "We believe in one God, Father, Son, and Holy Spirit," leaving the interpretation of these Bible words to the Christian believer, as God shall reveal himself in the clarified consciousness, so that the divine threeness shall not conflict with the divine unity.

That the worship of Christ may be and often is idolatrous worship; that it is the exaltation of the creature to the place of the Creator, of a finite suffering man to the place of God, we are by no means disposed to deny. We suppose it inevitable that many minds cling to the mere finite without rising clearly out of it. But we have no right to bring this as a sweeping charge against the orthodox denominations, as many persons do. Those who make these charges ignore the distinction which orthodoxy has always made in its doctrine of "the hypostatic union," the more interior union in Christ of the infinite and the finite. Christ as an object of prayer and of divine honors, stands for nothing finite and mortal to the mind of any intelligent worshipper, but rather for the Divine Logos, of which the finite suffering humanity was but symbol and scaffolding. To bring down the Christ within our human dimensions, and then project our shriveled conception into the creeds of our neighbors, and charge them with worshipping the Christ as we have constructed him, is not the device of truthful and honorable controversy. As the Mediator through whom alone the soul has been drawn up into the embrace of the divine love, what multitudes there are, both Trinitarian and Unitarian, who would say with tearful thanksgivings, "All I know of God is bound up in that name."

There is no ground for the charge of idolatry against those who worship God under the name of Christ, from that fact alone, any more than there is against the Naturalist, who sees God through the symbols of nature. The Naturalist, if a theist, sees in Nature God revealing himself, and he stands amid her blaze of magnificence, and adores. Am I to turn upon him, and charge him with Fetishism, with worshipping stones, and trees, and mountains, and not rather enter into his thought, in which stones, trees, and mountains, and the whole range of finite objects, are seen as the exponents of forces that lie within them and behind them, and these again resolved into the ground-force of all which is the adorable and eternal One. No catalogue of finite objects, however classified, exhausts your conception of Nature. It implies some power that lies within and behind them. If you ascribe to this power self-consciousness and personality, you are a theist and worship this power as God. But I should grossly belie your thought if I charged you with making deities of finite objects, whether stones and trees, or suns and stars, or men and women. Just as grossly do you misrepresent the Christian theist, when you charge him with worshipping a creature when he worships God in Christ. He forewarns you that while he sees Jesus the perfected man, finite, suffering, dying, he sees also the Eternal Word, that same Power which you see in nature. He sees it as he believes no longer dimly, but clothed in all the attributes of Divine Fatherhood, and of our own humanity in infinite degree; coming into the world through a more perfect and open way than that of nature, in order to take man's spiritual burdens upon himself, purify his child, and raise him up to the Divine communion. This is what he worships in Christ. He no more worships a finite and suffering man when he worships God in Christ, than you worship stones, trees, and mountains when you worship God in nature. But in a man though finite and suffering, yet unstained by sin, in a humanity not partial and one-sided but in complete and majestic proportions, and in which the Eternal Word is become man, he thinks he has access to the Godhead in his warm glories, and his forgiving and cleansing love, such as you can never have through material nature, nor yet in a humanity foul with the stains of moral corruption.

Between Unitarianism as Channing held it, and Trinitarianism, as Stuart held it, plainly the controversy ought to cease, as regards this single doctrine of the Divine Unity. In other respects, in details of doctrine, doubtless, the two systems greatly differ; but both tend to a sublimer unity in the Christ where artificial distinctions have fallen down. Channing's prime objection to creeds was that they come between the disciple and his Lord, and so are a hindrance to progress. He believed that Christianity as yet had been but half apprehended; that orthodox and heterodox alike were in the beggarly elements, and that their true progress lay not away from Christ, but towards Him. He seems to have worshipped God in Christ, at least, in his latest meditations, as much as any orthodox monotheist could consistently do, for in his last public utterance, which has been called the Swan-song of a Son of Light, he shows clearly that he had faith in what orthodoxy calls the "hypostatic union," though he believed it a doctrine too vast and mysterious to be packed into our human formulas.

"All the doctrines of Christianity," he says, "are more and more seen to be bonds of close, spiritual, reverential union between man and man; and this is the most cheering view of our time. Christianity is a revelation of the infinite, universal, paternal love of God towards his human family, comprehending the most sinful, descending to the most fallen, and its aim is to breathe the same love into its disciples. It shows us Christ tasting death for every man, and it summons us to take his cross, or to participate of his sufferings in the same cause. Its doctrine of immortality gives infinite worth to every human being, for every one is destined to this endless life. The doctrine of the 'Word made flesh' shows us God *uniting Himself most intimately with our nature, manifesting himself in a human form*, for the very end of making us partakers of his own perfection." [1]

When the denominations have done with the human creeds, and trust alike to the Word made flesh, they will meet together not by any compromise of opinions but in due course of Christian progress; not on any field of past controversy, but on those higher planes of thought where the beams of truth, once refracted and separated, are gathered and reunited into one ray of white light which reflects the sun in his original brightness. Theologians are evanescent and soon pass away. But the Word of God remains. A church founded upon it, such as Channing dreamed of and prayed for, fettered by no human interpretations but gathered only around him, in whom, to quote Channing's words, "the fullness of Divinity dwells," has all the future for its inheritance with none of the effete dogmas of the past; it may grow forever into the more perfect form and body of Christ till he lives in all its functions; its differences will be only as surface waves, while its unity of spirit will be as the deep, still currents beneath.

Experience thus far has shown that all attempts at progress by leaving out the Christ, have resulted

[1] This is from Dr. Channing's address at Lenox, his last public utterance. But it must not be inferred from this emphatic language, that he had adopted any received theory of the nature of Christ. We gather elsewhere from his writings that he considered himself a learner to the last.

in retrogression, not in a new unfolding of the wealth of the Gospel; that all movement out of the circle and beyond the influence of the personalities of the Bible, is not into the light that burns warmer and clearer. No foothold, that we can see, has ever been found, but one exceedingly slippery, between the naturalism that makes Christ a normal development of our nature, and the supernaturalism that asserts his essential Divinity. If we deny the latter, the whole New Testament must be reconstructed and vast portions of it expunged, and the Tübingen critics are right. Their method is the true one, and it depends on individual taste and idiosyncrasy, how much shall be expunged and how much shall be left, and whether anything. Not only so, but Christian history for eighteen hundred years has been developed from shadows, and the glorified company of saints have fed on husks that had no corn within them.

But why not teach the great truths of universal religion, God and the Holy Spirit and immortality and the duties of love to God and love to man without any other authority than the truths themselves? Because these words, — God, the Holy Spirit, and Immortality, — within the circle of Christian ideas and personalities are fraught with a meaning which they can never lose, but which grows more full and sufficing with all Christian progress; whereas outside that circle the meaning leaks out of them all the while, till they hang empty and float in air. No one who receives the Christ of the New Testament history, can lose faith in the personal fatherhood of God, in his universal providence, in the Holy Spirit as an effusive energy coming from above man to find him and renew him, in the existence of an angel-world, and in man as created for its abodes. Not only so, but these truths grow upon him and become the ever brightening scenery of his mind. On the other hand, outside the circle of Christian ideas and personalities, they freeze into abstractions, or fade off altogether, till God sinks into an impersonal force, and the spirit-world is swamped in the natural. If the idea of God, as held by such men as Herbert Spencer, and by men of equal ability nearer home, gets the essential qualities of a Divine Fatherhood strained out of it, leaving only an unknowable force for the evolution of phenomena, what reason have we to suppose that churches, founded not on Jesus Christ but on individual intuitions, may not exist with all the forms and titles of Christian theism, while all Christian thought is leaking out of its words and rituals?

There are "liberal Christians" among all sects; those, that is, who believe that Christianity is not yet learned out, that it is to have an auspicious future, since the hard features of the old creeds are softening and the old lines of division grow indistinct. These changes, as we read the signs, come not mainly from our controversies, nor from any visible appliances whatsoever. They come from the profounder currents of the Spirit within, which is bearing all of us, Trinitarians and Unitarians alike, towards higher realms of truth, and towards a more comprehending unity. This current sets not away from Jesus Christ and his Word, but toward larger views of both. The yearnings of this age, as we interpret them and as uttered out of the deepest wants of human nature, reach in this direction.

In America, the great denominations that move on with renewed vigor to the work of Christian civilization and education, do not make their theologies less Christian but more so, and the Christ in them gives to them both their aggressive power and their inspiring song. The antichristian Rationalism has not shown itself the advanced thought of the times, but the very smallest among the reflex eddies under the lee shore, while the vast current of the world's progress is sweeping grandly by. We can be set back on one of these side-eddies if we will, and then the other Christian bodies, advancing with the ideas which we shall have abandoned, will do the work which we ought to have done, — or as we pray and believe will be the case, we can be true to our historic urgencies and pledges, and then it is plain to see there is a point not far off in the distance, where we shall see the triumph of the divinest of all Unitarianism: "I in them and thou in me that they may be made perfect in one, and that the world may believe that thou hast sent me."

CHAPTER IX.

THE THRONES IN HEAVEN. — CONCLUSION.

"I SAW thrones," says the seer of the Apocalypse when describing the ritual of heaven. They appear in gradation rank above rank; and three grades are distinguished. There is the throne of the Supreme, who sits thereon encircled with rainbows, and the worshippers rest not day and night, saying, Holy, holy, holy Lord God Almighty, which was and is and is to come." There is the throne of the Lamb, who receives homage almost as great, who draws around him the alleluiahs of every creature which is in heaven and on the earth and in the under world and in the sea, whose name is coupled with that of God in receiving adoration; who sitteth down on the throne of God, or who is "in the midst of the throne;" so that the same throne is called "the throne of God and the Lamb." The same divine predicates are applied to him as to the Almighty, "Alpha and Omega, the Beginning and Ultimation, the First and the Last," and he feeds the saints from the midst of the throne, and judges the sinners who hide under rocks from "the wrath of the Lamb." There is a third and lower rank of thrones: those of the twenty-four elders, thrones of judgment for the redeemed who are to reign with Christ; and the promise is given that as Christ sits down with the Father on God's throne, so the saints shall sit down with Christ on his throne.

The reader knows very well what the literalists make of all this. It is the worship of a created being, so great and so exalted, that he sits on the throne of the Almighty, and receives a worship such as no enlightened pagan ever gave to inferior divinities. But it is not supreme worship, they say, but analogous to the homage paid to sovereigns and magistrates, only more magnificent, as to one more worthy; for does he not promise the same in kind to his saints who are to sit with him on thrones of judgment?

And what is the judgment-seat of Christ to which his saints are invited? Turn to Matthew, twenty-fifth chapter, and we shall see. The Son of Man comes in glory to summon all peoples to his bar, sits on the throne of his glory, and separates the saints from the sinners, — those to eternal life and these to eternal punishment. A singular judicial process, if the saints themselves are on the throne of judgment and not at the judgment bar!

This imagery of the Apocalypse only puts into concrete and objective form the figurative language of Christ in the Gospels. When events were moving on to their crisis, Peter came to Jesus with the question, "Behold, we have forsaken all and followed thee, what shall we have therefore?" Jesus assures his Apostles in reply: "When the Son of Man shall sit in the throne of his glory, ye also shall sit upon twelve thrones judging the twelve tribes of Israel." The ambition of two of them took fire at the prospect. They wanted the *highest* thrones, one on the right and one on the left of Christ; and soon after this they came with their mother secretly and applied for such promotion. What was the answer of Jesus? One of the most solemn rebukes of human ambition which it ever received, and one of the most touching lessons of humility and self-sacrifice: "Whoever will be chief among you let him be your servant. Even as the Son of Man came not to be ministered unto but to minister." Has Jesus left these lessons behind, and gone into the heavens, thence to address a more potent stimulus to our mean selfishness or our pompous vanities, than the empty grandeurs of earth could ever give?

When we undertake to interpret a symbolical book, we should not mix up symbol and letter into a jumble. We have seen into what a slough of insane nonsense the Apocalypse may thus be turned. But keep constantly to its symbolic meaning, and though we may not be drawn up to its sublime heights of vision, we shall have the same serene and blissful openings, that are given us in the fourth Gospel.

Persons in the Apocalypse, and the imagery amid which they appear, very often symbolize truths in a connected series ; even Christianity, as a system of truth, in its power of judging, regenerating, and saving mankind. What are the apostolic thrones ? Seats raised aloft with the fishermen of Galilee robed royally and sitting thereon, as the judges of their fellow men, they to whom the injunction first came, — Judge not that ye be not judged ? Not at all ; but the apostolic truths which they represented, applied in their royal power to subdue and save, and beneath which those twelve men have learned by this time to bring themselves in lowly self-surrender. And what is the worship of "God and the Lamb ?" Is it the worship of a created, dependent being, receiving the alleluiahs of the universe while seated on the throne of God ? Is this the worship received by a man who came to teach humility, and whose last office on earth was washing his disciples' feet ? Is it the kind of worship we render to sovereigns, magistrates, and prophets ? How John himself was taught to regard such worship, rendered not alone to magistrates and prophets, but to an angel of heaven of large commission, he has told us, for when he fell down to worship at the feet of the angel, though not rendering supreme worship, — for there is no intimation that he mistook the angel for the Almighty, — he was promptly rebuked, "See thou do it not, for I am thy fellow servant and of thy brethren the prophets, — *Worship God*."

I can worship neither sovereign nor prophet, nor archangel nor any created being whatever, placed on the throne of God and "in the midst of the throne," and my conviction is still the same, that if Christianity demands this of me it is as gross a system of idolatry as can be found among the religions of the earth. The Greeks who worshipped Apollo under Zeus did not place their sub-deity so high as this; did not make *him* the Alpha and Omega, the Beginning and the Ending, the First and the Last. No; I believe all this worship is rendered to the Logos of God who appeared as the Son of Man; to God speaking, or humanized to our finite conceptions and our deepest spiritual needs. It is the Word which was in the beginning with God, which is God in self-revelation, which is ever on the throne of judgment, and which by his unerring truth will judge the world at the last day; and who moreover ever brings forth to us the wealth of the Divine Nature, and its deepest and tenderest love. Does any enlightened person need to have it proved to him, that "the Lamb as it had been slain," appearing in the midst of the throne of God, and thence feeding those who hunger, and leading those who thirst by living waters, is neither a lamb literally, nor a man who had been put to death; but the Divine Logos rather, revealing the Eternal Father as Sacrifice, Mercy, and Love; love so tender that like our human love it can be wounded, can bleed for us, can give itself away for our redemption, yea, can be crucified or killed out from the impenitent soul; love of which the sacrifice on Calvary is only an outward sign, but the best, the truest, and the tenderest which our earthly annals can afford? We talk of the Fatherhood of God, and make it a cold and sounding generality, while God is far off in the unknown; and we might add mother and nurse or any other words of endearment from our human relations, without coming anywhere near to that experience of the divine love which the disciple finds in Christ as the Lamb of God who taketh away the sin of the world; which made Faber exclaim in excess of emotion,—

> "I thrill with painful joy, to find
> God's fatherhood so nigh."

I can see no reason why those Unitarians who receive the Gospel message in its integrity should forego the power, the inspiration, the renewing grace which the Logos doctrine has ever had among the followers of Christ. As held by the early Church it does not impinge in the least on the prime doctrine of Unitarian theology,— the essential oneness of the Divine Nature.[1] It has commended Orthodoxy to myriads of hearts and minds which draw this from it as its central and vital power; and I doubt not multitudes who are not called orthodox are in tacit acknowledgment of the same truth, but who would shrink from any fixed formulation of it, because human symbols are too poor for it. Between orthodox and unorthodox alike, it would be a bond of vital fellowship, giving them beneath all other forms and

[1] See the Appendix D.

theologies, however diverse, a common experience of a Saviour's deepest and tenderest love. It would, as we believe, invest every communion table with the almost visible presence of a Divine Redeemer and with the very fragrancy of heaven, for its worship would blend joyously with the worship around "the throne of God and the Lamb," and the church on earth and the church above would join in the music of one coronation song, — "Worthy is the Lamb that was slain to receive power and riches, and wisdom and strength, and honor and glory and blessing." For only when we can see "the Lamb in the midst of the throne," have we come into the heart of the Divine Mercy, where the throne is no longer invested with the thunderings and lightnings of Sinai, but clothed in rainbows in token that the storms are over.

THE DIVINE INCARNATION in the Lord Jesus Christ, we conclude to be the distinguishing doctrine of the Johannean theology. The other New Testament writers forecast it or reach towards it, and sometimes grasp it, but it beams forth in John as the sun of the whole Christian system, showing all its other truths in organic relations with it. Shall we not say too that all the other great religions prophesy towards it and find in it their fulfillment? Could Judaism have found its consummation in anything short of such a Divine Epiphany, revealing God not only as the Beginning but the End and Ultimation? What but this was to bridge the awful chasm between the world and Jehovah: He dwelling apart in his lonely solitudes, imposing law on his subjects and enforcing it with his thunders? Could a mere prophet, coming only in the line of the old ones, and saying their message over again, have given any culmination to the Jewish history? What would he have been but an earlier Mahomet with his endless iteration of "God is God," but with this other truth, GOD IS HUMAN, still withheld, instead of being given to the heart to soften its savagery and melt it down in the Divine Love? What but this truth was Judaism, as we find it represented in Philo reaching after and trying to clasp with its finest tendrils where Philo makes out two Jehovahs, and is feeling after the Logos as the Son of God and the angel of his nearer presence?

The two other great religions of the world, the religions of the Orient, have spent their force and have no future. Brahmanism is all centre. God is everything, and man and nature nothing, and belong to the world of illusion. God is the Alpha but never the Omega. Buddhism is all circumference. It affirms nature and humanity, but God is lost from both. Its *Nirvana*, though it promises eternal rest as the reward of self-renunciation, still leaves a vast *lacuna* as pertains to a spiritual world. Its morality, so near that of Christianity as to anticipate its entire moral code abuts upon nothing to give it support and inspiration; and as pertains to the truths that inlay the

Christian revelation, it is only the deep-drawn pensive sigh of human nature, towards the Word made flesh ; toward the Christ emerging out of the painful void, and lighting up both the spiritual world and the natural with the glories of the Godhead. Buddha only saw nature as a burden upon the spirit, to be denied and repudiated ; he never saw nature and spirit in harmony, one to be glorified by the other ; the natural, the clothing of the spiritual, and God pervading them both and making them sweet and sacred, by his transfigurations. Hence Buddhism was only a prophecy and preparation for that coming which should give it centre as well as circumference, and fill its painful chasm with divine reality. Its morality, sweet and pure as it is, has nothing behind it, and so lacks any impletion from the Divine Energy ; and though numbering nearly one third of the human race among its votaries, it has never organized any form of society which is really progressive. As applied to the wounds and sufferings of human nature, it is not a healer but a narcotic, to drown for the time being the consciousness of pain. "In the plan of the world's order," says Bunsen, "it seems even now producing the effect of a mild dose of opium on the raving or despairing tribes of weary-hearted Asia. The sleep lasts long, but it is a gentle one, and who knows how near may be the dawn of the resurrection morning?"

And if the Divine Incarnation, which reveals God not only as the Beginning but the Ultimation, is a truth towards which all the old religions prophesy out of the deepest wants of human nature, so again the modern religions which lead the world's progress, date from it and draw from it their impletion of life and energy. It is the focal centre of the world's history and unitizes the whole. Yea more; Origen is not only grandly comprehensive but strictly Johannean, when he makes Christ as the Logos the mediating and atoning power of the whole universe, angelic as well as human. Everything beyond the sphere of the Divine Existence is separated from God, and impure in his sight, and so Christ, the Eternal Word, is ever mediating to bring the universe into harmony with Him and fill it with Himself. This atoning work, says Origen, goes on in the heavens and upon the earth, and the cross is only its outermost earthly sign.[1] The Word becoming flesh puts him as never before in fellowship and correspondency with all mankind, and his atoning work in this world was not accomplished by a sacrifice made once for all, but is ever widening and will keep on till it fills the whole orb of humanity. In more inspired language than Origen's, John describes the one event in the world's history, which was to fulfill

[1] *Καὶ γὰρ ἄτοπον, ὑπὲρ ἀνθρωπίνων μὲν αὐτὸν φάσκειν ἁμαρτημάτων γεγεῦσθαι θανάτου, οὐκ ἔτι δὲ ὑπὲρ ἄλλου τινὸς παρὰ τὸν ἄνθρωπον ἐν ἁμαρτήμασι γεγενημένου, οἷον ὑπὲρ ἄστρων, οὐδὲ τῶν ἄστρων παντὸς καθαρῶν ὄντων ἐνώπιον τοῦ θεοῦ, ὡς ἐν τῷ Ἰὼβ ἀνέγνωμεν* (25, 5,) *εἰ μὴ ἄρα ὑπερβολικῶς τοῦτο εἴρηται.* — *Com. in Joh.*

The passage is quoted by Baur, *Versöhnung*, p. 65; and absurdly criticized, pp. 66, 67.

its prophet yearnings and assuage and finally banish its woes: "Behold the tabernacle of God is with men, and He will dwell with them, and they shall be his people, and God himself shall be with them, and be their God. And God shall wipe away all tears from their eyes; and there shall be no more death, neither sorrow nor crying; neither shall there be any more pain; for the former things are passed away."

APPENDIX.

A.

THE EASTER CONTROVERSY.

IT becomes necessary here to notice an alleged discrepancy between the fourth Gospel and the synoptics, touching the time of the last supper and the crucifixion of Christ. The synoptics — such is the objection — make the last supper fall on the 14th of the Jewish month Nisan, or on Thursday evening of Passover week, and the crucifixion on the 15th, or Friday; whereas the fourth Gospel makes no mention of the pascal supper at all, but describes an ordinary meal on the evening of the 13th, and makes the crucifixion fall on the 14th, the day following. That is to say, the fourth Gospel describes *a* supper on the evening of what we call Wednesday, which, therefore, was not the Passover, and places the crucifixion on Thursday, in entire inconsistency with the first three Gospels.

This supposed discrepancy would be of less consequence, even if it had turned out a real one, had not a controversy in the second century brought it to bear fatally, as some think, against the genuineness of the fourth Gospel. The controversy was this: The churches of

Asia Minor held an annual festival on the 14th Nisan, established, as Baur holds, in commemoration of the last supper, — the Passover meal of Jesus with his disciples. At Rome, on the other hand, the festival was held on Friday of paschal week, without any reference to the day of the month on which it might fall, and the churches of Asia Minor were blamed because they would not conform to the Roman custom. A warm controversy arose. The churches of Asia Minor appealed in behalf of their observance to apostolic tradition, and especially *to the authority of John himself*, then freshly preserved among them. Therefore, — such is the argument, — they could not have regarded the fourth Gospel as written by John, since its authority is directly against them. The fourth Gospel, say the critics, makes Jesus eat for the last time with his disciples, "*before* the feast of the Passover" (chap. xiii. 1), and describes him crucified on the next day, before the time of the Passover meal. It is palpable evidence that, on the very scene of John's labors, and near to his times, and among his own followers and churches, our fourth Gospel was not known, or if known, was not named as genuine.

We have stated the objection succinctly; but the reasonings which have grown out of it, the arguments and the answers, would make a small library. It has employed the time of such writers as Baur, Neander, Bleek, De Wette, Schneider, and Tholück, in Germany; of the best English theological writers; and Mackay, in a late treatise assailing the genuineness of the works of the New Testament, and the fourth Gospel in particular, fills page after page with this controversy, and closes in a tone of exultation that here is an argument which, if all others fail, puts the spuriousness of the fourth Gospel beyond debate. This controversy makes it expedient that we give a few pages to it; and there need be but few indeed.

The whole apparent discrepancy grows out of a confused rendering or reading of the introductory verses of the thirteenth chapter of John. They are as follows in our English version: —

"Now, before the feast of the Passover, when Jesus knew that his hour was come, — that he should depart out of this world, — having loved his own, who were in the world, he loved them unto the end. And, supper being ended, the devil having put it into the heart of Judas Iscariot, Simon's son, to betray him, Jesus knowing that the Father had given all things into his hands, and that he was come from God and went to God, he riseth from supper and laid aside his garments, and took a towel and girded himself" (xiii. 1–4).

Though a tolerably literal rendering, the passage as it stands, is obscure and ungrammatical. The important question is, Does the clause, "before the feast of the Passover," refer to the supper described soon after? The Tübingen critics say it does. Therefore it must have been a supper of a private nature, and not the Passover meal which it preceded. Therefore, according to the fourth Gospel, Jesus never ate the Passover at all, but only a private meal beforehand, and being crucified the next day, it must have been on Thursday, thus directly contradicting the synoptics, who make it fall on Friday.

Plainly this is a forced construction. The clause, "before the feast of the Passover," does *not* refer to the supper mentioned in the second verse, but to what immediately follows, namely, "Jesus knew that his hour was come." He knew it beforehand. It is in accord with all that he said and reiterated while in Galilee, and all the way thence to Jerusalem, that at the passover his hour of departure was to come. The whole passage, clearly rendered, is this: —

"Now Jesus, before the feast of the Passover, knew that his time to pass out of this world to the Father had come, and having loved his own, who were in the world, he loved them to the last. And when supper was proceeding, — the devil having put it into the heart of Judas Iscariot, Simon's son, to betray him, — Jesus, knowing that the Father had given all things into his hands, and that he came from God and was returning to God, arose from supper, and, putting off his mantle, took a cloth and girded himself."

The objection that the fourth evangelist does not say that this is the paschal supper, and go on to describe it as such, is trivial in the extreme. He is writing with the synoptics before him, on purpose to supplement them, and if he used common sense he would not tell their story over again. This very omission is highly significant. There is a tacit reference to what they had written, and needed not to be repeated. Still emphasizing the fact that Jesus had forecast the time of his death, and that the tender care which he had manifested for his own followers continued to the last, the whole passage is in beautiful harmony with all that precedes and follows. It is hardly a paraphrase to render: "Jesus knew his time was to come at the feast of the Passover, long before the time of that festival had arrived, and now that it had arrived, his love of his own was not remitted on account of his personal dangers, and so, the paschal supper being in progress, he even left the table to wash their feet."

Still, if there is any possible doubt as to the meaning of this passage, it will vanish as we read on. The evangelist proceeds to report the discourses of Jesus with his disciples in the four following chapters, which the synoptics had omitted entirely, but which John gives in full for the plain reason that they are in that high spiritual strain whose music touched his inmost thought, but which only fell on the external ear and mind of the other disciples. Then followed the scene in Gethsemane; and, on the next morning, the trial and the crucifixion. Describing the latter, the fourth evangelist says, "It was toward noon on the Preparation of the Passover" (xix. 14). What was "the Preparation"? It was the day before the Jewish Sabbath, or Friday. The word was just as much appropriated to designate that day, as our word Saturday is to designate the day before Sunday. The Passover festival continued seven days, during which unleavened bread and other sacrifices beside that of the paschal lamb were eaten; and the word "Passover" was used to cover the whole of that time; so that Mr. Norton very properly renders the above passage, "It was towards noon on the Preparation-day of passover week." Here, then, it is distinctly announced by the fourth evangelist that the crucifixion took place on Friday, in harmony with the synoptics, using the exact term which they employ, who call the Preparation "*the day before the Sabbath.*" See Mark xv. 42, compared with Matt. xxvii. 62. See also

Luke xxiii. 54, who says, speaking of the day of the crucifixion, "It was Preparation-day, *and the Sabbath was drawing on;*" thus making plain beyond all doubt that Preparation-day was Friday.

Still the Tübingen critics will have it that "the Preparation," as used by the fourth evangelist, means the day before the Passover, though without the faintest shadow of evidence. Pass on a little further, then, and let the fourth evangelist interpret himself. After Jesus had bowed his head and expired, the writer proceeds to say, the "Jews, as it was the Preparation-day, *that the bodies might not remain on the cross during the Sabbath, as that Sabbath-day was a high day*, requested Pilate that their legs might be broken, and they be taken away" (chap. xix. 31). The Sabbath-day of paschal week was a great day, commemorated with special pomp and ceremony, and would be profaned by the spectacle of dead bodies near Jerusalem, which rendered any one who came in sight of them legally unclean. Therefore the execution is hurried through, and, because late on Friday afternoon the two robbers were still alive, their bodies were broken to hasten dissolution; and, though Jesus was apparently dead, one of the soldiers pierced his side to make the fact perfectly sure, that the bodies might be taken down and put out of the way before the Sabbath drew on. Thus the fourth evangelist not only says that Jesus was put to death on Friday, but he is at pains to repeat his statement with circumstantial details as to how the execution was hastened lest they should encroach on the sanctity of the Sabbath-day.

Nor is this all. He repeats his statement yet again in

the closing verse of this same chapter, where he describes the removal of the body to Joseph's tomb. "There, then, they laid Jesus, *it being the Preparation-day of the Jews.*" If the fourth evangelist had foreseen this very controversy he could not have been more decisive and emphatic in his language, not only telling us once, but three times over, that Jesus was put to death on Friday, in exact agreement with the synoptics, furnishing minute details, which they had omitted, which serve for more complete and undoubted verification. That "the Preparation" meant invariably Friday, any one can abundantly verify from the parallel passages in the synoptics, and from Josephus, and from other writers, patristic and classical. See Norton's translation and commentary, *ad. loc.* The only other passage which would require elucidation is xviii. 28: "Then, early in the morning they carried Jesus from Caiaphas to the Prætorium. And they did not themselves enter the Prætorium, lest they should be defiled and prevented from eating the Passover." This was at the trial on the morning of the day of crucifixion; and, as the paschal lamb was always eaten the evening previous, it is argued that John here again makes the crucifixion fall on the day before the Passover. All this is quickly answered when we remember that "eating the Passover" meant not merely the paschal lamb of the evening before, but also the sacrifices and unleavened bread of the whole Passover week.

The reader may be surprised when we say that the objection, which these simple quotations banish clean out of sight, has been relied upon as the most stubborn of all against the genuineness of the fourth Gospel, but this is literally true. The very flood-gates of learning have been opened in order to cover with darkness a subject which in itself seems as clear as the light of noon-day.

B.

THE BIRTH OF CHRIST.

It is hardly necessary to say that the theory of evolution given in chapter iii., Part II., is not Darwinian. It is Darwin's theory of "natural selection" supplemented as far as it consistently goes by St. George Mivart's theory of "derivative creation." The latter, however, seems to me to have made a very lame and imperfect use of the truth which he handles. He supposes that nature or the Cosmos only as originally created was the immediate supernatural work of the Creator; that it had certain tendencies impressed upon it to be unfolded within it, such as tendencies to develop new species at certain times and eras. A clock-maker so constructs his time-piece that at certain hours the hammer will strike from one up to twelve successively without any foreign interference. So God made and *superintends* his Cosmos, but does not work immediately in it. But in due time a human body was evolved out of this Cosmical machine, with lower organizations for a basis; the original tendencies working upward till they produced a human form; or to keep to our illustration, the clock kept striking more and more till it struck the hour of noon. At this signal the Creator interferes. The Cosmos, though by its inherent power it could evolve a human body, could not put an immortal soul into it. Here the Creator comes in immediately and supernaturally, breathes a soul into the body, and so man appears on the earth. But why not acknowledge that God is immanent and interworking in his Cosmos as well as overlooking it; that He not only created it once but creates it freshly every day and hour? That done there are no difficulties in the theory of evolution, and Darwinism is supplemented by the only truth that can give it philosophic wholeness and consistency. "Natural selection" accounts for change of species within a certain range, but it breaks down when we apply it universally, as St. George Mivart clearly shows. It cannot pass the line between the animal, and the immortal being we call man, neither can it evolve the animal from the plant, nor the vegetable kingdom from the mineral without the acknowledgment of an immanent creative force acting intelligently, though acting through natural laws. Natural paternity only produces its kind, and when a higher kingdom of nature is evolved from a lower one, we must believe in the immanence of a power higher than either, or else break the continuity of rational thought.

The doctrine of the supernatural birth of Christ is placed on ground independent of all these analogies. They are only referred to for the purpose of showing the impotence of objections from mere naturalism, since naturalism cannot account for the original birth of man without acknowledgment of an immediate higher paternity. We receive the doctrine of the birth of Christ as given by the evangelic narratives, not merely because they have declared it, but because with the other facts of his life it makes a seamless, complete, and consistent whole. We understand Christ himself to claim it. See Matt. xxii. 41–45.

C.

THE PREEXISTENCE.

Mr. Norton renders John viii. 28: "Before Abraham was born I was he." Undoubtedly the words admit of this rendering as an instance where the present tense is used for the past. But the common usage requires that ἐγώ εἰμι should be rendered "I am," and by this rendering we think the significance of the passage is more completely given, though the difference would not affect in the least any theological doctrine which the text might be supposed to teach. If we supply the ellipsis by the pronoun "he" the question immediately returns, What is its antecedent? Plainly, "the Son" or "the Son of Man," occurring in immediate connection, — terms which Jesus used invariably in his colloquies with the Jews in the fourth Gospel, and which almost as invariably raised against him the charge of blasphemy. For the emphasis is always on the article. It is *the* Son, or the *only* Son. It is sonship in a sense that applies to him exclusively that Jesus here affirms. Not less than *nine times* in this same eighth chapter, and in this same conversation, Jesus asserts this sonship, by calling God "*my* Father," or by calling himself "*the* Son." In verse 28 he tells them, "When ye have lifted up the Son of Man, then shall ye know that I am," that is, that I *am* the Son of Man. In verse 25 they ask him to supply the ellipsis himself, which he does. He had told them, "If ye believe not that I am, ye shall die in your sins." "That you are *who?* " they ask him. "The same that I said unto you *from the beginning.*" What had he called himself from the beginning? If the reader will turn back he will see. In the conversation with Nicodemus he calls himself the *only begotten* Son of God" (iii. 16–18). In chapter fifth this sonship is asserted not less than eight times, so that the Jews seek to kill him because he made himself equal with God (ἴσον ἑαυτὸν ποιῶν τῷ Θεῷ). As Son of God he had abrogated the Sabbath, and annulled the law of Moses, thus arrogating to himself, they thought, the prerogatives of Jehovah. The reader need not be told that this charge in its very nature is of blasphemy, even were it not called so afterward, as it is twice over. It was punishable with death by stoning under the Jewish law (see Lev. xxiv. 16). This was at the second visit of Jesus to the Capitol after entering on his mission, and it was the standing accusation against him to the close, invariably for calling himself *the* Son of God, or Son of Man. Through five successive scenes the charge comes up when they seek to kill him. It came up at the fourth visit to Jerusalem (see John x. 33). It came up at the mock trial before the High Priest, who shook his robe saying, "He hath spoken blasphemy," because he had called himself "the Son of Man" (Matt. xxvi. 64). It came up before Pilate, where the Jews refer to their law requiring death "because he made himself the Son of God."

There can be no shadow of doubt, therefore, as to how

the ellipsis should be supplied in John viii. 58, or how John himself must have understood it who reports the words. He opens his Gospel by calling the Word made flesh, which was "in the beginning," "the only begotten of the Father," and "the only begotten Son of God." He reports Jesus as saying the same of himself, twice in the identical words of "only begotten Son," always in terms that involve that meaning. He had been saying it all through the preceding chapters, and nine times in this same eighth chapter, which led on to the declaration in verse 58, and he lay under the charge of blasphemy for saying it. It should read then "Before Abraham was born, I am the Son of God," or "I am the only begotten of the Father." *They took up stones*, and we cannot mistake as to what the accusation was. We come to the same result, by rendering in the past tense "From before the birth of Abraham I have been the only begotten of the Father," referring us directly to the Proem where "the Word" who was "from the Beginning," is "the only begotten Son." I have kept, however, to the rendering in the present tense, because the Eternal Word from which Jesus speaks, and which, as bread from heaven he calls *himself*, is timeless, and it seems to me that this is intimated in the text.

I can but notice here a common humanitarian argument, that the divinity of Christ is like that of other men because it is "derived." If we keep to the royal image of the Johannean writings, we shall see that this argument has no force. The WORD which became incarnate in Christ, which is God speaking, or, in the act of self-revelation, is called "Light," "the Light which coming into the world enlightens every man." So Christ as this Word calls himself "the Light of the World." In the Apocalypse his face is as "the Sun," and in heaven "the Lamb is the Light thereof." The Word is all that by which God is known or shines forth, whether in nature, in man, or supremely in Christ. The Word on the bosom of the Father, ever begotten from the depths of his love, is as the photosphere on the sun's disc, ever born of the solar fire, or if you will, forever *derived* or *given* from the solar deeps, without which the sun would be an invisible mass in the heavens, but by which he fills the universe with life and light. It no less belongs to the sun and is part of it from being "*derived.*" The image gives us the conception of the Divine Being, as not a bare point or dead unity, but a DIVINE ORGANISM which has eternal life and interaction in itself, even as the human being, God's image, has interaction in himself, with one power in derivation from another. Keep clearly to the royal image itself, and there is no confusion of thought in calling the Logos both essentially divine, and only begotten; nor is there any solecism in the language of the church, such as "eternal Son," or, "very God of very God," for the words do not mean that there are two Gods, but that God and his Logos are consubstantial. To say that all power in heaven and earth is "given" by one being to another, as if one person could confer omnipotence on another person, is gross solecism of language. To say that God could have an only Son, in any *natural* sense, "first born of the whole creation," yet not appearing till four thousand years after the creation, is most absurd anachronism. But all this disappears when we think of the Divine Being, neither as a bare point of unity, nor a stagnant deep, but having eternal activities within himself, a LIVING God, the motions of whose nature all this imagery serves to shadow forth. For a mortal man, or for an archangel as well, to announce that God is greater than *he* is, were profane egoism. But for Jesus speaking as the Word to say, "my Father is greater than I," is to say only that God as absolute, is more than God revealed.

D.

PERSONALITY AND PERSONIFICATION.

In this treatise we have regarded the Logos as *personified.* If our work were not expository rather than philosophical or ontological, it would require a dissertation on the distinction between personality and personification. Though the Word in the New Testament is personified, it is none the less regarded as hypostatized. It is not an abstract noun; not like human speech, something which can be broken off from the speaker and become dead letter. The divine substance is in it continuous and unbroken, though it is not a person exterior to God. It is that in which the One Divine Person is always revealed. Personality involves essentially the idea of Will or self conscious volition. Assuming that there are three persons in the Godhead, or three self-conscious Wills, is precisely where Trinitarianism breaks up in Tritheism; though as shown in the text there are forms of Trinitarianism which drop the word "persons" and avoid this danger. While the New Testament formula of Father, Son, and Spirit, declares three essentials of the Divine Being, we construe it in harmony with the strictest and purest monotheism. The Word and the Spirit may be separately *personified*, and are in the New Testament; but the moment we think of them as separate *persons* and not co-essentials of one Person, we have lost the Divine Unity, and are in the worship of three Gods. The debate of fifteen centuries has shown no possible escape from this alternative.

www.ingramcontent.com/pod-product-compliance
Lightning Source LLC
LaVergne TN
LVHW021239110826
845150LV00002B/358

* 9 7 8 1 4 2 5 5 6 1 9 4 9 *